The Muse
in Bronzeville

The Muse in Bronzeville

African American Creative Expression in Chicago, 1932–1950

ROBERT BONE AND
RICHARD A. COURAGE

FOREWORD BY AMRITJIT SINGH

RUTGERS UNIVERSITY PRESS
New Brunswick, New Jersey, and London

Library of Congress Cataloging-in-Publication Data

Bone, Robert, 1924–2007.
  The muse in Bronzeville : African American creative expression in Chicago, 1932–1950 /
    Robert Bone and Richard A. Courage.
      p. cm.
  Includes bibliographical references and index.
  ISBN 978–0–8135–5043–5 (hardcover : alk. paper) —
  ISBN 978–0–8135–5044-2 (pbk. : alk. paper)
  1. American literature—Illinois—Chicago—History and criticism. 2. African Americans—
    Illinois—Chicago—History—20th century. 3. African Americans—Intellectual life—
    20th century. 4. Chicago (Ill.)—Intellectual life—20th century. I. Courage, Richard A.,
    1946–   II. Title.
  PS285.C47B66 2011
  810.9'977311—dc22

                                                                                      2010045436

A British Cataloging-in-Publication record for this book is available from the British Library.

Visit our Web site: http://rutgerspress.rutgers.edu

Manufactured in the United States of America

810.9/BON

For Dorothea Bone,
partner in this project from its distant origins to its fruition

CONTENTS

ILLUSTRATIONS

Black-and-White Illustrations

Color Plates (between pages 146 and 147)

FOREWORD

At one point in a 1989 interview, Chinua Achebe, author of the definitive postcolonial novel, *Things Fall Apart* (1959), responds to the younger writer Nuruddin Farah and his provocative questions regarding Achebe's categorization of Nigerian literature written in English as "national literature" and Nigerian writing in Hausa, Ibo, and Yoruba as "ethnic literature": "We were pioneers and pioneers have to make statements. . . . [But] these statements need not stand for ever. If someone comes up with a better idea, let these statements be disconfirmed" (Institute of Contemporary Arts, London). Robert Adamson Bone, widely respected yet sometimes dismissed as the Euro-American author of *The Negro Novel in America* (1958; revised, 1965; Japanese translation, 1972) may have felt a similar impulse to respond to his detractors. But, as far as I know, he never did. Maybe he chose not to do so because, as a young socialist in the 1940s and 1950s, he had struggled deep within himself to come to terms with the imperatives of "race" and social justice in the United States, years before he chose to dedicate his career to the study of "Negro" history and literature.

Robert had, I believe, too much humility in the face of the complex subject he studied to assert himself solely based on his privilege as a pioneer. He chose instead to continue his writing and research in a field that he felt still needed further exploration and to which he gave both respectful affection and critical attention as a teacher-scholar for more than half a century. His second book, *Down Home: Origins of the Afro-American Short Story*, was published in 1975 and reissued in 1989. He also published a monograph, *Richard Wright* (1969), in the University of Minnesota's American Writers Series, as well as numerous reviews and articles on African American writing.

Like thousands of other students of African American literary tradition, I benefited from Bone's book—when I first read it during 1972–1973 while preparing my NYU dissertation. And yet I felt no obligation to agree with him on everything, including the honest if tough-minded criteria by which he had developed his summary "Recommended List" of fifteen novels in a book that offered a sweeping survey from the beginnings to the 1950s—a century of African American fiction. I learned later that he had developed a parallel reputation as not only a caring mentor but also a demanding professor and tough grader at Teachers College, Columbia University, where he taught from 1965 to 1990. I also found out that this "New Haven boy" had returned to the East Coast after he lost his tenure battle at UCLA by a close vote: twelve to thirteen, according to Dorothea Bone. The nay-sayers apparently regarded *The Negro Novel in America* as a nonbook because they did not view its subject to be worthy of serious study! One might note that the UCLA tenure vote on Dr. Bone was taking place roughly at the same time as the U.S. Congress was debating the passage of the historic Civil Rights Act.

A year after I completed my Ph.D. in 1973, my family and I had returned to our native India for nine years. Consequently, I didn't have an opportunity to meet Robert in person until the spring of 1985 at the International Symposium on Richard Wright organized by Maryemma Graham at Ole Miss. At this conference, Bone presented his pioneering essay, "Richard Wright and the Chicago Renaissance," which was to become the seed for later expansion of his insights. During 1991–1992, Robert and I were Du Bois fellows at Harvard University, and I became aware of his continuing book project on the Black Chicago Renaissance. During family visits in both Rhode Island and Nantucket throughout the following years, Robert filled me in on his steady progress. A few months before Robert died in November 2007, I was contacted by his friend and former student, Richard Courage, to whom Robert, facing debilitating health, had entrusted the task of finishing the manuscript that became *The Muse in Bronzeville*. Richard has demonstrated admirable courage, skill, and tenacity in bringing this rather complex work to fruition while honoring in word and spirit his mentor's high scholarly standards and distinguished career.

In 1985, Robert Bone challenged the scholars gathered at the Richard Wright Symposium at Ole Miss to undertake the task of recovering and evaluating black creative expression in Chicago in the 1930s and 1940s, a largely neglected phase and site of African American cultural history. In doing so, Bone suggested the rough outlines of a richer and more coherent account than the previously existing narratives of African American history from the Harlem Renaissance to the Black Arts Movement. Recovering this missing chapter demanded systematic attention to major artists in several creative fields, their works in various genres and media, and their historical context. In *The Muse in Bronzeville*, Robert Bone and Richard Courage offer the first comprehensive account of this creative awakening in Bronzeville, Chicago's South Side, from the 1930s through the early years of the Cold War.

The book synthesizes wide-ranging material, especially biographical profiles of figures—such as Richard Wright, Gwendolyn Brooks, Arna Bontemps, Horace Cayton, Charles White, Gordon Parks, Katherine Dunham, Mahalia Jackson, and Muddy Waters—into a compelling critical narrative. In writing that is both lucid and engaging, the book brings together much important information and many perceptive interpretations, valuable for scholar and general reader alike. At the core of *The Muse in Bronzeville* is Bone's contention, which is already gaining wide acceptance, that Black Chicago was the center of a creative awakening every bit as impressive as the more familiar Harlem Renaissance. We only need to recall that the first full-length critical treatment of the Harlem Renaissance did not materialize until Nathan Irvin Huggins's 1971 book and that, well into the 1980s, books such as *Cane* and *Their Eyes Were Watching God*—now featured regularly in courses in Modernism and American literature–were unknown to a majority of our students and colleagues. With new scholarship appearing in every decade since the 1970s, the Harlem Renaissance has begun to loom larger in our imagination and sense of the past. On the Black Chicago Renaissance, Bone's 1986 essay has already prompted important studies by scholars such as Carla Cappetti, Bill V. Mullen, and Anne Meis Knupfer, and I believe we will soon have as rich an array of scholarship on the Chicago literary phenomenon as we currently have on its predecessor in Harlem.

By grounding their examination of individual lives and careers during the years of the Great Migration, Depression, and Second World War, Bone and Courage illuminate the unique generational experiences and the sources of creativity for these artists. Especially valuable are discussions of such institutions as Parkway Community House, the South Side Community Art Center, the Art Institute of Chicago, the John Reed Club, George Cleveland Hall Library, the South Side Writers' Group, the Chicago Poets' Class, and the Illinois Art and Writers' Projects, all of which emerged as central sites where aspiring young black artists, writers, and intellectuals interacted, supported each other, honed their skills, and clarified their ideologies, while working with more seasoned professionals. This book is likely to raise further debate about whether the intense activity surrounding such institutions would supply an organizing heuristic, a magnet, or bonding glue, for the artists and intellectuals associated with the Black Chicago Renaissance.

A special strength of *The Muse in Bronzeville* is its elucidation of the cross-disciplinary nature of much creative work in "Bronzeville" or Black Chicago. Discussions of aesthetic issues such as the perceived tensions between the formal experimentation of modernist practice and commitment to address mass audiences are frequently enriched by examination of parallels in different art forms. As critics, Bone and Courage move astutely from close readings of novels and poems to richly informative analyses of musical performances and visual works of art. Discussions of the latter are enhanced by striking full-color reproductions of paintings by Archibald Motley, Charles White, Margaret Burroughs, Charles Sebree, and Eldzier Cortor.

This dynamic reappraisal of a neglected period in African American cultural history is based on deeply layered research in primary sources at major collections across the country. Through arduous and persistent archival work, the authors have unearthed historical gems that extend or challenge our understanding of how various actors situated themselves during this turbulent period. This is especially true of figures such as Charles S. Johnson and Arna Bontemps, who played roles in both the Harlem Renaissance and Black Chicago's creative flowering. In conjunction with the support offered by other Harlem Renaissance patrons and promoters, such as Alain Locke, James Weldon Johnson, and Carl Van Vechten, Charles S. Johnson's efforts in organizing and publicizing the Harlem artists are discussed in an early chapter, thus setting the stage for the surprise of a 1935 letter in which Johnson complains bitterly about Locke's public criticisms of his "wheedling gradualism."

In an analogous instance of an older figure struggling to find a vantage point amidst the political turmoil of the period, Bontemps comments to white novelist and radical Jack Conroy about Richard Wright's bitter public break with the Communist Party: "Perhaps if Dick had worn communism as a loose garment, this sad story would have been less sad. But he gave his heart without reserve, and I doubt that a creative spirit can ever do that." My own sense is that Bone and Courage offer a commendably balanced and insightful treatment of aesthetic and political controversies surrounding the period.

The Chicago artists have often been situated against the ideational and cultural framework of the Harlem Renaissance, and Bone and Courage helpfully identify points of both continuity and discontinuity between the two distinct generational milieus. The authors' treatment of their subject highlights the fluid boundaries between the two "movements," which may be viewed by some as fictional constructions needed by later-day cultural historians. Their examination of the influence of such "older" figures as Charles S. John-son, Bontemps, Locke, and Langston Hughes on the Bronzeville of 1930s and 1940s underscores elements of continuity, even as the artistic manifestos and actual output of the younger artists suggest a radical departure. Even Richard Wright, a quintessential figure of the Black Chicago Renaissance, was not without powerful Harlem links during the over-lapping years of the two movements. Wright had already moved to New York by 1937, when he published both his "Blueprint for Negro Writing" and his now infamous review of Hurston's novel, *Their Eyes Were Watching God*. But as I have noted elsewhere (see my essay in *Harlem Speaks*, 2006, edited by Cary D. Wintz), Wright's aesthetic positions have much in common with Wallace Thurman's, and maybe Wright (and Ralph Ellison) exhib-ited an extreme form of the "anxiety of influence" in denying their continuity with Harlem Renaissance writers and texts.

Overall, Bone and Courage make a powerful case for moving Chicago's Bronzeville, long overshadowed by New York's Harlem, from a peripheral to a central position within African American and American Studies. In closing, I cannot help but note how Robert Bone, who had begun to be perceived as part of our past in his final years, would eventu-ally leave us with a book that may mark the beginning of a new scholarly revival in U.S. literary and cultural studies.

Amritjit Singh
Ohio University

PREFACE

When Robert Adamson Bone died in November 2007, he left behind, besides a grieving family, a substantial but unfinished manuscript. Begun in the mid-1980s, this work was intended as the capstone of Bone's career, the book that would fully develop the core assertions of his seminal essay "Richard Wright and the Chicago Renaissance," published in 1986.[1] Focusing on such figures as Wright, Arna Bontemps, Gwendolyn Brooks, Margaret Walker, and Horace Cayton Jr., Bone argued that Chicago's South Side experienced a period of creative ferment during the 1930s and 1940s comparable in achievement and scope to the Harlem Renaissance, that it became for some fifteen years the center of African American writing, and that Richard Wright was "the towering figure" of his generation of black literary artists.

Bone's thesis was initially articulated in the closing pages of his 1975 work, *Down Home: Origins of the Afro-American Short Story*. That book concludes by musing on "a little-noticed but important essay" by writer Arna Bontemps, who lived in New York from 1924 to 1931 and Chicago from 1935 to 1943. Bontemps described "a second literary awakening" centered on the South Side among black writers employed by the Chicago office of the Federal Writers' Project. "If Bontemps is correct," Bone wrote, "literary historians should be thinking in terms of a Chicago Renaissance. . . . The torch was passing not only from Harlem to Chicago, but from one generation to the next."[2]

This idea took some time to gain traction, in part because it was first tentatively advanced in the midst of a series of important works that sparked a powerful upsurge in scholarly and popular explorations of the Harlem Renaissance.[3] Such serious and sustained attention to African American creative expression has proven to be a truly significant and positive phenomenon, yet an overly concentrated focus on a single cultural moment and a single place threatens to obscure the rest of the landscape. Like the storied Mount Kilimanjaro rising loftily from the Tanzanian plains, the mountain of books on Harlem in the 1920s and early 1930s seems to overshadow everything else within sight.

Coming nine years after that initial foray, Bone's essay was well received and widely noted. Since its publication, scholars such as Carla Cappetti, Bill V. Mullen, Maren Stange, Anne Meis Knupfer, Adam Green, and Davarian Baldwin have—from various perspectives—begun filling in the topographical details of this extensive area on the cultural map that was previously *terra incognita*.[4] Bone worked steadily on this book, initially titled *Lost Renaissance*, until illness slowed and then altogether stopped his progress. As his friend and former student, I began collaborating with him early in 2006 to bring the project to fruition.

In proceeding from essay to book, Bone had ambitiously expanded the scope of the study: moving synchronically out from literature across the disciplines of history, music, visual arts, and sociology while diachronically tracing a line of philosophical influence and institution-building from 1930s–1940s Chicago as far back as Booker T. Washington and

Tuskegee Institute in the 1890s. The expansive reaches of the partially completed manuscript presented challenges at every turn, especially for a scholar working at a community college and teaching African American literature only at the introductory level. While Bone's health still permitted active engagement, we discussed various issues related to focus, methodology, and periodization and considered how to balance and integrate the book's three distinct threads: historical/contextual, biographical, and critical.

One question we considered at some length was how best to address the influence of radical politics on black artists in Chicago. The importance of the question is posed indirectly by Randi Storch's study of the early history of the Communist Party in Chicago and directly by Bill Mullen's charge that "Bone systematically evades the possibility of radical political influence on Chicago."[5] What Mullen portrays as evasion might more fairly be characterized as an emphasis, within the brief span of an essay, on a different set of influences that Bone saw as both more central and less known, especially the sociological tradition associated with Robert Park and the University of Chicago. Along this line, Carla Cappetti has perceptively explored the manner in which sociology and realistic/naturalistic literature produced "two schools of urban writing" and "two groups of texts written [in Chicago] between 1915 and 1945" that were historically important and reciprocally influential.[6]

In our discussions, Bone and I became aware of how much our views were shaped by different generational experiences. We had both been profoundly influenced by Marxist thought and political organizations as young men. As national secretary of the youth group of Norman Thomas's Socialist Party in the late 1940s, Bone viewed the Communist Party as *the* political enemy, enjoying near-hegemony on the Left and usurping the mantle of Marxist and socialist leadership in the United States, even as it subordinated its own agenda to every tactical maneuver of Soviet foreign policy and covered up Stalin's monstrous crimes against the Russian people.

Coming of age in the New Left two decades later, I regarded the Party as a stodgy and irrelevant vestige of an earlier period. But many of my comrades in SDS and other organizations were "red-diaper babies," sons and daughters of communists, at odds with their parents' explicit political views, yet often proud of their specific deeds. One's father had fought with the Abraham Lincoln Brigade in Spain; another had organized Boston-area factories into the United Electrical Workers Union; a third had led the Massachusetts affiliate of Progressive Citizens of America, the organization that ran Henry Wallace for president in 1948. I became fascinated with the human drama of great ideas and passionate political commitments as they affected the experience of such individuals.

Bone and I eventually agreed that, in the post–Cold War era, we should endeavor to tell the story of how individual black artists in Chicago embraced, rejected, ignored, or otherwise interacted with the Communist Party during its period of greatest influence, in much the same way that we explored the influence of Parkian sociological thought, Bookerite black political conservatism, black nationalism, or New Deal liberalism—with the intention of neither valorizing nor demonizing but rather documenting and understanding.

I confronted many remaining challenges during what amounted to an intensive four-year apprenticeship in African American studies, graciously abetted by senior scholars in several disciplines. While many other friends, colleagues, and commentators are named below, special acknowledgment is owed to David Levering Lewis, whose study of the Harlem Renaissance has been a constant inspiration and whose early support helped me find the resolve to complete Bone's work; to Amritjit Singh, who has proven a good friend to both authors of this work and a scholarly mentor to me; to Christopher Robert Reed, who probably knows more about Black Chicago's past than any other living historian and who shares his knowledge with great generosity; to Patricia Hills, who welcomed me into the community of scholars and taught me something of the mysteries of the art historian's craft; to Michael Flug, former senior archivist at the Vivian G. Harsh Research Collection of Afro-American History and Literature, who offered sound advice, warm colleagueship, and a continually expanding trove of rich materials. To these must be added the names of a precious handful of community elders on the South Side, who have served as my guides, informants, hosts, and friends: Susan Cayton Woodson, the late Margaret Burroughs, Timuel Black, Charles A. Davis, and Clarice Davis Durham. This work, in its present form, would not exist without them.

Richard A. Courage
Westchester Community College, SUNY

ACKNOWLEDGMENTS

Because of this book's long gestation, thanks are due to many people, no fewer than three generations of scholars, archivists, community leaders, friends, and colleagues (including some no longer with us), who offered assistance and support to both authors. Limitations of space preclude offering the detailed, individual acknowledgment due to each, but this simple list of names is accompanied by a deep sense of gratitude from the family of Robert Bone and me: Dora Apel, Andrea Barnwell, Ken and Gwyneth Bohr, Martha Briggs, Quinn and Andrea Brisben, Ronald Brown, Valerie Gerrard Browne, Alice Browning, Marilyn Campbell, Beverly Cook, Bill Costanzo, Betsy Currier, Vera Davis, James de Jongh, Carlos Delgado, Alan Devenish, Sammie Dortch, David C. Driskell, Cynthia Fife-Townsell, Suzanne Flandreau, Henry Louis Gates Jr., Fern Gayden, Edmund W. Gordon, Maryemma Graham, Lawrence Graver, Adam Green, Tom Halsall, Joseph Hankin, Nathan Harpaz, Michael S. Harper, Michael Hays, Melanie Herzog, Beth Howse, Helen Hughes, Claudia Jacques, Lisa Jerry, Jeh Charles Johnson, Eileen Johnston, Chuck Jones, Beatrice Julian, Katie Keeran, Martin Kilson, James Sterling King, Daniel Klein, Donna Korey, Dale Leifeste, Irving Lippner, Robert Luckett, Frank Madden, Robert Mancell, Edward Margolis, Lawrence McClellan Jr., Rob Medina, Ethelbert Miller, Robert Miller, Leslie Mitchner, Archie Motley, Ray Nance, Heather Ostman, Louis Parascondola, Eugene Useni Perkins, Julia Perkins, Thelma and Toussaint Perkins, Kymberly Pinder, Linda Roberti, Chet Rogalski, Alexander Saxton, Nathaniel Sayles, Rebecca Schrader, Jody Schwartz, Patti Sehulster, Una Shih, Jessie Carney Smith, Frances Jones Sneed, Ruth Ann Stewart, Jon Christian Suggs, Trygve Tholfsen, John Edgar Tidwell, Karen Vanterpool, Jianping Wang, Elise Virginia Ward, Jerry W. Ward, C. Ian White, Sonja Williams, Ruth Wilner, Paul Wray, Scott Zaluda. A special note of appreciation is due to the other Courages in my life: my mother, Gloria, my former wife, Gretchen, and our children, Emilie and Stephen, for their love, support, and understanding of the struggles of a born-again scholar. I apologize to anyone I may have omitted.

I am grateful for the following forms of institutional support: a summer stipend from the National Endowment for the Humanities, a short-term fellowship in African American Studies from the Black Metropolis Research Consortium, a sabbatical granted by the Westchester Community College Board of Trustees, and research/travel support from the WCC Federation of Teachers and the WCC Center for Faculty.

For images and permissions to use images and various textual materials, I thank the following institutions and individuals: Art Institute of Chicago, Brooks Permissions, Valerie Gerrard Browne, Charles White Archives, Chicago History Museum, Chicago Public Library: Vivian G. Harsh Collection of Afro-American History and Literature and CPL Special Collections Division, Barbara Cordell, Donadio & Olson, DuSable Museum of African American History, the family of Garland J. Millet, Gordon Parks Foundation,

Harold Ober Associates, Howard University Gallery of Art, Jeh V. Johnson, Library of Congress: Prints & Photographs Division, Michael Rosenfeld Gallery, New York Public Library: Jerome Robbins Dance Division and Schomburg Center for Research in Black Culture, Newberry Library, Toussaint Perkins, Royal Opera House Collections, Alexander Saxton, Judith Siporin, Smithsonian American Art Museum, Melvin B. Tolson Jr., University of Chicago Special Collections Research Center, University of Georgia Press, University of Illinois in Chicago Special Collections, University of Illinois Press. Every effort has been made to contact all rights holders for images and unpublished materials. If you are the rights holder and have not been reached, please inform Rutgers University Press.

Richard A. Courage
Westchester Community College, SUNY

The Muse
in Bronzeville

Introduction

In 1945 social scientists St. Clair Drake and Horace Cayton described the South Side of Chicago as "a community of stark contrasts," at once an impoverished ghetto—densely populated, dirty, disease- and crime-ridden—and a mighty Black Metropolis—a city within a city boasting its own cultural and economic institutions, its own business, professional, and political leadership, and its own intellectual and artistic elite.[1] Geographically, it was a thin corridor, seven miles long and one and a half miles wide. For some three decades, the so-called Black Belt had slowly expanded southward. The area was hemmed in on all sides: to the north by the Loop and the skyscrapers of downtown Chicago, to the west by white working-class neighborhoods with borders defended by gang violence, and to the east by the lakefront properties of affluent WASPs and Jews, who sealed off their neighborhoods by restrictive covenants. Within these narrow confines were found not only crumbling tenement buildings, dilapidated shanties, and storefront churches but also tidy little homes, stone mansions, imposing church buildings, and elegant nightclubs.[2]

Most residents called this area the South Side, but the name Bronzeville, coined by one of its five weekly newspapers in the early 1930s, had become increasingly popular. If the term "South Side" was a neutral geographic description and if the designation "Black Belt" conjured images of southern segregation moved north, then "Bronzeville" was the name most closely associated with racial achievement on various fronts and with community pride and self-definition.[3]

In Bronzeville during the 1930s and 1940s, a remarkable group of creative artists came of age and laid the foundations for brilliant careers. Individually, their names are widely known—among them Richard Wright, Gwendolyn Brooks, Katharine Dunham, Gordon Parks, and Mahalia Jackson. Only in recent years, however, have scholars begun to explore their interconnections and to discern a generational milieu comparable in historical significance to the Harlem Renaissance. This study assumes the centrality of Black Chicago's cultural history to the recovery of a fully contextualized picture of early twentieth-century African American creative expression. The book documents the scope and achievements of Bronzeville's "Renaissance" through detailed accounts of institutional and intellectual origins, profiles of the leading artists and intellectuals, and interpretive readings of selected works of literature, visual art, and music.

A redrawn map of African American cultural history will give some comprehensible shape to the expansive terrain between the Harlem Renaissance and the Black Arts Movement that began three decades later. The process of historical revision promises to replace the current fragmentary view with a more synoptic perspective that stresses both generational contrast and continuity. The Harlem Renaissance will then seem not so much an isolated episode as one part of a larger movement unfolding in two phases, the first centered in New York and the second in Chicago. Both periods of cultural flowering extended across all the arts, and both may be seen as responses to the Great Migration. They were differentiated by the institutions and personalities involved, by the historical forces and events impinging on individual lives and imaginations, and by the specific nature of their aesthetic responses to the underlying phenomenon of urbanization.

A New Generation of Artists

Bronzeville's young artists and intellectuals were committed to the spheres of music and dance, painting and photography, fiction and poetry, journalism and social science, yet in the harsh Depression years, their futures seemed blighted before they could even launch careers. They turned to one another for support, shared ideas and aspirations, interacted daily across disciplinary boundaries, and created in the process a distinctive generational milieu. Needless to say, this milieu encompassed many more individuals and institutions than can be comprehensively discussed in a single volume. Instead, this work sketches a broad view of Black Chicago's artistic community of the 1930s and 1940s, while offering in-depth portraits of key figures and examining the institutions, events, and movements that influenced them.

Music was the precocious discipline of this "Renaissance."[4] The Methodist and Baptist churches established in the late nineteenth century by Black Chicago's "Old Settlers" esteemed European art music and, in the period of this study, produced classically trained musicians such as pianist/composer Margaret Bonds. In the 1920s, the South Side emerged as the center of African American musical innovation, and Louis Armstrong became the most influential jazz musician in the world. In the following decade, former Armstrong sideman Earl Hines and his NBC Orchestra contributed mightily to the development of big band jazz. Bill Broonzy and Muddy Waters, singer/guitarists from the Mississippi Delta, dominated Chicago's blues clubs and recording studios during this period and shaped a distinctive new musical genre. On the religious side of the folk tradition, Thomas A. Dorsey pioneered in the creation of urban gospel music, and the stirring voice of Mahalia Jackson achieved a massive following across the land. In the related performing arts, Katherine Dunham founded her dance troupe in Chicago, transformed African American concert dance, and interpreted diverse cultural practices to popular audiences around the world.

Dunham was a trained anthropologist, and her early career typified the interpenetration of creative expression and social scientific thought within her generation. This interaction is further illuminated by the friendship of Horace Cayton and Richard Wright. Cayton was a former student of pioneering sociologist Robert Park; Wright was a self-educated writer and product of the northern migration. Their professional collaboration on various fronts built on and extended the linked traditions of urban sociology and naturalistic fiction, both rooted deeply in Chicago. Cayton was involved, as community leader, social scientist, journalist, and patron of the arts, in nearly every significant cultural initiative within Bronzeville, while Wright became the leading black writer of his age.

Visual artists made signal contributions through representation of black urban subjects and the forging of a socially conscious aesthetic. Archibald Motley, an accomplished oil painter, was a transitional figure, spanning the generations. His 1928 solo exhibition in New York came at the height of the Harlem Renaissance, and he linked the urban realist tradition of the Ashcan School with the documentary spirit of the 1930s and early 1940s. Among notable younger artists, Margaret Burroughs painted, published poetry and children's books, and left an enduring legacy in the South Side Community Art Center and the DuSable Museum of African American History. In a class by himself was Charles White, known for his striking murals of African American history and magnificently dignified portrayals of ordinary black people. In an allied art form, the multitalented Gordon Parks, photographer for *Ebony* and *Life* magazines, composer, and filmmaker, spent nearly two years in Chicago learning the skills of documentary photography. Other noteworthy achievements in the plastic arts were made by sculptor Marion Perkins and painters Eldzier Cortor and Charles Sebree.

The verbal arts flourished in a wide range of forms and styles, most centered thematically on the Great Migration. Wright was the dominating presence in prose, and his earliest books, following the trajectory of his life, turn on a Mississippi-to-Chicago axis. *Uncle Tom's Children* (1938) and *Black Boy* (1945) are set primarily in rural Mississippi, while the posthumously published *Lawd Today!* (written about 1936) and *Native Son* (1940) explore the harsh realities of life on the South Side. Immediate best-sellers *Native Son* and *Black Boy* had a decisive impact on the future course of African American letters. Arna Bontemps authored two historical novels, *Black Thunder* (1936) and *Drums at Dusk* (1939), which echoed the tocsin of revolt and marked a generational shift from the myth of the primitive to the myth of Spartacus. Other novelists honing their craft in Chicago during these years included William Attaway, whose *Blood on the Forge* (1941) renders an unforgettable portrait of the migration, and Willard Motley, whose *Knock on Any Door* (1947) reveals the naturalistic novel as a literary form on the verge of exhaustion, its very success and longevity planting the seeds for a reaction against sociologically influenced fiction.

In poetry, three figures were preeminent. Gwendolyn Brooks published her first collection, *A Street in Bronzeville*, in 1945, joining a documentary impulse with the formal innovations of modernism. This was followed in 1949 by *Annie Allen*, as a result of which she became the first black writer awarded a Pulitzer Prize. Margaret Walker launched her career in the pages of Chicago-based *Poetry* magazine, where her poems appeared several times in the late 1930s. Her first book of poems, *For My People*, won the Yale Younger Poets Award of 1942. A third poet of lesser stature but still considerable power was Frank Marshall Davis, whose first collection, *Black Man's Verse* (1935), sounded the clarion call signaling the arrival of a new generation.

Crossroads Bronzeville

Creative individuals, however distinguished, do not of themselves constitute the conditions necessary for a broad flowering of the arts. A material base is needed: that complex of schools, libraries, churches, community centers, studios, galleries, concert halls, cafes and cabarets, public institutions and private homes where cultural events take place, where creative artists train, perform, exhibit, and interact, producing the necessary ferment and critical mass. Three focal points of the Harlem Renaissance, for example, were the 135th Street branch of the New York Public Library, where the Harlem Writers' Guild was launched, the offices of the National Urban League on Twenty-third Street, where Charles S. Johnson edited *Opportunity*, and the apartment on Sugar Hill where Johnson's private secretary, Ethel Ray, presided over the social life of the younger artists. Black Chicago too had its creative loci, which developed in the wake of the Great Migration.

The South Side had developed in successive waves, in accordance with the fluctuations of the migration and the degree of resistance from white Chicagoans. The first mighty surge occurred from 1916 to 1919, slowed somewhat during the 1920s, and subsided during the Depression years, but resumed with even greater force during World War II. In 1910 the black population of Chicago was about 44,000; by 1945 it had grown to 337,000—an increase of 666 percent.[5] From a nucleus in the vicinity of Sixteenth and State streets, the black enclave pushed southward in response to the swelling population. In the 1930s and 1940s, the geographical and cultural center was the intersection of Forty-seventh Street and South Parkway (today's Martin Luther King Parkway).

In a profile of Bronzeville published in *Holiday* magazine, Drake and Cayton wrote: "Within a half-mile radius of 'Forty-seven and South Park' are clustered most of the major community institutions, among them the Negro-staffed Provident Hospital; the George Cleveland Hall Library; DuSable High School; the South Parkway Branch of the YWCA; and Corpus Christi, the 'largest colored Catholic church in the country.' Here, too, are the Black Belt's Hotel Grand, the Parkway Community House, and the Michigan Boulevard Garden Apartments built by Julius Rosenwald in 1929 for middle and upper income Negro families."[6] The piece also identifies the most elegant of Bronzeville's nightclubs—the Rhumboogie, Club de Lisa, and El Grotto—and spotlights the Savoy Ballroom, whose central location at the crossroads of Forty-seventh and South Parkway attests to the primacy of big band music.

Further north was another important cluster of institutions. The Chicago Urban League had its headquarters at 3032 South Wabash. The black YMCA, at the corner of Thirty-seventh and Wabash, was the site where Carter Woodson's Association for the Study of Negro Life and History was founded in 1915. Three blocks away, at Thirty-sixth and Indiana, were the editorial offices of the *Chicago Defender*, the nation's leading black weekly. Near Thirty-sixth on Michigan was the South Side Community Art Center, a cooperative venture founded by black artists employed on the Federal Art Project. Near Thirty-ninth Street on South Parkway could be found the Grand Terrace Ballroom, where Earl Hines and his band broadcast live each night on a nationwide radio network, and at Thirty-ninth and State were the offices of all-black Local 208 of the American Federation of Musicians. Such was the distinctive and often contested physical terrain on which Bronzeville was born, its major institutions concentrated in a narrow strip roughly fifteen blocks long and five blocks wide.

Points of Reference

The institutions underpinning the South Side's creative efflorescence were established by the community's civic leadership to advance its interests in a generally hostile climate and to welcome, organize, educate, serve, and entertain the ever-growing mass of southern migrants who pressed against the boundaries of the so-called Black Belt. The historical origins, social functions, and guiding ideas of certain older institutions form the primary focus of the first section of this book, "An Account of Origins." These chapters trace the roots of Black Chicago's creative flowering deep into the soil of African American history, back to Tuskegee Institute and Booker T. Washington and to two whites who linked Tuskegee and Chicago. Robert Park, Washington's former publicity director, was not only a preeminent social scientist but also the first president of the Chicago Urban League, the most important organization attempting to ease the transition of southern migrants into life in the metropolis. Julius Rosenwald, chairman of the Sears & Roebuck mail-order empire and also a Tuskegee trustee, established a foundation that provided fellowships to promising black artists for two decades and contributed seed money to establish and sustain such key institutions as the Wabash Avenue YMCA, the local Urban League, Provident Hospital, and George Cleveland Hall Library.

Another central figure in the first section is African American sociologist and educator Charles S. Johnson, whose formal training in sociology and informal education in power politics were both conducted in Chicago under the tutelage of Robert Park and rooted in the philosophical and political assumptions of the Progressive Era. Later, as editor of *Opportunity*, Johnson played a strategic role in the organizational phase of the Harlem Renaissance. Although the legacy of 1920s Harlem was often treated as a negative model by Bronzeville's young writers, Johnson's vision of "a sociological and literary awakening" and his productive cross-disciplinary collaboration with philosopher and critic Alain Locke prefigured the alliance of Horace Cayton and Richard Wright in the following generation.[7] After moving to Fisk University in 1928, Johnson brought together two generations of black intellectuals, encouraged a rapprochement between Harlem aesthetics and Parkian sociology, and played a key role in the direction and deliberations of the Rosenwald Fund fellowship program.

With the growth of its black population, the South Side developed a racially assertive, entrepreneurial culture that made Chicago the growing edge of African American economic and political advancement before and during Harlem's emergence as the center of black creative expression in literature. *Defender* publisher Robert Abbott, its most representative figure, acknowledged a considerable philosophical debt to Booker T. Washington but joined a commitment to autonomous black institutional development with a defiant race pride and combativeness that were distinctly northern and urban. Within this milieu, black creative artists blazed trails that would be followed, with important differences, by the next generation. Louis Armstrong's trumpet, Archibald Motley's easel, and Fenton Johnson's pen may be regarded as harbingers of the flowering to come.

These early chapters provide points of reference essential to understanding the careers, events, institutions, and works of art discussed in the second section, "Bronzeville's Social

Muse": the institution-building initiatives of the South Side's civic leadership, often in collaboration with Rosenwald philanthropy; the influence of Parkian sociology on creative expression; the nonconfrontational civil rights strategy known as "the arts approach"; the achievements of white Chicago writers in free-verse poetry and naturalistic fiction; and the early achievements and organizational expressions of black Chicago visual artists, writers, and performing artists.

Generational Analysis

Generational analysis is the backbone of this study. Here is a working definition: a generation of artists is a group of men and women born about the same time, coming to maturity in the same historical epoch, and subject to the pressures of the same *Zeitgeist*. They read many of the same books and newspapers, listen to the same music, visit the same galleries, clubs, and social centers. They establish "little magazines," draw up manifestos, congregate in centers of culture like Boston, New York, and Chicago, and develop a strong sense of group identity. They become a contentious avant-garde disputing the rightness of things, and eventually they rise to the ascendancy, either joining the mainstream or transforming it. After enjoying their moment in the sun, they decline into obsolescence, having become passé. This generational affiliation permits the cultural historian to locate the individual artist within the dimension of time.

The following table demonstrates how this paradigm serves the present enterprise. Below are the birth years of eighteen individuals (creative in various mediums), whose careers are highlighted in the second section of this book. In conjunction with such older artists as Bill Broonzy, Thomas A. Dorsey, Florence Price, Archibald Motley, Arna Bontemps, and Langston Hughes, these figures formed the very center of Bronzeville's cultural ferment:[8]

1903	Horace Cayton	1912	Gordon Parks
1905	Frank Marshall Davis	1913	Margaret Bonds
1905	Earl Hines	1914	Charles Sebree
1908	Marion Perkins	1915	Margaret Walker
1908	Richard Wright	1915	Muddy Waters
1909	Willard Motley	1916	Eldzier Cortor
1909	Katherine Dunham	1917	Gwendolyn Brooks
1911	Mahalia Jackson	1917	Margaret Burroughs
1912	William Attaway	1918	Charles White

The average birth year of these artists and intellectuals was 1911, and on average they came of age in 1932, the early boundary of this study. Whereas artists of the Harlem Renaissance launched their careers during the postwar euphoria of the Jazz Age, Bronzeville's artists grew to maturity in a more somber time. Their outlook on the world, aesthetic values, and creative impulses were profoundly influenced by the traumas of the Great Depression and the searing reminders of white supremacy represented by the Scottsboro trials and the racial quarantining of their own community. Most of them were migrants or children of migrants, although not always from the South. While some Chicago artists came from the same sorts of striving middle-class backgrounds as the Harlem group, more typically their parents were sharecroppers, stockyard workers, domestics, or laborers.[9]

This generation first made its presence felt in the early and mid 1930s, a period when mere survival was a triumph. Many found employment on the Federal Writers' Project, the Federal Art Project, or the Federal Theater Project, agencies created by the Works Progress Administration (WPA) to provide work relief for desperate artists. During their young adulthood, many became members or sympathizers of the Communist Party, providing elements of hope and purpose through radical politics in an atmosphere of disintegration and despair. While the musicians generally kept to their own circles of status and affinity, would-be writers and visual artists regularly interacted through overlapping artistic circles. They struggled to eke out a living, obtain training, and find outlets for their work. Beginning with the Art Crafts Guild in 1932, several artists' groups functioned as hot centers of creativity and innovation. Besides the Guild, there were the South Side Writers' Group and, somewhat later, the Chicago Poets' Class. In forging their early careers, these artists also owed debts to institutions as diverse as the *Defender*, George Cleveland Hall Library, Associated Negro Press, Good Shepherd Church and Community Center, the Art Institute of Chicago, the South Side Community Art Center, the John Reed Club, and the cultural projects of the New Deal. The WPA projects and radical political groups were especially important points of contact across the color line among young artists from broadly similar socioeconomic backgrounds. Although Bronzeville's nightclubs certainly drew slumming white thrill-seekers, the projects brought together poor blacks from the South Side and poor Jews from the West Side, producing an interracial milieu profoundly different from that of the Harlem Renaissance.[10]

While a wide variety of specific aesthetic emphases, political commitments, and artistic styles could be found, Bronzeville's artists worked within a broad paradigmatic shift from the racially celebratory mood of the 1920s toward a new sensibility that was decidedly antiromantic, frequently militant, and fundamentally documentary or realist in spirit. Many visual artists looked to the urban realism of the Ashcan School or to Mexico's revolutionary muralists for inspiration. The poets were influenced by the free verse of not only Langston Hughes but also Carl Sandburg, Vachel Lindsay, and Edgar Lee Masters. The fiction writers joined such white counterparts as Nelson Algren and James T. Farrell in reworking the tradition of literary naturalism associated with the novels of Theodore Dreiser. The Bronzeville Renaissance owed as much to the (white) Chicago Renaissance of the 1900s and 1910s as to the Harlem Renaissance, and its artists generally incorporated diverse modernistic influences into mimetic art forms intended to address mass audiences.

By the end of the 1930s, the newcomers, establishing reputations and building new institutions, had wrested the ascendancy from artists associated with Harlem. By 1940, with the American Negro Exposition at Chicago's Coliseum, the landmark publication of Wright's *Native Son*, creation of the South Side Community Art Center, and the Dunham

Dance Company's performances on Broadway, the oncoming generation may be said to have captured the high ground. For a period of fifteen years—roughly 1935 to 1950—Chicago rather than New York was the focal point of African American writing and a major center of visual arts. To encompass its ascendant role as the crucible in which new forms of black musical expression developed, the early boundary of this study is set in 1932, the year that Margaret Bonds and Florence Price both won Wanamaker prizes for composition (Price for her milestone *Symphony in E Minor*) and Thomas A. Dorsey penned his most famous song, "Take My Hand, Precious Lord."

Richard Wright is the central figure in "Bronzeville's Social Muse," and discussions of his life and career thread through three chapters. His struggle to create a new aesthetic at the intersection of several literary and philosophical genealogies—literary naturalism, Chicago sociology, Marxism, and modernism—was embodied in his literary works as well as his photo-documentary book, *12 Million Black Voices*, a central text of the Bronzeville Renaissance. Wright's leadership among black and Leftist writers of his generation is exemplified through his organizing the South Side Writers' Group and the short-lived journal *New Challenge*, his manifesto "Blueprint for Negro Writing," his supervisory position with the Illinois Writers' Project, and his election as a vice president of the League of American Writers as well as by the gravitational pull exerted by the critical and commercial success of *Native Son*.

Bronzeville's leading role in African American creative expression persisted through the late 1940s, when the cultural climate of the Depression years gave way to that of the Cold War. The chilling effects of political repression on politically engaged artists were paralleled by aesthetic shifts from realism/naturalism to surrealist/absurdist fiction, high-modernist poetics, and abstract expressionism in the visual arts. Among black writers, a strong reaction was developing against sociologically influenced and protest literature. When Gwendolyn Brooks won the Pulitzer in 1950 for *Annie Allen*, a tour de force of formalist experiment, the award was a high point of Bronzeville's artistic achievements; it ironically also signaled the waning of the documentary spirit that had informed so many artistic endeavors among her peers. Bronzeville's moment of ascendancy was also undermined by the geographical dispersion of many of its creative artists and by social and demographic changes in Black Chicago that challenged the core cultural institutions of the South Side.

"Renaissance"?

The word "renaissance" is used herein with a certain hesitancy, occasionally placed in quotation marks but more often replaced by such terms as cultural flowering, ferment, awakening, or efflorescence. In 1986 Robert Bone wrote that "'Renaissance' is perhaps a pretentious word to describe the output of a literary generation. But if we wish to retain the usage 'Harlem Renaissance,' then we must accept the notion of a 'Chicago Renaissance' as well. For the flowering of Negro letters that took place in Chicago from approximately 1935 to 1950 was in all respects comparable to the more familiar Harlem

Renaissance."[11] Since then other scholars have rendered the phrase "Harlem Renaissance" increasingly problematic while retaining it as an established term of use. Several authoritative pronouncements serve to suggest a range of conceptual problems whose resolution lies beyond the already expansive scope of this study.

"The term renaissance is entirely appropriate," writes a noted literary scholar, "for in that decade or so a loose but united gathering of black artists, located most significantly in Harlem, *rediscovered the ancient confidence and sense of destiny of their African ancestors* and created a body of art on which future writers and musicians and artists might build and in which the masses of blacks could see their own faces and features accurately and lovingly reflected" [italics added].[12] This view employs the core etymological meaning of "renaissance"—rebirth—and follows a historiographical tradition traceable to Jacob Burkhardt's *The Civilization of the Renaissance in Italy* (1860), which associates creative flowering in a given time and place with a revival of ancient cultural elements.

An eminent historian writes: "If the Harlem Renaissance was neither exclusive to Harlem *nor a rebirth of anything that had gone before*, its efflorescence above New York's Central Park was characterized by such sustained vitality and variety as to influence by paramountcy and diminish by comparison the similar cultural energies in Boston, Philadelphia and Washington" [italics added].[13] This scholar avoids the larger claims of the first and, while acknowledging the geographical dispersion of African American creative work in the 1920s, rests his case on the "paramountcy" of Harlem's "cultural energies."

An essay by a third noted scholar argues that "today's African American renaissance is the fourth such movement in the arts in this century."[14] This discussion of four (!) periods of "high-quality ferment" ignores the generational milieu that is the focus of this study and intensifies terminological quandaries by rendering periods of black "renaissance" closer to the rule, rather than the exception, in twentieth-century African American cultural history.

The most judicious approach might be to avoid the term "renaissance" altogether, but that would unnecessarily marginalize this work from the current and emerging scholarly discussion. Instead, the term is used provisionally while primary emphasis is placed on changing generational dynamics. The existence of a geographical center exhibiting "paramountcy" within a given artistic generation is interrogated and questions are posed concerning the historical significance and specific "vitality and variety" of its "cultural energies." In assessing the questions engaged and the answers tendered, the reader should bear in mind that cultural history is ultimately as untidy and contentious a field as any other area of historical inquiry.

PART ONE

An Account of Origins

CHAPTER 1

The Tuskegee Connection

Nihil ex nihilo; all things have their beginnings. Humans are time-bound creatures, and in tribute to this reality Hesiod places Clio, the Muse of history, foremost among the nine sisters. When the mind encounters a strange phenomenon or new situation, it summons the historical imagination by looking for antecedents, forerunners, continuities with the past. These early chapters invoke Clio's assistance in the search for distant origins of Bronzeville's cultural efflorescence before attention turns to the aesthetic and intellectual currents that dominated the 1930s and 1940s.

The present chronological focus, the period marked by the ascendancy of Booker T. Washington within African American life, extends from his Atlanta Exposition speech of 1895 to his death in 1915. These years roughly correspond to the so-called Progressive Era. At the heart of this chapter is the relationship of white Progressives to both Washington and his network of influence. It describes the interracial collaboration that resulted in the founding of the National Urban League and profiles two whites, Robert Park and Julius Rosenwald, who linked Tuskegee Institute, Washington's power base, with the city of Chicago. Park, Rosenwald, and their circle effected a strategic alliance of social science and philanthropy that had a major impact on African American life and creative expression in Chicago and elsewhere for two generations.

The Wizard of Tuskegee

The last quarter of the nineteenth century witnessed a savage repression intended to destroy the limited social and political gains of Reconstruction and to restore southern white supremacy to its former sway. The plantation system was revived—no longer based on chattel slavery, but on sharecropping, debt peonage, and convict lease. Disfranchisement followed, and when such legal methods as the poll tax and "grandfather clause" failed, the Ku Klux Klan and lynch mob intervened. In the decades that followed the infamous Compromise of 1877, the legal foundations of the Jim Crow system were laid. As federal troops were withdrawn and Reconstruction governments deposed, state legislatures across the South began enacting laws that mandated racial segregation in all spheres of life, from travel and public accommodations to education and marriage. In the 1890s, these laws were upheld by the Supreme Court in a series of "separate but equal" decisions.[1]

The racial caste system established after 1877 was largely inimical to black education. Caste by definition is based on fixed positions in the social order while education's promise of social mobility potentially threatens such feudal arrangements. Education of the former slaves, moreover, had initially been an interracial endeavor built on staunch abolitionist sentiment. Yankee "schoolmarms" who came South during Reconstruction were the pioneers, along with Union Army officers such as Samuel Chapman Armstrong and Oliver Howard, founders of Hampton Institute and Howard University, respectively. Northern Protestant denominations established church-affiliated schools and colleges, and northern philanthropists provided crucial financial support, especially after the Freedmen's Bureau was closed in 1870. From the standpoint of the resurgent white South, however, to educate blacks "beyond their station" was to invite unrest and discontent. "When you educate a negro," South Carolina Senator Benjamin Tillman charged, "you educate a candidate for the penitentiary or spoil a good field hand." Mississippi Governor James Vardaman castigated Yankee philanthropy: "What the North is sending South is not money but dynamite; this education is ruining our Negroes. They're demanding equality."[2]

Blacks were deeply committed to the schooling of their children, however, and mounted stiff resistance to its curtailment. By century's end, Tuskegee Institute and its founder, Booker T. Washington, had become identified as symbols of their hopes. When Washington arrived in Alabama to start his school in 1881, he was about twenty-five years old. (Slave birthdates were unrecorded so he could not be sure.) He looked exceedingly young despite the handle-bar mustache he had grown for instant gravitas, but his "manly bearing," earnest manner, and cautious interracial diplomacy won over local officials.[3]

Born on a plantation near Hale's Ford, Virginia, he had moved with his family to Malden, West Virginia, after Emancipation, acquiring his sturdy frame working in salt furnaces and coal mines and acquiring his early education in a freedmen's school taught by a young black man from Ohio. He also came under the patronage of Malden's wealthiest family: businessman Lewis Ruffner, a former Union Army general, and his wife, Viola, once a teacher in her native Vermont, who bestowed books and the Puritan verities on her education-hungry houseboy. Maintaining good relationships with "the better class" of whites and promulgating the virtues of cleanliness, thrift, self-restraint, and hard work became central facets of Washington's lifework. At Hampton Institute, Washington found his hero and his educational philosophy. He became positively besotted with admiration for Samuel Armstrong, "the noblest, rarest human being" he ever met.[4] The heroic commander of the Ninth U.S. Colored Troops transformed himself during Reconstruction into the Great White Father of an educational institution for former slaves and Native Americans. With charisma, racial arrogance, unwavering self-confidence, and hyperkinetic energy, Armstrong kept Hampton afloat financially while offering his students a regimen of secondary-level book learning, manual labor, religious devotions, and military-style inspections and drills—all held in carefully measured, rigidly maintained balance. These elements fell under the vague rubric of "industrial education."[5] When the Alabama legislature authorized establishment of a normal school for blacks in Macon County, Washington seized the opportunity to reproduce the Hampton model near the very buckle of the southern "Black Belt."

The town of Tuskegee, with two thousand inhabitants, was the county seat and formerly a prosperous cotton market center, but Yankee money was financing more than schools in the South. Steel manufacture and railroad construction were the shape of the future, and little Tuskegee, five miles from the whistle-stop at Chehaw, was being left behind. "Macon has lost more in population in the last ten years than any County in the State," worried a *Tuskegee News* editorial three months before Washington's arrival.[6] Some blacks were leaving the land for the mines and mills of Birmingham. Others, anxiously observing resurgent white supremacy, had in 1879 joined Benjamin "Pap" Singleton's Exodusters, seeking homesteads on free government land in Kansas.[7]

The gains of Reconstruction were not, however, erased overnight. Republicans still held a tenuous grasp on political power in Alabama, and blacks still had the vote. Although Washington was not himself a party to the political deal that enabled the founding of Tuskegee Institute, its history is instructive of the climate in which he built his school. All deals contain an element of duress because that is the nature of power, but some are clearly more one-sided than others. When a former Confederate officer and Democratic candidate for state senate approached Tuskegee's leading black citizen, a successful tinsmith, to ask the price for his support in the 1880 election, the answer was simple and immediate: in return for their votes, blacks must be guaranteed a school to train elementary teachers. Blacks eventually lost the right to vote, but they got their school: Tuskegee Normal and Industrial Institute.

Fifteen years after that election, in his famous speech at the Cotton States Exposition in Atlanta, Washington offered a somewhat similar deal to the entire nation. His simple language, earnest mien, and homely anecdotes belied the mandarin subtlety with which the so-called "Wizard of Tuskegee" simultaneously addressed very different audiences: the southern black masses, the embryonic business class of the New South, and the more sophisticated precincts of northern Capital. Washington urged rural blacks hopeful of "bettering their condition in a foreign land"—such alien locales as Birmingham and Kansas—to "cast down your bucket where you are . . . in agriculture, mechanics, in commerce, in domestic service, and in the professions . . . [and] learn to dignify and glorify common labour." He urged southern whites to "cast down your bucket" with those who "tilled your fields, cleared your forests . . . the most patient, faithful, law-abiding, and unresentful people that the world has seen." The Wizard also exorcised the specter of social equality: "In all things purely social we can be as separate as the five fingers, and yet one as the hand in all things essential to mutual progress." He urged industrialists who might "look to . . . [employ] those of foreign birth and strange tongue" to look instead "among the eight millions of Negroes whose habits you know," who toil "without strikes and labour wars."[8] Washington sought a common denominator among his three audiences in the prospect of a literate, disciplined, and steadily employed black workforce, the basis for "a new era of industrial progress."

The Wizard delivered his speech in Atlanta seven months after the death of abolitionist lion Frederick Douglass. With its near-universal acclaim, whites across a broad geographical and political spectrum set about anointing Tuskegee's founder as the new spokesman for his people. He was hailed by the *Atlanta Constitution* as "a wise counselor and a safe leader" and by President Grover Cleveland as a harbinger of "new hope" for "our coloured fellow-citizens."[9] After the 1901 publication of Washington's autobiography, *Up From Slavery* (1901), northern millionaires flocked to the campus with tributes to a kindred spirit, and newly elected President Theodore Roosevelt invited Washington to dine at the White House, much to the mortification of southern whites. The book was translated into many languages, and, through disciples in Africa, Asia, and the Americas, Washington became the most famous black man in the world.

Tuskegee Institute in the early years of the century was at once a school and the power center of the Negro world, and Washington was one of the most influential figures in American public life. From this defensive bunker and command post, he built an empire that mirrored his own complexity. Its matrix of interlocking spheres embraced whites as well as blacks, northerners as well as southerners, Jews as well as Christians, and extended from the impoverished sharecropper's shack to a round dozen of the world's richest men, from the decrepit tenement to the White House.

Washington recognized the mailed fist beneath the velvet platitudes of American democracy, especially when it came to blacks, and he was prepared to bargain. He hoped to secure literacy and a share in economic growth for his people in exchange for acquiescence, or apparent acquiescence, in the imposition of Jim Crow segregation in the post-Reconstruction South.[10] With Roosevelt, he cut a different sort of deal: black votes in exchange for federal patronage. During the presidential elections of 1900 and 1904, his allies in such northern cities as Chicago, New York, and Boston delivered the black vote to the Republican Party, and in states where the balloting was close, these small margins made the difference. Black public opinion was effectively manipulated by secret subsidies and outright bribes to black newspapers, funded from the coffers of the G.O.P. and placed at Washington's disposal to use as he saw fit.

Like any turn-of-the-century political boss, Washington utilized patronage to build his personal machine. With national Republican leaders in his debt, he could count on their support for appointment of his key allies to posts in the federal government. At the height of his influence, he could command a wide range of appointments from recorder of deeds, custom house inspector, and assistant U.S. attorney to a federal judgeship and even collector of the federal revenue for the port of Charleston. A second source of power was Washington's skillful fund-raising among white industrialists, conducted from luxurious headquarters in a midtown Manhattan hotel midway between the millionaires' mansions and their offices. The fruits of these labors blossomed across the Tuskegee campus: Carnegie Library, Rockefeller Hall dormitory, and Collis P. Huntington Hall, a classroom building. "Steel, oil, and railroads!" the admiring visitor might exclaim.[11]

The less savory dimensions of the Wizard's power cannot be ignored, and they became especially apparent following publication of W.E.B. Du Bois's *Souls of Black Folk* (1903). The young scholar and incipient civil rights leader examined the rise of "Mr. Washington's cult" and acknowledged broad agreement with the Tuskegee philosophy of "Thrift, Patience, and Industrial Training for the masses." Du Bois nevertheless concluded with a forthright challenge: "So far as Mr. Washington apologizes for injustice, North or South, does not rightly value the privilege and duty of voting, belittles the emasculating effects of caste distinctions, and opposes the higher training and ambition of our brighter minds . . . we must unceasingly and firmly oppose [him]."[12] A leader who could brook no insubordination, Washington responded in the following years with increasing acrimony toward Du Bois, sometimes bordering on paranoia. Much of Washington's political maneuvering was conducted in a clandestine atmosphere described by his biographer, Louis Harlan, as "full of spies, whispered confidences, false datelines, and 'personal and confidential' correspondence."[13]

In the years before his death in 1915, the Wizard's power was waning due to urbanization of the black population, the civil rights militancy of the NAACP, and election of southern-born Democrat Woodrow Wilson as president in 1912. At the turn of the century, however, when Washington's personal eminence and power were at their apex and the status of blacks at its nadir, he sought to bargain and maneuver on behalf of his people, despite the overwhelming forces arrayed against them. He attempted, in the time-honored tradition of Brer Rabbit, to outsmart and outlast Brer Fox and Brer Wolf, exploiting the white man's vanities for his own ends and leaving a complex legacy of irony and ambiguity to future generations.[14]

The Progressive Era

Booker T. Washington shares center stage in the first act of this drama with four whites who had strong ties to Tuskegee Institute: William Henry Baldwin Jr., president of the Long Island Railroad and chairman of Tuskegee's Board of Trustees; his wife, Ruth Standish Baldwin, cofounder of the National Urban League; Robert Park, journalist and sociologist, who served for seven years as Washington's director of publicity; and Julius Rosenwald, president of Sears, Roebuck and a Tuskegee trustee. In their collaboration with Washington and such of his northern black allies as social worker George Haynes and physician George Cleveland Hall may be found the origins of institutional alliances and philosophical strains that would play an influential role in Black Chicago of the 1930s and 1940s.

All four were born during the Civil War. They were children when the Compromise of 1877 ended Reconstruction and betrayed the former slaves. They reached their majority in the 1880s, as railroad construction peaked in the United States. They turned thirty in the 1890s, when American manufacturing surpassed agriculture in its contribution to the gross national product. They witnessed, and in part presided over, the transformation of American society from its small-town, agrarian base to a preponderantly urban and industrial way of life.[15]

An increasingly obvious byproduct of this transformation was the running sore of squalid, polyglot urban slums. In response, a reform movement emerged with the new century: middle- and upper-class citizens challenged corporate rapacity, corrupt municipal government, exploitation of the poor, decrepit housing, adulterated foods, and other social ills. The Progressive movement, as it came to be called, engaged the best energies of the Baldwins, Park, and Rosenwald, as they sought to alleviate the worst abuses of laissez-faire capitalism and to improve the lot of poor immigrants from southern and eastern Europe as well as dispossessed African Americans.[16]

Northern whites of the Progressive generation first joined forces with blacks in defense of education in the South. Washington recalled that, on the day of his famous speech in Atlanta, his "personal friend" William Baldwin "was so nervous about the kind of reception that I would have, and the kind of effect that my speech would produce, that he could not persuade himself to go into the building, but walked back and forth in the grounds outside until the opening exercises were over."[17] Although whites had reached near-total consensus on racial subordination, Baldwin and other Progressives demurred from a policy of brute repression and urged strong support of black education—public schools, universal literacy, and opportunity to rise economically, if not politically. Curiously, many of these reformers had close connections with the railroad industry, a circumstance that prompts broad speculation on the nature of the age.[18]

The growth of railroads may provide a key to understanding Progressive ideology, for railroads were widely seen as the very embodiment of progress and modernity. Their seemingly magic power transformed sleepy hamlets into bustling commercial centers and middling cities into great metropolises while newly organized railroad trusts integrated and modernized the national economy. Walt Whitman's "Passage to India" (1870) offers a mythic vision of the first transcontinental railroad:

> I see over my own continent the Pacific railroad surmounting every barrier,
> I see continual trains of cars winding along the Platte carrying freight and
>   passengers,
> I hear the locomotives rushing and roaring, and the shrill steam-whistle,
> I hear the echoes reverberate through the grandest scenery in the world, . . .
> I behold enchanting mirages of waters and meadows,
> Marking through these and after all, in duplicate slender lines,
> Bridging the three or four thousand miles of land travel,
> Tying the Eastern to the Western sea. . . .

Devouring the miles, the iron horse overcame rural isolation, "surmounting every barrier" of mountain, desert, or river to achieve physical and even metaphysical unity.

In the closing decades of the century, track was laid at a frenzied pace, as if the nation embraced the potential of the railroad not only to create physical ties but also to reconcile a people divided and haunted by the wrenching traumas of the Civil War. The Compromise of 1877 signaled that the basis for unifying Blue and Gray was segregating black and white. Yet there remained a minority of wealthy whites, a vestige perhaps of the radical bourgeoisie, who hated the excesses of the racial caste system nearly as much as they hated labor unions. These captains of industry, and in particular the railroad industry, were prepared to support black education, even as they sought, through their alliance with Washington, to control its scope and content. Foremost among the benefactors of Tuskegee was William Henry Baldwin Jr., a young railroad executive from New England.

Origins of the National Urban League

During a meteoric career that lasted from 1886 to 1905, William Baldwin participated at top managerial levels in the economic integration of a continent.[19] He joined business acumen with a strain of moral idealism rooted in the abolitionist and Transcendentalist traditions of New England. A scion of Boston Brahmins, Baldwin graduated from Harvard College in 1885 in the midst of a decade that marked the peak of railroad expansion, and his talents and impeccable upper-class connections easily gained him entree to the growing industry. When Charles Francis Adams, chief executive of the Union Pacific Railroad, wrote to Charles Eliot, president of Harvard, in search of a promising young graduate to groom for leadership, Baldwin got the nod and soon found himself in the railroad's Omaha office, a former staging area for construction of the first transcontinental link. There he served a five-year apprenticeship, mastering the skills of railroad accounting, freight handling, and executive decision-making.

While in Nebraska, Baldwin married his college sweetheart, Ruth Standish Bowles, a descendant of Miles Standish and generations of Massachusetts Puritans, the most recent of whom had turned Unitarian in the early nineteenth century.[20] Her father, Samuel Bowles, a distinguished journalist and founding editor of the *Springfield [Mass.] Republican*, had been in the forefront of the tumultuous political struggle that brought Abraham Lincoln to the White House.

Bowles's friend Bret Harte helped shape the legend of the Golden West through his magazine fiction and poetry. Bowles's several journeys by stagecoach to the mythic landscapes of Colorado, Utah, and California resulted in two books, *Across the Continent* (1865) and *The Switzerland of America* (1868). What Mont Blanc had been to Percy Shelley, the Rockies and Sierras were to this American romantic; their snow-capped peaks and steep escarpments were emblems of the exalted soul.

After graduating from Smith College, Ruth Bowles worked for two years as secretary to its president, while her Harvard beau served his apprenticeship with Union Pacific. This proper Bostonian and fellow Unitarian shared her father's enthusiasm for the West. Baldwin and Bowles were married in October 1889, and their early years together in the frontier towns of Nebraska and Montana fulfilled Ruth's dream of an unorthodox, somewhat dangerous, and altogether bracing life.

In 1894 Baldwin became vice president of the recently consolidated Southern Railway Company. While working at its Washington, D.C., headquarters, he received a visit from Booker T. Washington, who carried a letter of introduction from Baldwin's father, head of the Christian Union of Boston, who had encountered the educator struggling with one too many heavy bags in that city's South Station. Offering assistance, followed by probing conversation, he had been much impressed by Washington's seriousness of purpose and suggested making the acquaintance of his influential son.[21]

The younger Baldwin initially greeted Washington with cautious skepticism. "I shall be glad to help you," he told Tuskegee's founder, "if on investigation, I find it is the real thing."[22] Some weeks later, he paid an unexpected visit, stopping his private car at

Chehaw station and proceeding to tour the campus. Baldwin scrutinized every department with the critical eye of a railroad trouble-shooter.[23] Apparently he found Tuskegee "the real thing," for he became a convert to Washington's philosophy of industrial education, joined the Board of Trustees, and became its chairman and dominating personality. He introduced the rigorous procedures of railroad auditing to improve the institution's solvency and frequently reviewed drafts of Washington's speeches in minute detail.[24]

In the early 1900s, Baldwin's work for Tuskegee shifted increasingly to fund-raising. Then president of the Long Island Railroad and living in New York, he developed contacts among the rich and powerful and solicited their support. In October 1901, for example, he and Washington spoke about Tuskegee at John D. Rockefeller's Bible class at Fifth Avenue Baptist Church.[25] In 1903 Baldwin was instrumental in securing an unprecedented gift of six hundred thousand dollars from Andrew Carnegie to build a library and underwrite the Wizard's extensive speaking tours.[26]

William Baldwin has been judged harshly for his willingness to tolerate racial segregation, yet some interpret his alliance with Booker T. Washington as a personal struggle to rise above the harsh contemporary consensus on race and embrace a Whitmanesque strain in the psyche of white America.[27] In any case, Ruth Baldwin developed, by all accounts, a more expansive social philosophy than her husband and claimed her own place in public life in the years following his death in 1905. Influenced by her nephew, Roger Baldwin, founder of the American Civil Liberties Union, she joined the Socialist Party of Eugene Debs and became a confirmed pacifist.

Active in campaigns for women's suffrage, in the founding of social welfare agencies, and in movements of the Left and labor, Ruth Baldwin never lost focus on the plight of black America. At the time of her husband's death, black migration to northern cities was little more than a slow trickle, yet she grasped the implications of the vast population shift that was just beginning. Ruth threw herself into a new phase of the work that she and William had undertaken together. She became deeply involved in establishing three social welfare agencies, which merged in 1911 to form the National Urban League.[28]

While working at a Philadelphia settlement house, Baldwin's friend Frances Kellor had discovered a shadow-world in which unscrupulous employment agencies lured black women to northern cities by promising well-paying jobs but instead trapping them in lives of prostitution. A social worker of strong activist bent, Kellor organized protective societies in Philadelphia and New York, and the movement spread to other cities. A meeting in December 1905 at Mount Olivet Baptist Church on West Fiftieth Street, then the heart of Manhattan's black community, led to the founding the following year of the National League for the Protection of Colored Women. Its chief concerns were safe lodgings, wholesome recreation, and job training for female migrants. Baldwin was active in the New York branch and became national president after Kellor.

Another leader of the organization's New York branch was William Bulkley.[29] Born a slave in 1861 in Greenville, South Carolina, he attended a Freedmen's Bureau school and then Claflin University, a black institution in Orangeburg. After completing a Ph.D. in Greek and Latin at Syracuse University, he became a public school teacher and principal.

In January 1903, Bulkley attended a private conference called by William Baldwin to discuss economic conditions among blacks in New York.[30] Not much was accomplished, but a few seeds were sown, and two years later, Bulkley established a night school at predominantly black P.S. 80 to offer job training to adults, many of them recent migrants from the South.[31] For help with placement, he approached sympathetic white businessmen, including William Jay Schieffelin, a Tuskegee trustee and president of the Armstrong Association, which raised funds for both Hampton and Tuskegee. Schieffelin prodded his fellow philanthropists to take an interest in northern blacks, an initiative that led in 1906 to formation of the Committee for Improving the Industrial Condition of Negroes in New York. With Schieffelin as chairman and Bulkley as secretary, the group held its first public meeting at Mount Olivet Baptist, and Booker T. Washington delivered the keynote speech. Ruth Baldwin contributed financially and served on the committee's executive board.

In January 1910, Baldwin assembled some thirty-eight leaders at her Manhattan townhouse. Ray Stannard Baker, muckraking journalist and author of *Following the Color Line* (1908), was the featured speaker. Other whites in attendance included Schieffelin and Robert Park, Tuskegee's publicity director and the Wizard's frequent emissary. Among the blacks were Fred Moore, editor of the *New York Age*, Eugene Roberts, a prominent New York physician, and Henry Phillips, rector of an Episcopal church in Philadelphia. All three were staunch "Bookerites," as followers of Washington were familiarly known. The meeting appears to have been orchestrated by the so-called "Tuskegee Machine." There was much talk of "cooperative work" and "non-duplication of effort," as the groundwork for a merger was being prepared. Meanwhile, a black graduate student from Columbia University assumed a prominent role.

George Haynes was born in Pine Bluff, Arkansas, in 1880 and earned his bachelor's degree at Fisk University in 1903.[32] He completed a master's in sociology at Yale and worked for the YMCA until enrolling in a graduate program jointly administered by Columbia University and the New York School of Philanthropy, where he became the first African American to earn a doctorate in sociology.[33] Early in 1910, Haynes approached Ruth Baldwin and Frances Kellor at the offices of the National League for the Protection of Colored Women, pressing on their attention the need for trained black social workers to serve newcomers from the South. So compelling were his arguments and so impressive his credentials that Baldwin and Kellor's first impulse was to hire him as executive secretary of the Committee for Improving the Industrial Condition of Negroes, but, upon encountering opposition in that quarter, they decided to found a new organization. On May 19, 1910, Baldwin chaired a meeting at the New York School of Philanthropy at which the Committee on Urban Conditions among Negroes was born. In its first year, Haynes served as director, leaving his stamp on the organization in its emphases on both sound research informing policy and the training of black social workers, effected through a special arrangement with Fisk University, whose faculty he soon joined. After the three groups merged in October 1911, these perspectives were incorporated into the program of the National Urban League.

In its formative years, the leadership of the Urban League included patrician reformers like Baldwin and Schieffelin, social workers like Haynes and Kellor, and blacks in other professions such as Hall and Moore. A shared understanding of the Great Migration, sociological at base, brought together these leaders. As its name implies, the league responded to the urbanization of American blacks by securing decent housing and jobs, promoting health and safety, and providing sorely needed social services.

Washington served on the league's executive board during the last year of his life, his wife Margaret replaced him in that office, and she was replaced in turn by Robert Moton, his heir at Tuskegee. This dynastic succession bespeaks the respect of Urban Leaguers, black and white alike, for the Wizard of Tuskegee. Eugene Kinckle Jones, director of the organization for many years, maintained that Ruth Baldwin undertook to found the league at Washington's behest.[34] If so, his motives seem transparent. Since the founding of the NAACP in 1909, with his sharpest critic, W.E.B. Du Bois, in a leadership role, Washington must have felt the need for a rival organization. Baldwin's personal loyalty to the Wizard was well known. If she served as the instrument of his factional intrigues, then it was apparently a case of founding the right league for the wrong reason.

Robert Park and Tuskegee

In September 1905, a white man of tall stature, wearing a full beard of Victorian cut, alighted from a train near a small town in Alabama. In July and August, Robert Ezra Park had traveled across the South, observing the racial caste system at first hand, in preparation for his new responsibilities. At the age of forty-one, he had accepted the invitation of Booker T. Washington to assume the post of publicity director at Tuskegee Institute. For nearly eight years, he served as Washington's amanuensis, ghost-writer, and intellectual-in-residence. Decades later, after he had become America's leading sociologist, Park recalled: "I probably learned more about human nature and society, in the South under Booker Washington, than I had learned elsewhere in all my previous studies."[35]

Park was born in 1864 on a farm in Pennsylvania, but grew up in Red Wing, Minnesota, a frontier town on the west bank of the Mississippi, forty miles south of Minneapolis.[36] His father was a Union Army veteran and prosperous merchant. The youth majored in philosophy at the University of Michigan, where he studied with John Dewey. Park was deeply influenced by the philosopher's pragmatic conception of "thought and knowledge . . . as incidents of and instruments of action."[37] Along the way, he mastered Greek, Latin, French, and German and studied English and German literature. After a brief stint teaching high school, Park moved to Minneapolis to become a newspaperman, a phase of his career which lasted eleven years. As reporter and city editor in Minneapolis, Denver, Detroit, New York, and Chicago, he acquired a thorough knowledge of the newspaper industry and the big city and later credited his "wide acquaintances in the slum district" with awakening an "interest in sociology."[38]

In 1898 Park returned to the world of books and enrolled at Harvard for a master's degree in philosophy under the tutelage of William James and Josiah Royce. He proceeded to Berlin, Strasbourg, and Heidelberg, where he worked with the giants of European social science. From sociologist Georg Simmel, he absorbed a basic theoretical orientation to human interaction, a commitment to establishing sociology as a distinct discipline with valid claims to scientific knowledge, and an abiding interest in investigating city life.[39] He studied the history of Germany's agriculture and its peasantry with historian and statistician Georg Friederich Knapp. Under the direction of philosopher Wilhelm Windelband, he wrote his doctoral thesis on the newspaper and society.

Returning to Cambridge in 1903, Park found employment as a philosophy instructor at Harvard, where he put the finishing touches on his dissertation, *Masse und Publikum* (*The Crowd and the Public*). Published the following year in Switzerland, the study advanced an abstract theory of collective behavior and social change, arguing that a *crowd* (ruled by instinct and capable of mob violence) can be transformed into a *public* (ruled by reason and capable of rational decision-making) by means of newspapers and their role in creating awareness of pressing social issues.[40] *Masse und Publikum* also marked Park's early attempts to assimilate Simmel's pioneering work in conflict theory.[41] The winter months in which he toiled to finish his dissertation ushered in a period of malaise. Four years of recondite theoretical work left him "sick and tired of the academic world" and yearning "to get back into the world of men."[42]

Park was eager to test in practice his theories about the nature of public opinion and the journalist's role in a democratic society. Opportunity knocked in the person of Thomas Barbour, secretary of the Baptist Missionary Association, who recruited Park to help organize an American branch of the Congo Reform Association. This lobbying group, composed primarily of Protestant missionaries and their supporters, sought to arouse world opinion against the brutal colonial regime of King Leopold II of Belgium and incidentally to counteract Leopold's favoritism toward Catholic missions.

In 1884 the rival imperialist powers France, Great Britain, and Germany had recognized the Congo Free State as a neutral zone under the "civilizing" stewardship of Leopold, who promptly defied his international mandate and installed himself as absolute ruler of a nine-hundred-thousand-square-mile domain in equatorial Africa, turning its native inhabitants into his tenants. The Africans became subject to a "labor tax," which effectively turned them into slaves forced to extract rubber and ivory for Leopold and the various foreign concessions to which he leased parts of his territory. Those who resisted were shot, tortured, and maimed by mercenaries in the king's service. The Congo Reform Association was established to protest such atrocities.

Park and Barbour launched their campaign in 1904 with Park as secretary and publicist. He assembled a prestigious board of directors, including Lyman Abbott, editor of *Outlook* magazine, Samuel Clemens/Mark Twain, whose antislavery and anti-imperialist views were well known, and Booker T. Washington. Park and Barbour organized public lectures and published indignant exposés so successfully that in 1907 the United States Senate passed a unanimous resolution condemning abuses in the Congo. Within a week, the British Parliament followed suit, and in 1908 the Congo Free State ceased to exist as both a separate legal entity and the king's personal satrapy.[43]

Park and Washington first met in the spring of 1904 at a board meeting of the Congo Reform Association. "I went after an article by Booker T. Washington," Park recalled. "He said he would do it if I got the facts together. I wrote up something, and then he said for me to go ahead and write it up for publication and he would sign it."[44] The article appeared in *Outlook* under Washington's signature; "Cruelty in the Congo Country" was Park's first ghost-writing assignment for his future employer.[45]

At another meeting, Park described to Washington what he had learned about an educational experiment on the Cape of Good Hope, where missionaries were teaching European trades and work methods to their converts: "I told Washington that I was thinking of going to Africa; that there was . . . at Lovedale, South Africa, an industrial school for natives, and that if there was any solution for the Congo problem, it would probably be some form of education." Washington responded with an invitation to visit Tuskegee. As usual, the Wizard had ulterior motives. His white ghost-writer and advisor, Max Thrasher, had died suddenly in 1903, and he had Park in mind as replacement.[46]

Park saw Tuskegee for the first time on February 18, 1905, and that sufficed. He was impressed by the beautiful 3,000-acre campus and, even more, drawn to Washington's educational philosophy with its emphasis on practical training, hard work, and acquisition of property. In an article published three years later, Park called Tuskegee "the greatest mission station in the world."[47] Its success appeared to support a theory taking shape in his mind: the "Negro problem" in the United States was best understood "as an aspect or a phase of the native problem in Africa; . . . a problem which, like slavery, had arisen as an incident in an historical process and as a phase of the natural history of civilization."[48] This "natural history" entailed disruption and butchery on a grand scale as formerly isolated societies came into contact and subsequent conflict: warfare between territorially adjacent peoples; invasion and conquest, as in the Congo; or forced deportation, as in the slave trade. Gradually such bloody conflict gave way to a process of "accommodation," in which a new social order was established and status relations among competing social groups were temporarily fixed.[49] "Progress," Park learned early, "is a terrible thing," and he saw at Tuskegee some hope of ameliorating the most brutal aspects of this seemingly inevitable process.[50]

Park returned to Tuskegee in September to take up his new position as publicity director. The expansive, well-tended grounds were alive with late summer foliage and green lawns, honeysuckle and wisteria vines, neat privet hedges and graceful magnolia trees, giving the impression of a lush green oasis amid the exhausted red soil and sun-bleached shacks of the surrounding countryside. Washington's fame was then at its height, and for the next seven years, Park would be exposed to a fascinating apprenticeship in the ways of power, whose closely guarded secrets had tantalized him since his newspaper days. To watch the Tuskegee Machine in action from the vantage point of its inner circle was to receive instruction in the arts of Machiavelli comparable to a tour of duty in the British foreign office or a senior appointment to the diplomatic staff of the Vatican. Park was perforce drawn from time to time into Washington's factional intrigues against his critics. The original Wizard of L. Frank Baum's Emerald City of Oz was revealed to be a confidence man, and Park was well aware that Tuskegee's Wizard needed the wiles of a confidence man to maintain his empire.

Park wrote Washington's speeches, offered advice on policy, handled correspondence, and supplied the national press, both black and white, with a steady flow of news releases, primarily intended to generate publicity in support of institutional fund-raising. Contacts from his days as a working journalist proved invaluable. His ghost-writing responsibilities involved researching, drafting, or revising "most of Washington's writings for publication between 1905 and 1912," according to Louis Harlan, who specifies the full-length manuscripts that Park brought to fruition: *The Life of Frederick Douglass* (1907), *The Story of the Negro* (1909), *My Larger Education* (1911), and *The Man Farthest Down* (1912). The first three were signed by Washington alone, while Park was acknowledged as coauthor of the fourth.[51] The Wizard apparently wished to enjoy the fruits of authorship without having the trouble of writing books, and Park in turn was habituated, through years of newspaper work, to getting a job done without excessive concern over bylines.

In September 1906, a bloody race riot, erupting in Atlanta, left eleven dead, dozens injured, and widespread property damage in black neighborhoods. Washington hastened to the city in an effort to defuse further violence. W.E.B. Du Bois, who was teaching at Atlanta University, voiced his outrage in "A Litany of Atlanta," one of his most famous poems. Ray Stannard Baker, a white journalist of Progressive views, launched a series of articles on race for *American Magazine*. In November Washington invited Baker to visit Tuskegee in preparation for an investigative tour of the South, and Park had an opportunity to meet his fellow journalist. In the ensuing months, Baker consulted frequently with Washington and sent drafts of his articles to be read by Washington, Park, and another trusted lieutenant, Emmett Scott. These pieces were subsequently published as *Following the Color Line* (1908).[52]

This early involvement in what might very broadly be called riot prevention played a crucial role in Park's response to the larger and more devastating riot that occurred in Chicago during the summer of 1919. In the aftermath of the bloodshed in Atlanta, Park began increasingly to draw on Georg Simmel's dialectical view of conflict as "the resolution of the tension between the contraries" and thus an inescapable element of human interaction and powerful engine of progress. "That which was negative and dualistic," Simmel wrote, "may, after deduction of its destructive action in particular relationships, on the whole, play an entirely positive role."[53] From this perspective, the deepest crises contain the seeds of the most profound changes. Park believed that, in modern societies, the press can ease the path toward mutual understanding between conflicting groups through what he called "scientific reporting."[54]

Park also approached social groups and social interactions from a comparatist perspective. To help his employer gain a similarly broad viewpoint on American race relations, he arranged a European tour in 1910. Early in their itinerary was a trip to the north of Scotland to pay a courtesy visit to Andrew Carnegie at Skibo Castle. Otherwise, Washington had little interest in castles and cathedrals. "I have never been greatly interested in the past," he wrote, "for the past is something that you cannot change. My experience is that the man who is interested in living things must seek them in the grime and dirt of everyday life."[55] Hence on their travels through England, Germany, Austria-Hungary,

Italy, Poland, and Denmark, Washington and Park focused on meeting rural peasants, urban proletarians, and even homeless drifters. The product of this trip was a little book titled *The Man Farthest Down*, which placed the status of southern blacks in international perspective.

Park's last major project in Alabama was to organize an International Conference on the Negro in April 1912. Speaking to an audience composed largely of missionaries, he posed the question, "How far is it possible by means of education to abridge the apprenticeship of the younger to the older races, or at least to make it less cruel and inhuman than it now frequently is?"[56] Another speaker was William I. Thomas, professor of sociology at the University of Chicago, who had read some rather sophisticated prose emanating from Tuskegee and was curious to discover its source. Park and Thomas discovered many shared theoretical interests, including peasant life, urban migrations, and race relations. A correspondence ensued, in the course of which Thomas urged his new friend to join the Chicago faculty. Park's decision, so pregnant for the future of American social science, was swiftly made, and he moved to Chicago in the fall of 1913.

Julius Rosenwald, American Citizen

Robert Park taught at the University of Chicago for more than twenty years, officially retiring in 1933 but lecturing occasionally until he moved to Fisk in 1936. He gave his last lecture in Rosenwald Hall, a building endowed by Julius Rosenwald, whom Park first met at Tuskegee in 1911.[57] With Tuskegee as a common bond, the two men collaborated productively on several fronts, not least of which was the founding of the Chicago Urban League. Millions of Americans, including two generations of African American creative artists, benefited from the remarkable generosity of Julius Rosenwald, the son of a Jewish peddler who became president of Sears, Roebuck.

Rosenwald was born in Springfield, Illinois, in 1862. His father had arrived from Germany eight years earlier and succeeded in exchanging a peddler's pack full of kitchen utensils, cloth, and sewing materials for a successful clothing store that supplied uniforms to the Union army. The boy grew up in a comfortable neighborhood, one block west of Abraham Lincoln's former residence. He was a typical middle-class, middle-American youth, save for the fact that his family worshipped at a Reform Temple rather than a Protestant church. At seventeen he was sent to New York to serve an apprenticeship with his uncles in the garment district. In 1885 he moved to Chicago, where in partnership with a cousin, he established a firm manufacturing lightweight men's suits. Chicago was a boomtown in the years following the devastating 1871 fire, and the business was modestly successful until the depression of 1893.[58]

Meanwhile, Richard Sears, a young Minnesotan with a genius for marketing, quit the Great Northern Railroad and went into business with Alvah Roebuck, a watch-maker from Indiana. They began by selling watches to farmers through a network of railroad station agents doubling as salesmen, and they soon added furniture, wagons, household goods, patent medicines, clothing, and numerous other items to their catalog. Needing capital to expand and with Roebuck eyeing retirement, Sears offered a half-interest in the business to Aaron Nussbaum in 1895. Nussbaum in turn offered his brother-in-law, Julius Rosenwald, a quarter-interest for $37,500, an investment described by Rosenwald biographer Peter Ascoli as "one of the most brilliant decisions in American business history."[59]

The growth of Sears, Roebuck at the turn of the century was phenomenal. In 1895 the firm employed about eighty people; by 1908 its workforce exceeded eight thousand. Much of this increase occurred after the organization built a forty-acre complex of warehouse facilities, manufacturing units, administrative offices, printing and advertising building, power plant and railroad terminus on Chicago's West Side in 1906.

Rosenwald's personal rise was no less phenomenal. Bringing much-needed adminis-trative and organizational skills, he moved from minority stockholder to vice president, and in 1901 he and Sears bought out Nussbaum for $1.25 million. Sears resigned seven years later, and Rosenwald became president.[60] Presidential trappings followed in due course, including a spacious mansion on Ellis Avenue, near the University campus in Hyde Park, and a country estate in Ravinia on the shores of Lake Michigan, capstone of Chicago success.

Just as the railroads helped integrate the national economy by providing physical access to remote corners of the continent, so Sears, Roebuck—strategically located in the nation's railroad hub—provided access to a common market for mass-production in-dustries. Everywhere the railroad went, the telegraph followed. Sears had originally been a railroad telegraph operator and recognized the commercial value of speedy communica-tions. While the telegraph allowed quick processing of orders, the system of Rural Free Delivery, inaugurated by the U.S. Post Office in 1896, ensured prompt delivery. Thus was formed the infrastructure of the country's greatest mail-order house.

The glossy pages of the Sears catalog, more than a thousand pages long and distrib-uted free of charge, reached millions of potential buyers in the hinterland and joined the Bible and *Farmer's Almanac* as primary diversions of rural households. America's Book of Desire broke the dam of Puritan self-denial and opened the sluice gates of consumerism. Caught in this historical transition, general stores folded right and left, for they could hardly rival these glorious visions, much less compete with the ruthless efficiency of the modern corporation. Sears, Roebuck undersold them consistently and changed the buying habits of a nation.[61]

Sometime after Rosenwald turned forty, he began directing his millions toward wor-thy causes. Another prominent Chicago Jew influenced this dramatic change. Emil Hirsch emigrated to the United States from Luxembourg when he was fourteen, studied at the universities of Pennsylvania, Berlin, and Leipzig, and briefly served as a rabbi in Baltimore and Louisville, before assuming the pulpit at Chicago Sinai Temple in 1880.[62] The temple, at Twenty-first Street and Indiana Avenue, was an impressive edifice, built in 1876 and designed by famous architects Louis Sullivan and Dankmar Adler. Hirsch's congregants included such wealthy businessmen as Rosenwald, shoe manufacturer Siegmund Florsheim, and the principals of clothier Hart Schaffner & Marx.[63]

Hirsch quickly gained national recognition as a writer, scholar, and civic leader. He was founding editor of the *Reform Advocate*, in whose pages he conducted a running skirmish with spokesmen for Conservative and Orthodox Jewish traditions, urging rapid "Americanization" and such radical reforms as Sunday services and elimination of Hebrew readings and prayers. Acutely aware of social differences separating German Jews from the Yiddish-speaking *shtetl* Jews of Eastern Europe, he noted their possession of greater "wealth, culture, education and liberalism over [the] Russian brother of late arrival." Hirsch argued that religious obligation, social justice, and self-interest required extending assistance to fellow Jews. In 1900 he was instrumental in founding Associated Jewish Charities of Chicago, and eight years later Rosenwald became its president.[64] Hirsch's discomfort with the religious conservatism of Eastern European Jews complemented his assimilationist sentiments. "If we come to consult really who are our co-religionists," he remarked in one sermon, "we shall discover that we have much more in common with the Unitarians and Ethical Culture people than with the orthodox Jews."[65] Hirsch's views spurred Rosenwald's desire to become involved in liberal religious circles and Progressive reform movements.

Progressivism was intimately associated with the settlement house movement and the Social Gospel, and Chicago was a center of both. Rather like secularized versions of foreign missions, settlement houses sought to ameliorate living conditions and impart WASP values in impoverished, immigrant neighborhoods. Ideologically, they were rooted in a non-Marxist, Christian-socialist tradition, believing with their most famous proponent, Jane Addams, in "the common interest of labour and capital" and "the gradual interpenetration of the two classes."[66] They were broadly sympathetic to the labor movement and organized consumer cooperatives to purchase coal and food supplies at wholesale prices. Sharing Addams's view that "the blessings which we associate with a life of refinement and cultivation . . . must be made universal if they are to be permanent," settlement houses brought high culture to the masses through lending libraries, art and music lessons, concerts, galleries, and theater groups.[67]

Addams founded Hull House in 1889 in a teeming West Side neighborhood populated by Italians, Bohemians, Greeks, and Eastern European Jews. Its female staff tended the sick and buried the dead, provided kindergarten classes, taught English language and literacy to adults, organized a boys' club, and offered sewing and art classes.[68] After 1899 some Hull House residents served as probation officers for the municipal Juvenile Court, the first such institution in the country.[69] A few blocks north, Chicago Commons was founded in 1894 by Graham Taylor, a Congregational minister and professor of "Christian sociology" at Chicago Theological Seminary. Taylor became a noted proponent of the Social Gospel through weekly columns in the *Chicago Daily News*, a nationally circulated newsletter, *The Commons*, and a book called *Religion in Social Action* (1913).[70]

In an era before racial violence and restrictive covenants locked the vast majority of blacks into the tightly bounded South Side ghetto, several settlement houses on the South Side were sites of interaction between the races. Institutional Church and Social Settlement was founded by African Methodist Episcopal minister Reverdy Ransom in 1900.

With a day nursery, kindergarten, employment bureau, gymnasium, and 1,200-seat auditorium, Institutional was, according to Ransom, "not a church in the ordinary sense . . . [but] a Hull House or Chicago Commons founded by Negroes."[71] In 1905 white Unitarian minister Cecilia Parker Woolley established Frederick Douglass Center on South Wabash, which became a popular location for "the best whites and blacks" to interact at concerts, forums, and teas.[72] In the same year, Jenkin Lloyd Jones, a white Union Army veteran and Unitarian minister, opened the Abraham Lincoln Centre on Oakwood Boulevard. The five-story complex was designed by his nephew, Frank Lloyd Wright, and intended as a showcase experiment in adult education and interracial cooperation.[73]

Seeing organic connection among ministry, social service, and higher education, Graham Taylor accepted an invitation from University of Chicago president William R. Harper to teach a downtown extension course for social workers in training. In 1906 he joined other Progressive civic leaders in organizing an independent venture that became the Chicago School of Civics and Philanthropy. Its curriculum included courses in social investigation, local government, industrial relations, philanthropy, and rehabilitation of juvenile delinquents as well as fieldwork placements at some twenty agencies. Sophonisba Breckinridge, an instructor of political economy at the University of Chicago and close associate of Jane Addams, became director of the school's research department in 1908. Breckinridge in turn persuaded Edith Abbott to leave the economics department at Wellesley College.[74]

Embracing this milieu enthusiastically, Julius Rosenwald contributed both his wealth and administrative skills. In 1902 he became a trustee of Hull House, and he maintained a series of substantial annual pledges to Chicago Commons. When the School of Civics and Philanthropy was incorporated, he agreed to serve on its board, "equivalent to a 'living endowment'" in Taylor's judgment.[75] Rosenwald became a University trustee in 1912 and donated a lifetime total of $4.5 million to its support. In the realm of municipal reform, he was a major financial backer of the 1912 mayoral campaign of political science professor Charles Merriam and enthusiastically campaigned for him in Jewish and African American wards.[76]

Abetted by his friend Paul Sachs, junior partner in the investment banking firm of Goldman Sachs, Rosenwald forged ties between white Progressives and African Americans. Sachs frequently traveled to Chicago to serve the financial needs of Sears, Roebuck, and, after the day's business was concluded, the two men often found themselves discussing their common interest in reform movements. During a trip in the spring of 1910, Sachs was full of news concerning his recent involvement with Ruth Standish Baldwin and her associates. That summer, he sent Rosenwald a gift—a slim volume titled *An American Citizen: The Life of William Henry Baldwin*.[77]

This inspirational biography portrays the socially conscious businessman as hero and role model. Writing to his daughters, Rosenwald described the book as the "glorious . . . story of a man . . . whom I shall endeavor to imitate or follow as nearly as I can." He added that Baldwin "was a good friend to Booker T. Washington and made great study of the Negro problem along common sense, helpful lines."[78] Perhaps equally compelling to this second-generation immigrant was the title, for Rosenwald aspired to be an American citizen in every conceivable sense. In the end, he validated his American identity through his role in Progressive circles and by ameliorating the grim legacies of that most American of institutions, chattel slavery.

A Saul who had seen a blinding vision, Rosenwald lost no time in pursuing philanthropic initiatives on behalf of African Americans. In December 1910, Dr. Jesse Moorland, a black Congregational minister and administrator of the Colored Men's Department of the YMCA, headquartered in Washington, D.C., traveled to Chicago at the invitation of L. Wilbur Messer, general secretary of the local (white) YMCA. Moorland's mission was to raise funds for the construction of a facility to serve the South Side. Rosenwald invited the two men to lunch at the Sears headquarters and offered then and there to donate twenty-five thousand dollars to build a YMCA in any black community in the nation that raised seventy-five thousand dollars on its own.[79]

Formal announcement of the grant program was made on New Year's Day 1911. Speaking to an audience of five hundred African Americans, Rosenwald linked their fate with that of the Jews, referring to pogromist violence in Russia and anti-Semitism in the United States.[80] The *Chicago Defender* gave front-page coverage to the campaign to raise matching funds on the South Side, emphasizing community self-help and a ringing endorsement from Booker T. Washington.[81] Eventually, twenty-five cities took advantage of Rosenwald's offer, and Chicago's Wabash Avenue YMCA, a handsome five-story brick structure with 114 dormitory rooms and recreational and meeting facilities, opened its doors in June 1913. In years to come, the Wabash "Y" would be the site of many of the South Side's most important political and cultural initiatives.[82]

Washington first met Rosenwald during a fund-raising trip to Chicago in May 1911. In October the philanthropist hired a private railroad car and took a group of friends, including Emil Hirsch, Graham Taylor, and L. Wilbur Messer, to Macon County. He shared his first trip to Tuskegee with Progressive leaders from Chicago in order to lay a strong foundation for their future collaboration. Meeting publicity director Robert Park was an important element in the emergence of this political alliance. On February 12, 1912, Lincoln's birthday, Rosenwald was appointed to Tuskegee's board, a post in which he served for the remainder of his life.[83]

Later that year, Washington approached Rosenwald with a proposal to foster the spread of literacy by constructing rural elementary schools. The philanthropist responded with a plan to match building funds raised by local black communities. In 1913 a pilot project under Washington's personal supervision began in the vicinity of Tuskegee. The program was soon extended throughout Alabama and, thereafter, to the entire South. By 1932, the year of his death, Rosenwald had helped build 5,357 modern, attractive elementary schools for black children.[84] The schools functioned within the context of a Jim Crow system—far less than full justice, to be sure, but a substantial dent in the problem of illiteracy. By the late 1920s, an estimated two out of every five black schoolchildren in the deep South attended one of the so-called "Rosenwald schools."[85]

Such were the lines of force radiating from Tuskegee Institute toward the end of the Progressive Era: the New England idealism and organizational sophistication of William

1. Julius Rosenwald and Booker T. Washington, 1914.
Special Collections Research Center, University of Chicago Library.

and Ruth Baldwin joined with Washington's northern allies such as George Cleveland Hall and George Haynes, culminating in the founding of the National Urban League; the intellectual discipline and high seriousness of Robert Park shifted from Tuskegee to Chicago; and the powerful leverage of Julius Rosenwald's private fortune combined with his social vision. Chapter 2 describes the manner in which these vectors converged in 1915 and 1916 with the founding of the Chicago Urban League. A fruitful interpenetration of philanthropy, social work, and social science resulted, from which emerged institutional infrastructures and intellectual paradigms that powerfully enabled and influenced African American creative expression. A central figure in this interracial collaboration was black sociologist Charles S. Johnson.

CHAPTER 2

Charles S. Johnson
and the Parkian Tradition

Robert Park was forty-nine years old and on the threshold of a new career when he taught his first classes at the University of Chicago in 1913. In less than a decade, he emerged as the dominant star in a brilliant constellation known to posterity as the Chicago School of Sociology. Not the least of his achievements was creation of a cadre of African American social scientists to carry on a tradition of inquiry, much of it centering on the Great Migration. Among them was Charles S. Johnson, whose life and career weave together many threads in this narrative.

While studying at the University, Johnson also worked with Park at the Chicago Urban League, where he documented the living conditions of blacks on the South Side. He nearly perished in the 1919 riot, which convulsed the city as whites reacted savagely to destabilized race relations and shifting neighborhood boundaries. When the governor convened an investigative commission, Johnson assumed a key role, overseeing research on the riot's background. He served as principal author of the commission's report, *The Negro in Chicago* (1922), a landmark of social scientific inquiry and a testament to his optimistic faith in the power of scrupulous research, reasoned discourse, and interracial contact to improve race relations. As editor of the National Urban League journal *Opportunity* from 1923 to 1928, Johnson extended Parkian notions about the relation between public opinion and social change in an effort to organize a full-fledged literary and cultural movement centered in Harlem.

The Teacher

As Park settled into a new position at an institution that was itself barely two decades old, his first task was to master his own discipline. He had studied philosophy at five universities, but his only formal instruction in sociology was a single course with Georg Simmel at Berlin. His apprentice years were devoted to extensive reading in sociology, anthropology, and social psychology, under the mentorship of his friend William Thomas, who was about the same age, but already an established figure in the field. Park found a congenial intellectual atmosphere at the University. His undergraduate professor, John Dewey, had moved from Michigan to Chicago in 1894 and taught there for ten years while developing his pragmatic philosophy in dialogue with sociology and other disciplines. George Herbert Mead, Dewey's colleague in the philosophy department, taught at Chicago from

1894 to 1931, and his course "Advanced Social Psychology" profoundly influenced graduate students and faculty in the social sciences.[1]

Park was initially appointed professorial lecturer in the Divinity School, based on his "special knowledge of the Negro" and expertise in collective psychology.[2] In 1914 he introduced a course in the department of sociology called "The Negro in America." This was its catalog description: "Directed especially to the effects, in slavery and freedom, of the contacts of the white and black race, an attempt will be made to characterize the nature of the present tensions and tendencies, and to estimate the character of the changes which race relations are likely to bring about in the American system."[3] Park next offered a course titled "Crowd and Public," which addressed such topics as "crowds, mobs, panics, manias, dancing crazes, stampedes, mass behavior, public opinion, fashion, fads, social movements, reforms and revolutions."[4]

As Park's exploratory reading progressed, he added new courses. "The Newspaper" grew out of his earlier career as journalist and focused on the influence of the press on public opinion amid the rapidly changing conditions of city life. "The Survey" addressed methodological problems in studying urban environments. Shortly after American entry into World War I, Park developed a fifth course, "Race and Nationality," which linked his knowledge of black life with broader theoretical interests in migration and cultural assimilation.

Park is best remembered for some thirty essays on race, ethnicity, and culture published during his tenure at Chicago.[5] His central contribution was the concept of a race relations cycle through which alien peoples necessarily pass once they are brought into close proximity.[6] Park identified four successive stages: contact, conflict, accommodation, and assimilation. Throughout human history, he observed, cross-cultural contacts have occurred as a result of war, commerce, and migration, while in modern times dramatic changes in modes of communication and transportation have mobilized formerly isolated peoples. Initial contact zones, which Park described as cultural or racial frontiers, become arenas of competition and conflict, where Darwinian struggles for survival prevail. Gradually, however, conflict gives way to some form of accommodation in which "status, subordination, superordination, control" become temporarily fixed and regulated by custom or law.[7] Eventually, if diverse populations remain in contact over long periods of time, some degree of assimilation or amalgamation occurs.

Park's belief in the inevitability and ultimately progressive nature of these historical processes today appears largely a product of Progressive Era optimism and ethnocentrism. His formulations on race have been critiqued and refuted from various perspectives, yet they remain among the earliest efforts of the human mind to treat the complexities of cross-cultural contact in a systematic way and to develop a theory of socially constructed behavior and belief that contradicted earlier views of innate racial essences and racial hierarchy.[8] Whatever its limitations, Park's theory of a race relations cycle served as a core premise for a generation of American social scientists.[9]

Park became involved in new areas of applied research as a result of the intensifying nativism that accompanied American participation in World War I. Immigrant organizations such as the Sons of Italy and the Deutsch-Amerikanischer Bund came under suspicion of potential disloyalty during the war, and calls for instant "Americanization" of the foreign-born became common. Hoping to deflect mounting hysteria and threats to civil liberties, the Carnegie Corporation commissioned ten studies of immigrant groups in the fall of 1917. Park was invited to direct a survey of the foreign-language press, which he undertook in Chicago and New York and produced a report entitled *The Immigrant Press and Its Control* (1922).[10] The book's nuanced conclusions recognized immigrant organizations and newspapers as cultural bridges between countries of origin and American society. Park observed that immigrants' efforts to preserve their mother tongue and cultural heritage through ethnic newspapers led paradoxically to their gaining access to knowledge that facilitated greater acculturation. His primary exemplar was the Yiddish-language *Jewish Daily Forward*, edited by Abraham Cahan.[11]

From the age of twenty-three, when he left the prairie town of his youth for a newspaper in Minneapolis, Park had a love affair with the city, which he perceived as a transformative force. Influenced by Simmel and Thomas, he conceptualized the modern metropolis as a place where social forces of attraction and repulsion, organization and disorganization, eventually find dynamic resolution. This dialectical synthesis, born of urban diversity and productive conflict, permits human consciousness to reach a higher plane. In Park's sociological terrain, *city* functions as the antipode of *hinterland*; it is the terminus of all migrations, the fulfillment of an evolutionary imperative, "the natural habitat of civilized man."[12] Little wonder that some should identify his crowning achievement as his work in urban sociology. In 1915 Park published a seminal essay on the city as a primary site for "investigation of human behavior." Ten years later, a book-length expansion, with contributions from several coauthors, appeared while he was president of the American Sociological Association (ASA).[13] He proposed "the city" as the theme for the society's annual meeting and solicited papers from a roster of distinguished sociologists. Park's biographer, Winifred Raushenbush, describes that conference as a "maturing point for American sociology. . . . [and] the acme of Park's sociological career."[14]

Park's research in urban sociology required a setting where data could be gathered and theories tested. His department chair, Albion Small, proposed that Chicago itself serve as laboratory. Park took charge of fieldwork projects and persuaded the University Press to underwrite a series of monographs on urban life, most of them authored by his students. Among the more famous were Nels Anderson, *The Hobo* (1923), Louis Wirth, *The Ghetto* (1926), Frederick Thrasher, *The Gang* (1927), and Harvey Zorbaugh, *The Gold Coast and the Slum* (1929). Under Park's leadership, Chicago—both city and university—became the acknowledged center of urban studies in the United States.

Such was the formidable array of theories and investigative methods confronting Park's graduate students. Much was expected of them, for they were being trained for leadership in their discipline, but much guidance and support were provided. Park met often with doctoral candidates, suggested dissertation topics, monitored their prose at sentence level, and later wrote introductions to their books and offered advice far into their careers. By mid-century eight of his former students had succeeded him as president of the American Sociological Association.

Among Park's students were a number of African Americans recruited to the University through his professional connections across the country. Among them were such future distinguished scholars and educational leaders as Charles S. Johnson, E. Franklin Frazier, Bertram Doyle, Horace Cayton, St. Clair Drake, Horace Mann Bond, Lewis Wade Jones, Oliver C. Cox, and Earl Moses. By the early 1930s, Johnson and Frazier chaired the departments of sociology at Fisk and Howard, flagship institutions among black colleges and universities. In 1945 Bond became the first African American president of Lincoln University in Pennsylvania; two years later, Johnson became the first black president of Fisk. Frazier became first African American president of the ASA in 1948. Drake and Cayton's *Black Metropolis* (1945) stands as a landmark sociological study and a central document of Bronzeville's cultural flowering.

The Student

Charles Spurgeon Johnson was born in 1893 in Bristol, Virginia, about 150 miles from Hale's Ford, Booker T. Washington's birthplace. Johnson much admired Washington and, like him, was a southerner to the marrow of his being, conceiving his leadership role from a southern perspective.[15] His father, Charles Henry Johnson, was a Baptist minister trained at Richmond Theological Institute (later known as Virginia Union University). Although born into slavery, "he had the rare good fortune," according to his son, "to be reared in the house of a quiet Greek scholar . . . so aloof from the burning political controversies of his time that he could devote himself to the education of his own and his servant's son without apology."[16] Having been tutored by this Virginia gentleman, who may have been his father, Charles Henry was sent with his benefactor's white son to Richmond to complete his education. After graduation he became a missionary traveling the Virginia mountains. In 1888 he married Winifred Lee Branch of Lynchburg, and the young couple undertook a mission to the railway workers of Bristol, a raw frontier town. There Reverend Johnson served for more than forty years as "spiritual adviser, legal and business counsel, guardian and banker, nurse and doctor, tutor and social worker."[17]

Turn-of-the-century Bristol was a typical town of the upper South, marked by certain relaxations of racial mores. "My parents," Johnson recalled, "knew all of the Negro families and most of the white families that had any standing at all; and they lived on terms ranging from tolerant indifference to restrained cordiality with all of them."[18] Nonetheless, the growing boy witnessed a hardening of the color line, as the legislatures of Virginia and other southern states passed a profusion of Jim Crow laws.

When Johnson was twelve or thirteen, he witnessed the prelude to a lynching, as a mob of besotted whites dragged their victim through town en route to a public hanging. He watched in amazement as his "diminutive but courageously righteous father stood alone in the center of the street through which they passed, shouting solemn warnings against their reckless and ungodly lawlessness."[19] The crowd streamed around the preacher. Some snickered at his outrage, but none dared threaten him. Johnson thus grew up with both a deep hatred of racial injustice and an understanding of the limits of individual bravery in confronting it.

At fourteen the youth was sent to Wayland Academy in Richmond, a preparatory school, operated under Baptist auspices, for sons of the black elite,. At Virginia Union University, Johnson managed the football and baseball teams, edited the school newspaper, became president of the student council, and delivered the valedictory address. He graduated in 1916 after only three years.[20] His community service included delivering food baskets and making home visits among desperately poor blacks in Richmond, in the course of which this offspring of Virginia's black bourgeoisie experienced stirrings of empathy for "children classed as delinquents, . . . impoverished tobacco workers, . . . men in prison, . . . humble people who made up the families on the left side of the tracks."[21] Such feelings pointed in the direction of graduate study in sociology to better understand, and perhaps change, an unjust social order.

Johnson arrived at the University of Chicago in 1916, just three years after Robert Park. Son of a Baptist minister, named for a Baptist evangelist, and educated under the stern regimen of Baptist missionaries, he had chosen the University in part for its sectarian affiliation. Nothing in his provincial past, however, prepared him for the intellectual stimulation he found in Park's courses. From formal contacts in the classroom, the relationship between Park and Johnson progressed to the journeyman/apprentice stage and then to a deep friendship lasting almost three decades. The turning point came, according to Johnson, "when it dawned on me that I was being taken seriously and without the usual condescension or oily paternalism of which I had already seen too much."[22]

Johnson took full advantage of his mentor's intellectual resources, emerging from his apprenticeship with a comprehensive grasp of urban and migration theory, the race relations cycle, and the case-study method. But perhaps Johnson's greatest debt to Park was his exposure to the scientific ethos. Christian altruism and reform instincts, he soon realized, would not pass muster in this new milieu. The ameliorative impulse of his youth must be tempered by the rigors of scientific method. "The first thing you have to do with a student who enters sociology," Park wrote, "is to show him that he can make a contribution [even] if he doesn't try to improve anybody. . . . Sociology should not help to build up reform programs, but it should help those who have to build these programs to do it more intelligently."[23]

As a disciple of John Dewey, Park was firmly committed to the principle of learning by doing. To enhance Johnson's academic work, he arranged for him to acquire practical skills in research and administration. Park had attended the founding convention of the National Urban League in 1911, and, when a Chicago branch was formed five years later, he became its first president. Determined that "the League should be a source of knowledge and insight as to what actual conditions were," Park created a research department and hired Johnson as part-time director.[24] After compiling extensive files on black life in Chicago, Johnson undertook three field studies: an examination of juvenile court records to document instances of police brutality, an investigation of housing conditions among migrants on Wabash Avenue, and a broad survey of the economic and social status of blacks in Milwaukee.[25]

Meanwhile, Park was drawing on Tuskegee connections to advance his protégé's career. Two years after Washington's death, his former confidential secretary, Emmett Scott, was invited by the Carnegie Endowment for International Peace to study black migration. When Scott consulted Park about suitable research assistants, Johnson was recommended and given a leave of absence from the Urban League. His territory was the Mississippi River Valley, and in late 1917 he made an extensive field trip through Mississippi, Missouri, Illinois, Wisconsin, and Indiana, producing a series of reports that Scott incorporated into his book *Negro Migration during the War* (1920).[26]

Johnson's memoir attests to his fascination with "the Negro migrants, then moving in millions in a current too vast for them to comprehend."[27] This surging tide of black humanity engaged his imagination and best scientific energies, and he emerged during the 1920s as the nation's most knowledgeable expert on the subject.[28] For him, as for Richard Wright and Horace Cayton in the next generation, the northern migration became the central reality of African American life.

"Freedom Train"

In 1900, 90 percent of the black population of the United States lived south of the Mason/Dixon line. The percentage declined to 79 by 1930 and to 53 by 1970.[29] This dramatic demographic shift occurred in two great waves, each triggered by a world war. From 1910 to 1920, New York City's African American population increased by 66 percent, Chicago's by 148 percent, and Detroit's by a phenomenal 611 percent, with most of the growth occurring during World War I.[30] As Europe was caught up in the slaughter, young men were conscripted, and immigration to the United States virtually halted. American factories ramped up production to supply the wartime needs of France and Britain even as the labor force was contracting. When the United States entered the war in 1917, labor shortages reached crisis proportions, and northern industry turned to the South to find new workers. To a black population groaning beneath Jim Crow segregation, endemic poverty, soil erosion, and the ravages of the boll weevil, this was opportunity speaking to desire. The Great Migration was a watershed in African American history, a time of transition from the Age of Washington to an era generally designated as the New Negro movement or the Harlem Renaissance.

Migration was encouraged by labor agents promising good jobs and high wages, by friends and family who had already moved North, and by Robert S. Abbott and his *Chicago Defender*.[31] Abbott, a native Georgian, had moved to Chicago in the late 1890s and founded the weekly *Defender* in 1905. Within a decade, it achieved the largest paid circulation of any African American newspaper, eventually surpassing an estimated 230,000 copies with two-thirds of the readership outside Chicago. On September 2, 1916, Abbott ran a front-page photograph captioned "The Exodus," depicting a massive crowd of "northward bound" blacks waiting for a labor train outside Savannah. From that point on, he preached migration with evangelical zeal. "MILLIONS TO LEAVE SOUTH" shouted his banner headline of January 6, 1917. Utilizing a network of news dealers, black railway workers, traveling entertainers, barbershops, and churches, the *Defender* penetrated every nook and cranny of the Black Belt, from Maryland to Texas, with a simple exhortation: "COME NORTH!"[32]

And come they did. From 1916 to 1919, half a million southern blacks resettled in northern cities. They were in fact the advance guard of a far larger exodus, an estimated total out-migration of five million between 1910 and 1960.[33] From the deep South, they surged northward in two great streams: one up the Mississippi River Valley toward Chicago, the other up the Atlantic seaboard toward Philadelphia and New York. From the upper South, many made the shorter trip to Detroit, Cleveland, or Pittsburgh.

Whatever their individual destinations or transportation modes, the migrants shared collective memories of railroad journeys that brought so many out of Pharaoh's land and into something resembling freedom. Such journeys reinforced the archetypal image of the freedom train within the African American cultural tradition. This motif runs from folk tales, songs, and narratives of escape on the metaphorical Underground Railroad through what Albert Murray called "locomotive onomatopoeia"—railroad sounds absorbed and echoed in the music of the blues and jazz.[34] The freedom train also appears frequently in twentieth-century poetry and fiction. A scene early in Toni Morrison's novel, *Jazz* (1992), for example, portrays migrants Violet and Joe Trace leaving rural Virginia in the Jim Crow car of the Southern Sky. As they approach New York, their feet begin to tap in joyful anticipation. Too excited to sit still, they begin to dance in the aisle, swaying to the rhythm of the train: "They weren't even there yet and already the City was speaking to them. They were dancing. And like a million others, chests pounding, tracks controlling their feet, they stared out the windows for first sight of the City that danced with them, proving already how much it loved them."[35]

Within the portion of this great saga that is the present focus, the "Freedom Train" was literally the Illinois Central Railroad, which ran circa 1910 from a passenger terminal in downtown Chicago south to Cairo, Illinois, crossed a corner of Kentucky and Tennessee, and extended the length of Mississippi, through Jackson to New Orleans, roughly approximating the course of the Mississippi River. From western Tennessee, a branch line diverged in a southeasterly direction to Birmingham, Alabama, where the IC connected with a subsidiary line leading to Columbus and most of central Georgia. In short, the IC and its feeder lines linked Chicago to the heart of the Black Belt: Louisiana, Mississippi, Alabama, Georgia, Arkansas, and Tennessee.[36]

Within months of Booker T. Washington's death, black farmers and laborers, whom he had exhorted to "cast down your bucket where you are," began to move en masse. Seemingly overnight, as if to defy the great river's sense of direction, the Illinois Central became the conduit of a relentless northern flow. They came from the Louisiana bayous and the Mississippi delta, the red clay farms of Georgia and Alabama, the hills and valleys of Arkansas and Tennessee, converging on Cairo and moving on to the great midwestern metropolis. James Grossman estimates that, between 1916 and 1919, some fifty to seventy thousand blacks moved north to Chicago.[37] That may not seem large in absolute numbers, but the rate of growth is impressive. From 1910 to 1920, the black population of Chicago increased by at least 148 percent, a figure that dwarfs the 24-percent growth rate for the city as a whole. In 1910, blacks constituted 2 percent of total population; in 1920, 4.1 percent; and in 1930, 6.9 percent—an almost exponential growth curve.[38] By any measure, the absorption of tens of thousands of migrants was no small task. To serve their needs, the Chicago Urban League was founded.

The Chicago Urban League

In December 1916, two leaders of the National Urban League headed for Chicago to establish a local branch.[39] Executive Secretary Eugene Kinckle Jones, having made several preliminary trips, stayed only long enough to oversee the founding ceremonies, but T. Arnold Hill, his assistant and protégé, remained for eight years, serving as local executive secretary under several presidents, beginning with Robert Park. Jones and Hill had both grown up in Richmond and, like Charles Johnson, attended Wayland Academy and Virginia Union University.[40] All three men, being black Virginians of their time and place, shared a deep admiration for Booker T. Washington. All three belonged to Alpha Phi Alpha, the first and still most prestigious black fraternity, with a strong tradition of leadership and service.[41] All were active in the early affairs of the Chicago Urban League and served as functionaries of the national organization in the 1920s: Jones as executive secretary, Hill as director of industrial relations, and Johnson as research director and editor of *Opportunity*.

Three white Chicago residents were already connected with the National Urban League when Jones and Hill arrived in the city. Robert Park had been present at the organization's founding in New York, Sophonisba Breckinridge was a member of the board of directors, and Julius Rosenwald was a major contributor. All were enthusiastic about the prospect of a local branch. While Park was a relative newcomer to the city and professionally skeptical of idealistic reformers, Breckinridge and Rosenwald were mainstays of the Chicago Progressive movement.[42] Breckinridge and her friend Edith Abbott promoted the league among social workers and enlisted the support of Jane Addams of Hull House, Mary McDowell of the University of Chicago Settlement, Celia Parker Woolley of the Frederick Douglass Center, and Amelia Sears of the Juvenile Protective Association.[43]

Rosenwald and his confidential secretary, William Graves, helped line up other potential board members.[44] Heading the list was George Cleveland Hall, chief surgeon at Provident Hospital and a well-known black leader, who soon joined Breckinridge on the national board and also became vice president of the Chicago chapter. Because legal challenges might be expected, several lawyers were approached for support, including Judge Edward Brown, white president of the Chicago NAACP, and Albert George, who later became the first black appointed to the city's municipal bench. Two newspaper publishers, Robert Abbott of the *Defender* and Victor Lawson of the *Daily News*, likewise agreed to serve on the board, ensuring sympathetic press coverage.

Jones and Hill convened a planning session in December at the Wabash Avenue YMCA. Those present included representatives of a dozen social service agencies, including such black leaders as Alexander L. Jackson, executive secretary of the Wabash "Y," Joanna Snowden Porter and Jessie Johnson of the Chicago Federation of Colored Women's Clubs, and Mrs. William Carry of the Baptist Women's Congress. Hall presided; a constitution and bylaws were proposed, a slate of officers endorsed, and a budget for the first year approved. On January 10, 1917, a general session, at the same location, ratified these proposals and began the process of formal incorporation.

With substantial financial support from Rosenwald, Robert Park presided over the fortunes of the Chicago Urban League during its formative years from 1916 to 1918. In his first annual report, he observed that the problems of blacks became "more intelligible" when considered "in the same category with other immigrants—the Jew, the Italian and the Slav." Those common problems were "work and wages, health and housing, the difficulties of adjustment of an essentially rural population to the conditions of a city environment, and to modern life." He added, however, that "the European immigrant is not subject to racial discrimination," associated with "the fixed and permanent form of caste" experienced by blacks.[45] Park focused the league's energies on concrete projects in the spheres of jobs, housing, and social services. Such programs, he believed, must be based on accurate information; hence, he created a research department and appointed Charles Johnson as its director in June 1917. While Park, as president and ranking social scientist, largely set the league's agenda, Hill, as executive secretary, took charge of day-to-day administration, fund-raising, staff appointments, and membership recruitment. Beyond these routine duties, he began, in the spring of 1917, to cultivate the goodwill of white employers and trade unions, for his special responsibilities were job placement and follow-up inspections at work sites.[46]

As migrants arrived at the Illinois Central terminal, they were greeted by black volunteers from the Urban League, working under the supervision of the Travelers Aid Society. Cards were distributed with the league's address and telephone number, offering assistance in the search for housing and employment. League headquarters housed an employment bureau where college-educated blacks screened job applicants and referred them to prospective employers. Between March and November 1917, the league placed 1,792 migrants with such firms as Swift, Armour, International Harvester, Montgomery Ward, and Sears. In 1918 the organization found jobs for 6,861 clients, and in 1919 the number rose to 12,285.[47] In 1918 the league added a children's department with a full-time staff member to address the ill effects of poverty and transplantation. It organized a day care center for children of working mothers, sponsored a citywide conference on juvenile delinquency, established liaison with public schools to address truancy, and investigated police brutality in the treatment of juvenile offenders.

Through such programs, the league emerged from the war years as the leading social agency in Chicago's growing black community. Toward the end of 1917, the organization had some five hundred members, of whom perhaps fifty might be considered activists: officers and staff, board members, committee chairmen, and dedicated volunteers.[48] Politically,

2. Job seekers in the waiting room of the Chicago Urban League, c. 1919.
Chicago Urban League Records, 1916–2000. Series 1, box 1, folder 3. CULR_02_0001_0003_0001.
University of Illinois at Chicago Library.

its inner circle consisted of Robert Park, Julius Rosenwald, and George Cleveland Hall, each with strong ties to Tuskegee.

A Vestige of the Tuskegee Machine

George Cleveland Hall was born in Ypsilanti, Michigan, in 1864, but his family moved to Chicago when he was five.[49] The son of a Baptist minister, he was educated in public schools, at Lincoln University in Pennsylvania, and at Bennett Medical College in Chicago, where he earned his M.D. in 1888. Following two years of private practice, he joined the staff of Provident Hospital, founded in 1891 with an interracial staff of doctors and nurses serving both black and white patients. Hall became chief surgeon in 1894 and established undisputed control in 1912 by displacing black surgeon Daniel Hale Williams, the institution's founder. Williams, better trained than Hall, is best known as the first doctor to perform successful open-heart surgery. But Hall possessed, according to historian Christopher Reed, "a steely will . . . that allowed for bureaucratic combat" and "an ability to interact well with powerful, successful figures," which he used effectively to secure the financial resources necessary to serve the needs of a neighborhood growing increasingly black and poor.[50]

Hall won his battle to control Provident with the aid of Booker T. Washington. As a rising professional, he had joined the National Negro Business League, founded and led by Washington, and he soon became a member of its national committee. In the winter of 1907, he was invited to Tuskegee, where he attended to an ailment of his host's son and

3. George Cleveland Hall, c. 1920.
Vivian G. Harsh Research Collection
of Afro-American History and Literature,
Chicago Public Library. Hall Branch
Archives 145.

presumably met Robert Park. Some months later, Dr. and Mrs. Hall were entertained at the Washingtons' summer home in Huntington, Long Island. Hall's medical skills so impressed Tuskegee's founder that he invited the Chicagoan to become his personal physician. Although both Hall and Williams were loyal Bookerites, the former ultimately proved more useful to the Wizard's hope of continued national political influence. Hall served on the executive committee of the Hyde Park Republican Club and campaigned vigorously for Washington's favored candidate, William Howard Taft, in the 1908 presidential election.[51]

In the dynamics of the Tuskegee machine, one good turn deserved another. In 1910, as the struggle for control of Provident Hospital neared a climax, Washington wrote to Hall requesting a photograph and biographical sketch. A few weeks later, the surgeon received a marked copy of the *Baltimore Afro-American*, containing a full-page spread celebrating his professional accomplishments. The article appeared simultaneously in thirty-five black newspapers.[52] The skillful orchestration from Tuskegee bore the unmistakable stamp of its publicity director, Robert Park. In the same year, Hall chaired the fund-raising campaign for the Wabash Avenue YMCA and met the other Tuskegee stalwart, Julius Rosenwald. From 1911 until his death in 1932, the philanthropist made substantial annual contributions to Provident Hospital.[53]

Hall collaborated with Park and Rosenwald in several important ventures in Chicago. The prime mover in the first was pioneering black historian Carter G. Woodson, who had overcome early hardships to complete a Ph.D. at Harvard and become a high school teacher in Washington, D.C. Woodson was visiting Chicago and staying at the Wabash

"Y" in the summer of 1915. He enjoyed passing evenings in the company of Hall, chairman of the Y's board, and its director, A. L. Jackson, a recent Harvard graduate. On the
evening of September 9, Woodson, Hall, Jackson, and two friends sat in the lounge, discussing D. W. Griffith's *Birth of a Nation*. That incendiary film had been released in the
spring and was playing to packed houses across the country. Some dramatic gesture, the
men felt, was required to counter its venomous racism. Woodson proposed that they
found, then and there, an organization devoted to studying Negro history. Adjourning to
a nearby office, they committed their dreams to paper.[54]

Hall's four companions chose him to serve as first president of the Association for the
Study of Negro Life and History. One of his initial tasks was to approach Rosenwald and
request support to establish a journal. Always a cautious investor, the Sears president
waited for the appearance of the first issue under Woodson's editorship in January 1916
and then pledged four hundred dollars a year to the quarterly *Journal of Negro History*. Hall
served as president of the association for two years, until its first nationwide meeting in
Washington in August 1917. He was succeeded by Robert Park, who was no mere figurehead, but an active fund-raiser, soliciting support from such Tuskegee supporters as philanthropists George Foster Peabody, James H. Dillard, and J. G. Phelps-Stokes. Rosenwald
also attended the convention and joined the executive council along with Hall's protégé
Jackson, research director Woodson, and national YMCA executive Jesse Moorland.[55]

The second major collaboration of Hall, Park, and Rosenwald was founding the
Chicago Urban League. Rosenwald may in fact have taken the lead in this project.
According to Horace Bridges, leader of the Chicago Ethical Culture Society and Park's
successor as Urban League president, "There is some reason to think that Mr. Rosenwald
had earlier intimated to the officials of the National organization his hope that a branch
would be started in Chicago."[56] Consistent with Rosenwald's cautious habits, such "inti-
mations" were presumably accompanied by his pledge of financial support and advance
commitments from Park and Hall to serve as president and vice president.[57]

In physics, the law of Conservation of Energy holds that energy can neither be created nor destroyed, but only converted to another form. Some such law seems likewise to
govern human affairs. The cultural energies generated at Tuskegee during Booker T. Washington's lifetime did not disappear with his death in 1915 but were transformed by his
admirers. Through the Chicago Urban League, Park, Hall, and Rosenwald adapted
Bookerite values and methods to the circumstances of northern urban life. The symbolic
shift from Tuskegee, Alabama, to Chicago, Illinois, from rural South to urban North, constituted a dramatic change in the social base of African American life. What remained
constant was a central value that defined both Tuskegee and the Urban League: concern
for practical solutions to the problems of "the man farthest down." Washington, in his
context, focused on providing black farmers with the rudiments of literacy and modern
agricultural methods. Park, in his, focused on providing black migrants with jobs, housing,
and social services—the rudiments of civil life. But their motives were essentially the
same. For this reason, *The Man Farthest Down* (1912), which bears the names of both men,
is a crucial link in African American cultural history.[58]

Park, Hall, and Rosenwald were politically sophisticated men. Each had seen enough of the Tuskegee machine to absorb something of its ethos and techniques. They knew how to create an organization and shape it to their will, how to handpick a slate and get it elected. As occasion required, they could be visible, presenting a suitable façade to the outside world, or invisible, working secretly behind the scenes. They knew how to deal and how to circumvent, when to speak and when to remain silent. They knew how to defeat adversaries and, in hostile encounters, were as full of wiles as Brer Rabbit. Each man honed these skills in his own professional world but found a common role model in the Wizard of Tuskegee.

The Chicago Urban League is thus best understood as a vestige of the Tuskegee machine, reconstituted in the city of Chicago, not long after Washington's death.[59] Within its purview, Park, Hall, Rosenwald, and their allies sought to create an organizational infrastructure to ease the settlement of black migrants in their new home. Elsewhere in the city, there was only neglect or overt hatred. In the summer of 1919, eight months after Germany's surrender ended warfare on the Western Front, the hatred infecting Chicago metastasized into race war. While the streets ran with blood, the Urban League was put to the test, and its efforts to defuse the crisis called for all the political finesse the Tuskegee network could muster.

"Cry Havoc!"

American entry into World War I interrupted Charles Johnson's studies for a year. He enlisted in the 103rd Pioneer Infantry, was sent to France, and rose to the rank of sergeant-major. His regiment took part in the vast, bloody Meuse-Argonne offensive and was under fire for twenty-two days. Early in July 1919, Johnson was transported by troop train to the port of Brest, gateway for American soldiers entering or leaving France. There he embarked for Virginia, but not before witnessing a clash between white and black troops in the streets of Brest. He was mustered out in Newport News, but in nearby Norfolk he again observed the violence of white soldiers and sailors, who perhaps wished to remind their black comrades-in-arms that the "home of the brave" was anything but free. Traveling from Norfolk to Chicago by way of Washington, he observed similar episodes in the nation's capital. Johnson arrived in Chicago on the evening of July 21. Six days later, that city exploded in an orgy of bloodletting.[60]

The postwar world that Johnson confronted was a breeding ground of political reaction. During the war years, winds of change had swept across Europe. The Bolshevik revolution was the eye of the hurricane, and everywhere the propertied classes trembled. By 1919, however, a fierce backlash was under way. In Hungary, Germany, and Italy, bids for power by the Left were thwarted, and the seeds of fascist dictatorship sown.[61] Nor was the United States immune from the general hysteria. Within a few months of the Armistice, an American expeditionary force was dispatched to Siberia in support of Admiral Kolchak and his counterrevolutionary "White" armies. Back on home territory, Attorney General A. Mitchell Palmer was hunting down, jailing, and deporting immigrant radicals and union militants with the zeal of a Puritan witch-hunter.[62]

This period of global repression was the background of the bloody summer of 1919. The Great Migration and the Great War had destabilized American race relations by disrupting the fixed patterns of southern life and bringing unprecedented freedom of movement to the black masses. But in the war's aftermath, new boundaries were drawn and old taboos reinstated. Competition for jobs and housing was the proximate cause of the riots, but their deeper motive was to reestablish the *status quo ante*, to remind blacks of their place. Riots swept through twenty-six American cities from May to October, and the epicenter of the convulsion was Chicago.

"Very hot—100 degrees," Reverend Graham Taylor noted in his diary on July 27.[63] As a faint breeze stirred the surface of Lake Michigan, a black youth named Eugene Williams floated on a log raft with four companions, enjoying the cool water. The boys were unaware of a vicious fight taking place on shore as a group of blacks attempted to swim at the previously all-white Twenty-ninth Street beach. As they drifted across an invisible racial boundary in the lake, a white man at the end of a breakwater began hurling rocks. Williams was struck in the forehead, lost his grip on the raft and drowned. When a white policeman refused to arrest Williams's assailant, despite positive identification by the other youths, fighting broke out again, escalated with an exchange of gunfire that left a black man dead, and the Twenty-ninth Street beach became the flashpoint for rioting that spread across the city.[64]

Pitched battles were fought on the South Side, along the boundaries of the ghetto, and in nearby white neighborhoods. Blacks living in isolated enclaves in other parts of the city were especially vulnerable. Gangs of armed whites roamed the streets, shooting at random and torching houses. Blacks were dragged from streetcars and beaten. Several were murdered by mobs near the stockyards, located in the Irish, Polish, and Lithuanian neighborhoods west of Wentworth Avenue. The rest stopped reporting to work. The surface cars and elevated trains stopped operating. "Race riots and street car strike menace city," Taylor recorded on July 28.

Embattled blacks fought back, sometimes in disciplined self-defense, sometimes in random retaliation. A. L. Jackson posted a group of veterans at windows and fire escapes to protect the YMCA. Years later he recalled carloads of armed whites speeding into the area: "Cars came through, and they came directly east and turned north on Wabash . . . shooting as they came. My boys, of course, returned the fire."[65] After five days of violence, the state militia established martial law. Thirty-eight Chicagoans lay dead; of those, twenty-three were black and fifteen white. At least 537 persons of both races were seriously injured, and an estimated 1,000 were left homeless. For the city, indeed for the nation, the readiness of South Side blacks to exchange blow for blow was now established fact.[66]

On the second day of the riot, Robert Park must have awakened with the guilty joy of a seismologist shaken out of bed by an earthquake measuring eight points on the Richter scale. Always the scientist, but never merely the scientist, his first move was to organize a delegation to press the chief of police to enforce the law in a racially even-handed manner and specifically to bring charges against the policeman who had refused to arrest the killer of Eugene Williams.[67] He next accepted chairmanship of a Joint Emergency Committee formed by the Urban League, the Union League Club, the Wabash Avenue YMCA, and other groups in an effort to protect the civil rights of blacks arrested during the rioting. This decisive action took place in the context of a relatively passive response by the Chicago branch of the NAACP.[68] Park also activated the concept of a governor's commission, with a broad mandate to investigate and publicize the underlying causes of the riot. Central to his plan was to gain control of the editorial process by placing his protégé Charles Johnson in a key position.[69]

After returning from France, Johnson had resumed his duties as research director of the Chicago Urban League. Early on July 28, he began walking toward his office on Wabash Avenue. "He saw a man stabbed to death on the steps of the building," reports a biographer. "He himself was shot at. Cut off by the milling mobs from his rooms near the University, he ran onto fresh bursts of rioting all the way from the Loop to the Midway."[70] The experience of such random violence, following hard upon the even-greater horrors he had witnessed in the European trenches, strengthened Johnson's determination to transform dangerous crowds into rational publics through the patient labors of research, education, and reasoned discourse.

As the city reeled from the violence, the local Tuskegee network was swinging into action. Prominent settlement house director Graham Taylor, an ally of Park and Rosenwald, called an emergency meeting of business executives, reform leaders, and representatives of major black institutions. Eighty-one concerned citizens assembled on August 1 at the influential Union League Club. Their chief order of business was to draft a letter asking Governor Frank Lowden to appoint a commission to investigate the riot. A committee of six was chosen to "wait upon the Governor," of whom three—Taylor, William Graves, and T. Arnold Hill—were members of the Urban League.[71]

Lowden equivocated at first, but under pressure from such powerful men as Rosenwald and industrialist Cyrus McCormick III, he capitulated, turning the matter over to Francis Shepardson, his cabinet member for education. Shepardson had previously been a history professor and Park's colleague at the University of Chicago. He served as vice chairman of the Chicago Commission on Race Relations throughout its existence and, on its demise, he became executive secretary of the Rosenwald Fund. Shepardson proposed a commission of twelve members, six white and six black. Rosenwald referred him to A. L. Jackson for suggestions about black members. On August 20, Shepardson announced the names of his blue-ribbon panel. Four commissioners had direct ties with Tuskegee Institute: Julius Rosenwald, George Cleveland Hall, Robert Abbott, a friend of Washington's, and prominent attorney Edgar Bancroft, the commission's chairman and a Tuskegee trustee. Two others, Victor Lawson and Edward Brown, were members of the Urban League's executive board. With Shephardson's tie-breaking vote, the Tuskegee network was firmly in control.[72]

The most pressing issue when the commission first met on October 9 was selection of a full-time executive secretary, and the body authorized a search committee composed of Rosenwald, Hall, Jackson, and Shepardson. By late November, there were two finalists: Graham Romeyn Taylor, white, age thirty-nine, and Graham Taylor's son; and Charles Johnson, black, age twenty-six, and Robert Park's protégé. Taylor had served as special assistant to the American ambassador to Russia during the war and returned to Chicago about two months after the riots.[73] After extensive discussion and behind-the-scenes negotiations, the body agreed to hire both an executive and an associate executive secretary. The senior appointment and larger salary went to the white man, an unmistakably American arrangement.[74]

On December 11, Taylor and Johnson submitted an outline of their proposed study to the commission. By late January, they had rented office space and "secured a list of people available as paid investigators."[75] An interracial team of ten field investigators was hired, three of whom were Park's students.[76] Their research took most of the year to complete and encompassed six areas: racial clashes, housing, industry, crime, racial contacts, and public opinion. These analytical categories were expanded to ten chapters in the final report. Writing and editing the report consumed the first half of 1921, and finally the commission submitted a 672-page document to the governor. The University of Chicago Press published *The Negro in Chicago* (1922) in its entirety with wide circulation and wide acclaim. In years to come, it served as a model for many race relations surveys, including Johnson's own *Patterns of Negro Segregation* (1943), Gunnar Myrdal's *An American Dilemma* (1944), and St. Clair Drake and Horace Cayton's *Black Metropolis* (1945).

Despite its official corporate authorship, *The Negro in Chicago* is today generally acknowledged as the first of Charles Johnson's many books, the work he wrote (or mostly wrote) in lieu of a doctoral dissertation. Two years of on-the-job training in the formal investigation of race relations marked the culmination of Johnson's apprenticeship with Park and served as the foundation of his scholarly career.[77] The circumstances were unorthodox, to be sure, but the notion of academic apprenticeship, with its core of supervised research, remained intact.

Standing in the role of mentor, Park broadly influenced the design of the study, its methodology, content, and presentational strategies.[78] Early on, Johnson and Taylor reported to the commission about "helpful interviews" with several consultants, including Park, fellow sociologist Ernest Burgess, and T. Arnold Hill.[79] Two months later, they reported that their plan for investigating public opinion was improved by "certain amplifications suggested by Professor Robert Park."[80] Park insisted that a race relations survey was "inevitably . . . a study of public opinion," and *The Negro in Chicago* concludes with two substantial chapters on the subject, together constituting one-quarter of the book.[81] One deals with mutual perceptions of blacks and whites; the other consists of detailed studies of both black and white newspapers. The fifty photographs illustrating the book gradually progress from shocking images of violence to images of restored order to images featuring blacks and whites interacting harmoniously at work and play. Park's guiding concepts, if not direct hand, are evident in this sequence, signaling an intention to confront white readers' racial misconceptions by controlling the image-making function.

In his work for the Lowden Commission, Johnson first encountered the Tuskegee machine running at full throttle. From his unique vantage point, he observed how Park, Hall, and Rosenwald circumvented official inertia and harnessed power to their own purposes. At his initial interview with the search committee, Johnson met Hall and Rosenwald, and he reportedly "worked closely" with the philanthropist during the subsequent study.[82] Familiar with the crucial distinction between having the name and having the game, the young scholar must have carefully studied the process of his own appointment, the necessary fiction of a white figurehead, and the subsequent isolation of that figurehead from actual editorial control. In these crucially formative months, Johnson was maturing as both sociologist and wizard, acquiring mastery of not only books, theories, and research methods but also the political realm, and learning how to work the levers of power to make things happen in the world. Some months before *The Negro in Chicago* appeared, Johnson's achievements were validated by the offer of a new job, which brought him and his wife, Marie Burgette, to New York. There he found a new arena in which to deploy the knowledge, skills and competencies, political stratagems and philosophical assumptions he had absorbed in Chicago.

Strategist of the Harlem Renaissance

When Johnson joined the National Urban League staff as director of Research and Investigation in July 1921, he was expected to produce the sort of dispassionate, densely factual surveys for which he himself had provided so exemplary a model in Chicago. During his seven years at league headquarters, he investigated and reported on the economic and social conditions of blacks in Baltimore, Pittsburgh, Buffalo, Los Angeles, and other major cities. Johnson proceeded from the Parkian premise that information media potentially constitute a fulcrum with which to move public opinion in a positive direction.[83] While in Chicago, he had drafted a brief paper on propaganda and race relations. Against "racial propaganda" intended to demean and dehumanize blacks, Johnson counterposed "educational and correctional propaganda . . . directed toward the white public principally . . . to change public opinion by providing a foundation in actual fact."[84]

At league headquarters, Johnson began pressing for a broader definition of his duties. He persuaded the organization's officials to replace a modest newsletter, the *Urban League Bulletin*, with a more ambitious monthly, *Opportunity: A Journal of Negro Life*, and to devote a substantial portion of an annual $8,000 grant from the Carnegie Corporation to its costs of publication.[85] From the journal's first issue in January 1923, its editor sought to document the realities of race and race relations in order to effect the slow transformation of an unreasoning *crowd* into a potentially rational *public*. For "Facts," in the Parkian scheme, "are . . . only facts in a universe of discourse . . . something which has come into existence to enable individuals associated in any . . . common purpose, to think consistently and to act understandingly, and in some sort of concert."[86]

The establishment of a common set of facts and common universe of discourse across racial lines was no small task in the years following the premier of *The Birth of a Nation* in 1915 and the "Red Summer" of 1919. Arnold Rampersad has noted with bitter irony that Harlem's cultural "renaissance" was most immediately preceded by "the renaissance of the Ku Klux Klan."[87] And virulent "Nordic" supremacy was hardly confined to lower-class whites. Despite such notable exceptions as Park and his colleagues at the University of

Chicago and anthropologist Franz Boas at Columbia, the American academy in this period was busily producing, through its various disciplines, a vast body of literature that rationalized racial inequality.[88] Johnson used *Opportunity* to challenge this "prostitution of science," penning article after article with such titles as "Mental Measurements of Negro Groups" (February 1923), "The Verdict of 'Common Sense'" (June 1923), "Public Opinion and the Negro" (July 1923), and "Blind Spots" (January 1924).[89]

The editor was also attuned to the freshening winds of cultural awakening and in sympathy with what the multitalented writer, diplomat, and NAACP leader James Weldon Johnson called "the art approach to the Negro problem."[90] Early in 1922, the latter's *Book of American Negro Poetry* was published by Harcourt. Its introductory essay explored the achievements and vernacular roots of black poetry and asserted that "nothing will do more to . . . raise his status than a demonstration of intellectual parity by the Negro through the production of literature and art."[91] In the spring of that year, Claude McKay's collection, *Harlem Shadows*, set a new standard of high seriousness for the younger poets. In the summer and fall, the early poems of Countee Cullen and Langston Hughes were showcased in *The Crisis*, the NAACP journal. In 1923 Jean Toomer's stunning debut, *Cane*, was published by Boni and Liveright. Such "fugitive and disconnected successes of certain of the generation of Negro writers now emerging" spurred Charles Johnson's resolve to organize a full-fledged literary and cultural movement and to challenge the NAACP for leadership in the cultural arena.[92] His strategy unfolded along three lines: (1) discovery of new talents and their concentration in New York, to achieve a critical mass; (2) creation of a milieu where ties could be developed between black and white intellectuals; and (3) cultivation of sympathetic whites in the New York literary world who, by virtue of their reputation or role as power brokers, could offer access to major magazines and publishing houses.

In July 1923, *Opportunity* published an article called "A Librarian in Harlem." Its author, a white woman named Ernestine Rose, had directed the 135th Street branch library since 1920 and, through a series of strategic appointments, had successfully integrated its previously all-white staff.[93] Among the African Americans hired by Rose were Catherine Latimer, Sadie Peterson (Delaney), Nella Larsen, Regina Anderson, and Harold Jackman.[94] They were joined by a talented cadre of volunteers that included Gwendolyn Bennett, Jessie Fauset, and Ethel Nance.[95] In alliance with Charles Johnson and the Urban League, the 135th Street branch became a focal point of the emerging Harlem Renaissance, hosting art exhibits, poetry and fiction readings, lectures on literature and current events, and amateur theatricals. An especially important milestone was the spring 1923 launching by Sadie Peterson of the Book Lovers' Club, which met regularly at the library to discuss books by and about Negroes.[96]

In August 1923, *Opportunity* invited submissions of drawings, paintings, fiction, poetry, and essays on cultural subjects, heralding a major turn toward the creative arts. In the fall, Countee Cullen and Eric Walrond took the lead in transforming the Book Lovers' Club into a more formally structured organization called the Writers' Guild. Walrond was elected president, and monthly meetings were relocated to Urban League offices on Twenty-third

Street and Madison Avenue.[97] Cullen was then an undergraduate at New York University, where he acquired the solid grounding in English verse traditions that proved the under-pinning of his career.[98] A native of British Guiana, Walrond had passed his adolescent years in Panama, where he got a start in journalism. From December 1921 to April 1923, he served as associate editor of Marcus Garvey's journal, *Negro World*. By the time he became president of the Writers' Guild, Walrond had turned away from Garvey's Black Zionism and toward the young writers and intellectuals calling themselves New Negroes. [99] With the assistance of a white literary agent, he began publishing essays and short fiction in such journals as the *New Republic*, *Smart Set*, and the *New York Times* Current History supplement.[100] Some of these pieces focused on the Great Migration and showed the influ-ence of Charles Johnson's research and, more broadly, of Parkian sociology.[101]

As the Writers' Guild strategized means to gain wider exposure, two members, Regina Anderson and Gwendolyn Bennett, approached Johnson with a promising idea for rap-prochement with the white literary world. The *Opportunity* editor swiftly set the scheme in motion with the assistance of William Baldwin III, son of Ruth and William and sec-retary of the Urban League's board.[102] On March 21, 1924, about a hundred guests gath-ered for a black-tie banquet at the Civic Club. Ostensibly celebrating publication of Jessie Fauset's first novel, *There Is Confusion*, the event was primarily intended by Johnson "to present this newer school of writers."[103] Located on Twelfth Street near Fifth Avenue, not far from Henry James country and the heart of Old New York, the Civic Club was an ideal site for Harlem's young talents to be introduced to such white magazine editors and book publishers as Paul Kellogg of the *Survey Graphic*, Freda Kirchwey of the *Nation*, Carl Van Doren of the *Century*, Horace Liveright of Boni and Liveright, and Frederick Lewis Allen of Harper and Brothers.

The black contingent at the Civic Club evening featured six members of the Writers' Guild, official sponsors of the event.[104] The younger generation had the moral support and public endorsement of such elder statesmen as NAACP leaders W.E.B. Du Bois and James Weldon Johnson and Urban League leaders Eugene Kinckle Jones and George Haynes. Other distinguished blacks, such as bibliophile Arthur Schomburg, Jesse Moorland of the YMCA, and Montgomery Gregory, head of Howard's drama department, lent further dig-nity to the occasion. Charles Johnson made the opening remarks, with Alain Locke serv-ing as master of ceremonies. Countee Cullen and Gwendolyn Bennett read several poems, and guests were encouraged to socialize. From such face-to-face contacts flowed magazine acceptances, publishing contracts, and fellowships.

The most momentous exchange of the evening took place between Charles Johnson and Paul Kellogg, who proposed a special issue of *Survey Graphic* devoted to Harlem and written largely by its young talents.[105] Titled "Harlem: Mecca of the New Negro," the issue appeared in March 1925 and provided an unprecedented opportunity to publicize what Locke described as an unfolding movement "for group expression and self-determination." Forty-two thousand copies, more than double the journal's normal circulation, were sold.[106] In November Albert and Charles Boni brought out Locke's anthology, *The New Negro: An Interpretation*, based in large part on materials from the special *Survey Graphic*.

Three days after the Civic Club banquet, Johnson offered his private version of what transpired in a letter to Ethel Ray Nance, a Minnesota native and Urban League activist who shortly thereafter came to New York to serve as his confidential secretary: "You could have been of enormous assistance to me this past week *when I was arranging for the 'debut' of the younger Negro writers.* It was a most unusual affair. . . . All of the younger Negro writers . . . met and chatted with the passing generation . . . and with the literary personages of the city" [italics added].[107] In a euphoric mood following the event's success, Johnson claimed credit in a manner at once uncharacteristic and wholly appropriate.

Nance became a key figure in Johnson's network. Her first assignment was to assemble dossiers on writers and artists in the hinterlands, with a view to enticing them to New York. Johnson and his new assistant bombarded likely candidates with letters that coaxed, cajoled, and challenged, until prudence or timidity was overcome. Arna Bontemps and Wallace Thurman came from Los Angeles; Zora Neale Hurston and Rudolph Fisher from Washington, D.C.; Dorothy West and Helene Johnson from Boston; Aaron Douglas from Kansas City. Inspired by news of the Civic Club dinner, they came to New York secure in the knowledge that they would find support from the Johnson network. In some cases, they left behind literary circles and fledgling journals that may be regarded as significant outposts of the New Negro movement.[108]

On her free evenings, Nance volunteered at the 135th Street library, where she befriended Regina Anderson. In the summer of 1924, they went apartment hunting together and, along with a third young woman, took a spacious flat at 580 St. Nicholas Avenue, one of the toniest addresses on Harlem's Sugar Hill. They soon established what David Lewis describes as "a sort of Renaissance USO, offering a couch, a meal, sympathy, and proper introduction to wicked Harlem for newcomers on the Urban League approved list."[109] The apartment's function as social center for aspiring young talents led to its becoming known as "Dream Haven."

One chilly evening in November 1924, the inner circle gathered at "580" to welcome the nomadic Langston Hughes back from Europe. Among those present, in addition to hostesses Anderson and Nance, were Locke, Fauset, Charles and Marie Johnson, and the three leading lights of the Writers' Guild: Cullen, Walrond, and the guest of honor. Clad in a plaid mackinaw, Hughes entertained his rapt audience with tales of his adventures as a dishwasher in a Parisian *boîte de nuit* and as a beachcomber in the port of Genoa. He read several new poems based on his sea voyages, followed by his favorite jazz-inflected pieces. Arna Bontemps, then a newcomer meeting Harlem's writers for the first time, cemented a close, lifelong friendship with Hughes. Years later, Bontemps recalled Charles Johnson that evening excitedly discussing plans for a literary competition. "He had found a donor, and substantial prizes would be awarded. . . . The contest would be open to Negroes anywhere in the nation, and would be judged by panels of the most respected pundits."[110] In the pages of his journal, Johnson promoted the contest as a means to create a broad audience for black writers, to bring them "into contact with the general world of letters . . . ; to stimulate and foster a type of writing by Negroes which shakes itself free of deliberate propaganda and protest."[111]

4. On the roof at 580 St. Nicholas Avenue, 1924;
left to right: Langston Hughes, Charles S. Johnson, E. Franklin Frazier,
Rudolph Fisher, Hubert T. Delaney.
Photographs and Prints Division, Schomburg Center for Research in Black Culture,
The New York Public Library, Astor, Lenox and Tilden Foundations.

This vision was consummated in May 1925, when more than three hundred guests assembled for an awards dinner at the fashionable Fifth Avenue Restaurant, its gold-mirrored dining room reflecting the cultural opulence on display that evening. More than seven hundred manuscripts had been submitted—short stories, poems, plays, essays, and personal experience sketches—and judged by such pillars of the literary establishment as Carl Van Doren, Eugene O'Neill, Van Wyck Brooks, Alexander Woollcott, Fannie Hurst, and Robert Benchley. The very presence of these luminaries made the proceedings news-worthy. Among the prizewinners were Cullen, Hughes, and Walrond and three newcomers to Harlem: Zora Neale Hurston, who won awards for both a short story and a one-act play, and E. Franklin Frazier and Sterling Brown, who captured first and second places in the essay contest.[112] Lavish, well-attended awards dinners were also held in 1926 and 1927, and public recognition, as well as cash prizes, was conferred on a range of talent extend-ing well beyond the original members of the Writers' Guild.

In retrospect, the *Opportunity* contests themselves seem of less significance than the publicity surrounding them. They enabled Johnson to mount a relentless promotional campaign with some sort of coverage in his journal every month for three years. His prime objective was to open white markets to black writers, and his prime leverage consisted of the contests and the free advertising that they generated. Prospective publishers, it goes without saying, kept an eye on the bottom line, and from a strictly economic point of view, this free publicity was creating demand for books that had yet to be written. It was a strategy no different in principle from a thousand negotiations between the Urban League and prospective employers of Negro labor. Elements of the white power structure took a calculated risk, and the league did everything in its power to reduce that risk to a minimum.[113]

During Johnson's five-year tenure at *Opportunity*, the journal published the early poetry of Countee Cullen, Langston Hughes, and Arna Bontemps, the early fiction of Eric Walrond, Zora Neale Hurston, and Rudolph Fisher, and the early artwork of Gwendolyn Bennett and Aaron Douglas. Johnson also effected a close liaison with leaders of the younger generation through his employment of Ethel Nance as confidential secretary and of Eric Walrond, Gwendolyn Bennett, and Countee Cullen as members of the *Opportunity* staff. The editor cultivated black literary and visual artists, created a supportive interracial milieu, and performed the countless organizational tasks required to realize his vision of "a sociological and literary awakening."[114]

The Johnson/Locke Collaboration

Johnson raised the essential political skills of making contacts and forming alliances to the level of a fine art. One key alliance resulted from his opening the pages of *Opportunity* to Alain Locke, professor of philosophy at Howard University and one of Black America's most distinguished public figures. Working in close collaboration for several years, when the cultural awakening was in its formative stages, Johnson and Locke attempted to pro-vide a programmatic basis for the New Negro movement, shaping and guiding the younger generation, bridging the gap between the social sciences and humanities, and turning *Opportunity* into the premier journal of black creative expression to emerge in the period between the wars.

Locke was born in 1885 into what he called the "frantic respectability" of Philadelphia's black middle class, his ancestors having been free prior to the Civil War.[115] His father was a school principal and civil servant, and his mother a high-school teacher who surrounded her son with good books, art, and music. At Harvard College, he studied philosophy with William James, Josiah Royce, and George Santayana, and English literature and composition with Barrett Wendell, George Lyman Kittredge, and Irving Babbitt; Locke graduated magna cum laude in 1907. He won a Rhodes scholarship to study at Oxford, the first member of his race to be so honored. From 1907 to 1911, he studied philosophy, literature, and Greek at Oxford and then Berlin, but he did not complete a graduate degree until resuming studies at Harvard and receiving a doctorate in philosophy in 1918.

Locke returned from his sojourn abroad in 1911. By this time, he was something of an Edwardian dandy, and along with W.E.B. Du Bois, one of the two most highly educated black men in America. Despite his impeccable credentials, however, he faced an uncertain future. With little chance of finding a teaching post at a white institution, he wrote to Booker T. Washington for advice and was invited to accompany the Wizard and his personal physician, George Cleveland Hall, on a fund-raising tour through Florida. It was Locke's first trip to the deep South, and, much to his dismay, white Floridians proved true to form, at one point threatening Washington's entourage with violence. The young scholar changed his itinerary, making brief visits to John Hope, president of Atlanta University, and Emmett Scott, Washington's chief lieutenant at Tuskegee. Clearly Locke was exploring employment opportunities at southern Negro colleges while assessing the psychological price that such a situation might exact. Eventually the Tuskegee machine secured his appointment at Howard. Through the intervention of Booker T. Washington, a member of Howard's Board of Trustees, Locke was offered an assistant professorship in the teaching of English and the philosophy of education in August 1912.[116] Save for an interlude in New York from 1925 to 1928, he remained on the Howard faculty for four decades.

In 1915, when *The Birth of a Nation* was befouling the silver screen, Locke petitioned the administration for approval of a course in race relations. The trustees rejected the proposal on the ground that such a course might provoke an uproar in the halls of Congress; Howard had been federally funded since its inception in 1867. Locke quietly arranged for the university's NAACP chapter and the campus Social Science Club to sponsor an extension course in the spring semesters of 1915 and 1916. In the same mode of discreet defiance, he published his lecture notes in pamphlet form, under the title "Race Contacts and Inter-Racial Relations." One intriguing entry in the list of source materials is "Park, R. E., 'Racial Assimilation in Secondary Groups.'"[117]

Scrutiny of Park's essay, which appeared in 1914, suggests a significant contribution of Chicago sociology to Locke's *Weltanschauung*. A distinctive feature of Parkian methodology was its relentlessly comparatist approach, which placed the status of American blacks in global perspective, drawing parallels with the German peasantry, eastern European

Slavs, Japanese immigrants in California, and other social groups. Echoes of this perspective may be found in Locke's lecture notes of 1916, and nine years later in his introduction to *The New Negro*: "Harlem has the same role to play for the New Negro as Dublin has had for the New Ireland or Prague for the New Czechoslovakia." Locke saw Harlem, like Dublin or Prague, as "a race capital," a cosmopolitan center where the "many diverse elements of Negro life" could for the first time come together and achieve "a common consciousness," rather than simply endure "a common condition."[118]

Park observed that "Nationalist sentiment among the Slavs, like racial sentiment among the Negroes, has sprung up as the result of a struggle against privilege and discrimination based upon racial distinctions." He recognized a distinctive contribution of creative artists to this process: "Literature and art, when they are employed to give expression to racial sentiment, and form to racial ideals, serve, along with other agencies, to mobilize the group and put the masses *en rapport* with their leaders and with each other. [They] are like silent drummers which summon into action the latent instincts and energies of the race."[119] Alain Locke became acquainted with Park's ideas as a young professor at Howard; Charles Johnson encountered them as a graduate student at Chicago. In retrospect, the Parkian paradigm may be seen as an important element of the powerfully enabling vision that brought Locke and Johnson together in the 1920s.[120]

As Johnson steered his journal toward Parnassus and the fountain of the Muses, he found himself in largely unfamiliar waters, in need of a pilot who was better grounded in traditional art forms and conversant with the modernist currents swirling through the contemporary art scene.[121] Who if not the Harvard-educated aesthete and professor of philosophy? Locke in turn was delighted with the prospect of becoming a regular contributor to *Opportunity*. Prior to 1923, his writing career had been sporadic, with seven articles appearing over a period of twenty years, and with never more than one piece in the same journal. Now Johnson was offering a reliable publication outlet, with no new editors to cultivate, no referees acting out of prejudice or whim, and no rejection slips from white arbiters of taste. His output soared from the outset of this new arrangement, and his affiliation with *Opportunity* extended from 1923 to 1942, encompassing the bulk of his always engaging and sometimes brilliant essays.

Locke's attempts to shape the aesthetics of the New Negro movement can be traced through his many reviews and articles in *Opportunity*, *Survey Graphic*, and other journals. "The Negro's Contribution to American Art and Literature," a major piece published in 1928, is a succinct overview of his theoretical perspectives of the 1920s.[122] The animating concept is cultural pluralism, a set of ideas about the interplay of ethnic and American identities that Locke was developing in dialogue with philosopher Horace Kallen, a friend since his days at Harvard and Oxford.[123] Locke observed that the collective experiences of black Americans tended "to intensify . . . group feelings, group reactions, group traditions" and to serve as "the basis of the Negro's characteristic expression." In the work of Harlem's young artists, he discerned a maturing of such expression from spontaneous vernacular forms "to conscious control and intelligent use," in the process transforming what had been perceived as a "social handicap and class liability" into "positive group capital and [a] cultural asset." Locke observed that it had become "apparent, both to white and black observers, that the folk-products of the peasant Negro are imperishably fine and . . . constitute a *national asset* of the first rank" (italics original).

These were radical assertions in an age of forced Americanization and resurgent white supremacy, but they resonated with the work of such white artists as Eugene O'Neill and DuBose Heyward and with ideas emanating from avant-garde circles in New York and Chicago.[124] In journals such as *Seven Arts*, *Poetry*, *Secession*, *Little Review*, and *Others*, Van Wyck Brooks, Waldo Frank, Randolph Bourne, Harriet Monroe, Alfred Kreymborg, Carl Sandburg, Sherwood Anderson, Carl Van Vechten, and others spearheaded their generation's attack on the genteel literary tradition, on nineteenth-century moral values, and on the cultural bankruptcy of a business-worshipping civilization. Brooks's *America's Coming of Age* (1915), Frank's *Our America* (1919), and Bourne's *The History of a Literary Radical* (1920) called for a spiritual transformation of society through the arts. Michael North refers to these intellectuals collectively as "the Americanist avant-garde," in light of their sustained attention "to American popular culture, to the multiracial heritage of the Americas, and above all to modern writing in 'plain American,'" and in contradistinction to the "transatlantic modernism" of such writers as T. S. Eliot, Gertrude Stein, Ezra Pound, and James Joyce, marked by an emphasis on formal experimentation, a self-consciously complex, often allusive style, and elitist conceptions of audience.[125]

In their efforts to forge an American cultural tradition independent of English and European antecedents, the Americanist avant-garde embraced a Whitmanesque ethos that challenged so-called "Nordic racial integrity" and laid a basis for interactions between white modernist circles and the Harlem writers. Van Vechten was but the most important and consistently involved of a number of white intermediaries. Brooks, for example, had been Locke's classmate at Harvard, influenced some of his theorizing about the New Negro, and served as a judge for the 1925 *Opportunity* literary contest.[126] Locke was also greatly influenced by philosopher Josiah Royce's vision of a "Beloved Community," which permeated the views of Bourne, Brooks, and others in their circle.[127] Frank reviewed and promoted works by Harlem Renaissance authors and forged a close friendship with Jean Toomer.[128]

In "The Negro's Contribution to American Art and Literature" and other writings, Locke argued for freedom of the black artist from "didactic emphasis and propagandist motives," for "realistic folk portrayal" in drama and fiction, for the literary use of genuine folk idioms instead of a caricatured dialect, for an embrace of vernacular musical forms ranging from spirituals and folk songs to contemporary "folk derivatives" such as jazz and blues, and for aesthetic exploration of "the motives and technical originalities of primitive African sculpture and decoration." Such movement toward distinctively racial expression on the part of young black artists would lead, Locke argued, to "profitable exchange and real cultural reciprocity" across the color line.[129]

In rallying widespread support for this avant-garde perspective, Johnson and Locke established a productive division of labor. Johnson, with his experience in the Urban League and the Chicago Commission on Race Relations as background, played the role of strategist: mobilizing the troops, deploying them to maximum advantage, and executing details of the battle plan. As the primary theorist and publicist, Locke articulated an aesthetic for the New Negro movement, defining its central tenets and popularizing them for a broad audience. In playing the game of cultural politics to win, Johnson adopted a familiar stance of self-effacement, generally leaving center-stage to his more artistically inclined confrere. The Johnson/Locke collaboration in New York serves as a striking example of the deliberate and fruitful interpenetration of social and aesthetic thought and practice—a crossing of disciplinary boundaries, a meeting of minds that would recur in the following decade—in a different city, among different actors, and in a radically transformed situation.

CHAPTER 3

The New Negro in Chicago

In December 1918, Chicago Urban League president Robert Park observed that the World War had "disturbed the equilibrium of the races." "What is going to happen," he wondered, "when the negro troops return from France?" Three months later, white civic leaders gathered at the City Club to hear A. L. Jackson, director of the Wabash Avenue YMCA, describe the dramatic increase in black population, the cramped misery of tenement housing, and the pervasive health problems of the Black Belt. Jackson added that black veterans were returning from Europe with a new "sense of manhood" and "consciousness of power hitherto unrealized." In response, social philosopher George Herbert Mead, president of the club, wondered whether Chicago was "far-sighted enough to avoid a calamity."[1] Mead got his answer in late July, as hospitals and morgues filled with victims of the calamity he feared.

In an editorial written while violence raged in the streets, *Defender* publisher Robert Abbott thundered: "America is known the world over as the land of the lyncher and of the mobocrat. For years she has been sowing the wind and now she is reaping the whirlwind. . . . A Race that has furnished hundreds of thousands of the best soldiers that the world has ever seen is no longer content to turn the left cheek when smitten upon the right."[2] "[Whites] really fear," wrote the *Chicago Whip*, "that the Negro is breaking his shell and beginning to bask in the sunlight of real manhood."[3] Nor were these isolated voices. According to a contemporary survey, "Self-defense is applauded and advocated . . . by [nearly] the entire colored press."[4]

In November Attorney General Palmer issued a report equating such expressions of "insolence" with anarchy and sedition. "The increasingly emphasized feelings of a race consciousness in many of these publications [are] always antagonistic to the white race and openly, defiantly assertive of its own equality and even superiority."[5] The 1919 riots thus proved a watershed in the history of Chicago: on one side of the color line, altering perceptions of an isolated, nearly invisible racial minority so that it now appeared the city's foremost social problem; on the other side, underpinning defiant race pride, commitment to black institutional development, and avoidance of or conditional alliances with whites.

Bookerism Sui Generis

Race pride was increasingly associated with the phrase "New Negro," which had predated Alain Locke's famous anthology by at least a quarter century, serving as the key term in

Booker T. Washington's *A New Negro for a New Century*, published in 1900, the same year the Wizard's supporters founded the National Negro Business League and elected him president. By the time he died in 1915, the league had six hundred local chapters with thousands of members around the country and was, according to Louis Harlan, "the organizational center of black conservatism." The league promoted Washington's view that rather than placing "hope . . . in politics and in the ballot . . . the Negro has settled down to the task of building his own fortune and of gaining through thrift, through industry, and through business success that which he has been denied in other directions."[6]

Reshaped in the urban North, Washington's strategy of racial progress through self-reliance and entrepreneurship may be seen as an alternative pole of attraction to both the civil rights militancy of *Crisis* editor W.E.B. Du Bois and the "arts approach" associated with Alain Locke and Charles Johnson, providing another nexus of values, goals, and tactics associated with the elusive term "New Negro." A fourth perspective could be found in the New York–based *Messenger*, edited by Chandler Owen and A. Phillip Randolph, who viewed the New Negro as "a militant, card-carrying, gun-toting socialist who refused to turn the other cheek."[7]

Proponents of all four strategies, as well as the Black Zionism of the Garvey movement, could be found on the South Side in the late 1910s and 1920s, often in alliances that have challenged subsequent scholarly attempts to draw neat philosophical or political boundaries.[8] An especially important strain among the black civic leadership might be labeled "Bookerism sui generis." This phrase describes a pragmatic orientation to racial progress expressed in deeds as much as words and represented by, among others, surgeon George Cleveland Hall, YMCA executive A. L. Jackson, publisher Robert Abbott, bankers/businessmen Jesse Binga and Anthony Overton, Republican political leaders Edward H. Wright and Oscar DePriest, and gambling/music hall impresario Robert Motts—all of whom first rose to local prominence during the period of Washington's national ascendancy among blacks.[9]

Chicago's New Negroes generally admired Washington, shared his belief that the color of freedom was the green of the dollar bill, often joined his National Negro Business League, and worked to build black-controlled institutions. Tuskegee's founder made frequent fund-raising visits to the city and, in 1910, told an audience in Quinn Chapel: "You meet severe competition here in Chicago. . . . I have recently been in southern Europe, where the people talk slow, and walk slow, and work slow. Why, we can keep up with those white people easily. But here in Chicago it is different. You can't keep up with this northern white man . . . so easily."[10] In years to come, "beating the white man at his own game" would become the foremost criterion of success and popular admiration on the South Side.[11] While Washington's own dependence on a series of white benefactors extending from Samuel Chapman Armstrong to William Baldwin and Julius Rosenwald was well known, less so were such sentiments as those expressed in a 1913 letter to his friend Robert Abbott: "Another thing we must learn sooner or later . . . is that no matter how much a certain type of white people may promise to do for us in the way of securing 'rights' in the last analysis, we have got to help ourselves."[12]

Despite their admiration for the Wizard's accomplishments, few members of Black Chicago's professional and business elite were actually indebted to him for their positions, and they lived and worked in a dramatically different social, political, and economic environment. They had no compunctions about leveraging the residential concentration of blacks into a source of local political power or speaking in a register of militant group assertion unheard in Macon County, Alabama. Black supporters of the local Urban League such as Abbott, Hall, and Jackson did not hesitate to aid the Chicago NAACP on occasion and by the late 1920s had produced an "interlocking directorate" of the two organizations' boards.[13] It might be said that, in an era of racial retrogression, these leaders took the best of Washington and left the rest.[14] "Between 1890 and 1915," writes James Grossman, "they established a bank, a hospital, a YMCA, an infantry regiment, effective political organizations, lodges, clubs, professional baseball teams, social service institutions, newspapers, and a variety of small businesses."[15] In the following decade, the South Side became the growing edge of African American economic and political advancement contemporaneously with Harlem's emergence as the center of black creative expression in literature.

Robert S. Abbott and the New Negro

Robert Sengstacke Abbott was perhaps the most famous exemplar of Chicago's New Negroes. Born in 1868 to former slaves Thomas and Flora Abbott on St. Simon's Island, near Savannah, Georgia, he was raised by his mother and Afro-German stepfather, John H. Sengstacke, who pursued careers as teacher, clergyman, and journalist. Abbott studied the printer's trade at Hampton Institute and then moved to Chicago, where he earned a degree at Kent College of Law, the only black graduate in the class of 1899. After unsuccessful attempts to establish a law practice, he launched the *Defender* in 1905, working at a folding card table in a rented room and selling his publication door-to-door.[16]

Despite lack of capital and competition from three other Chicago-based black weeklies, Abbott built the *Defender* into the most successful African American newspaper in the country. His success formula was a brilliant combination of two elements: sensational news coverage with screaming headlines resembling the yellow journalism of William Randolph Hearst and bold denunciations of racial oppression in its many forms. In response to a growing wave of lynchings, the *Defender* in 1915 inaugurated a slogan—"If you must die, take at least one with you"—resulting in both greater national prominence and heightened suppression in some parts of the country.

Abbott relentlessly promoted migration, thereby increasing his market in Chicago and spreading his newspaper's circulation throughout the South. He also associated migration with the phenomenon of the New Negro although, in a January 1920 editorial, he suggested that "awakened" was a "better word" than "new" to characterize the Negro's shift in consciousness. Citing the momentous events of 1919 and economic opportunities in the North, the publisher wrote that "the same old tinted individual [has been] roused into self-consciousness, awakened to his own possibilities, with stiffened backbone, with new ambitions, new desires, new hopes for the future."[17]

Although the *Defender* was nominally independent in politics, Abbott generally allied himself with the black Republican political machine led by Edward H. Wright, the basis for Carl Sandburg's 1919 characterization of "the Black Belt of Chicago [as] the most effective unit of political power, good or bad, in America."[18] Wright was a major power broker and supporter of three-term Republican mayor William Hale Thompson. While flamboyant, Stetson-hatted "Big Bill" Thompson, first elected in 1915, became notorious for overseeing graft- and crime-ridden regimes, he delivered a broad range of political appointments to blacks. "Iron Master" Wright's tenure as Republican committeeman for the South Side's Second Ward also saw the election of the first black municipal judge, first state senator, and fourth state representative. Wright's fortunes rose and fell contrapuntally with those of rival Oscar DePriest, a former housepainter who was elected the first black alderman (city councilor) in 1915 but politically sidelined following a corruption trial two years later. Tenaciously rebuilding his political base among the migrant masses of the Third Ward and securing Thompson's support, DePriest became in 1928 the first black elected to Congress since Reconstruction and the first ever from a northern state.[19]

Abbott preached his gospel of economic achievement to both the masses in Chicago and the talented tenth in training at black institutions. One such student was Blyden Jackson. Later a venerable professor of literature at Fisk University and the University of North Carolina at Chapel Hill, Jackson was an undergraduate at Wilberforce University in the late 1920s when he witnessed "the epiphanic vision of Abbott's emergence from the plush recesses of a chauffeur-driven Rolls Royce." He never forgot the dark-skinned publisher telling the assembled students "that in Chicago his money was enabling him to pass for white. He spoke . . . as an Old Testament prophet dutifully expounding holy writ. His audience listened in a hush of unfeigned reverence. For his audience knew of Jesse Binga, . . . Oscar DePriest, . . . Daniel Hale Williams."[20] Abbott's *Defender* trumpeted a "Promised Land" of lucrative careers for the black middle class and good jobs in northern industry for the masses breaking free from the shadow of the plantation. Like much of the emergent South Side elite, the publisher's personal fortunes were tied to growth of the migrant population and development of a black consumer market.[21]

The migrants themselves dreamed of not only higher wages and greater dignity but also education and social advancement for their children. The reality they encountered was mixed. As a result of residential segregation, schools in the Black Belt were increasingly characterized by overcrowding, racial concentration, aging physical structures, and inadequate facilities. Teachers were overwhelmingly white and often prejudiced, and nothing in the curriculum reflected African American history or culture. Despite such obvious drawbacks, Chicago offered significant educational opportunities. In 1920, 92 percent of black children between the ages of seven and thirteen were regularly attending school, a proportion higher than that of the city's white immigrants and qualitatively superior to the black experience in the South. Education-hungry black adults made the evening program at Wendell Phillips High School the largest in Chicago. The school itself, a focal point of community pride, offered a full range of academic and extracurricular activities.[22]

The *Defender* and other black newspapers encouraged and benefited from the growth of literacy, which was for them both a sign of racial progress and a pragmatic issue of the marketplace. One of Abbott's strategies for enhancing the *Defender*'s readership was to establish "Bud Billiken" Clubs wherever the newspaper was sold. The club's name derived from the nom de plume given the editor of the children's page. In December 1922, thirteen-year-old Willard Motley, a future best-selling novelist, became children's editor, earning three dollars a week for writing a column filled with drawings, poems, jokes, and letters from young readers.[23] Bud Billiken and the *Defender Junior*, with its masthead slogan "School Study Sports Home Play Work," became symbols of youthful exuberance, ambition, and community advancement.

In November 1928, hundreds of excited club members marched from the *Defender*'s building at Thirty-fifth and Indiana through rain-drenched streets to "Bud's First Regal Party," attended by four thousand youths and their parents at the magnificent new Regal Theater at Forty-seventh and South Parkway.[24] The Wendell Phillips High School Band led the way, followed by two motorcycle policemen, Abbott's flag-draped limousine, a line

5. Dignitaries at Bud Billiken Parade, 1934.
Front, right to left: John H. Sengstacke III, Robert Abbott, Edna Abbott;
back, third from right: Earl Hines; *fifth from right*: Duke Ellington;
second from left: Noble Sissle.
Vivian G. Harsh Research Collection of Afro-American History and Literature,
Chicago Public Library. Abbott-Sengstacke Family Papers 1501.

of fifty more vehicles, and Billiken clubs from across the city. At the theater, the crowd was entertained by the Regal Symphony Orchestra, assorted musical and comedy acts, a horror movie starring Lon Chaney, and a greased-pole climbing contest.[25] The Billikens included ten-year-old Nathaniel Coles, later known as Nat King Cole, along with other future jazz greats such as Lionel Hampton, Milt Hinton, and Ray Nance.[26] In August 1930, Abbott officially launched the Bud Billiken Day Parade and Picnic, crowning the decade's achievements—cultural, economic, political, educational—while providing welcome distraction from the deepening gloom of the Depression. The annual parade remains the South Side's most important and distinctive public celebration.[27]

Crucible of Jazz Creativity

Some older members of the crowd at "Bud's First Regal Party" would have remembered Robert Motts's famous Pekin Theater, a popular beer garden and gambling hall at Twenty-seventh and South State streets, which in 1905 added a 1,200-seat "theater for Colored people of this city." Although his gambling business catered to an interracial "sporting crowd," Motts, an African American originally from Iowa, carefully cultivated the support that the black community and its leaders were inclined to give nearly all forms of black enterprise. He made contributions to local churches and donated his theater and orchestra for a fund-raising performance to benefit the Frederick Douglass Center. The all-black Pekin Stock Company presented dramas and musical comedies to complement the performances of touring vaudeville troupes. The "famous Pekin Orchestra," directed by pianist/composer Joe Jordan, offered mixed musical fare including ragtime and pre-jazz popular music. Motts, also a reliable prop of the Second Ward Republican Party machine, paid some of his customers to register black voters and turn them out on Election Day. At his funeral in 1911, prominent banker Jesse Binga served as a pallbearer.[28]

The Pekin was an institutional predecessor of the cabarets where jazz stopped over on its evolutionary journey from New Orleans to New York. On the South Side—in the Apex Club and the Dreamland, Lincoln Gardens, Sunset, and other cafes—the syncopated rhythms and collective improvisations of transplanted southern musicians made Chicago a crucible of jazz creativity in the 1920s. This development was, in its early years, a product of the interaction of a black entrepreneurial culture with two distinct faces of the northern migration: the wartime influx of thousands of unattached young men and women, drawn by bright lights and urban diversions as well as job opportunities; and a movement of professional musicians from New Orleans. From these migratory streams came a musical elite and its most receptive audiences.[29]

Many of the musicians, among them Sidney Bechet, Barney Bigard, Freddie Keppard, and Jelly Roll Morton, were born and bred among the New Orleans Creoles of color—an elite caste of mixed ancestry, descended from the original French and Spanish settlers and their African slaves. A longstanding social separation of downtown Creoles from uptown blacks, reflected in the composition of local brass and dance bands, was undercut by an 1894 residential segregation ordinance and by the 1897 creation of an official red-light district, soon called Storyville. The best performers from each group found employment in the saloons, dance halls, and bordellos along Basin Street, where they formed mixed bands and exchanged musical ideas.

After the district was closed by the U.S. Navy in 1917, some displaced musicians followed the sporting establishments to surrounding neighborhoods or toured the country with carnivals, minstrel shows, or vaudeville troupes. Others made their way to clubs in Chicago where a good sideman could find steady work and earn about forty dollars a week plus tips, no small sum in those days.[30] The urbane and highly competitive environment of South Side cabarets and theaters generated new standards of dress and deportment, fast-tempo performance, familiarity with musical notation, and instrumental versatility.[31]

Musicians of this caliber cut the early jazz recordings on "race record" labels and set the pace for the postwar decade that F. Scott Fitzgerald dubbed the Jazz Age. Among them was Joseph Oliver, a 250-pound cornetist with lungs like bellows, who had been proclaimed "King" in Storyville after blowing the competition off the streets. In 1918 he brought to Chicago a loud, hot, ragged sound that blended blues, ragtime, marches, and folk songs into a musical gumbo first served up in Basin Street honky tonks, on Mississippi riverboats, and in the parades and funeral processions that wound through the Crescent City. In 1919 Oliver accepted an offer to lead his own six-piece Creole Jazz Band and to hold court nightly at the Dreamland, described by the *Defender* as "a first class resort owned by a member of the Race"—prominent music entrepreneur William Bottoms.[32]

The Dreamland was located at Thirty-fifth and State in the very heart of the nightlife district called the Stroll. Langston Hughes visited in 1918 and later recalled "a teeming Negro street with crowded theaters, restaurants, and cabarets. And excitement from noon to noon. Midnight was like day. The street was full of workers and gamblers, prostitutes and pimps, church folk and sinners. The tenements on either side were very congested. For neither love nor money could you find a decent place to live." Venturing "outside the Negro district, over beyond Wentworth, [he] was set upon and beaten by a group of white boys. . . . That was the summer before the Chicago riots."[33] Hughes's memoir suggests the social complexities of a richly creative milieu within an overwhelmingly poor and racially quarantined community.

In 1922 King Oliver left the Dreamland for a lengthy engagement at another black-owned cabaret, the Lincoln (formerly Royal) Gardens. In July he summoned his young disciple, Louis "Satchmo" Armstrong, to play second cornet.[34] In the next two years, the younger musician completed an apprenticeship begun the previous decade in New Orleans. Born in 1901 in a shack on James Alley, Armstrong was raised by his mother and grandmother. He had his first exposure to instrumental music during two years in the Colored Waifs' Home, after which he learned his art in local bands, most importantly under the King's tutelage.

Armstrong spent six years in Chicago, an initial two years alongside Oliver and a second stint between 1925 and 1929.[35] An intervening year was spent in New York with Fletcher Henderson's big band, where his sight-reading skills and knowledge of orchestration grew as he worked with Don Redman's arrangements, harmonically more complex

than the simple chord progressions with which he was familiar. Although still a shy hay-
seed in appearance and manner, Armstrong took command during his solos and with his
jagged rhythms, melodic surprises, and blues-inflected notes taught the New York band
what swinging was all about.[36]

Returning to Chicago, Satchmo worked with several bands including wife Lil Hardin
Armstrong's combo at the Dreamland, Carroll Dickerson's band at the Sunset, and Erskine
Tate's Vendome Theater Symphony Orchestra, which accompanied silent films and played
concerts at the 1,500-seat theater.[37] During this time, he switched from cornet to trumpet
and made a series of recordings with groups called the Hot Five and Hot Seven. These
were produced for the race records division of Okeh Record Corporation, which was dramatically expanding the audience of black jazz and blues musicians.[38]

With Armstrong in the original Hot Five line-up were trombonist Edward "Kid" Ory,
Lil Hardin on piano, Johnny Dodds on clarinet, and Johnny St. Cyr on banjo and guitar.
Later studio sessions included drummers Baby Dodds and Zutty Singleton, Peter Briggs on
tuba, and a dapper young pianist named Earl Hines. These recordings gave Satchmo a
chance, after his New York sojourn, to cut loose with some small-combo, down-home
"Gut Bucket Blues" and also to push traditional forms in new directions with his guttural
vocals and scat singing on "Heebie Jeebies," the extended cornet solo that ends "Potato
Head Blues," and the daring stop-time chorus of "Cornet Chop Suey."[39]

In April 1926, Armstrong began playing at the Sunset Café, owned by whites connected with Al Capone's mob. It was the best-known of the "black and tan" cabarets,
which drew white tourists, neighborhood blacks, and aspiring jazz musicians of both races
to hear the South Side's top talent.[40] Across from Satchmo on the bandstand sat twenty-
year-old Earl Hines, originally from Duquesne, a steel town southeast of Pittsburgh. Born
into a middle-class family, Hines had been a piano prodigy training classically with a German music teacher who stressed discipline as much as technique. He began to win awards
and get his picture in the local newspaper, but at fifteen, he heard the enticing sounds of
jazz in an after-hours club and soon forgot Chopin's preludes. He found a job with Lois
Deppe, a Pittsburgh-based (male) singer in desperate need of an accompanist who could
read music and play in more than three keys. After much musical experience and several
risky encounters in clubs along Wylie Avenue, the commercial strip in the city's Hill District, Hines moved to Chicago in 1923.[41] He was part of a second-generation cohort of
musicians who learned their art in such Mississippi Basin cities as St. Louis, Chicago,
Kansas City, Detroit, Cleveland, and Pittsburgh. Their arrival in clubs and recording studios signaled that, despite the weight of New Orleans traditions, jazz had become an
American music and was no longer merely a regional curiosity.

As Hines's reputation grew, his extraordinarily strong, dexterous command of the key-
board generated tall tales of an invisible third hand. Carroll Dickerson invited Hines to
join his big band on a national tour of vaudeville theaters. After a couple of years on the
road, Dickerson reorganized the group into a smaller combo and settled into the Sunset.
Hines had met Armstrong at the offices of the black musicians' union, Local 208, and persuaded him to leave King Oliver and join Dickerson's band as lead trumpet. As the band-

leader succumbed to a drinking problem, Armstrong took his place, and Hines became musical director.[42]

For some thirty months, Armstrong and Hines traded twelves on the bandstand and became the talk of a jazz-mad town. They also recorded such classic moments as their sweetly mournful rendition of "West End Blues" and the competitively charged perfection of their duet on "Weather Bird," both compositions by King Oliver.[43] For this brief period, Armstrong and Hines jointly dominated the jazz world, two musicians in their twenties and at the top of their form, the number-one trumpet player in the world and arguably the number-one jazz pianist of his era. Elevating their art to new levels of complexity on the very threshold of the swing era, they were inventing "the seminal rhythmic language of ensemble jazz."[44]

Spring of 1928 found Armstrong headlining at the Savoy Ballroom at Forty-seventh and South Parkway, a veritable palace of dance with a flower-strewn lobby, half-acre dance floor, and checkroom holding six thousand coats and hats. Its Grand Inaugural Ball the previous November had drawn such prominent figures as Robert Abbott, Jesse Binga, George Cleveland Hall, and Oscar DePriest. Chicago's Savoy was built by a group of white investors organized by I. Jay Faggen, who at various times owned the downtown Roseland and uptown Savoy ballrooms in Manhattan as well as dance halls in Brooklyn, Philadelphia, and Chicago's Loop. In February 1928, this same financial group opened the Regal Theater next door to the Savoy, definitively signaling relocation of the South Side's commercial and entertainment center. The continuous southward movement from the Pekin on Twenty-seventh to the cabarets of Thirty-fifth to the entertainment emporiums of Forty-seventh Street closely tracked the population growth and geographic expansion of Black Chicago as well as the struggle between white and black capitalists.[45]

In the late 1920s, cabarets and dancehalls were pummeled by tighter enforcement of Prohibition, onset of the Depression, and encroachment by white gangsters.[46] Many clubs simply shut down. The Savoy moved from nightly performances by house orchestras to performances by touring bands and more varied attractions, including weekly boxing matches. When Faggen began handing Satchmo a hard-luck story instead of his pay envelope, opportunities in New York suddenly gleamed more brightly. Armstrong took a brief engagement at the Harlem Savoy, recorded at Okeh's New York studio, and was hired for a long run in the wildly popular black musical revue *Hot Chocolates*.[47] He would call New York home for the rest of his life.

While recording with Satchmo, Earl Hines played late-night gigs with master New Orleans clarinetist Jimmie Noone at the Apex Club. Benny Goodman, Bix Beiderbecke, Eddie Condon, and other white musicians came to listen and learn. Hines was soon invited to lead his own big band at the Grand Terrace Ballroom, which opened in December 1928. There he would ply his trade for a dozen years and broadcast nightly over the NBC radio network. Always smiling, always elegantly attired, he was all the while indentured to the jazz slave masters of the Capone syndicate.

The association of jazz with the sporting life and divers forms of criminality began in Storyville, continued on the South Side, and complicated the music's reception among blacks.

6. Forty-seventh Street with Regal Theater and Savoy Ballroom, 1941.
Photo: Russell Lee. Library of Congress, Prints & Photographs Division,
FSA-OWI Collection, LC-USF34–038808-D.

Although "Maurice Ravel [would] sit for hours at the Apex Club listening to Jimmy Noone's band," David Lewis noted, "upper-crust Afro-Americans still mostly recoiled in disgust from music as vulgarly explosive as the outlaw speakeasies and cathouses that spawned it."[48] Lewis's observation has greater relevance to the black "upper-crust" in New York, Philadelphia, and Washington, D.C., than in Chicago. Robert Abbott and his peers were more inclined to share Ravel's enthusiasm for superb musicianship, support African American music entrepreneurs, and ignore threats to respectability. The absence of cabarets like Harlem's Cotton Club and Connie's Inn, which did not allow blacks as customers, probably helped, but even more pertinent was Charles Johnson's observation that the South Side's "social set" was "lacking in definite standards of ancestry and culture and even wealth." "New countries are always democratic," he remarked.[49]

Chicago's black weeklies reflected a spectrum of views on jazz. Of the five that existed in the mid-1920s, the *Broad Ax* was the oldest; the paper generally expressed Victorian attitudes and defended the hard-won dignity of Chicago's "Old Settlers," that small minority who had planted roots in the city long before the wartime migration. Its editors deplored jazz, cabarets, and the "ugly, low, nasty dances" performed therein by a raucous migrant crowd rubbing elbows and other body parts with slumming whites.[50] The most influential newspaper, the *Defender*, had tied its fate to the migration and provided enthusiastic coverage of popular leisure pursuits ranging from South Side sports teams to boxing matches, from locally produced black films to the music pouring forth each night from State Street clubs. To Abbott's instinctively hyperbolic writers, the Stroll was "a Mecca for Pleasure" rivaling the cultural attractions of Rome, Athens, and Jerusalem.[51] The *Whip* had been established by Joseph Bibb in 1919 with financial help from the Dreamland, Deluxe, and Royal Gardens and militantly advocated the linked causes of black music and black entrepreneurship.[52] Samuel Floyd puts the matter succinctly: "The music of the rent-party, theater, and cabaret worlds was separate from, yet ironically supportive of, some of the New Negro ideals."[53]

New Negroes of the Easel

Greater social distance could hardly be imagined than that between the Dreamland Café and Chicago's ultimate monument to respectability, the Art Institute. With its classic façade rising grandly above Michigan Avenue and its broad steps guarded by Edward Kemeys's bronze lions, the Institute has been both art museum and academy since its founding in 1879.[54] Its school at times has claimed the largest enrollment in the country and also acquired the distinction of opening its doors to blacks in an era when the vast majority of art academies, North and South, followed Jim Crow admissions policies.[55]

At the School of the Art Institute of Chicago (SAIC), instruction in the fundamentals of line and color, composition and design, and figurative representation was infused with lofty ideals of form and inspirational content. Associated with the neoclassical style of the École des Beaux-Arts in Paris, an emphasis on "beauty and character" was in part intended to counter the image of "the city of the Big Shoulders" as a raucously corrupt and materialistic outpost of civilization.[56] To most SAIC faculty in the 1910s and early 1920s, modernism was anathema and the 1913 Armory Show a manifestation of European decadence. Their guiding principle was mimesis, mixed with Midwest populism and a touch of Victorian gentility. Such was the institutional ethos as increasing numbers of black students enrolled, among them Richmond Barthé, Charles Dawson, Arthur Diggs, William McKnight Farrow, Archibald Motley Jr., Robert Pious, William Edouard Scott, Dox Thrash, and Ellis Wilson.

Scott, a native of Indianapolis and the first black art teacher in that city's schools, was an early star to rise; he established himself as an important easel painter, muralist, and illustrator and studied in Paris with expatriate African American painter Henry Ossawa Tanner. In 1915 he journeyed to Tuskegee Institute at the invitation of Booker T. Washington, a visit that sparked a deep interest in representing black life in the South. W.E.B. Du Bois also commissioned him to provide illustrations for *Crisis*.[57] In 1931 Scott received a Rosenwald fellowship to spend a year in Haiti, where he created more than a hundred paintings and five hundred sketches of daily life in the American-occupied black republic.[58]

Farrow and Dawson took the lead in creating organizational expressions of the New Negro spirit among the city's African American artists. In 1923 Farrow founded the all-black Chicago Art League to sponsor group exhibitions and public lectures, most of them

7. The Chicago Art League, c. 1927; William Edouard Scott (*top row, center*),
Richmond Barthé (*middle row, third from left*), Charles Dawson (*front row,
second from left*), William McKnight Farrow (*front row, second from right*).
Charles C. Dawson Collection, DuSable Museum of African American History.
Gift of Mrs. Mary R. Dawson.

at the Wabash Avenue YMCA. A month before the Harlem issue of *Survey Graphic*
appeared, he delivered a slide-illustrated lecture on art history intended to show "the
direct connection between the later African work and that of Egypt and to indicate by
that means the historical background from which the Negro of today may draw much
inspiration." Farrow's presentation indicates that South Side artists were engaging the
question of what Alain Locke called "the ancestral arts" at the same time as their Harlem
counterparts.[59]

Dawson, the league's vice president, earned his livelihood as an illustrator and provided the catalog cover drawing for the breakthrough "Negro in Art Week" exhibition,
held in November 1927 at the Art Institute and sponsored by the Chicago Woman's Club.
Dawson's design juxtaposed images of an Egyptian pharaoh, an African sculpture, and
modern black performers in formal attire. The exhibition included sculptures from the
Belgian Congo, and Locke was on hand to lecture about Negro art. Catalog illustrations
and titles indicate, however, that pastoral landscapes and portraits were the dominant

types of contemporary paintings exhibited, while the most distinguished participant, Henry O. Tanner, was represented by several narrative scenes drawn from the Bible. Although there was little evidence of the "realistic folk portrayal" advocated by *Opportunity*, there was much evidence of artistic achievement in "Negro in Art Week," the first exhibition of black artists at a major American museum.[60]

Black Chicago's most accomplished artist of the 1920s and 1930s, Archibald Motley Jr., refused to join Farrow's and Dawson's Art League.[61] This life-long maverick was born in New Orleans in 1891.[62] Envious white competitors forced Motley's father, a prosperous storekeeper of Creole stock, to flee the South, and in 1894 the family settled in Chicago, where Archibald Sr., found employment as a sleeping-car porter. In an era before the residential color line had become firmly fixed, the Motleys moved into the white neighborhood of Englewood. Archibald Jr., attended the neighborhood high school, which had a strong art department that sent many graduates on to SAIC. Its four art rooms were reputedly the best equipped in the city, and the faculty exhibited at the Paris Salon, New York Watercolor Club, and the Art Institutes of Chicago and Atlanta.[63]

After graduating from SAIC in 1918, Motley initially hoped to make his mark as a portrait painter. He began by painting members of his family, creating a series of dignified representations of blacks that challenged racial stereotypes. In *Portrait of the Artist's Father* (1921, color plate 1), Archibald Sr., is formally attired in a black suit with a black tie, Windsor-knotted and pinned beneath a starched collar. A partially obscured painting above his head shows a pair of thoroughbred horses. The table on which his arm rests holds a book and colorful figurine. Most important is the open book in his hand, symbolic of leisured refinement. The effect is heightened by light, focused on the right side of his face to emphasize a well-shaped forehead, steel-rimmed glasses, and a stern expression.

By the mid-1920s, Motley had created a second portrait series with such titles as *A Mulatress* (1924), *The Octoroon Girl* (1925), and *The Quadroon* (1927). This multihued spectrum of elegant and sophisticated "Negro" women explored "the full gamut, or the race as a whole . . . [from] terribly black [to] very light."[64] While subtly undermining popular media images of African American women, the artist was no doubt also exploring the intraracial color hierarchy in which his light complexion and Creole heritage accorded him a privileged position. Although these paintings exhibited impressive technical expertise, Motley was generally disappointed in his efforts to sell them.

Consequently the artist shifted to multifigure compositions. Technically, Motley stretched his expertise in the "breaking up of space," use of varied color schemes, and the interplay of different types of light. Thematically, he created scenes that "tell a story," especially "night scenes where you find a lot of these people of my race."[65] In portraying cityscapes, Motley turned to the decidedly antiacademic influence of George Bellows, a painter associated with the Ashcan School, which emphasized individual expression and techniques that captured the energy, speed, and tension of modern city life. Bellows had a major exhibition at the Art Institute in 1919, followed by a two-month residency at SAIC, during which Motley attended his lectures. Bellows's influence encouraged many young Chicago artists to unite a "traditional emphasis on illustrational realism with a heightened emotional response to everyday reality," in the process creating what Charlotte Moser identifies as a historically important "local version of American Scene painting."[66]

Motley biographer Amy Mooney deftly characterizes him as "an outsider with insider privileges" and enumerates those facets that placed him outside the core experiences of black migrant life: his light skin and Creole heritage, status as pre-migration settler, devout Catholicism, marriage to a white woman, professional training and four-year degree from SAIC, and residency in Englewood on the white side of Wentworth Avenue.[67] But in painting such exuberant Jazz Age scenes as *Black and Tan Cabaret* (c. 1921), *Syncopation* (1924), and *Stomp* (1927), not only Motley's race made him an insider but also the long association of New Orleans Creole culture with jazz and blues. Some middle-class blacks may have condemned "low-life" music and the highly sexualized atmosphere of the cabarets, but this artist celebrated jazz and the nonhierarchical association of blacks and whites of all classes on crowded dance floors.

The genre scenes document Motley's move away from academic influences and toward something akin to Locke's aesthetic. In 1925 William Farrow attempted to discourage him from submitting *Syncopation* to be juried for the Art Institute's annual exhibition of Chicago-area artists. His fellow black painters, Motley recalled, "were awfully afraid years ago to send anything that was Negroid to any of the exhibitions." He ignored Farrow's advice, submitted the piece, and won a cash award.[68] Despite such successes, the artist could not support himself solely by painting and began offering private classes. One student, Richmond Barthé, a future sculptor of distinction, embraced New Negro ideas of distinctively racial art as a result of Motley's influence.[69]

Motley's slow accumulation of professional successes reached critical mass on a chilly February morning in 1928 when the *New York Times* heralded an extraordinary event: "One-Man Show of Art by Negro, First of Kind Here."[70] With a solo exhibition of twenty-six oil paintings at Madison Avenue's prestigious New Gallery, arranged by Art Institute director Robert Harshe, Motley became the first African American painter of his generation so honored. Coming at the crest of the Harlem Renaissance, the show proved a huge success. Twenty-two paintings sold, netting substantial income. Harlem's enthusiasm at this breakthrough for the race may have been dampened, however, by the fact that the Chicagoan's heady triumph overshadowed the first annual Harmon Foundation exhibition uptown at International House, which included the work of such rising black artists as Augusta Savage, Palmer Hayden, Aaron Douglas, and Hale Woodruff.[71]

The exhibition included Motley's best portraits and genre paintings and five new works, executed at the gallery owner's request for "pictures showing . . . negro life in its more dramatic aspects . . . perhaps . . . the voo-doo element as well as the cabaret element." Motley knew plenty about cabarets; "the voo-doo element" was something else again. Nevertheless, he set his talented brush to the task, creating such fanciful African scenes as "Kikuyu God of Fire," "Devil-Devils," and "Spell of the Voodoo."[72] *Times* art critic Edward Alden Jewell responded ecstatically to this invocation of the primitive. In 1925 Alain Locke had soberly observed that "There would be little hope of an influence of African art

February 25th through March 10th, 1928

EXHIBITION OF PAINTINGS
BY
ARCHIBALD J. MOTLEY, JR.

The New Gallery

600 MADISON AVENUE · NEW YORK

NOTE: The first one-man exhibition in a New York art gallery of the work of a negro artist is, no doubt, an event of decided interest in the annals of the American school of painting. It seems, however, worth while to record the fact that the invitation to Mr. Motley to show his paintings at The New Gallery was extended prior to any personal knowledge concerning him or his lineage and solely because of his distinction as an artist.

8. Cover of New Gallery catalog for *Exhibition of Paintings by Archibald J. Motley, Jr.,* New York City, 1928. Chicago History Museum.

upon the western African descendants if there were not at present a growing influence of African art upon European art in general."[73] In contrast to Locke's measured hope that black artists might consciously join their white modernist counterparts in turning to "the ancestral arts" for inspiration, Jewell perceived in Motley's African exotica a manifestation of "the subconscious . . . of his race." "Here," he effused in near-Conradian prose, "are steaming jungles that drip and sigh and ooze, dank in the impenetrable gloom of palm and woven tropical verdure. . . . Glistening dusky bodies . . . silhouetted against hot ritual fires. Myriad age-old racial memories drift up from Africa."[74] Jewell meant to praise Motley's work, but in the process he revealed the nod to primitivism often required of black artists seeking to gain the attention of white critics and patrons.

On the strength of his New York show and earlier achievements, the artist won a Guggenheim fellowship to study abroad, embarking for France with his wife, Edith, in the summer of 1929. There he executed one of his most famous works. *Blues* (1929, color plate 2) takes the viewer inside a little Parisian café favored by the Motleys as a place to escape the pressures of American racial mores.[75] Dancing couples, jazz musicians, and seated spectators are jammed together like the Chicago El at rush hour—a crowded canvas for the crowded conditions of modern urban life. Arbitrary cropping of bodies and heads, varied repetition of flat monochromatic blocks, such emblems of pleasure as closely pressed bodies, glasses of wine, musical instruments, and smoke rising from a cigarette—all combine to create a scene of rhythmic gaiety.

This cosmopolitan scene embodied Motley's goal of creating "pictures portraying . . . the dance, the song, the hilarious moments when a bit of jazz predominates. . . . to bring about better relations, a better understanding between the races, white and colored." His Guggenheim application had invoked "the art approach [as] the most practical, the most durable" solution to "the race problem."[76] After a year in Paris, he and Edith returned home to a city and nation in the tightening grip of the Great Depression. They soon saw the art approach challenged and eclipsed by philosophies and programs that aimed to do no less than make the world anew.

The New Negro and the New Poetry

In 1920 Archibald Motley was launching his career, King Oliver's cornet was shaking the walls of the Dreamland Cafe, Robert Abbott was putting a Chicago face on the image of the New Negro, and Charles Johnson was spearheading research for the Chicago Commission on Race Relations. That same year, prominent journalist and critic H. L. Mencken dubbed Chicago the "Literary Capital of the United States." The Sage of Baltimore was looking back on a decade of extraordinary creativity in fiction, poetry, and drama, at the end of which, he declared, it was difficult to find any significant literary trend "that did not originate under the shadow of the stockyards."[77] Mencken was impressed by the manner in which writers in the "most thoroughly American" city were creating a vital national literature freed of its Anglophile traditions and cultural inferiority complex and rooted in the diversity of American experience and its polyglot vernaculars.[78]

The white writers who made Chicago a literary capital had moved to this fastest-growing of the world's great cities from "remote wheat-towns and far-flung railway junctions": Theodore Dreiser from Indiana; Sherwood Anderson from Ohio; Susan Glaspell from Iowa; Edna Ferber and Ben Hecht from Wisconsin; Carl Sandburg, Edgar Lee Masters, Vachel Lindsay, and Floyd Dell from downstate Illinois. Collectively, their works explored both ends of the migratory trail: from the tales of village "grotesques" in Anderson's *Winesburg, Ohio* (1919) to the grinding gears of great Chicago industries in Dreiser's novels (1900–1947), from the distant voices of those "sleeping on the hill" in Masters's Spoon River cemetery (1915) to the brawny tumult of Sandburg's Chicago poems (1916). Dreiser's works, in particular, with their focus on impersonally brutal social forces that shape and often crush individual lives, were echoed in later decades in the naturalistic novels of black Chicago writers Richard Wright, William Attaway, Alden Bland, and Willard Motley. But the most immediate influence of white Chicago writers on African American letters was in the realm of poetry.

"The poets of to-day," declared Harriet Monroe in 1917, "seek a vehicle suited to their own epoch and their own creative mood." Born in 1860, this Victorian product of a Washington, D.C., finishing school dedicated herself to overturning Victorian standards in poetry. The journal that she and Alice Corbin Henderson launched in Chicago in September 1912 advocated "modern speech, simplicity of form, and authentic vitality of theme."[79] On its pages *Poetry: A Magazine of Verse* united such "educated sons of pioneers" as Sandburg, Masters, and Lindsay with future avatars of transatlantic modernism: William Butler Yeats, Ezra Pound, Hilda Doolittle ("H.D."), and T. S. Eliot. The midwestern contingent of the Americanist avant-garde constitutes the present focus.

Lindsay's "General William Booth Enters into Heaven" appeared as the lead piece in the January 1913 issue of *Poetry*. With its simple diction, musical directions, and frequent refrain—"Are you washed in the blood of the Lamb?"—drawn from a well-known gospel hymn, the dramatic poem was intended to be performed before popular audiences, and so it was, with increasing frequency as Lindsay's fame spread. The March 1914 issue carried several free-verse poems by Sandburg, including "Chicago."[80] Monroe revealed in a memoir that she initially found its opening line, "Hog Butcher for the World," "a shock," but "took a long breath," read on and eventually decided to use it as lead poem.[81] The piece was in fact a calculated assault on traditional notions of poetry as an embodiment of transcendent ideals of morality, beauty, and symmetry. "Chicago" explored an urban reality acknowledged as "wicked," "crooked," "brutal," and "fierce as a dog." Sandburg, a socialist and sometime itinerant laborer, turned back the "sneer" of an imagined bourgeois critic with a defiant song of praise for his city, "so proud to be alive and coarse and strong and cunning." Monroe and Henderson called the work they published "the New Poetry," maintained an open door to poets as different as Sandburg and Pound, and created new possibilities for other writers working in the genre.[82]

Among Chicago's poets at this time was Fenton Johnson, born in 1888 into one of the city's longest-resident and more prosperous African American families.[83] His father, Elijah, was a railroad porter and later a bail bondsman, his mother, Jessie, was a prominent clubwoman, and his aunt Eudora married Jesse Binga. Fenton studied at Northwestern and the University of Chicago, met all of Black Chicago's elite, and was known as "a dapper fellow who drove his own electric automobile."[84] He was inclined toward the literary arts from an early age, wrote news articles and features for the *Defender*, and had plays and musical reviews performed by the Pekin Stock Company. The Pekin's owner, Robert Motts, was a former employee of Fenton's well-known uncle, gambling czar John "Mushmouth" Johnson.[85]

Between 1913 and the early 1920s, Johnson published three books of verse at his own expense and successfully placed individual poems in *Poetry*, *Crisis*, *Others*, and *The Liberator*. His first collection, *A Little Dreaming* (1913), is a motley of decorous Victorian lyrics, a long biblical allegory, and dialect poems—not only sentimental plantation verses modeled after Paul Lawrence Dunbar but also pieces in the popular music-hall vein purportedly representing Irish, Scottish, and Yiddish dialects ("Mine Rachel iss der Ghetto rose," begins one). *Visions of the Dusk* (1915) and *Songs of the Soil* (1916), however, foreshadow in their more interesting poems the New Negro literary project of reclaiming a racial past and idiom freed from the minstrel mask. The first collection includes "Ethiopia," a long historical poem paying tribute to Toussaint L'Ouverture, Nat Turner, Frederick Douglass, Booker T. Washington, and W.E.B. Du Bois. Another piece underscores the ironic reliance of European empires on their colonial armies during World War I: "London shall be saved an age / By the fighters of the dusk; / Zulu, robbed of land and home, / For the robber bares his heart."[86] Alongside poems in the Dunbar mode, Johnson wrote his own spirituals in an attempt to give literary form to the sorrow songs. In these pieces, he successfully conveyed the rhythms and powerful concrete imagery of the vernacular without the usual device of pseudo-phonetic eye-spelling ("Oh, my soul is in the whirlwind, / I am dying in the valley, / Oh, my soul is in the whirlwind / And my bones are in the valley.").

Songs of the Soil contains "Harlem: The Black City," apparently "the very earliest rendering of black Harlem in creative literature."[87] The poem had its origins in the two years that Johnson lived in New York while studying at the Columbia University School of Journalism. For the next six years, he worked in Chicago as a journalist, launching two monthly magazines and doing nearly all the writing for them. *The Champion Magazine* (1916–1917) included prose and poetry, surveyed black achievements in music, sports, and theater, and announced as its goal "to bring about a literary Renaissance."[88] The longer-lived *Favorite Magazine* (1918–1921) contained political commentary, fiction, and poetry and grew to an impressive eighty-four pages in length. One issue stated this credo: "We desire the race to prepare for its materialistic needs. . . . The walls of Jericho are very hard to raze until we have the money to raze them. The *Favorite Magazine* is very anxious . . . to see the race become a race of millionaires."[89]

In 1920 Johnson published two prose collections culled from his magazines: *Tales of Darkest America*, composed of eminently forgettable short stories, and *For the Highest Good*, a group of political essays that reveal him to be a staunch supporter of the Republican Party and Mayor Thompson, an advocate of the settlement house ideal of harmony between classes and races, and an opponent of Bolshevism. These magazines were impor-tant milestones in the history of black periodical publishing as well as the history of the New Negro, but, despite family support, a timely inheritance, and enthusiastic coverage in the *Defender*, both ventures ended in financial disaster.

Harriet Monroe corresponded with Johnson and published several of his spirituals, no doubt finding in them the "simplicity of form and authentic vitality of theme" that were for her essential elements of the New Poetry. Other discerning poet/editors such as William Stanley Braithwaite, James Weldon Johnson, and Alfred Kreymborg anthologized his work. Fenton Johnson's connection with the last figure is especially illuminating. Dur-ing its short existence, Kreymborg's *Others: A Magazine of the New Verse* (1915–1919) was as important as Monroe's and Henderson's journal in stimulating modern trends in Amer-ican poetry.[90] Kreymborg coedited the journal with William Carlos Williams and Maxwell Bodenheim from an artists' colony in Ridgefield, New Jersey, with regular treks to Green-wich Village. Well-connected with the Chicago poets through his friendship with Carl Sandburg, Kreymborg exemplified the aspirations of the Americanist avant-garde for a spiritual rebirth of society through the arts and a renaissance of the arts through deeper connection with the diverse wellsprings of American culture. The white editor on the East Coast discovered the black poet in the Midwest as the latter's work was undergoing a major transition in dialogue with the New Poetry.

The friendship between Kreymborg and Johnson was marked in a highly public man-ner by the appearance of Kreymborg's Whitman-like "Red Chant" in the November 1917 issue of *Crisis*. "There are veins in my body, Fenton Johnson—" the poem begins, "veins that sway and dance because of blood that is red." A series of parallel images and struc-tures establishes the consanguinity that symbolizes their common humanity and bond. "Let me think of loving you, / Let you think of loving me," the speaker rhapsodizes, "Let us go arm in arm down State Street." History does not record whether Johnson and Kreymborg ever took that interracial stroll down the Stroll, but the 1919 anthology culled from *Others* did contain a generous selection of eight of Johnson's poems alongside pieces by Sandburg, Lindsay, Williams, Marianne Moore, Lola Ridge, and Robert Frost.

Those poems were part of a group that Johnson intended to publish as his fourth col-lection, to be called *African Nights*, but apparently he never found the wherewithal to implement his plans. The eight pieces, including "Tired," "The Banjo Player," and "The Scarlet Woman," are essentially character sketches in free verse. Six of eight speakers tell their own stories, much like the monologues in Masters's *Spoon River Anthology*. Each piece offers some implied element of social commentary in the description of the dis-appointments and cramped boundaries of black lives nearing their end. In tone and mood, the poems run a gamut from the despairing pessimism of "Tired" to the lighter irony of "The Banjo Player," whose unexamined life of simple pleasures is disrupted only when a woman calls him "a troubadour," a word whose utter strangeness puzzles and dismays him. These pieces exhibit the unadorned naturalism of Sandburg's Chicago poems, but where Sandburg's shorter works often create scenes with compressed imagistic detail, Johnson's sketches derive their strength from the poet's ability to create—in a few brief lines—a voice, a situation, a mood, a story. In his best work, Johnson gave a racial inflection to the New Poetry, just as New Poets Sandburg and Lindsay explored jazz, black folk songs, and African American history as source material for their free-verse experiments.

Johnson's financial setbacks and professional disappointments caused him much suffering, as a 1920 memoir reveals, but Jean Wagner's well-known characterization of him as "the poet of utter despair" is misleading.[91] In selecting pieces by Fenton Johnson for *The Book of American Negro Poetry*, James Weldon Johnson balanced "Tired" and "The Scarlet Woman" with two poems expressing the racial pride and optimism of the New Negro. The exhortatory pieces "Children of the Sun" and "The New Day" are not Fenton's best literary work, but they do indicate a broader range in his postwar poetry than some commentators acknowledge.

Johnson essentially disappears as a significant presence in African American letters after 1922. Only a few references to organizational activities and some unpublished work in connection with the Illinois Writers' Project document his later years. One contemporary source places him in 1927 among "a group of young people of Chicago and a number of seasoned writers [who] formed a circle for the appreciative criticism of literary production" and planned to publish a quarterly called *Letters*.[92]

Johnson and his mentor, newspaperman and poet William H. A. Moore, constituted the "seasoned writers" in the *Letters* group. Younger members included sociology student Horace Bond, who wrote criticism, philosophy student Albert Dunham, who worked in drama, Dewey Jones, who wrote book reviews and edited a poetry column for the *Defender*, and poet Lucia Mae Pitts, who also published in the *Defender*. Newly arrived from Kansas at the age of twenty-one, journalist Frank Marshall Davis attended a few meetings, but was so irritated by Moore's "caustic tongue" and dominating manner that he soon left.[93] At one point, members of the group communicated with the Harlem writers centered around Wallace Thurman to explore the possibility of publishing a follow-up issue of *Fire!* in Chicago.[94]

Like Davis, Richard Wright arrived in Chicago in 1927. He later recalled a "Negro literary group . . . of a dozen or more boys and girls, all of whom possessed academic learning, economic freedom, and vague ambitions to write." Sorely lacking the first two qualities, Wright was ill at ease with blacks who were "more formal in manner than their white counterparts . . . wore stylish clothes and were finicky about their personal appearance. . . . In speech and action they strove to act as un-Negro as possible, denying the racial and material foundations of their lives."[95] As their experiences with the *Letters* group suggest, both Davis and Wright found the South Side in the late 1920s a generally inhospitable climate for literary work. It was a good place to make money, to make music, and—for a handful of trained professionals—to make art, but it had not yet developed the institutions and social milieu necessary to sustain creative writers.

That Fenton Johnson achieved as much as he did evidences individual talent and determination as well as the empowering spirit of both the New Poetry and the New Negro movements. Coming from the black elite, Johnson began his career with money, education, and connections, but to sustain careers, artists need seasoned mentors, training, serious colleagues, a means of support, outlets for their work, and ultimately an appreciative audience—the sorts of things in fact that Charles Johnson attempted to engineer in 1920s Harlem. Fenton Johnson's vaulting ambitions were thwarted by the limitations of self-financed publication, the walls of American apartheid, the relative thinness of Black Chicago's literary milieu, and the absence of a significant number of blacks with an interest in reading material more challenging than the *Defender*.

The newly arrived migrants, Wright and Davis, were each beginning a long struggle to survive economically and to establish themselves as writers. The former challenge required Wright's attention for years, but Davis had certain advantages. Unlike the Mississippian, he had attended nominally integrated schools in his native Kansas and gone as far as the state college in Manhattan, where he studied journalism. He was confident and "excited" on first encountering "this . . . mighty monster of a metropolis. . . . [with] more than a quarter of a million blacks, more than two and a half times as many as lived in all Kansas."[96]

With five weekly newspapers, the South Side offered Davis an opportunity to use his talents and training within a black environment. Frustrated in his attempts to secure a job with the *Defender*, he began working for the smaller-circulation *Whip*. On the side, he wrote crime stories and poetry, the latter much influenced by Masters, Lindsay, and especially Sandburg, whom Davis "considered the nation's greatest poet." He "did not identify with . . . Eastern writers," black or white. As a reporter, he became acquainted with the South Side's best-known residents: entrepreneurs, musicians, sports legends such as boxing champion Jack Johnson and All-American Fritz Pollard, as well as the gambling czars and vice lords. The young Kansan came to love the city "despite its coarseness, its blatant vulgarity, its raw corruption," and he would celebrate it in his free-verse poetry of the 1930s and 1940s.[97]

The Cube Theater and the Negro Ballet

Richard Wright described the aspiring writers of the *Letters* group as "hover[ing] on the edge of Bohemian life." Albert Dunham, in particular, had significant connections with the long-established white bohemian enclave on Fifty-seventh Street. Between the University of Chicago and Jackson Park was a cluster of low wooden buildings that had served as souvenir shops, storage facilities, and stables during the Columbian Exposition of 1893. In later years, they became cheap studios and makeshift dwellings for such creative artists as Floyd Dell, Carl Sandburg, Sherwood Anderson, and Maxwell Bodenheim. Late-night gatherings over gin and chop suey attracted lively crowds that included downtown lawyer-poet Edgar Lee Masters, downstate vagabond-poet Vachel Lindsay, *Poetry* editor Harriet Monroe, and *Little Review* editor Margaret Anderson. Many of the most important works of what Bernard Duffey and other scholars later called the (white) Chicago Renaissance were read aloud at these soirees.[98]

Albert Dunham's involvement with this colony of free spirits began sometime before he helped his younger sister transfer from junior college to the University of Chicago.

Katherine Dunham was just nineteen and had spent the greater part of her childhood and adolescence in Joliet, a suburb some thirty-five miles southwest of the metropolis. Her mother died when Katherine was just four, and she and Albert were entrusted to an aunt living on the South Side. Their father, Albert Sr., remarried, bought a dry-cleaning establishment, and attempted to reconstitute the family. Despite his social prominence among the few blacks in Joliet, he was profoundly unhappy and subjected his children and second wife to a steady onslaught of verbal and physical abuse, which eventually drove his son from their home. Always a brilliant student, Albert Jr. made his way on scholarship at the University of Chicago, studying philosophy with George Herbert Mead.[99]

Albert graduated Phi Beta Kappa in 1928, the year Katherine joined him in Chicago. About that time, he became involved in The Cube, successor to a black amateur theater group called Masque, which had been organized in March 1927 by the society editor of the *Defender*. Masque gave private performances and identified with the "Little Theater movement," which was best known for the Provincetown Players in New York but actually began in Chicago in 1912 when director Maurice Browne established his Little Theater in a Fifty-seventh Street studio.[100] Albert and Katherine Dunham and an interracial group of University students collaborated with former Masque players in The Cube, "an independent venture of students and artists interested in all forms of modern art."[101] The *Defender* covered one of the group's fund-raising events, calling it "a delightful concert" highlighted by performances presented by such locally prominent musicians as violinist and band director Walter Dyett and baritone John Greene. Composer W. C. Handy attended and "pronounced the movement a forward step."[102]

As an expression of the Americanist avant-garde, the little theater movement sought to present material from culturally diverse sources. For The Cube, this often meant plays relating to the experience of African Americans. Two early offerings were by white southerners. Paul Green's *In Abraham's Bosom*, winner of a 1927 Pulitzer Prize, centered on a struggling black teacher in North Carolina and his eventual murder by the Klan. A dramatization of DuBose Heyward's *Porgy* presented life on Charleston's Catfish Row with a ground-breaking attempt at realism. Such plays drew the attention of Alain Locke, who offered a curtain speech at one performance; they also expressed Albert Dunham's hope that "all bids fair for a vital folk theater in Chicago."[103] The Cube functioned from 1929 to the mid-1930s and attracted radicalizing young blacks, who expanded the repertoire with Leftist political dramas in the manner of Clifford Odets. Participants included Ruth Attaway and Canada Lee (actors), Charles White and Charles Sebree (graphic artists and set designers), St. Clair Drake (consultant in anthropology), and Mary Hunter Wolf (director).[104]

Katherine Dunham was involved in the whirl of activities around the group and appeared in at least one production—a stage adaptation of a Scott Fitzgerald story.[105] At one point, she shared a studio/loft with William Attaway, a student at the University of Illinois, and his sister Ruth, also a student and aspiring actress. While Katherine taught children's dance classes, Ruth taught acting, and Bill, who became a novelist, listened to music and worked on his early pieces.[106] Involvement with The Cube extended Dunham's cultural contacts on both sides of the color line, enriched her knowledge of stagecraft, and prepared her for the role of choreographer, which became integral to her career.

But dance, not theater, was the center of Dunham's dreams. In January 1930, she met Mark Turbyfill, *jeune premier* of the Adolph Bolm Ballet and an avant-garde poet who once filled an entire issue of *Poetry* with a single work. Turbyfill agreed to train Dunham in ballet and to collaborate in realizing her dream of creating a Negro ballet troupe. He rented a studio on Fifty-seventh Street, and he and Dunham gathered an interracial advisory board. Turbyfill involved such pillars of the white cultural establishment as composer Eric DeLemarter, assistant conductor of the Chicago Symphony Orchestra, while suavely handsome sculptor Richmond Barthé approached such "really elite Negroes" as Robert Abbott.[107] Turbyfill also published an article about this bold enterprise in the November 1930 issue of *Abbott's Monthly*, a glossy magazine newly launched by the *Defender* publisher.[108]

Dunham and Turbyfill collaborated for nearly a year, but their inability to maintain a reliable troupe of dancers led them to suspend the effort. The young woman was determined, however, and soon began working with Russian ballet teacher Ludmilla Speranzeva. In December 1932, Dunham and five other dancers performed at the Stevens Hotel Beaux Arts Ball, premiering the *Fantasie Nègre in E Minor* of composer Florence Price, choreographed by Speranzeva and accompanied on piano by Margaret Bonds.[109]

The names of most of the young African Americans who collaborated in Dunham's dance troupe, The Cube, the *Letters* group, and the Art League went unrecorded in the annals of cultural history, but the careers of many of the most talented were advanced at crucial stages by a unique fellowship program established in Chicago in 1928. This select group of fellows included William Attaway, Richmond Barthé, Horace Bond, Margaret Bonds, Horace Cayton, Frank Marshall Davis, St. Clair Drake, Albert Dunham, Katherine Dunham, John Greene, Dewey Jones, Willard Motley, William E. Scott, Charles Sebree, and Charles White.[110] This is but a small subset of the nearly one thousand fellowships awarded to African Americans across the country by the Julius Rosenwald Fund, but these recipients suggest the Fund's strategic importance to Black Chicago's rising artists and intellectuals. Its story is consequently a significant part of the larger narrative of Bronzeville's Renaissance and of differences in the cultural arena between the 1920s and the following decades. Charles S. Johnson, a central figure in the organizational phase of the Harlem Renaissance, was also central to the Rosenwald Fund's decision-making processes.

The Julius Rosenwald Fund Fellowship Program

Johnson left New York for Nashville in the summer of 1928, two years after Thomas Elsa Jones, a white Quaker, assumed the presidency of Fisk University at a moment of deep institutional crisis. Jones had acted swiftly to restore financial stability, initially through a fund-raising tour of 130 southern black churches. The remarkable success of that effort caught the attention of the Rockefeller Foundation, Carnegie Corporation, and Julius Rosenwald Fund, which jointly stepped forward with sufficient aid to pay off Fisk's remaining debts and establish a million-dollar endowment.[111] In addition, the Laura Spelman

Rockefeller Memorial Fund committed an annual grant of twenty-five thousand dollars to develop a strong department of social sciences.

Beardsley Ruml was director of the Rockefeller Memorial Fund from 1922 to 1929. Working at the interface of government agencies, corporations, universities, and foundations, he was part of a shadow-world that exercised great power over public policy without the impediment of accountability that theoretically accompanies public office. During seven years with the Memorial Fund, Ruml disbursed an estimated fifty-eight million dollars. He supported institutional development of southern black colleges, contributed to the Atlanta-based Commission on Interracial Cooperation, and helped launch such organizations as the Social Science Research Council in New York, the Institute for Research in Social Science at Chapel Hill, and Robert Park's Local Community Research Committee in Chicago.

Ruml's philosophy was shaped by his mentor, James Rowland Angell, with whom he had studied while completing a Ph.D. in psychology at the University of Chicago. When Angell left the University for a brief stint as president of the Carnegie Corporation, he brought Ruml along as confidential secretary and shortly thereafter arranged his appointment as director of the Memorial Fund. The Angell/Ruml philosophy can be summarized in three propositions: foundation giving should be governed by the scientific ethos; empirical research in the social sciences should be a primary focus; and the new scientific philanthropy should take the form of substantial institution-building grants in order to create centers of public policy expertise.[112] Their vision of society, technocratic in essence, moved ineluctably in the direction of social engineering, embodied in the 1930s by the policies of the New Deal.

The Memorial Fund's substantial grant to Fisk advanced Jones's plan to hire a cadre of distinguished black faculty for this flagship black institution. Another crucial step was the recruitment of Charles Johnson, who brought scholarly expertise, administrative experience, and a national network of black professional associates—just the package to help Jones realize his dream of "a Greater Fisk." The president made his first overtures in May 1927, and ten months later Johnson accepted his invitation to chair the department of social sciences.

With Jones's assurance that, as department chair, he would control the annual disbursements from Ruml's Fund, Johnson began deploying his network of contacts to assure decisive input into the hiring of new faculty.[113] He drew on connections with both the Harlem intelligentsia and Chicago social scientists. Of the Harlem Renaissance figures who in effect followed Johnson to Nashville, there were Arthur Schomburg in 1929, James Weldon Johnson in 1931, Aaron Douglas in 1937, and Arna Bontemps in 1943. On the Chicago side were Horace Bond and E. Franklin Frazier. The son of prominent Nashville pastor James Bond, Horace had specialized in the sociology of education at the University of Chicago. At Fisk he worked as Johnson's research assistant, taught courses in history and education, and studied black schools in Alabama, North Carolina, and Louisiana for a program financed by the Rosenwald Fund.[114] With a doctorate from Chicago, Frazier had taught sociology at Morehouse College from 1922 to 1927, while publishing in *Opportu-*

nity and Locke's *New Negro* anthology. After joining the Fisk faculty in 1929, he published *The Negro Family in Chicago* in 1932 and gained a reputation as one of the more politically radical of Robert Park's students.[115]

Through the faculty appointments Johnson engineered, he created what Blyden Jackson, a Fisk professor from 1945 to 1954, called "the last salon of the Harlem Renaissance."[116] The intellectual ferment generated by these eminent figures contributed to the cultural capital of the Bronzeville Renaissance, symbolizing a paradigmatic shift from the racially celebratory mood of the 1920s toward a new sensibility that was decidedly antiromantic, frequently militant, sometimes economic determinist, and decisively influenced by Chicago social science. At Fisk itself and through an expanding national network, Johnson pursued his vision of "a sociological and literary awakening" as a key to racial advancement. During the political upheavals of the Depression, he appeared something of a Janus-figure, facing in opposite directions like the Roman god of gates and doors. One face of that metaphorical door opened toward the past—the 1920s, the arts approach, and the Harlem Renaissance; the other faced the future—the 1930s, Chicago sociology, and the liberal social engineering of the New Deal.

Johnson advanced his strategic vision through involvement in the Julius Rosenwald Fund, which underwent major reorganization in the same year that he moved to Fisk. In 1927 Rosenwald turned sixty-five and was preparing to retire as president of Sears and also to restructure his philanthropic initiatives. The fund had been established under exclusive family control in 1917 primarily to oversee the southern school-building program. In 1928 it was placed under the professional management of full-time officers overseen by an active Board of Trustees that included Beardsley Ruml.[117]

Searching for a suitable candidate for chief executive officer, Rosenwald decided on Edwin Rogers Embree, vice president of the Rockefeller Foundation. Born in Nebraska in 1883, Embree was the grandson of a heroic Kentucky abolitionist, Reverend John Fee, who had founded the village of Berea as a model of "anti-slavery, anti-caste, anti-rum, anti-sin" righteousness. By 1857 the little community in the foothills of the Cumberland Mountains included a small church and school built on the bedrock of abolitionist principle.[118] Decades later, Embree attended Berea College with both black and white classmates before moving on to Yale, where he majored in philosophy and in 1907 went to work in the Yale alumni office. For ten years, he edited alumni publications and oversaw the scholarship program. In 1917 he moved to New York to serve as confidential secretary to fellow Yale graduate George Vincent, head of the Rockefeller Foundation. For the next decade, Embree worked with Vincent, learning to think on a foundation scale and absorbing the ethos of the new scientific philanthropy. Rosenwald served concurrently as a trustee of the Rockefeller Foundation, became personally well acquainted with Embree, and developed great respect for Embree's administrative skills and social vision.

In luring Embree away from the prestigious Rockefeller Foundation, Rosenwald offered both a higher salary and greater freedom to pursue innovative ideas.[119] Embree assumed his new position on January 1, 1928. Rosenwald gave the reorganized fund an initial endowment of twenty million dollars' worth of Sears stock with the observation that "more good can be accomplished by expending funds as Trustees find opportunities for constructive work than by storing up large sums of money for long periods of time," a philosophy unprecedented in the world of large foundations.[120] Embree carried out the philanthropist's wishes and spent the fund out of existence by 1948, sixteen years after Rosenwald's death.

The fund's priorities were clear from the beginning of Embree's twenty-year tenure: "to better the conditions of Negroes, especially through education, and to improve race relations." Embree wound down the school-building program within four years and launched new initiatives in higher education, health services, librarianship, teacher education, race relations, and "fellowships to unusually promising Negroes . . . to enable them to engage in advanced study, in special field work, or in other experiences which would further qualify this selected group for distinguished service."[121]

A Committee on Fellowships was established in 1928, and the fund disbursed a total of $1,655,911 over two decades, encompassing 999 awards to blacks and 538 to southern whites. The latter were specifically intended to "strengthen the liberal movement in the South." "On the committee throughout its whole course," according to Embree, "were the president of the Fund, Dr. Will Alexander, and Dr. Charles Johnson, three men with wide acquaintance in the Negro group and the South."[122] A broad division of labor emerged in the screening process, with Alexander reading dossiers of southern whites, Johnson focusing on blacks, and both reporting their findings to Embree and other program officers. By one account, Alexander planted the seed that blossomed into the fellowship program.

Like Embree and Johnson, Will Alexander was a native of the upper South. Born in 1884 in the Ozark region of southwestern Missouri, he was a descendent of southern abolitionists, one of whom had been lynched.[123] He attended a one-room country school through twelfth grade, studied at a small denominational college of fundamentalist persuasion, and then did graduate work at Vanderbilt University, in preparation for ministry. Prior to living in Nashville, he had never seen an elevator, never attended a theatrical performance, nor ever met anyone from another country. His clerical career was short, as he discovered that "the people expected their preachers to love the Lord, but they would not tolerate a minister who loved Negroes."[124] He escaped parish work in 1917, when the National War Work Council invited him to serve as a chaplain at Fort McPherson, Georgia. Among the soldiers were many illiterate rural blacks. The solicitous chaplain soon found himself reading and writing letters of an intimate nature. These interracial contacts foreshadowed his new career in the postwar years.

The return of black soldiers after World War I signaled a brutal repression that began with isolated incidents but steadily escalated into full-scale riots that engulfed twenty-six cities in 1919. In January of that year, a small group of concerned southerners gathered in Atlanta to explore means of defusing tensions. They compiled an index of potential members, raised start-up funds, and conducted leadership training institutes. Early in 1920, they incorporated as the Commission on Interracial Cooperation (CIC), with headquarters in Atlanta and Will Alexander as director, a post he held for a quarter-century. By July the advisory council had twenty-one black members, including Robert Moton, principal of Tuskegee Institute, and John Hope, president of Morehouse College.

The CIC was at bottom a decentralized association of volunteers. At its peak strength in the 1930s, it had eight hundred affiliated committees in counties across the South, engaged in such local projects as establishing a tuberculosis sanatorium for blacks, opening a tax-supported hospital to black doctors, and reforming a Georgia prison farm. Regional agendas included campaigns to abolish the white primary and the poll tax and to dismantle a quasi-feudal system of agricultural peonage, based on imprisonment for debt. The most dramatic campaigns were a running battle with the Ku Klux Klan, directed personally by Alexander, and the valiant efforts of Jessie Daniel Ames and her Association of Southern Women for the Prevention of Lynching to fight southern barbarism from within, by discrediting the sexual pretext for most lynchings.

One day in 1927, the head of the Phelps-Stokes Fund wrote to Alexander that he had a potential donor "who wished to use some money in ways that would be helpful to the South." Recalling his own process of deprovincialization at Vanderbilt, the CIC director suggested scouting southern colleges for talented youngsters and offering financial support for their graduate training at major research universities. In mid-summer a telegram arrived from Julius Rosenwald inviting Alexander to Chicago. "I saw that memorandum that you sent to Dr. Stokes," the philanthropist remarked over lunch. "Here's a check for fifty thousand dollars. If you can take this and demonstrate that there are people of the sort you say, . . . I'll put some real money into it." Alexander set up a pilot project and identified seventy students, black and white, who were motivated to attend northern universities before returning home to address the South's most pressing problems. The success of this pilot influenced the decision of the Rosenwald Fund to launch a full-scale fellowship program shortly after Embree took the helm.[125]

That program supported talented blacks in fields as diverse as agriculture, chemistry, visual arts, creative writing, education, library science, music, nursing, philosophy, social work, and sociology. Within this broad range, all forms of creative expression were represented, and many artists had significant ties to Chicago. As a patron of African American artists, the Rosenwald Fund was unprecedented in scope and influence.[126] In the 1930s, such new patrons as the cultural apparatus of the Communist Party and the arts-oriented projects of the New Deal entered the field, but the ongoing role of Rosenwald philanthropies in supporting creative individuals and providing seed money to build community institutions constituted an absolutely necessary, if not sufficient, condition for the flowering of the Black Chicago Renaissance.

PART TWO

Bronzeville's Social Muse

CHAPTER 4

Year of Transition

By all accounts, A'Lelia Walker had a splendid funeral, one of the finest Harlem had ever witnessed. The bejeweled and silver-turbaned heiress of Madam C. J. Walker's hair-straightening empire, hostess of the Dark Tower and Villa Lewaro, had expired suddenly on August 13, 1931—victim of a fatal combination of high living and high blood pressure. Like the lavish parties that drew the rich, famous, and clever of all hues to her mansion on 136th Street, her apartment on Sugar Hill, and her Irvington-on-Hudson estate, Walker's funeral was by invitation only, and once again far too many invitations had gone out. The exclusive little chapel simply could not hold all the family, friends, and admirers who thronged Seventh Avenue, many of them desperately waving their engraved invitations above one another's heads. Those who found a way inside heard a stirring eulogy by Reverend Adam Clayton Powell Sr., pastor of Harlem's mighty Abyssinian Baptist Church, and an address by educator and civil rights leader Mary McCleod Bethune. A female quartet put a swing tempo to Noel Coward's "I'll See You Again," actor Edward Perry read Langston Hughes's poem "To A'Lelia," and young women from Walker beauty shops across the nation heaped flowers high about the silver casket.[1]

Sitting among the mourners that day, Hughes sensed that far more than one woman's life was over: "That was really the end of the gay times of the New Negro era in Harlem, the period that had begun to reach its end when the crash came in 1929 and the white people had much less money to spend on themselves, and practically none to spend on Negroes, for the depression brought everybody down a peg or two. And the Negroes had but few pegs to fall."[2] Walker had willed her thirty-four-room Villa Lewaro to the NAACP, but the venerable civil rights organization had lost thousands of dues-paying members and was forced to put the estate up for auction.[3]

Of the hard Depression years, 1931 was perhaps the hardest, and the unique convergence of personalities and institutions responsible for a luminous decade of African American creative expression centered in New York was quickly unraveling. Several years earlier, W.E.B. Du Bois had steered *Crisis* away from the cultural scene, largely in reaction to the defiant bohemianism of the younger writers.[4] The *Opportunity* awards competitions were gone, and Charles S. Johnson had left for Fisk University; in 1931 James Weldon Johnson joined him there. Alain Locke, who had returned to Howard, pointedly employed past tense when discussing the literary movement in a February 1931 essay: "The much exploited Negro renaissance was after all a product of the period of inflation and over-production."[5] With drastically reduced resources, white publishers, producers, galleries, and patrons no longer courted young black talents. What had been a struggle for artistic recognition and success became a struggle for sheer survival, and many of Harlem's brightest lights were forced into the hinterlands.

Among them was Arna Bontemps, whose poetry had won prizes from both *Opportunity* and *Crisis*. His novel *God Sends Sunday* was published in 1931 to fine reviews but few sales, and, within weeks of its debut, the private school where he taught closed its doors.[6] Bontemps fled New York with his wife, Alberta, and two young children.[7] "The Depression," he recalled, "brought instant havoc to the Harlem Renaissance of the twenties. . . . The jobs we had counted on to keep us alive and writing in New York vanished . . . quicker than a cat could wink." The family "wandered into northern Alabama . . . to wait out the bad times."[8] Arriving in the cotton-mill town of Huntsville the same month that A'Lelia Walker died, they settled into a decaying plantation house on the grounds of Oakwood Junior College, where Arna had accepted a teaching position.

Northern Alabama was farm country in those days, its red-clay soil an eye-pleasing contrast to the green foliage of rolling hills. The collapsing cotton market had forced many to shift from the South's ubiquitous cash crop to subsistence agriculture, but at least a farm family did not starve.[9] Bontemps was struck by the "primitive beauty" of the countryside outside Huntsville—"a green Eden," he called it.[10] Yet there was something sinister in that landscape, some specter from the past he would prefer to ignore, if that were possible. "This is a good place for writing," he wrote to Countee Cullen, "if I am not worked too hard. The place was originally a slave plantation. I live in the ruined 'old mansion' and have found it haunted by ghosts."[11]

To Langston Hughes, who was planning to visit for the winter holidays, Bontemps wrote, "Scottsboro is not far from here but I have not had a chance to go there yet."[12] Behind his matter-of-fact tone lay a domestic drama of some intensity. Just months before the Bontemps arrived in Huntsville, the nearby town of Scottsboro had emerged from sleepy obscurity to become center of the decade's cause célèbre.[13] Arna was keen to witness the unfolding events, but his employers had warned him to stay away. Nor would Alberta hear of such a reckless journey. Her husband was an educated black man, newly arrived in a small southern town, with a growing family to support, and already raising eyebrows by his choice of friends and reading material. Prudence dictated that he stay well away from Scottsboro. By the end of 1931, Arna had become painfully aware that his new-found Garden of Eden had more than its share of snakes.

One day in March of that year, a score of hoboes, both black and white, had hopped a freight train as it left Chattanooga's Southern Railroad yards headed west to Memphis. When as many as an estimated two million desperate Americans rode the rails each day in search of work, food, shelter, or any other form that hope might take, the event was at first quite unremarkable.[14] The train followed the Tennessee River as it wound across the state line down into Jackson County. Then, some thirty minutes after it passed through Stevenson, Alabama, a startled station master was confronted by a group of bruised and bleeding white youths, claiming that blacks had forced them off the speeding boxcars.

Telephone calls to local authorities revealed that the train was approaching Paint Rock. Word went out to every white man in the vicinity to grab his gun and head for the depot. The hastily deputized posse combed all forty-two cars that day and found nine black youths and three whites, but two of the white "boys" in overalls and caps turned out to be Victoria Price and Ruby Bates. Soon the dreaded word "rape" was uttered, and the nine were facing capital charges and a gathering lynch mob outside the jail in Scottsboro, the county seat. Four mounted machine guns and a detachment of National Guard held the crowd at bay.

One by one, local court-appointed defense attorneys found reasons to withdraw from the case. Finally one Scottsboro attorney, reputedly near-senile, stepped forward and was joined by another lawyer on retainer from Chattanooga's leading black citizens. The Tennessean had drunk so much whiskey to fortify his nerves that he could barely stagger to his chair. With no preparation, this duo purported to represent nine youths facing the electric chair. Eight were quickly sentenced to die, while the case of the youngest ended in mistrial.

Ranging in age from thirteen to nineteen, the defendants were dirt-poor, unemployed, and nearly illiterate. One was almost blind; another so cankered from syphilis that he hobbled with a cane. While the NAACP initially wavered at the appalling prospect of associating the Talented Tenth with a bunch of hoboes accused of gang rape, the Communist Party stepped into the breach through its International Labor Defense. The ILD provided a skilled and combative legal team to appeal the verdicts and launched a massive agitational campaign. The effectiveness of its protest meetings and marches was bolstered by the frequent presence of the defendants' mothers and later of Ruby Bates, who recanted her charges of rape in 1933. The slogan "Free the Scottsboro Boys" soon echoed across the United States and major cities of the world.

The Scottsboro affair was just nine months old as the Bontemps family contemplated their first Christmas in Alabama. Arna worked quietly on a children's book, *Popo and Fifina*, coauthored with his good friend Langston. The poet, on a tour of southern black colleges, was giving readings and selling his collections *The Weary Blues* and *The Negro Mother*. Traveling in a car purchased with a Rosenwald fellowship, he hoped to "build up a sustaining Negro audience for [his own] work and that of other Negro writers," for he believed strongly that black writers needed black readers "if their work is to be racially sound."[15] Since the campuses emptied out over the holidays, Hughes looked forward to a restful week exchanging news of the writer's trade with Arna and sharing family meals beneath Alberta's warmly welcoming gaze.

The two men must have spoken incessantly about the Scottsboro case, as the campus where they walked was a mere thirty miles from Alabama's seething cauldron, and Hughes had just published a powerful one-act play, "Scottsboro Limited," in the November issue of *New Masses*. That Leftist cultural journal was becoming his major outlet as he moved into the political orbit of the Communist Party.[16] Always the more cautious of the two, Bontemps produced, sometime later, a fine short story, "Saturday Night: Portrait of a Small Southern Town, 1933," vividly portraying the tensions that surrounded him.[17] These works joined a swelling chorus of outrage, making the case a common point of reference for an entire generation of writers and artists and the very name "Scottsboro" a shorthand and synonym for racial oppression.

Hughes resumed his southern tour early in 1932, leaving in his wake an irate white principal at Oakwood College, who lost no time in harassing Bontemps for the "subversive" company he kept. One chill February day, the principal burst into Bontemps's private quarters and demanded that he destroy whatever books and magazines might incriminate him in the eyes of local officials. Bontemps was no revolutionary, but he knew that when the authorities threaten to start burning books, it is clearly time to leave.

Temporizing while exploring a narrowing range of options, Arna eventually moved his family to Chicago. He and Alberta were dismayed by what they found: staggering unemployment, a violent crime wave, frigid winters, residential segregation, decayed housing, and garbage-strewn streets. "We had fled from the jungle of Alabama's Scottsboro area to the jungle of Chicago's crime-ridden South Side," he recalled, "and one was as terrifying as the other."[18]

The Depression had devastated the South Side and made a distant, painful memory of the employment boom that had fueled the Great Migration. "Last hired, first fired," black workers suffered the ravages of joblessness sooner and longer than whites. At its worst, in January 1931, black unemployment in Chicago stood at 58.5 percent for women and 43.5 percent for men.[19] In a single week in August 1930, three banks closed their doors and, according to the *Defender*, "threw the South Side into a turmoil." Most traumatic was the fall of the Binga Bank, whose deposits of $1.2 million made it the largest black-owned bank in the nation. Overextended in real estate loans just as property values plummeted, the bank's assets were frozen, and thousands lost their life savings.[20] Bills, rents, and mortgages went unpaid. Evictions followed on a massive scale, and dazed families sitting amidst their wrecked furniture became a common sight on the streets. Robert Abbott exhorted *Defender* readers to "have faith" and return to "common sense," assured them that "millions will be raised for relief" from private sources and "none will suffer" and censured "no account good-for-nothing loafers" looking for handouts.[21] His editorials increasingly seemed detached from the grim reality and the mood of ordinary South Side residents.

The Depression was disrupting lives and drowning hopes in a manner so fundamental as to shake the confidence of blacks in the constellation of leaders and institutions that had largely defined community life in the 1920s.[22] In March 1931, a bankrupt Jesse Binga was jailed on charges of embezzlement. The following month Republican Mayor Thompson was overwhelmingly defeated in his bid for a fourth term.[23] Although he still prevailed in South Side wards, his majorities declined significantly, an early rumble of the seismic shift in African American party loyalty that would result in the 1934 defeat of Oscar DePriest by black Democrat Arthur Mitchell.[24] The Chicago Urban League had lost the financial backing of Julius Rosenwald in 1929, threatening its social welfare programs just when they were most needed.[25] The *Defender* was briefly overshadowed by the *Whip*, which galvanized the community with the militant rhetoric, protests, and boycotts of its "Don't Spend Your Money Where You Can't Work" campaign.[26] Churches that had grown and built lavishly in the 1920s found themselves swamped by debt and widely regarded as just another "racket."[27]

If the established race leadership appeared paralyzed, communists seemed to be everywhere on the South Side: haranguing crowds at the open-air forum in Washington Park, parading down major thoroughfares, rallying at relief offices, canvassing for their electoral candidates.[28] Black newspapers followed the Scottsboro case closely, and the ILD's central role bolstered the Party's reputation as an opponent of racial oppression. In just three months following the initial April 1931 trial in Alabama, communist-controlled organizations such as the ILD, League of Struggle for Negro Rights, and Young Liberators of Chicago held fourteen protest meetings on the South Side and began receiving invitations to speak at black churches and clubs.[29]

Even more effective were communist-led unemployed councils and their campaigns for relief and against evictions. One newcomer to Chicago, black sociologist Horace Cayton, was astonished by the sight of "a long uninterrupted line" of "dirty, ragged Negroes" marching "in a serious and determined fashion" to the site of an eviction. The marchers braved police clubs and guns in order to "put back into the house the few miserable belongings of the evicted tenants."[30] A series of similar confrontations reached their climax on August 3, when police killed three blacks who were part of a crowd restoring an elderly woman's furniture to her flat. Two of the bodies lay in state for five days, guarded by Party members in military formation beneath the portrait of a steely-eyed Lenin. An estimated sixty thousand blacks and whites followed red banners down State Street in the funeral procession.[31]

Arna Bontemps arrived in the stricken city four years after that outpouring of grief and rage. He lived there from 1935 to 1943 and witnessed "a second awakening" of African American creative expression, "less gaudy but closer to realities," which brought a new generation to the forefront. "Chicago was definitely the center," he observed, and Richard Wright "the most typical as well as the most famous" of the writers.[32] The rising artists paid homage to all the Muses (including perhaps one or two that eluded ancient Greeks), and their approach might be described as documentary, sociological, or mimetic in spirit, and decidedly antiromantic, in reaction to the primitivist effusions of the 1920s. If the era of the New Negro was a time of challenging stereotypes through racial self-definition, then the era that followed represented a testing of that self—a time of hardship and struggle for which the Depression and Scottsboro may stand as potent symbols and 1931 as a year of transition.

CHAPTER 5

Birthing the Blues and Other Black Musical Forms

In the flowering of African American creative expression in Bronzeville, music was the precocious discipline, blossoming earliest, most spectacularly, and with the broadest audiences. The South Side was the hot center of jazz creativity in the 1920s, but in fact European art music had a considerably longer history among black Chicagoans. Building on deep roots in the community, classical musicians such as Margaret Bonds and Florence Price made landmark achievements that establish the early boundary of this study as 1932. In the same year, Thomas A. Dorsey penned his most famous song, "Take My Hand, Precious Lord," setting in motion both a stellar career and rapid evolution of urban gospel music. The achievements of gospel musicians Dorsey and Mahalia Jackson, the work of bluesmen Bill Broonzy and Muddy Waters, and the jazz masterpieces of King Oliver, Louis Armstrong, and Earl Hines—all bear testament to Chicago's singular importance as birthplace and incubator of distinctively African American musical genres arising in the wake of the Great Migration. Chicago was also the birthplace of Katherine Dunham's troupe, which transformed African American concert dance and interpreted dance forms of the African Diaspora to audiences around the world.

The Precocious Discipline

The *Defender*'s society page of December 15, 1928, included the photograph of a carefully coiffed, tan-complexioned girl, her round cheeks dimpled by a demure smile. The caption, "PRODIGY," aptly described fifteen-year-old Margaret Bonds, whose piano performances had been deemed newsworthy since she was six years old. At eight she won a scholarship to the Chicago Musical College—"in competition with 30 or more white pupils," music critic Nora Douglas Holt duly noted. Herself a talented musician, holder of a master's degree from the college, and publisher of the journal *Music and Poetry*, Holt had cofounded the National Association of Negro Musicians in 1919 to promote talents just like this. For "little Margaret Bonds, daughter of Estella Bonds, well known pianist and accompanist," was one of Black Chicago society's own.[1] Her father, Monroe A. Majors, was a pioneering physician and medical researcher.[2] Her mother was a music teacher and organist for Berean Baptist Church, one of the old-line black churches where musical tastes ran to such works as Haydn's *Creation*, Mendelssohn's *Elijah*, and Rossini's *Stabat Mater*.

Chicago's African American churches had by the 1890s become closely associated with classical music. The majority of black Christians attended such venerable institutions as Quinn Chapel African Methodist Episcopal (founded in 1847), Bethel A.M.E. (1862), Olivet Baptist (1862), St. Thomas Episcopal (1878), Bethesda Baptist (1882), and Grace Presbyterian (1888). Led by college-educated ministers trained in homiletics, these congregations were accustomed to worship in the subdued manner of their white counterparts. European art music was incorporated into services and into broader institutional life through church-sponsored concerts, vocal competitions, choral societies, and community orchestras.[3]

Margaret began playing alongside her mother at Berean Baptist and was soon performing throughout Bronzeville. With "a collector's nose for anything that was artistic," Estella made their home a lively gathering place for musicians, writers, and artists. Margaret recalled meeting "all the living composers of African descent," and she studied piano and composition with her mother's friends William Levi Dawson and Florence Price.[4] The latter was especially important as a teacher, friend, and collaborator.

Florence Price was born in Little Rock, Arkansas, in 1887.[5] Her father, James Smith, was a dentist whose lucrative practice in the Chicago Loop had been destroyed in the Great Fire of 1871, after which he moved to Little Rock and became the first black dentist in a city known as the "Negro Paradise" for its Reconstruction-era opportunities. Her mother, Florence Irene, was a teacher, businesswoman, and talented pianist, who nurtured her daughter's musical abilities. The Price family and the family of William Grant Still moved in the same social circles, and the two future composers began a lifelong friendship as children.

After graduating from Little Rock's public schools, Price enrolled in the prestigious New England Conservatory of Music to study piano and organ. She was also accepted as a composition student in the private studio of conservatory director George Whitefield Chadwick, who supported her exploration of folk materials. Only a few years earlier, Antonin Dvorak had encouraged American composers to create a national music based on "Negro melodies and Indian chants" and lit the path with his own "New World" *Symphony No. 9.*[6] Florence returned home to teach and then became head of the music department at Atlanta's Clark University, a post she resigned to marry attorney Thomas Price in 1912. She taught privately, continued composing, and frequently submitted pieces to competitions. In 1926 and again the following year, she won second prize in the composition contest sponsored by *Opportunity.*

The Prices and their two daughters moved to Chicago in 1927, the year that an ever-worsening racial climate in Little Rock reached its horrific nadir with a lynching in front of a church in a middle-class black neighborhood. Florence found a vitally sustaining musical environment in her new home. She pursued further study in composition at Chicago Musical College and the American Conservatory of Music, performed frequently, gave private lessons, and was actively involved in black organizations affiliated with the National Association of Negro Musicians and also in predominantly white women's musical groups. Her compositional output was prolific and eclectic, ranging from teaching pieces for piano and organ, to classical works for solo and ensemble performance, to popular songs for theater and radio.

Price taught composition to Margaret Bonds and became intimately associated with her family. The Bonds' household served as refuge after the composer divorced her husband in 1931. The younger artist recalled that Price was in "bad financial shape," when she and her daughters moved in. "During the cold winter nights . . . we used to sit around a large table in our kitchen—manuscript paper strewn around, Florence and I extracting parts for some contest deadline. . . . When we were pushed for time, every brown-skinned musician in Chicago who could write a note, would 'jump-to' and help Florence meet her deadline."[7] Both women won Rodman Wanamaker prizes in 1932: Bonds for her song "The Sea Ghost," and Price for her *Piano Sonata in E Minor* and her *Symphony in E Minor*. These prestigious awards brought both artists to national attention and mark 1932 as a milestone for the unfolding of the Black Chicago Renaissance.

Another of Price's compositions, the *Fantasie Nègre in E Minor*, caught the interest of ballet teacher Ludmilla Speranzeva, who was then training Katherine Dunham and her first black dance troupe. Speranzeva choreographed the piece, and Bonds, well known for fluent interpretations of her friend's work, accompanied the dancers when the work was premiered at the Beaux Arts Ball in December 1932.[8] In February Price and Bonds performed as soloists at Metropolitan Church in the second annual memorial concert for Julius Rosenwald.[9] Among the honors that marked the progress of their interlocked careers, perhaps most important was their participation in "The Negro in Music," a June 15, 1933, program held in conjunction with the Chicago World's Fair, "A Century of Progress."

Presented in the Auditorium Theater, the city's largest music venue, and broadcast over NBC radio, the concert celebrated the contributions of African American artists and musical forms to the classical repertory. Renowned concert artist Roland Hays sang a Berlioz aria, a piece by Afro-British composer Samuel Coleridge-Taylor, and arrangements of two spirituals. Margaret Bonds played the solo in a jazz-based concertino by John Alden Carpenter. In the audience Robert Abbott experienced "a feeling of awe" as "The Chicago Symphony Orchestra . . . swung into the beautiful harmonious strains of a composition by a Race woman," namely Price's *Symphony in E Minor*.[10]

That year Bonds was awarded a Rosenwald fellowship to support graduate study at Northwestern University. That training would support her future work as concert pianist, teacher, arranger, and composer. She set the poems of her friend Langston Hughes to music. Her popular songs were recorded by Glenn Miller, Woody Herman, Peggy Lee, and others, and her arrangement of "He's Got the Whole World in His Hands," commissioned by Leontyne Price, would became world famous.

Price's *Symphony in E Minor*, composed in 1931, stands with William Grant Still's *Afro-American Symphony* (1930) and William Dawson's *Negro Folk Symphony* (1932) as one of the first three symphonies by African American composers performed by major American orchestras. In "Echoes of the Harlem Renaissance," Rae Linda Brown observes that, in their interweaving of black folk idioms with classical music structures, the symphonies "represent the culmination of a black cultural awakening . . . in the 1920s."[11] Only in the case of Still's symphony, however, can Harlem—as actual place rather than imaginary locus of *all* African American creative expression—take any credit. Price was a pillar of the Chicago musical scene from her arrival in 1927 until her death in 1953. Dawson lived there for five years before returning to his alma mater, Tuskegee Institute, in 1930 to create a professional music school. He studied at Chicago Musical College, completed a master's at Chicago's American Conservatory, served as music director at Ebenezer Baptist Church, arranged and edited music for local publishers, played first trombone in the Chicago Civic Orchestra, and began composing his *Negro Folk Symphony* while living on the South Side.[12]

Bill Broonzy and the Blues Tradition

In 1940 Florence Price wrote: "In all of my works which have been done in the sonata form with Negroid idiom, I have incorporated a juba as one of the several movements because it seems to me to be no more impossible to conceive of Negroid music devoid of the spiritualistic theme on the one hand than strongly syncopated rhythms of the juba on the other."[13] For Price and many educated, middle-class black artists, aesthetic engagement with such traces of slavery as the sorrow songs and juba dances was much like discovering a vestigial organ. To William Lee Conley Broonzy, the "Negroid idiom" seemed closer to his own heartbeat.

Certain details of his early life are in dispute, but this much is certain: Bill Broonzy was, like Richard Wright, a product of that great inland flood plain called the Mississippi Delta, the former dominion of King Cotton, where black lives still passed in the shadow of the plantation. Both artists spent part of their formative years in rural Arkansas and made their way to Chicago as young men. Both surmounted the disruptions and tensions of the migrant's life and made the migratory experience a pillar of their art. Wright transmuted that experience into prose, Broonzy into the blues.

Broonzy was born on a plantation near Scott, Mississippi, a few miles north of Greenville.[14] The year was 1898, or perhaps 1893, depending on the source.[15] His parents were sharecroppers and former slaves, struggling to raise seventeen children. The family moved to Arkansas when Bill was quite young. His formal schooling was meager, but his music-making started early. With the help of an uncle who played banjo, he made a fiddle out of a cigar box, becoming sufficiently accomplished to organize a jug band that played for picnics and dances. The youth absorbed a wide array of musical styles, including minstrel songs, syncopated dance tunes, gospel hymns, field hollers, and mournful Delta blues.

Broonzy briefly laid music aside to follow his parents' strict Baptist faith and preach the gospel. Eventually he saved enough money to get married and buy a small farm, but when a drought destroyed his crop, he turned to common labor to earn a living. For several years, he worked with a railroad section gang, laying track between Texarkana, Arkansas, and St. Louis, Missouri. The young chanter calling out the work songs that kept the gang moving at a steady pace was Sleepy John Estes, a legendary figure in blues history.[16]

During World War I, Broonzy was drafted and shipped to the port of Brest with a labor battalion. Not directly involved in combat, he acquired the rudiments of literacy and saw a bit of France. After this heady experience, he returned to the deep South, where the rituals of racial subordination were being reinscribed with the blood of black veterans. Like many of his comrades-in-arms, Broonzy left for Chicago, arriving there in February 1920 and finding work as a maintenance man with the Pullman Company.[17]

Chicago in the 1920s was a good place to sing the blues. At the Monogram, Grand, and other vaudeville theaters on State Street, such artists as Ma Rainey, Bessie Smith, Mamie Smith, and Alberta Hunter could be heard regularly. These reigning queens of the blues were constantly on tour, playing the eighty or more theaters in the Midwest and South connected with the Theater Owners Booking Association. Such male talents as Blind Lemon Jefferson, Tampa Red, Georgia Tom Dorsey, and Papa Charlie Jackson could be heard close-up at house-rent parties and after-hours joints. These settings reproduced the communal energy of honky-tonks in the Delta or East Texas, creating a very different atmosphere from big theaters and jazz cabarets.[18]

The musicians who performed in these blues joints, when not playing on street corners, drew from a deep well of sound first heard in post-Reconstruction days—in juke joints and barrelhouses, levee camps and prison farms, picnics and dances, indeed nearly all social functions except church affairs because the blues had a distinctly disreputable aura. The sound was spread across the South by musicians who were forever on the move, hopping freights, bedding down in hobo jungles, being jailed for vagrancy, being drunk and disorderly, embroiled in disputes over women. Guitars strapped to their backs, these black bards became cultural icons, the rambling men of song and story. In a society characterized by immobility, blues men were symbols of freedom and movement.[19]

The actual origins are various and obscure, but if the music had a father, it was W. C. Handy, and if a mother, Ma Rainey; for Rainey gave the bastard a name, and Handy claimed paternity. The first professional blues singer to gain national recognition, Gertrude "Ma" Rainey remembered hearing the plaintively haunting sound for the first time in 1902, while she toured Missouri with a minstrel troupe. She later claimed to have named this music "the blues" in response to repeated queries about what to call the new songs she had added to her act.[20]

In his autobiography, *Father of the Blues*, William Christopher Handy recalled a night in 1903 while he waited for a train at Tutwiler station, deep in the Delta. "A lean, loose-jointed Negro," dressed in rags, "commenced plunking a guitar. . . . He pressed a knife on the edges of the guitar. . . . [producing] the weirdest music." Handy was then leading a brass band in Clarksdale, the center of what he called "Mississippi Mud." He immersed himself for years in the "low folk forms" of the region before moving upriver in 1909 to Memphis.[21] He took the sounds he heard, embellished and invented. Albert Murray described the result: "Once W. C. Handy had arranged, scored and published 'The Memphis Blues' (1912), 'The St. Louis Blues' and 'Yellow Dog Blues' (1914) and 'Beale Street Blues' (1916), it was no longer possible to restrict blues music to the category of folk expression."[22] Handy founded a small publishing house to market his compositions, which standardized a twelve-bar, three-line stanza with a repeated line, and an "aaa" rhyme scheme. In 1918 he and partner Harry Pace moved to New York to expand their business.

Bill Broonzy arrived in Chicago at a seminal moment in the evolution of the blues. The forces of migration had gathered a cadre of talented country musicians with eclectic backgrounds and an ear for the new music. Handy had made a repertory of classic blues songs available on sheet music, and the blues queens had popularized them on the vaudeville circuit. The phonograph-cylinder was displaced in the 1920s by the relatively inexpensive 78-rpm phonograph-disk. Seeing a potential new market, recording companies such as Paramount, Okeh, and Columbia established race record divisions and hired talent scouts. J. Mayo "Ink" Williams, an African American graduate of Brown University, represented Paramount in Chicago.[23] Sales of his mid-1920s recordings of Blind Lemon Jefferson, Charley Patton, Papa Charlie Jackson, and other country bluesmen demonstrated a significant audience for down-home sounds among migrants in the North, an example of what Farah Jasmine Griffin calls "the South in the city," that longing for things familiar that lodged itself in the heart of the transplanted southerner.[24] Urbanization of the blues thus began, ironically, when a mass-production industry based in northern cities made possible the permanent recording and widespread dissemination of the music in its rural southern forms as well as its more sophisticated classic versions.[25]

Broonzy teamed up with several co-workers from Pullman and began performing again, initially making a few dollars playing his fiddle at rent parties. He bought his first guitar in the open-air Maxwell Street market on the West Side, the former epicenter of Jewish immigrant life that was rapidly becoming Chicago's second black population center. Broonzy was tutored on his new instrument by guitarist John Thomas and banjo player Charlie Jackson, who taught him "how to make [his] music correspond to [his] singing."[26] He learned "slide" or "bottleneck" guitar, the distinctive style that Handy had heard in Tutwiler, involving use of a glass or metal tube or pocket-knife to slide down the guitar neck and produce a whining glissando.

In 1927 Ink Williams recorded several sides by Broonzy and Thomas, but sales were unimpressive. The following year, Williams released "It's Tight Like That" by the guitar/piano duo of Tampa Red and Georgia Tom. The upbeat number, spiced with double entendre, sold nearly a million copies at seventy-five cents each and sparked a dance craze called "hokum."[27] This low-down, good-time sound ushered out the last of what would soon be remembered nostalgically as Bronzeville's "fat years."

No sooner had Broonzy made his first recordings for Paramount and Gennett than both firms fell beneath the hammer blows of the Depression. But several companies held on, and in 1934, white businessman Lester Melrose was hired by RCA Victor to breathe life back into its Bluebird subsidiary. He had a good ear for talent and an eye for the bottom line. He gathered the best blues musicians in Chicago, signed them to long-term contracts, and recorded them regularly in combo and solo performance.[28] The bottom line required paying artists a pittance, and Broonzy worked as a laborer even while he was a Bluebird recording star.[29] Melrose's musical assembly line included Broonzy, Tampa Red (Hudson Whittaker, guitar), Memphis Minnie (Minnie Douglas, guitar), Black Bob (Bob

Alexander, piano), Josh Altheimer (piano), Bill Settles (bass), Fred Williams (drums), Washboard Sam (Robert Brown, Broonzy's half-brother), and Sonny Boy Williamson (harmonica).

Broonzy and Tampa Red, mainstays of the Melrose organization from 1934 until its demise in 1950, contributed both as recording artists and song-writers, producing a constant stream of new material for Bluebird artists. Tampa Red was born Hudson Woodbridge in rural Georgia but raised in Florida by his maternal grandmother, whose name, Whittaker, he took as his own. In his early years, he traveled across the South, playing guitar wherever he could earn some money. Dubbed "The Guitar Wizard," Whittaker perfected an open tuning, bottleneck technique used to equal advantage on up-tempo dance numbers and slow blues. In the early 1930s, he and Broonzy became close friends, hunting and fishing together when they were not in recording studios or performing at the Bee Hive, Triangle Inn, Tempo Tap, or other blues bars. Whittaker and his wife Frances rented a large house at Thirty-fifth and State. With ample living quarters and rehearsal studio, they kept open house for southern bluesmen visiting Chicago to record, many of them recruited by Broonzy, who doubled as talent scout for Melrose. Broonzy meanwhile was installed as in-house singer at Ruby Gatewood's Tavern, otherwise known as "The Gate," an important venue where veteran blues performers and young contenders displayed their virtuosity. Whittaker and Broonzy were largely responsible for keeping "the Bluebird beat" steady, and Broonzy in particular became "the venerable father figure of the Southside blues community."[30] Chicago was the center of the developing industry in black recorded music, and Whittaker and Broonzy were the most-recorded blues artists between 1928 and 1942, with 251 sides attributed to the former and 224 to the latter.[31]

Many of the blues that Broonzy wrote during the Depression shifted in theme from personal sorrows to the dislocations and traumas of urban life and hard times. The song that became his signature piece memorializes the migration: "I got the key to the highway, yes, I'm billed out, and I'm bound to go. / I'm gonna leave here runnin,' because walking is most too slow." "Billed out" means roughly "with all accounts settled" and refers to the system of peonage that bound sharecroppers to the land by keeping them perpetually in debt. Other migration-related songs included "IC Blues," "Going Back to Arkansas," "C and A Blues," and "I'm a Southern Man," which reflect the migrants' ambivalence and sense of displacement. Alongside a continuing string of good-time songs about drinking, sex, and nightlife, Broonzy recorded "Starvation Blues," "Unemployment Stomp," "WPA Rag," and "Romance without Finance." His songs "When Will I Be Called a Man?" "Black, Brown, and White," and "Police Station Blues" draw their power from revulsion at racist treatment of blacks. During the Depression, blues artists increasingly functioned as chroniclers of black, working-class experience.[32]

Broonzy was invited to participate in a December 1938 concert at Carnegie Hall intended to showcase the full range of African American music. Concert organizer John Hammond was a jazz critic and freelance music producer, who shortly thereafter became a major power at Columbia Records. Both a wealthy descendent of Vanderbilts and Benny Goodman's brother-in-law, Hammond had been a regular at Harlem cabarets since the

1920s. He secured financial backing from *New Masses* magazine and set off in his Terraplane convertible on a talent search in the deep South. He had hoped to sign Robert Johnson, but the Delta bluesman was murdered earlier in the year. Hammond found his next choice, Blind Boy Fuller, in a North Carolina jail. Broonzy was apparently a last-minute recruit to fill the slot of "primitive blues singer." After nearly two decades in Chicago, he was an accomplished studio and club musician with a versatile repertory, a fine wardrobe, and a Cadillac sedan. Nevertheless, for his performance in the "Spirituals to Swing" concert, Hammond asked him to wear overalls and pretend to be a shy sharecropper. Jazz singer Helen Humes, who fronted Count Basie's big band, was assigned the role of coaxing Broonzy from behind the curtain. "Don't worry about the way you're dressed," Humes called from centerstage, "or what people will think of you. Just . . . imagine you're in the country singing to the cattle." Despite this degrading bit of minstrelsy, Broonzy's musicianship soared, and his appearance at the concert lifted him a notch above local celebrity to national recognition.[33]

The war years brought new challenges. Not long after Pearl Harbor, the recording industry was hit by the rationing of shellac, used to manufacture both records and aircraft. Then in 1942 a labor dispute in the music industry stopped recording altogether. Musical sensibilities were also undergoing profound shifts as the bop revolution roiled the jazz world and the vocal scene was being transformed by rhythm and blues, on one hand, and the smooth love ballads of Nat King Cole and Billy Eckstine, on the other.

In 1943 a gifted young blues musician named Muddy Waters (McKinley Morganfield) arrived in Chicago from Rollingfork, Mississippi. He played bottleneck guitar and had a vocal style that was particularly intense and guttural. He found, at first, that "the blues didn't move anybody in the big city. They called it sharecropper music."[34] Broonzy recognized the younger man's drive and ability, introduced him to the house-party circuit, and helped him establish a presence on the club scene, where he began making his mark after switching to amplified guitar.

World War II produced another great migratory wave, which carried a new generation of blues musicians on its crest. Muddy Waters found his Lester Melrose in the persons of Phil and Leonard Chess, owners of the 708 and Macamba clubs. Noticing a rapidly growing audience for blues, the brothers formed a new record company in 1947, and within a year, Muddy Waters was their rising star.

While Chess Records, an upstart independent label, grew and built the bridges that led from Chicago blues to early rock and roll, the established record companies were shutting down their race record divisions. In 1950 RCA Victor terminated its Bluebird label.[35] Broonzy reinvented himself, with the help of a new interest in folk music among middle-class white audiences, especially in England and Europe. He breathed new life into his career by presenting himself as something like the "primitive blues singer" he had pretended to be for John Hammond.

Broonzy's life and work may be read as metaphors for the Great Migration. The movement, on either plane, is from simplicity to complexity, from innocence to sophistication. Consider the instrumentation available at successive stages of his career. From a one-string, cigar-box fiddle, appropriate for country dances, Broonzy progressed to guitar and learned how to blend it with his voice. With the start of his recording career, he mastered the musical dialogue of the guitar/piano duo. With the addition of bass, drums, and harmonica for recording sessions and club dates, he became in effect a bandleader. By the early 1940s, he was playing an amplified guitar. His music became more complex through instrumental augmentation and the influence of such vital forms as the boogie woogie piano style of Chicagoan Albert Ammons, who accompanied him at Carnegie Hall. Broonzy's musical development paralleled the transition from an agrarian, tradition-bound, church-centered folk culture to an urban, innovative, secular way of life. The country blues that went North with the Great Migration were transformed in a relentless process of triage. Folk values, including musical styles, were subjected to the weight and pressure of a great metropolis—some diluted or discarded, others salvaged in whole or part. Mississippi Delta versus "Sweet Home, Chicago": these polarities are crucial to an understanding of Broonzy and his generation.

One Way to Heaven

Historically, the boundaries between secular and sacred modes of African American life, between so-called sinners and saints, have been markedly fluid, despite the best efforts of those on the sanctified side of the aisle to maintain barriers. No life better exemplifies this observation than that of Thomas Andrew Dorsey, also known as Georgia Tom, prominent blues pianist, but more widely recognized as the father of gospel music. A man of many aptitudes, he worked extensively in both secular and sacred modes, functioning variously as performer, composer, teacher, voice coach, choir director, and musical evangelist. With as many guises as Ralph Ellison's Rinehart, he was part P. T. Barnum, part Billy Sunday, and part Booker T. Washington.

Dorsey was born in 1899 in Villa Rica, Georgia, a small town west of Atlanta.[36] His father, Thomas Madison Dorsey, was a graduate of Atlanta Baptist College, now called Morehouse. Trained for the ministry, he was unable to find a pulpit and resorted to itinerant preaching and then sharecropping, drawing ever closer to the margins of subsistence. Witnessing his father's defeats left the boy was with a dual legacy: pride in his father's priestly calling and shame at his worldly ineptitude. Dorsey's mother, Etta Spencer, was a widow of some substance when she remarried in 1895. She owned a bit of farmland, was an active church worker, played piano, and could provide whatever music a preacher-husband might require. In this devout household, hymns and family "sings" provided the earliest foundations of Dorsey's musical career.

In 1908 the family moved to Atlanta's West Side, where Dorsey's father found employment as a porter, his mother as a laundress. Left to his own devices, the boy dropped out of school around the age of thirteen. He spent much of his time at a vaudeville theater, where he hawked popcorn and soda. There he first heard Ma Rainey sing the blues. Her powerful presence reinforced the boy's association of the blues with rebellion and the romance of the open road, personified within his own family by maternal uncle

Phil Plant, a blues guitarist who hoboed across rural Georgia. Meanwhile, Dorsey continued his musical education by taking lessons from a piano teacher with Morehouse connections, but her commitment to classical training was of little value to a youngster bent on solving the mysteries of syncopation. Beyond the rudiments, he relied on his quick ear to master his instrument and by sixteen had become one of the top blues pianists in Atlanta. He played at teenage dances, rent parties, and on occasion at bordellos in the red-light district.

Dorsey relocated to Chicago in 1919, as the recently enacted Volstead Act was driving Demon Rum underground and creating opportunities for musicians in speakeasies and after-hours joints. Although there were many jobs, there were also many musicians to fill them, and the young pianist needed to upgrade his skills if he hoped to get an edge on the competition. Dorsey took lessons in composing and arranging and began to write his own songs. In 1923 he copyrighted seven blues pieces, one of which, "Riverside Blues," was recorded by King Oliver's Creole Jazz Band.

Dorsey was working as a freelance arranger for Paramount when the company signed Ma Rainey. As she was about to launch a southern tour, they learned that her regular accompanist was unable to leave Chicago, but Dorsey was available and prepared to travel. The two musicians were fellow-Georgians, thoroughly conversant with the blues style of the piedmont region. Dorsey was hired as Rainey's accompanist, arranger, and director of her touring band. In April 1924, they opened at Chicago's Grand Theater, and the pianist rose suddenly to the summit of the blues world.

Dorsey toured with Ma Rainey for two years, perfecting his musical and theatrical skills under her tutelage. His next partnership, lasting four years, began one evening in 1928 when Tampa Red dropped by his apartment with a handful of blues lyrics and asked him to set the words to music. The result was the raunchy hit record "It's Tight Like That." Elated by their success, the two musicians collaborated on some sixty more records and played every venue that mattered on the South Side.

But Dorsey's story is, ultimately, a tale of metamorphosis: from Georgia Tom, seasoned bluesman, to Thomas A. Dorsey, father of gospel choirs and gospel songs. What caused this unlikely transformation? Pain, sorrow, the death of loved ones—in a word, the human condition. As early as 1920, the pianist experienced a nervous breakdown that sent him home to Atlanta for a year, where his mother nursed him back to health. A second affliction struck in 1926, in the form of a deep depression that lasted for years. Each crisis was followed by a religious conversion, and each conversion by a relapse into the secular environment of the blues. Spiritual doubts and vacillations persisted until August 1932, when Dorsey's wife died in childbirth, along with his newborn son. These tragic events prompted him to compose his masterpiece, "Take My Hand, Precious Lord." Henceforth he confined himself to sacred song, worshipping his God through the medium of gospel music.

Dorsey undertook to blend religious texts with musical elements best described as blues-like, marked by syncopations and signifying embellishments: the clapping, swaying, moans, hollers, bent notes, and displays of religious fervor characteristic of the down-home church. To legitimize this new sound among Chicago's old-line black congregations required the utmost tact and shrewdest political stratagems, for it was a point of pride in these churches to avoid embarrassing reminders of slavery times and to erase any lingering Africanisms from worship services.

Against these legions of respectability, Dorsey had the sheer weight of the southern migration. It proved to be enough. As tens of thousands of migrants passed through the portals of the Illinois Central, they brought with them a style of worship that was participatory, revivalist, and ecstatic. These new arrivals did not conveniently disappear into Holiness or Pentecostal sects; most joined Baptist or Methodist mainline denominations, where they constituted an awkward, unassimilated presence. Astute pastors were quick to grasp the necessity of compromise between rural and urban modes of worship.[37] Dorsey rode this migratory wave to fame and fortune. He began by composing gospel songs and founding a small publishing house to produce the sheet music. Campaigning judiciously on the fringes of the larger churches, he built a network of sympathetic pastors, choir directors, and singing evangelists. As his sphere of operations expanded, he enlisted vocalists to join him in demonstrating the power of gospel music. Slowly the tide turned, as he was able to satisfy the longing of southern migrants for a sacred music warmer and more familiar than the somber tones of northern hymns and anthems.

Dorsey was primarily responsible for creating the institutional base of the gospel movement. In August 1930, the National Baptist Convention gathered in Chicago, some fifteen thousand strong. One of Dorsey's songs became instantly popular, and, before the sessions ended, he had sold four thousand copies.[38] The Baptist imprimatur vastly enhanced his access to the larger black churches. In the fall, the Metropolitan Community Church Choir became the first to use his songs. In 1931 he was called to the post of choir director of Ebenezer Baptist, and the following year he was asked to organize and direct a gospel chorus at Pilgrim Baptist, with a membership of seven thousand souls. From these commanding heights, he established the Gospel Choral Union of Chicago and, in August 1933, became founder and first president of the National Convention of Gospel Choirs and Choruses.

During this time, Dorsey searched for a singer who could match his own skills as accompanist, tour with him, and demonstrate his songs to best advantage. Two female vocalists became his chief collaborators. The first, Sallie Martin, was a former blues-shouter turned gospel singer, who joined Dorsey on the road, performed, organized choirs, kept his books, and helped promote his publishing ventures. Their partnership lasted from 1932 until 1939, when Martin left to form a rival publishing company.

Dorsey's second collaborator was a young singer from New Orleans named Mahalia Jackson. She was born in 1911 in a three-room shack situated between the railroad tracks and a levee on the Mississippi River. Her father was a stevedore who toted cotton bales by day, barbered in the evening, and preached on Sunday. Her mother died when Mahalia was only four, and her father, overwhelmed by the burden of raising six children, placed the girl and her brother William with their mother's sister. Aunt Duke was a stern disciplinarian and beat them mercilessly for any infraction. Mount Moriah Baptist Church soon became Mahalia's refuge, both from her aunt's tyranny and from the temptations of

9. Mahalia Jackson, c. 1945.
Vivian G. Harsh Research Collection of
Afro-American History and Literature,
Chicago Public Library. Ebenezer
Baptist Church Archives 067.

the port city famed for its red-light district. Jackson sang in the children's choir and, at the age of twelve, stepped to the mourner's bench, confessed her sins, and was baptized in the Mississippi.[39]

Mahalia's cousin Fred offered a bridge to the secular world.[40] An aspiring musician, he played the forbidden sounds of jazz and blues on his gramophone. Through him the girl discovered Bessie Smith, whose version of "Careless Love" she listened to over and over again.[41] Bessie Smith's blues were to haunt Jackson throughout her life, producing a deep ambivalence and sharp repression. At thirteen she promised herself never to sing the blues, thus repudiating the fallen world of "Careless Love." She was more receptive, however, to Fred's encouragement to escape Aunt Duke by moving to Chicago.

In 1927 Jackson boarded the Illinois Central, aided by another aunt, who offered to share her South Side flat. Employed at first as a laundress, chambermaid, and factory hand, she later became proud proprietor of Mahalia's Beauty Salon. Shortly after her arrival, Jackson joined the Greater Salem Baptist Church and rose to lead soloist in the choir. In the early 1930s, she joined a vocal group called the Johnson Singers, consisting of three male and two female voices, with Mahalia singing contralto. Based at Greater Salem, but performing chiefly on the storefront circuit, this quintet was, according to Jackson, "the first organized gospel group to circulate the city."[42]

In the early 1940s, Jackson's musical life was dominated by her partnership with Dorsey, whom she initially approached for formal vocal training. Dorsey focused on her timing and encouraged her to build steadily to a climax, rather than "start off shouting."

Young and headstrong, Jackson frequently clashed with her voice coach. Nevertheless, they managed to achieve a partnership of five years' duration, in the course of which Dorsey wrote many songs for Jackson, while she joined him in a series of extensive tours that spread the gospel style from Chicago to most of Black America.[43]

In 1946 Jackson began recording with a small company called Apollo Records. About a year later, Studs Terkel, a white radio journalist and disk jockey, was browsing in a record store on Michigan Boulevard when the owner pressed on his attention a newly minted recording called "Move On Up a Little Higher." It was love at first sound. Terkel had never heard of Mahalia Jackson, but after some detective work, he visited Greater Salem and directly witnessed the power of her music. Jackson accepted an invitation to perform on Terkel's weekly program, followed by a second session that included a leisurely interview. Like some magic carpet, Mahalia's first radio broadcasts lifted her above ghetto walls and put her down in living rooms across the city. "Move On Up a Little Higher" eventually sold more than two million copies and put her on the path to financial independence.[44] Working for eight years with Apollo's owner, Bess Berman, Jackson produced a stunning series of recordings that many critics regard as her finest work.[45] In 1950 she performed at Carnegie Hall, and the National Baptist Convention named her its official soloist.

From Swing to Bebop

In the winter of 1935–1936, Richard Wright was assigned by the Federal Writers' Project to compile a report on Bronzeville's recreational facilities. "The most attractive place of entertainment," he noted, "is the Grand Terrace Dine and Dance Cafe. . . . It possesses a splendid dance floor, accommodating about two hundred. Its seating capacity is five hundred and fifty. . . . The most distinctive feature of the Grand Terrace is Earl Hines' NBC orchestra which is known the nation over. . . . Four floor-shows are given nightly; it is an all-Negro revue. The place opens at 10 P.M. and runs till 5 A.M."[46] The Grand Terrace opened in December 1928 and closed some twelve years later. Throughout this span, Hines led the band, played piano, and "emceed" floor shows that featured a dozen or more chorus girls and visiting entertainers such as Buck and Bubbles, Ethel Waters, and Bill "Bojangles" Robinson. When not on tour, the fifteen-piece band performed six or seven nights a week. As "Fatha" Hines slipped his long legs under his white Bechstein piano, patrons knew that the place was about to rock.

Radio was a major cultural force in the 1930s, and it served to amplify Hines's sound a thousand fold. From 1933 onward, live broadcasts from the Grand Terrace Ballroom were relayed nightly, coast to coast, by the NBC blue line (to New York) and red line (to California and Canada). Top pianists shook their heads in grudging admiration, while bandleaders of stature strove to match Hines's level of proficiency. In far-off Macon County, Alabama, Albert Murray and other Tuskegee students gathered surreptitiously each night in the darkness of Sage Hall lounge, listening to Hines's after-curfew broadcasts.[47]

Bronzeville had a luxurious entertainment center in the Grand Terrace, but behind its plush facade, the Chicago underworld was at work. One day late in 1930, five of Al Capone's gorillas appeared with the precision of a S.W.A.T. team. Without preamble, the chief enforcer announced, "We're going to take twenty-five percent." "You must be losing your mind," the outraged owner replied. When the visitors suggested, in that exquisite gangster understatement, that it might not be too good for the health of his children if their father refused protection, the argument ended. Henceforth five of Capone's soldiers were placed at strategic intervals around the club, to assert their territorial rights and serve as bouncers.[48]

How did the musicians respond? "It was a case," Hines recalled, "of the three monkeys: see no evil, hear no evil, speak no evil."[49] If he complied with the arrangement and did as he was told, Capone himself would sometimes lean toward the bandleader, straighten his handkerchief, and leave a hundred-dollar bill in his breast pocket. This was the way of the world, as Hines had known from his adolescence in Pittsburgh. Moreover, it was the fate of the black musician to be pushed toward the fringes of society. The price of steady work, celebrity, and relative comfort was all too frequently a state of servitude. After the mob took over the Grand Terrace, they signed Hines to a contract binding him for life, in exchange for a salary of one hundred and fifty dollars a week.[50] When three of his sidemen decided to leave and work with Don Redman's band in Detroit, calls were made from a Capone operative to Owney Madden, mobster boss of New York's Cotton Club, who relayed the message to a member of the Purple Gang in Detroit. Redman's manager got the word via gangster telex and sheepishly sent the errant musicians back to Chicago. Not that such events were unique to Hines's band. Underworld bosses controlled the bookings and salaries of such distinguished bandleaders as Louis Armstrong, Duke Ellington, and Cab Calloway.[51]

Chafing at his exploitative contract and at a schedule that increasingly kept him on the road, Hines had by 1940 determined to free himself at all costs. He had the full support of Harry Gray, the pugnacious leader of all-black Local 208, one of the most powerful affiliates of the American Federation of Musicians, and Gray and Hines had backing from the national union. It took a year of lawsuits and periods of forced musical inactivity, but eventually Hines was his own man again.[52] Without a stable Chicago base, he had lost several musicians to other bands and soon lost others to the wartime draft. Like other big band leaders, Hines saw audiences dwindle as smaller rhythm and blues combos gained in popularity. Yet he was always a master of improvisation and managed to keep a band more or less intact through the war.

One strategic addition was Billy Eckstine, a smoothly handsome baritone who joined Hines as male vocalist in late 1940. Another was Sarah Vaughan, whom he hired early in 1943, just after she won the amateur-night competition at Harlem's Apollo Theater. "She didn't give a damn about *nothing* except Charlie Parker's music," Hines recalled.[53] Hines had heard Parker at Minton's, a little uptown Manhattan club where young musicians escaped the big bands that employed them and jammed with one another while trying out their boldest ideas.[54] He shared Vaughan's enthusiasm for the innovative saxophone player from Kansas City. In mid-1943, Hines hired Minton's veteran John Birkes "Dizzy" Gillespie on trumpet and, a few months later, with an opening for a second saxophonist, he called Parker.

Hines's collaboration with these musical revolutionaries is not documented in the normal manner because it occurred during a period when a dispute between the musicians' union and company executives prevented the recording of instrumental music. The recollections of participants are all that remain. Gillespie left this account: "We were playing around with bebop ideas in New York . . . in the later '30s and early '40s, but the whole thing came together when I was in the Earl Hines band. . . . Although Earl did not need another saxophone player, he hired Charlie Parker because Charlie was unique. . . . In 1943 the Hines band was doing things that were ahead of their time. I don't think people realize the kind of contribution Earl Hines made, not just to piano-playing, but to music in general."[55] Hines himself recalled: "All Dizzy was thinking of in those days was getting over his horn. He never thought too much of tone. I used him on up-tempo numbers, but for tone I would use somebody else in the trumpet section. Same way with Charlie Parker. He didn't have the tone on alto that you'd like to hear in playing a ballad." Hines remembered Gillespie doing "quite a bit of writing then," including two of his most famous works: "'Night in Tunisia,' a title I suggested because World War II was raging and there was a lot of action in Tunisia. Dizzy also did a vocal on 'Salt Peanuts,' the two words of the title! He was very serious about music and he and Charlie Parker were always working on the exercise books they had accumulated."[56]

Eckstine left Hines to form his own band in the spring of 1944, taking Gillespie and Parker with him, and some months later, "the divine Miss Sarah" also joined him. The founding fathers of bebop played with Hines night after night during a crucial moment in its evolution, and on that basis the Hines band may be considered an incubator of the new style. Stepping back for perspective, it becomes apparent that Earl Hines was playing a familiar role. In the late 1920s, as New Orleans jazz was evolving into swing, he joined Louis Armstrong in creating new forms. In the early 1940s, when big-band dance music was giving way to the radical deconstructions of bebop, Hines offered hospitality, if not total concurrence, to the young rebels. He was, in short, among the rarest of his guild—a pioneering jazz musician everlastingly receptive to the new.

The Worlds of Katherine Dunham

Dancer/choreographer/educator Katherine Dunham came from the same sort of Talented Tenth background as Florence Price and Margaret Bonds, classically trained musicians with whom she collaborated in the early 1930s. A businessman's daughter from Joliet, Illinois, she shared certain formative experiences with other leading figures of the Bronzeville Renaissance: the challenges of racial discrimination, the influence of Chicago social science, employment on the cultural projects of the New Deal, a fellowship from the Rosenwald Fund, and an artistic career shaped in the interplay and tension among classical European forms, modernist influences, and the folk legacies of the African Diaspora.

Katherine had followed her brother Albert to the University of Chicago in 1928 and shortly thereafter began pursuing her dream of creating a black troupe. Her dream was thwarted by lack of funds, however, and beyond that problem lay the question of which dance form she would pursue. This issue surfaced in the *Defender*'s account of Dunham's 1932 collaboration on *Fantasie Nègre* with Price and Bonds. The anonymous writer (who may have been Dunham herself) described the dancers' aspiration to "interpret the music, moods and life phases of the Race in the expressive movements of the modern dance as it is inspired by the emotions and voices from within, rather than in the steps of formal ballet."[57] Dunham's most important teacher, Ludmilla Speranzeva, had offered eclectic training that combined classical ballet with modern dance, musical theater, and ethnic dance, and clearly the young woman was searching for her métier.

While Dunham struggled to build a troupe and find a form best suited to her talents, she worked in a library, took classes at the university, and taught dance. One studio was in an unheated former coach house, where students in her "primitive" and ballet classes "bundled up in long woolen underwear under their tights, and two or three sweaters or scarves."[58] In her early academic career, Dunham was often "late to classes, fail[ed] to get papers in on time, and skip[ped] class now and then." The university did not have a dance program so she turned elsewhere for training and was continually torn between academics and performing arts.[59]

Aware of Katherine's diverse interests and adventurous nature, her brother suggested anthropology as a field of study. That department had separated from sociology in 1929 to focus on "the simpler cultures and the more primitive languages" that were rapidly disappearing. The department's founding members were pioneers of the discipline: Edward Sapir, Fay-Cooper Cole, A. R. Radcliffe-Brown, and Robert Redfield. The latter, who was Robert Park's son-in-law and protégé, had a decisive influence on Dunham. Focusing on what he called "folk societies"—physically isolated communities with simple social structures and cohesive value systems and customs—Redfield made his reputation with a famous study of a Mexican village that he called Tepotzlan. He also had broad interests in the arts and encouraged Katherine to connect her two areas of focus by exploring the social origins of contemporary dance forms.[60]

Dunham's academic turn toward anthropology coincided with a breakthrough in her dance career. In 1933 Ruth Page, ballet director for the Chicago Opera Company, was choreographing a piece called *La Guiablesse*, based on a Martinique folk tale of a she-devil who lures a young man to destruction. With music by William Grant Still, *La Guiablesse* was part of an all-ballet program presented in conjunction with the Century of Progress. Page invited Dunham to perform a supporting role, along with such other talented young blacks as Talley Beatty and Charles Sebree. When Page was unavailable to serve as prima in a December 1934 performance at the Opera House, she arranged for Dunham to dance the lead and take charge of the entire company.[61]

A few weeks earlier, Dunham had submitted a fellowship proposal to the Rosenwald Fund. Noting that modern dance pioneers such as Isadora Duncan and Ruth St. Denis had explored only "the Greek and the Oriental," she proposed an ethnographic study in a broader range of cultures to discover "fundamental and universal" elements to "incorporate into a basic dance form which has not yet been developed by the modernists."[62] She was invited to Fund headquarters to explain her ideas in greater detail. "Do you mind if I show you?" she asked. Slipping off her tailored suit in front of the startled fellowship committee, she pirouetted in a leotard and played a lovesick swan, before noting "that is the kind of dancing being taught in Chicago." She then performed a strenuous imitation of an African ritual dance. "That is the way people dance in other places," she commented. "I want to go where they dance like that. I want to find out why, how it started, and what influence it had on the people."[63]

With strong support from Charles Johnson and other committee members, Dunham was awarded a substantial grant with the stipulation that she first spend a semester at Northwestern under the tutelage of anthropologist Melville Herskovits. An expert on Haiti and West Africa, Herskovits helped Dunham focus her study plan and complete her training in fieldwork methods.[64] She decided to concentrate on Afro-Caribbean societies, where "one finds forms completely primitive as well as those in a process of acculturation. African forms still survive vigorously."[65]

The same month that Dunham applied for a fellowship, Zora Neale Hurston was in residence at the South Parkway YWCA and directing a pageant of folklore and song called *Singing Steel*. Dunham made her studio available for Hurston's rehearsals and gave a party in her honor. Members of the Rosenwald family saw *Singing Steel* and suggested its director apply for a fellowship to support doctoral study. Consequently both Hurston and Dunham received grants in 1935, as did a third black anthropology student, St. Clair Drake, who was at the University of Chicago concurrently with Dunham. He later observed that "most black graduate students in those days . . . depended upon the Rosenwald Fund for financial aid at crucial moments."[66] The striking simultaneity of these awards underscores both the fund's role in identifying outstanding black talents early in their careers and the interrelationship of creative arts and social science in many fellowship awards.

In May 1935, Dunham embarked on a year-long research trip to the Caribbean. Her itinerary included brief visits to Martinique and Trinidad and longer stays in Jamaica and Haiti. A full six months were devoted to Haiti, and that "island possessed," as she would title one of her books, became the focal point and culmination of her anthropological studies. Her professors at Chicago and Northwestern had trained her to approach dance in terms of its role in the social structure. In Haiti she discovered that dance was closely entwined with a whole system of customary practice and religious belief called Vodun, or voodoo, that was central to folk society.

"If all goes well in Haiti," Dunham wrote to Herskovits, "I shall have a little controversy with you." Not one to settle for half-measures, she determined to probe the mysteries of the Vodun by becoming initiated, "which means that I will probably have to do away with the typewriter and picture machine for a while."[67] Through contacts in Port-au-Prince, she gained access to the Rada-Dahomey cult.[68] After several months of preparation, she was ready for the lavé-tete, or head-washing ceremony, required of all initiates. While Dunham's mentor in Evanston fretted about her "going native," she spent three days in the company of eight other initiates—male and female, old and young—lying spoon-fashion on the damp earthen floor of a small hut. Fasting, mildly drugged, and entranced by an incessant, subdued drumbeat, she emerged from her ordeal and ended the ritual by placing a wedding ring on her finger, for she was now a bride of Damballa, serpent-god of the Rada-Dahomey.[69] The ceremony concluded with a communal dance in which Dunham experienced "the sheer joy of motion in concert, of harmony with self and others."[70] Her initiation was a particularly radical, intense form of participant-observation, the culminating moment of an extended fieldwork experience that proved life-changing.[71]

Dunham returned to Chicago in May 1936. She made her report to the Rosenwald committee, illustrated with photographs, recordings, and a short dance during which Herskovits accompanied her on drum.[72] She then faced a decision of enormous consequence: the choice of career. One path led toward graduate school, a Ph.D. in anthropology, and a scholar's life. The other led toward dance, choreography, and her dream of building a black troupe. This dichotomy between analysis and performance, between the Apollonian and Dionysian aspects of her temperament, was a source of considerable personal turmoil, and she sought help from both Redfield and Herskovits in designing a suitable graduate program. She produced two manuscripts based on her fieldwork, one of them intended to serve as master's thesis. But in the end, she apologized profusely to her mentors and departed academia.

To earn a living during this time of transition, Dunham sought employment on the Federal Writers' Project. Redfield had read her manuscript *Journey to Accompong*, based on a month spent among the Maroon people of Jamaica, and recommended that she present it as evidence of her writing and research skills.[73] She applied to the project's office in Chicago with Redfield's letter of recommendation, her study, and a proposal for investigating "the cults burgeoning in Chicago and their relationship to deprivation."[74] The director, John T. Frederick, was suitably impressed and hired her to supervise the study, which took some six to eight months.

As her work for the Writers' Project was winding down, Dunham approached the local unit of the Federal Theater Project with a work she had written called *L'Ag'Ya*, based on dances of Martinique and set in an eighteenth-century fishing village. She was hired to produce the piece and auditioned "out-of-work cooks, chauffeurs, maids, typists," until she assembled a cast of nearly fifty dancers.[75] Dunham described the story-line in her memoir "Minefields": "Loulouse loves Alcide and is desired by Julot." Rejected by the beautiful Loulouse and "filled with hatred and desire for revenge," Julot seeks aid from the King of the Zombies and secures a love charm to win his object of desire. "The following evening . . . is a time of gaiety, opening with the stately creole mazurka . . . and moving into the uninhibited excitement of the beguine. . . . Julot . . . exposes the [love charm]. Even Alcide is under its spell. Now begins the majumba, love dance of ancient Africa." Alcide suddenly breaks loose from his trance and challenges Julot to "the l'ag'ya, the fighting dance of Martinique," but he dies in the ritual combat that follows.[76] Chicago audiences had never seen such a combination of dramatic intensity, sensuality, and theatrical elegance; the effect was heightened by the costumes and sets of John Pratt, a white painter, costume and set designer, who became Dunham's second husband and her master of the mise-en-scène.

L'Ag'ya was a sensation, running from January to March 1938 at the Great Northern Theater. More good fortune followed when Louis Schaeffer of the New York Labor Stage

10. Katherine Dunham in *L'Ag'Ya*, 1952.
Roger Wood Photographic Collection, Royal Opera House Collections;
Photograph courtesy of Jerome Robbins Dance Division, The New York Public Library
for the Performing Arts, Astor, Lenox and Tilden Foundations.

saw Dunham perform and invited her to New York as dance director for the popular labor-oriented musical *Pins and Needles*. This was her entree to Broadway. By February 1940 the Dunham Company were performing their revues *Tropics* and *Le Jazz Hot* at the Windsor Theater. In the fall, they appeared in the all-black musical drama *Cabin in the Sky* at the Martin Beck, and Dunham shared choreographic responsibilities with George Balanchine.[77]

Dunham took *Cabin in the Sky* on tour, ending in California, where her company appeared in the film *Stormy Weather* (1943) as part of an all-star cast that included Lena Horne, Cab Calloway, and Bill Robinson.[78] Thereafter, the Dunham Company embraced touring as a way of life, traveling the country with her *Tropical Review*, managed by famed impresario Sol Hurok. In several cities en route, Dunham boldly challenged segregated accommodations or theater seating.[79] After the war, she undertook a North American tour, followed by a world tour with *Caribbean Rhapsody*, and found warm welcomes and growing fame in the capitals of Europe.

In 1950, at the peak of her celebrity, Dunham acquired an abandoned sugarcane plantation in the hills above Port-au-Prince. Intended as a refuge from incessant touring, Habitation Le Clerc also allowed her to reestablish spiritual ties with the Vodun and connection with the Haitian people. Dunham's long periods of residence there reflected the profound transformation she had undergone during her first visit to the country and her ability to move among vastly different cultural worlds. She had come to the Vodun as a social scientist, but she had embraced anthropology through dance. Dance ultimately allowed her to experience the world kinesthetically and communally, becoming both her art form and her most profound way of knowing.

In Dunham's early career may be found a prototype for many of the most accomplished Bronzeville artists. Chicago social science provided the intellectual paradigm within which she conceptualized her art. In her anthropological studies of dance, she explored the survival of African-derived cultural forms least changed by contact with European practices. While Richard Wright's prose works explored transformations of African American folk culture in the processes of urbanization and modernization, Dunham's dance works attempted to reproduce rural Afro-Caribbean folk dances in their purest form. The two artists worked at opposite ends of Robert Park's acculturative cycle, yet within its general frame of reference and with a shared documentary impulse.[80] The Rosenwald Fund (for Wright the Guggenheim Foundation) eagerly underwrote this synthesis of creative expression and social thought. As a dancer and choreographer, Dunham built on classical and modern European forms while placing Afro-Caribbean and African American dances at the center and on an equal plane with European dances. Perceiving the underlying similarity of social function behind different cultural practices, "It never seemed important" to Dunham "to portray . . . the behavior of other peoples as exotics."[81] The cultural projects of the New Deal provided financial support, exposure to new aesthetic perspectives, and collegial interaction across the color line. Dunham moved from the Federal Theater Project to Broadway, Hollywood, and beyond as an acclaimed modern artist, pioneering figure in African American concert dance, and interpreter of diverse cultures to popular audiences around the world.

CHAPTER 6

Bronzeville and the Documentary Spirit

In the friendship and professional collaboration of Richard Wright and Horace Cayton in the early 1940s, the Black Chicago Renaissance may be seen *en petit*. Like Alain Locke and Charles S. Johnson in 1920s Harlem, Wright and Cayton brought complementary skills, values, and bodies of knowledge to a productive alliance that advanced their careers while enriching and even shaping the cultural milieus within which they worked. The fiction writer and the sociologist understood their areas of expertise as cognate disciplines animated by a common impulse to document, interpret, and ultimately change the realities of a society built on racial and class oppression. Indeed, the kinship of realist/naturalist fiction and urban sociology had a long and notable lineage largely centered in the city of Chicago.

Each man was profoundly influenced by Parkian sociology as well as Marxist radicalism. Each pushed against the received wisdom and common practice of his own professional field: Wright struggled to carve a place for human agency and subjectivity within the determinism of the naturalistic novel; Cayton sought to infuse activist urgency into the social scientific enterprise. Their individual talents and training, their rich cross-disciplinary collaboration, and their extensive social and institutional networks supported the creation of such central texts of Bronzeville's creative flowering as Wright's *Native Son* and *12 Million Black Voices* and Cayton's coauthored study, *Black Metropolis*.

"A Poetic Little Negro"

At their first encounter in the halcyon sanctuary behind university walls, each man was acutely aware of the different world from which the other had come. The Mississippian stood five feet, eight and a half inches in height, had a ninth-grade education, was malnourished and on relief. Knocking at the office door of sociologist Louis Wirth, he was perhaps startled when another African American greeted him. "Hello. What do you want?" asked a tall, barrel-chested, copper-colored man from Seattle, who felt rather superior in his status as doctoral candidate and research assistant to the eminent professor.[1]

Born in 1903, Horace Cayton Jr. was the son and namesake of a pioneering newspaper editor and leader in the Washington State Republican Party. His maternal grandfather was Hiram Revels, the first black U.S. senator and founder of Mississippi's Alcorn University. His earliest years were spent in a stately two-story home with carriage house, horse and buggy, and Japanese servant. Horace and his four siblings were sent to school each day with the parental injunction "Go out and achieve." Living among whites in the city's most affluent neighborhood, at a time when Seattle's African American population was tiny and the residential color line had not yet been drawn, they were frequently reminded by their father that "Colored society starts with us!" Horace began graduate work in sociology at the University of Washington with R. D. McKenzie, a former student of Robert Park, but transferred to Chicago in 1931 at Park's invitation.[2]

Four years earlier, Richard Wright had disembarked at the Illinois Central's Twelfth Street station, the Ellis Island of Chicago-bound migration. No one had invited him, but nineteen years of desperate, driven wandering across the Mississippi Delta had infected him with a bad case of "northern fever." He was born in 1908 in a log cabin on the old Rucker plantation twenty-two miles east of Natchez, "too far back in the woods to hear the train whistle."[3] He was four when his father, Nathan Wright, an illiterate sharecropper, abandoned him, his mother, and younger brother, Leon. Ella Wright had been a schoolteacher before the marriage but worked as a cook after her husband left. Crippling illness soon prevented her doing work of any sort and pushed her sons and her to the brink of starvation. Anxiously, they depended on other family members, moving from household to household and town to town. Richard's last two years in the South were spent in Memphis, where he worked for an optical company and read everything he could get his hands on—from the local newspaper to the *Atlantic Monthly* and *American Mercury*, from lurid pulp fiction to Sinclair Lewis and Sherwood Anderson.[4]

Nothing in Horace Cayton's previous experience—not even the wandering years when he shipped out as steward, cook, and ship rigger and worked as coal miner, prizefighter, and deputy sheriff—nothing had prepared him for the South Side of the early 1930s: "Never had I seen so many Negroes," he later wrote, "this sea of black, olive, and brown faces everywhere. On a narrow tongue of land seven miles long and a mile and a half wide were packed more than 300,000 Negroes." Bronzeville, from the viewpoint of an ambitious young social scientist, was one great laboratory: "Beneath the surface were patterns of life and thought, attitudes, and customs. . . . Understand Chicago's black belt and I would understand the black belts of a dozen other large American cities."[5] But the scientist himself bore the blood of Africa in his veins, and he and his white wife, Bonnie Branch Hansen, had to live inside this walled-in laboratory. At first, they shared a one-room kitchenette, but life improved when Unitarian minister Curtis Reese invited them to live at the Abraham Lincoln Centre.[6]

While Cayton dreamed of launching a successful academic career from the very epicenter of American sociology, Wright's "expectations were modest. I wanted only a job."[7] A job and perhaps something more—a shred of dignity, a respite from the naked race terror of the South, and a place in the world that might match his capacious imagination and questing intellect. But even a steady job, his most basic aspiration, proved elusive. He was employed at first as a delivery boy and then a dishwasher, until he qualified for temporary work in the post office. Passing the written exam was easy, but he failed the physical at first and had to stuff himself relentlessly to meet the 125-pound minimum weight requirement.

And when the Depression struck, he was laid off. His mother and brother had come North in 1928, and with them and an aunt, Wright shared a series of cramped kitchenettes. These shabby flats were soon filled with ugly emotions and bickering, often over the young man's strange, solitary habit of reading books and his even more outlandish dream of becoming a writer. The arrival of maternal grandmother Margaret Wilson, a devout Seventh-day Adventist who considered modern literature "the devil's work," only exacerbated family tensions.[8]

With a University fellowship arranged by Robert Park, Cayton studied full-time for two years and then began a series of research positions working with prominent academics. Park encouraged him to accept an invitation to spend the summer of 1932 at Tuskegee, his first trip south. "You may not like what you see," his mentor warned, "and I doubt that it would be possible for your wife to go with you. But you'd better have a look around down there if you can possibly manage it."[9] Cayton found time to travel outside Tuskegee and learn something of the elaborately ritualized code of behavior that governed black life below the Mason-Dixon Line. He found himself "standing one day near the highway which cuts across a portion of the campus when a caravan of speeding cars passed. Men were riding on the running boards with rifles and shotguns in their hands." While Cayton stood gaping, "everyone else on campus had suddenly disappeared." Later, someone cautioned him, "When you see a bunch of rednecks like that, it's best to get out of the way." He learned that the armed men were pursuing "a young Negro accused of insulting a white girl." He had seen his first lynch mob.[10]

The hell that Horace Cayton briefly glimpsed that summer was seared into every nerve and fiber of Richard Wright's being. When he was eight, his family moved in with his aunt and uncle, Maggie and Silas Hoskins, in Elaine, Arkansas. Their white bungalow was neat and well-appointed, their dinner table full of tasty food. Silas owned a saloon, and they lived well, apparently too well for black folks in Arkansas. One morning, Silas did not come home from work. The family learned that he had been shot and that whites were threatening to "kill all his kinfolks." Packing whatever they could fit into a farm wagon, they fled under cover of darkness. About eight years later, while living in Jackson, Mississippi, Wright learned with horror that the brother of a classmate had been castrated and murdered when his furtive involvement with a white prostitute was discovered. The specter of the lynch mob haunted him and would appear repeatedly in his writing.[11]

Both Wright and Cayton broke into print in 1931. *Abbott's Monthly* published Wright's suspense tale "Superstition" in April. He never received payment, however, and his hopes of finding work on a black newspaper failed to materialize.[12] One morning, without a scrap of food for breakfast, he stifled his pride and turned to the public dole: "As I walked toward the Cook County Bureau of Public Welfare to plead for bread," he recalled, "I knew that I had come to the end of something."[13] While on relief, he worked as a street-cleaner, ditch-digger, and hospital orderly. Cayton's first published piece, appearing in the September issue of *The Nation*, described a confrontation with the police during a communist-led attempt to block an eviction. The ragged, angry protestors seemed to the sociologist like people "who had awakened from a pleasant dream to find that reality was hard, cold, and cruel. . . . A few years ago [they] had migrated from the South . . . with prayers to the Almighty for deliverance. . . . Now they were virtually starving to death."[14]

One of those starving migrants, Richard Wright, was also beginning to take notice of communist soap-boxers, their unemployed councils, and their campaign to save the Scottsboro defendants. At the invitation of a former postal coworker, he joined the Party's cultural affiliate, the John Reed Club, in the fall of 1933. The national network of clubs served as a combination of Marxist discussion groups, free university, gallery, and publishing house and offered elements of hope and direction to some twelve hundred radical young artists and writers.[15] Encouraged by his new comrades, Wright began publishing poems in Leftist journals and quickly became the club's secretary. Shortly thereafter, he joined the Party itself. He organized a lecture series for the John Reed Club and invited prominent artists, writers, and intellectuals, including sociologist Louis Wirth, who spoke about Jewish ghettoes in the United States.[16]

Wirth was a preeminent figure in the second generation of Chicago social scientists. Jewish and born in a rural German village in 1897, he emigrated to the United States and joined his sister in Nebraska in 1911. He began studies at the University of Chicago as a premedical student, but electives in sociology brought him into contact with William Thomas, Robert Park, and Ernest Burgess, who inspired him with the belief that "a science of human behavior was not only possible but indispensable."[17] Wirth trained with Park, joined the faculty in 1930, and, by the time of his John Reed Club lecture, had established a national reputation as an expert on urban life and minority group behavior.[18]

One other connection brought Wright to Wirth's office in the winter of 1933–1934. Mary Wirth, the professor's wife, was assistant supervisor of an emergency relief center where Wright had turned for help, and he made a strong impression on the social worker during his intake interview. When Cayton curtly asked, "What do you want?" Wright replied, "Mrs. Wirth made an appointment for me to see Dr. Wirth." Cayton became "a little more respectful" and invited him in. Wright continued, "Mrs. Wirth said that her husband might help me. I want to be a writer." Cayton began showing Wright their research files. "We were very empirical," he recalled. "We were going out studying every facet of the city . . . the Italian district, the Polish district, the Irish district, the Negro community." "You've got all of your facts pointed," Wright responded, "pinned to the wall like a collector would pin butterflies." What "a poetic little Negro," thought Cayton.[19]

The two men did not meet again for some six years. When they reestablished contact, Wright was a best-selling author living in New York and about to fly to Chicago on assignment for *Life* magazine. Cayton, a prominent researcher and settlement house director, met Wright's plane, and thus began a warm friendship and productive professional collaboration with profound consequences for intellectual life and creative expression in Bronzeville.

A Certain Family Resemblance

Wirth gave Wright a list of sociological works that an undergraduate major would typically read. At their second meeting, the professor was impressed by the alacrity and thoroughness

11. Horace Cayton and Richard Wright examining census maps
of the South Side, 1941.
Vivian G. Harsh Research Collection of Afro-American History and Literature,
Chicago Public Library. Horace Cayton Papers 015.

the young man demonstrated in his self-directed course of study. The contemporary reader may wonder why someone who wanted to write fiction would approach a sociologist for help, but, to an apprentice writer living in 1930s Chicago, a basic grasp of sociology was self-evidently valuable. The novel of urban life and the sociological study of the city then seemed first cousins, each inhabiting a separate domicile, but bearing a certain family resemblance.

The modern novel, like most contemporary art forms, was spawned in those vast metropolitan centers that, for better or worse, set the tone of life in the twentieth century. Paris, Berlin, Prague, London, Dublin, New York, and Chicago left indelible imprints on modern fiction. In the United States in the early twentieth century, novels by Frank Norris, Stephen Crane, Theodore Dreiser, Upton Sinclair, Sinclair Lewis, and others defined a new form that came to be called literary naturalism. Such writers were influenced on the scientific side by Charles Darwin and Herbert Spencer and on the literary side by European novelists, especially Emile Zola. They considered their approach objective and scientific, focusing on the epic forces that shape human destinies, often crushing helpless individuals in the process. Norris wrote that "No one could be a writer until he could regard life and people . . . from the objective point of view—until he could remain detached, outside, maintain the unswerving attitude of the observer."[20] Naturalistic writers aspired to create novels as big and brutally powerful as the cities and industries they portrayed. It was no coincidence that many began their careers as newspaper reporters, immersed in the drama and details of urban life—sensational acts of violence, civil conflicts, corruption in high places.[21]

Chicago, the youngest of the world's great cities, frequently yielded setting and subject matter. Fighting suppression and censorship, these writers challenged an earlier tradition of literary gentility, which had produced fiction that Norris ridiculed as "safe as a graveyard, decorous as a church, as devoid of immorality as an epitaph."[22] According to Carl S. Smith, the Chicago novels of Norris and Dreiser, like Sandburg's poems, expressed a sense that "art forms that the 'cultured' world favors cannot begin to match [the] drama of power enacted by the city itself."[23]

In Wright's account of his earliest reading of "serious" novels, he credits the influence of H. L. Mencken, editor of *The Smart Set* and *American Mercury*, who satirized anachronistic, small-minded traits in American life. The critic attacked "colorless and inconsequential" strains in American literature and championed cultural independence from Victorian England, attention to real life in American cities and towns, and literary language rooted in the vernacular.[24] Wright responded enthusiastically to Mencken's iconoclasm and read the authors whom he favored: "All my life had shaped me for the realism, the naturalism of the modern novel, and I could not read enough of them." Lewis's *Main Street* led Wright to perceive his boss at an optical company in Memphis "as an American type." Dreiser's *Jennie Gerhardt* and *Sister Carrie* left him "silent, wondering about the life around me."[25] Such works provided an angle of vision on human experience that focused on the social panorama, rather than on individual acts of heroism, social and moral conventions, or subjective experience. From this perspective, a fictional character may be perceived as representative of a social type and individual life experiences as a history unfolding against a backdrop of social institutions and processes.

When Wright crossed the invisible barrier separating the solidly black world he inhabited from the Hyde Park environs of the University of Chicago, he entered a milieu associated with sociology from its very birth. Landmarks of that discipline's history include the simultaneous founding of the University and its sociology department, first in the nation, in 1892; establishment of the *American Journal of Sociology* at the University three years later; appointment of William Thomas to the department in 1896; appointment of Robert Park in 1914; publication in 1918 of the first two volumes of Thomas's and Florian Znaniecki's *The Polish Peasant in Europe and America*, described by Lewis Coser as "the first great classic in American empirical sociology"; publication in 1921 of Park's and Ernest Burgess's *Introduction to the Science of Sociology*, "by far the most important textbook-reader in the early history of American sociology."[26]

Comparable milestones in the history of the naturalistic novel are these publications: Stephen Crane, *Maggie: A Girl of the Streets* (1893); Frank Norris, *McTeague* (1899); Theodore Dreiser, *Sister Carrie* (1900, reissued 1911); Norris, *The Octopus* (1901); Norris, *The Pit* (1903); Jack London, *The Sea-Wolf* (1904); Upton Sinclair, *The Jungle* (1906); Dreiser, *Jennie Gerhardt* (1911); London, *Martin Eden* (1913); Sinclair Lewis, *Main Street* (1920); Lewis, *Babbitt* (1922); Dreiser, *An American Tragedy* (1925).

Norris, Dreiser, and Sinclair all had significant connections with Chicago. Sinclair, for example, spent nearly two months researching the city's meat-packing industry for *The Jungle*. He lived among the immigrants who worked in the packing houses and, like a good reporter or empirical sociologist, recorded everything he observed, what knowledgeable people said, and what the newspapers reported.[27] "If there is an American city that supplies a terrain for literary naturalism, it is Chicago," Richard Lehan observes.[28]

The leading figures in the early days of Chicago sociology were quite conscious of their affinities with literary artists. The department's founder, Albion Small, became known in the city as a strong advocate of social reform and, toward that end, published a didactic novel called *Between Eras: From Capitalism to Democracy* (1913).[29] William Thomas had been a language and literature professor before coming to the University. In a proposal outline for the Carnegie Corporation, he observed that sociologists had paid much attention to social organization but little to "the field of behavior," which they left by default to "literary men—Zola, Ibsen, Shaw, Meredith—and psychiatrists."[30] As an undergraduate, Robert Park's imagination had been stirred profoundly by Goethe's *Faust*. During his days as a journalist, he wrote a novel, *The Isle of Enchantment*, exploring the social complexities of life in Manhattan.[31] The Park/Burgess textbook observed: "The novel which emphasizes 'milieu' and 'character,' as contrasted with the novel which emphasizes 'action' and 'plot,' is a literary device for the analysis of human nature and society."[32]

Engagement with literature as a cognate discipline continued into the second generation. Social anthropologist Robert Redfield observed: "No one is more deeply engaged in the examination and understanding of human nature than are the dramatist and the novelist. . . . I doubt that the results so far achieved by the social scientists are more communicative of the truth about human nature than are the results achieved by the more personal and imaginative records of the artist." Lecturing on such topics as "The Deserted Village" and "The City in Literature," Louis Wirth illustrated his descriptions of the processes of urbanization with poems and novels.[33]

In the second novel of his *Studs Lonigan* trilogy, James T. Farrell, a former social science major at the University, paid tribute to the Chicago School. John Connolly, "King of the Soap Boxers" in Washington Park, challenges the racism of white listeners by citing "ideas presented by members of the Department of Sociology at the University of Chicago, and developed from [their] . . . community research programme." Another speaker reports that the "new science" of anthropology has "proven as a scientific truth that no one race is superior to any other race." This episode falls, ironically, between a white gang's violent fantasies about ethnic cleansing of the changing neighborhood and their mugging of "a passing Negro hot-tamale-man."[34] Such explicit references suggest the strong sociological influence on Farrell, Wright, and other writers working in the naturalist tradition.[35]

Richard Wright and the Sociological Imagination

Wirth and Cayton shared a certain missionary zeal toward their profession, which inspired Wright to add a new and vital element to his growing understanding of the world and his place in it. His reading habits, always omnivorous, tilted for a time toward social science. He later wrote: "I lived half hungry and afraid in a city to which I had fled with the dumb yearning to write, to tell my story. But I did not know what my story was, and it was not until I stumbled upon science that I discovered some of the meanings of the environment that battered and taunted me. I encountered the work of men who were studying the Negro community, amassing facts about urban Negro life, and I found that sincere art and honest science were not far apart, that each could enrich the other."[36] A welcome opportunity to join "sincere art and honest science," while also putting food on the table, appeared in the summer of 1935 when Wright was hired by the newly created Federal Writers' Project.

In April Congress had passed the Emergency Relief Act giving President Franklin Roosevelt broad powers to meet the ongoing unemployment crisis. On May 6, the Works Progress Administration (WPA) was created by executive order to provide relief for the needy and work for employable people on the relief rolls. Although the public image was of manual laborers working on construction sites, Roosevelt and his aides, most notably Harry Hopkins, had included language in the authorizing legislation that provided some budgetary allotment for unemployed cultural workers. Forty thousand men and women, more or less skilled in their respective arts, comprised the initial cohort of what was known collectively as Federal One, divided administratively into four agencies, each with its own national director and staff.[37]

The Writers' Project was a godsend for Wright. Mary Wirth, who now worked for the WPA's Division of Employment, helped with the hiring process. A copy of *New Masses* containing a poem that Wright had written was sufficient for him to qualify as an editorial supervisor with a monthly wage of $125, more than double what he had been earning as a laborer on work-relief.[38] His first assignment was preparing copy for *Illinois: A Descriptive and Historical Guide*, one of a series of state guidebooks that consumed the time and talents of project employees across the land.

While Wright's responsibilities were largely editorial, he also undertook original research, including a brief history of the Chicago Urban League and block-by-block surveys of amusement and entertainment facilities in Bronzeville.[39] A more substantial piece, "Ethnological Aspects of Chicago's Black Belt," focused on the Great Migration and the problems of adjustment blacks faced in a northern city. Parkian concepts are evident in some passages: "From an extremely simple set of rural relations in the South, Negroes were transported to more complex relations based on more elaborate distribution of responsibilities. Thus it happens that contacts in the public schools, politics, business, industry, sport, colleges, clubs, and housing were points of contact [between the races] making for friction, comment, antagonism, resentment, prejudice, or fear."[40] The sociological influence is reflected in the restrained analytical language, the notion of urbanization as a transition from simple to complex modes of social organization, and references to the first two stages in Park's race relations cycle, contact and conflict. An appended bibliography includes works by Chicago-affiliated scholars E. Franklin Frazier, Charles Johnson, Robert Park, and political scientist Harold Gosnell.

Compiled two years *before* publication of *Uncle Tom's Children*, this bibliography demonstrates Wright's familiarity with Chicago sociology from the outset of his literary career. The reports themselves, however amateurish, reveal the young poet and short-story writer seeking to expand his range, experimenting with a new medium, expository prose, and a new voice, that of empirical investigator. They contain the seeds of his documentary book, *12 Million Black Voices* (1941). Moreover, even as he decisively turned his attention from poetry to fiction, his true métier, his initial exploration of social science left its trace.

Wright's first three books—*Lawd Today* (c. 1935), *Uncle Tom's Children* (1938), and *Native Son* (1940)—are structured on the principle of contrast. Either the foreground is the city of Chicago and the background the rural South (*Lawd Today* and *Native Son*) or vice-versa (*Uncle Tom's Children*). One or the other milieu is dominant, but in each instance a polarity develops between contrasting social systems, reflective of both Wright's own experience and Parkian paradigms.

Lawd Today, unpublished in Wright's lifetime, is a fictional projection of his experiences working in Chicago's central post office, a huge brick building on the corner of Clark Street and Jackson Boulevard. The giant mail-order firms of Sears, Roebuck and Montgomery Ward rendered it the largest postal facility in the world. Most of the novel's characters are black migrants, and polarity develops on two levels: geographically, between rural South and urban North, and temporally, between past and present. At one pole is Mississippi, birthplace of protagonist Jake Jackson, and at the other, Chicago, his treacherous city of refuge. Jake and his friends try constantly to repress painful memories of the South, but the past returns to haunt them, in headlines about lynchings or bitter-sweet recollections of rural childhood. The post office is their way station and gateway to the modern world, yet the pressures of working the night shift and the killing pace of the mail-sorting assembly line make them yearn sometimes for the natural rhythms of rural life. They are caught, like all exiles, between the upper and lower millstones, undergoing a process of triage; some adjust successfully to their new environment while others fall before its hardships and anxieties.

Wright's first published book, *Uncle Tom's Children* (1938), was a collection of novel-las, which drew in part on material he had gathered previously in life-history interviews of black communists in Chicago, all of them migrants from the deep South. Wright had probed the early experiences of his comrades to discover the sources of their militancy by eliciting details of the racist violence they had endured, or witnessed, in the region of their birth.[41]

The lead story in the collection, "Big Boy Leaves Home," reproduces the same polar-ity in the imaginative landscape as *Lawd Today!* The setting is rural Mississippi, but that terrain is crisscrossed by tracks of the Illinois Central line, linking Mississippi and Chicago, as hinterland to metropolis. Train whistles and talk of trains are omnipresent. Against this symbolic backdrop, the action unfolds. Big Boy, a black teenager, and three companions go skinny-dipping in a creek on a white man's farm. They are discovered by a white woman and her lover, who is carrying a rifle. In the ensuing scuffle, two of the boys are shot dead, but Big Boy wrests the weapon away and kills the man. The rest of the tale is an escape drama. Concealed in a brick kiln, Big Boy watches the horrific lynching of his friend Bobo, but with help from the black community, he is secreted away and carried to safety in a truck headed for Chicago.

Native Son (1940) may seem at first glance to violate this pattern of polarity. Chicago is represented in considerable, if not always loving, detail, while the South appears nowhere to be found. A careful reading reveals, however, that here too Mississippi casts its long shadow over Bronzeville. The crucial episode takes place well into Book One. Two young whites—heiress Mary Dalton and her communist lover, Jan Erlone—have instructed Bigger Thomas, the Dalton family chauffeur, to join them for a meal in Ernie's Kitchen Shack, a Black Belt eatery. Warmed by rum and fried chicken, Jan tries to get acquainted:

"Where were you born, Bigger?"
"In the South."
"Whereabouts?
"Mississippi."
". . . . Did you go to school in the North or South?"
"Mostly in the South. I went two years up here."
"How long have you been in Chicago?"
"Oh, about five years."

Because the reader is told elsewhere that Bigger is twenty years old, it follows that he migrated from Mississippi at fifteen. The conversation continues:

"Where's your father?"

"Dead."

"How long ago was that?"

"He got killed in a riot when I was a kid—in the South."

". . . And what was done about it?"

"Nothing, far as I know."[42]

Bigger's southern antecedents form a crucial plot element, a key to understanding his psychic life and his behavior at key moments in the novel. *Native Son* will be further discussed in a later chapter, but, for the moment, suffice it to note that Mississippi and Chicago formed the antipodes of Wright's imaginary landscape in these early works and that the conceptual apparatus of Parkian sociology helped him navigate the terrain.

Horace Cayton and "The *Known* City"

While Wright struggled to build a career as a fiction writer, Cayton pursued his work in sociology. Early on, senior faculty took note of his obvious talents and ease of access to black communities. Harold Gosnell engaged him as research assistant for a book on black politicians in Chicago. Sometime later Cayton was assisting Louis Wirth in research on teenage suicide when another of Park's protégés suggested a more enticing possibility. From his post at Fisk, Charles Johnson was acquiring considerable influence in certain quarters of the New Deal and offered to arrange a choice appointment for the promising young sociologist. Harold Ickes, a former mainstay of Chicago Progressive circles, was serving as Roosevelt's interior secretary and looking for a special assistant to study the effects of recent labor legislation on African American workers.[43]

Cayton leapt at the opportunity and, for five months in 1934, traveled back and forth across the Northeast and Midwest, an eyewitness to the beginning of the greatest labor-organizing drive in American history. Newly formed, industrywide unions were breaking with their predecessors' Jim Crow practices and organizing black and white workers together. Eventually, the unions came together under the banner of the Congress of Industrial Organizations (CIO).[44] Aided by two consecutive Rosenwald fellowships, Cayton's research resulted in publication of his first book, *Black Workers and the New Unions* (1939), coauthored with Columbia University economics professor George Mitchell.[45]

The grueling schedule of constant travel and work impaired Cayton's health and emotional stability. In September Johnson sent a solicitous letter: "I learned just before leaving Chicago that you were showing some of the effects of this sustained drive in your physical condition," he wrote. "I feel that I should . . . insist that you take at least a couple of weeks in a sanitarium and follow this with . . . less arduous labor, perhaps in the Department at Fisk."[46] For most of the following year, Cayton was in recovery, briefly working once again as Wirth's research assistant and then traveling in Europe. Upon his return to Chicago, he accepted a one-year teaching appointment at Fisk. He found the atmosphere congenial. Writing to Wirth shortly after his arrival in October 1935, he reported: "Dr. Park has the office next to mine and seems hard at work most of the time."[47]

Cayton was delighted to have such ready access to his mentor, who had accepted Johnson's invitation to move to Fisk as scholar-in-residence after retiring from the University of Chicago. "Dr. Park and I have spent a lot of time talking," Cayton told Wirth. "I have been working on a study of class stratification in the Negro group which I think will shed some light on many problems and especially that of the Negro college. Dr. Park seems to be very interested in this project."[48]

While Cayton resumed his professional life under Johnson's watchful eye, Park and Johnson moved well beyond the teacher/student relationship to become close friends and colleagues. With their reputations joined at the same institution, Fisk's prestige, further enhanced, attracted even more scholars of the first rank. Park remained there, actively engaged in teaching and research, until his death in 1944.[49]

Since his years in New York, Johnson had continued to pursue the strategy of a two-pronged attack on the racial status quo that was at once scientific and artistic. Cayton's apprentice year at Fisk ultimately helped advance both his own career and Johnson's strategy. His letter to Wirth tells part of the story: "I am spending all of my spare time on [the study of class stratification] and hope to use it for my thesis," he wrote. "I hope to trace the development of a group from a caste to what Dr. Park calls a Minority Group i.e. a group with functional economic upper classes." In Park's view, during slavery and its immediate aftermath, blacks had constituted a social caste with no significant internal differentiation, but gradual development of professional and business classes had altered their status to that of minority group, a change that opened, at least "in a long historical perspective," the possibility of "a common culture and a common social order" with whites.[50] Cayton's discussions with Park (and presumably with Johnson) became the basis not for research on "the Negro college," but for *Black Metropolis*, his magisterial study of Bronzeville, coauthored with St. Clair Drake.[51]

In the fall of 1936, Cayton moved back to Chicago as a research assistant for social anthropologist W. Lloyd Warner, who had recently secured WPA funding to study juvenile delinquency on the South Side. Cayton was appointed project superintendent, and he and Warner developed an ambitious research agenda exploring all aspects of life in Bronzeville. He proved an able administrator, cobbling together financing from federal, state, and local agencies and hiring more than one hundred staff members, 90 percent of them black. Cayton's field workers combed written records and spread across the city, conducting some eight thousand interviews over a three-year span. The voluminous data served as the basis for numerous articles, theses, dissertations, and books and augmented the "mountains of facts piled up by the Department of Sociology" to make Chicago "the *known* city" (italics original). "Perhaps more is known about it," Wright observed, "how it is run, how it kills, how it loves, steals, helps, gives, cheats, and crushes than any other city in the world."[52]

Cayton had told Wirth of his intention "to describe the social world of the Negro upper classes and their struggle to create this world apart from both the black masses and the unaccepting white community."[53] This was the world he inhabited on the South Side, and the very conditions documented by his research—segregated housing, a racial "job

ceiling," and an all-black parallel universe of social clubs, service organizations, frater-
nities, sororities, and church congregations—suggested that he might remain permanently
behind the walls of American apartheid. In *Black Metropolis*, he and Drake wrote that "the
Cayton/Warner Research . . . revealed what happens in a ghetto when the successful and
ambitious can't get out and when the city does not provide the poor and vicious with
enough living space, or enough incentive and opportunity to modify their style of life."[54]

With a high-profile WPA position, a Parkian flair for publicity, and a grievance of his
own, Cayton became a prominent Chicago "race man," defined in *Black Metropolis* as
someone "who has a reputation as an uncompromising fighter against attempts to subor-
dinate Negroes."[55] He personally ensured that information on black unemployment and
job discrimination, health and educational problems, and especially the South Side's
housing crisis was widely disseminated through the press and at public forums. He became
a well-known community spokesman, much in demand as guest speaker and member of
numerous committees. "It is the responsibility of the Negro community," he wrote in the
Defender, "to formulate for itself a complete and comprehensive housing program."[56]
Cayton added a distinctly activist bent to the Parkian faith in gradual improvements of
race relations through naturally unfolding social processes. In this, he was a spiritual
descendant of another crusading African American social scientist, W.E.B. Du Bois, and
direct heir to his own father's history as outspoken advocate of racial equality.

Meeting of the Minds

Cayton's talent for bringing attention to issues was enhanced by the dashing figure he cut
with wide-brimmed hat, ascot, cane, and long cigarette holder. Langston Hughes described
him as a "Genuine character, ace sociologist, A-1 administrator, amateur psychiatrist, bon
vivant, good party giver, art lover, and a man with a beard."[57] Cayton and second wife Irma
Jackson, whom he met at Fisk, had many friends on the South Side and in Hyde Park: "the
younger intellectuals . . . a mixed lot of Negroes and whites, many with left-wing lean-
ings."[58] They lived in the Michigan Boulevard Garden Apartments, a Rosenwald-financed
residential complex for professionals and middle-income residents of the South Side.

The Cayton/Warner project was initially housed in the basement of Good Shepherd
Congregational Church, a middle-class black church with a long record of providing assistance to poorer members of the community. With funding from the WPA and Chicago
Board of Education, its Yale-educated pastor, Harold Kingsley, created a full-service community center in 1938. In December of the following year, Cayton became director and
undertook the institution's transformation in line with his developing vision of racial
advancement through broad interaction among social science, social work, and community organization. A key step was the purchase in October 1940 of the former Chicago
Orphan Asylum at Fifty-first Street and South Parkway. The six spacious buildings of
Good Shepherd Community Center, renamed Parkway Community House in 1942, encompassed an entire city block. This campus soon contained a nursery school, health
clinic, relief office, selective service office, reading room, summer camp, theater, gym-

nasium, performance space, dormitory, staff apartments, meeting rooms, and classrooms. The *Defender* described Parkway as "the warp and woof of the community."[59]

While Cayton was settling into his new position as settlement house director, Wright was experiencing sudden fame. *Native Son* was chosen as a Book-of-the-Month Club selection for March 1940, an unprecedented coup for a black writer. Even before the novel's official release, a check for advanced sales had paid for a new wardrobe and a trip to Chicago, where Wright bought his family a small house.[60]

Wright was now a literary celebrity and New York resident. His earliest trip to the city had occurred in April 1935, when he hitchhiked from Chicago to attend the first American Writers Congress. There the impoverished youth bravely defended the John Reed Clubs despite the Communist Party's plan to dissolve them. He described the colleagueship and opportunities the clubs provided aspiring writers like himself, politically fervent yet slight in artistic achievement. But a loose network of bohemian radicals would not help the Party as it followed the Communist International's turn from the confrontational campaigns and ultrarevolutionary rhetoric of the so-called Third Period toward the more muted tones of the People's Front against Fascism. American Party leaders now sought broader appeal and greater respectability in their efforts to defend the Soviet Union against the growing threat from Nazi Germany.[61]

The 1935 Writers Congress voted overwhelmingly to abolish the John Reed Clubs and in their place launched the League of American Writers, whose more selective ranks included some of the most well known literary figures in the country.[62] Abolition of the clubs remained a sore point for Wright but did not prevent him from joining the new organization. When he visited Chicago in 1940, he was one of the league's honorary national leaders, along with Ernest Hemingway, John Steinbeck, Upton Sinclair, Van Wyck Brooks, Malcolm Cowley, and Langston Hughes.[63]

As *Native Son* shot up the best-seller lists, *Life* magazine hired its author to consult on a photo-essay about the South Side, necessitating another brief trip in late February. Wright boarded "a huge, sleek, steel plane and flew above the clouds" to Chicago.[64] Horace Cayton had agreed to meet him at the airport and offered guest accommodations at Parkway. Meeting again after some six years, the two men discovered they had much in common, despite very different social backgrounds. The writer was fascinated by sociology, impressed by Cayton's research on the South Side, and in need of his professional guidance.[65]

The sociologist in turn was a friend of Chicago writers and had a thick file full of his own unpublished stories, most based on the nomadic wanderings of his youth.[66] Horace shared the fiction-writing habit with his mother, the remarkable Susie Revels Cayton. A letter from Mother Cayton, written about a year after his arrival in Chicago, suggests a further point of affinity between the sociologist and the writer. After critiquing one of Horace's stories and promising to send a draft of her own, Susie adds: "I have helped to sponsor a 'Scottsboro group' of the ILD. We have about 17 members and meet each Monday night. . . . Revels [Horace's brother] is in Cleveland, Ohio, as a delegate to some convention there. He went by bus and doubtless had a hard ride but 'the party' means so much

I fancy it made the seats seem softer and the miles seem shorter."[67] The Depression was a great leveler, and as it completed destruction of the family's fortunes in Seattle (the letter reports their home is in foreclosure), Horace Cayton's mother and younger brother joined the Communist Party.

Horace himself always kept the Party at arm's length and was especially critical of its wartime policy of subordinating racial issues to "national unity." He strongly advocated the so-called "Double-V" strategy—victory over fascism abroad and victory over Jim Crow at home—and lambasted segregation in the armed forces and defense industries even as communist leaders sought to maintain social peace and downplay organized struggles against discrimination. Cayton's criticisms of the Party nevertheless expressed apprecia-tion of its earlier achievements, which suggested something in the nature of a family quar-rel on the Left tinged with nostalgia for Third Period militancy.[68]

Cayton and Wright cemented their friendship, moreover, at a time when the writer was still a nominal Party member but undergoing a profound crisis of faith preceding a highly public break in 1944. The complementary values and intellectual strengths they discovered in one another eventually quickened their hopes of creating a radical black "school of thought" independent of the Communist Party. They would explore several joint publishing projects that Cayton suggested could "blend a Marxian economic analy-sis with a psychological content from the psychoanalysts, stated in a literary form."[69]

Following publication of *Native Son*, Wright basked in the warmth of successful authorship and of the sun that shone reliably on Cuernavaca, where he and first wife Dhimah Meidman spent a honeymoon that lasted nearly as long as the marriage itself. Meanwhile, letters from important figures in the theater, cinema, and publishing industry arrived almost daily at their Mexican villa. In May Orson Welles and John Houseman, famous for their work with the WPA Theater Project and the Mercury Theatre, offered to produce a stage version of the novel, and Wright suggested that Pulitzer-winning play-wright Paul Green collaborate on the script. July found him back in Chicago, where he stayed with Cayton for two weeks, spoke at Good Shepherd Church, and obliged former Writers' Project colleagues Jack Conroy and Nelson Algren with a star turn at a fund-raising party for their *New Anvil* magazine.

Life magazine never published the planned photo-essay inspired by *Native Son*, but the idea of a photo-documentary book captured Wright's imagination. He had recently learned to use a camera from his friend Frank Marshall Davis, a skillful portrait photogra-pher as well as a journalist and poet.[70] Wright was thus eager to collaborate when con-tacted by Edwin Rosskam, an editor in the photographic section of the Farm Security Administration (FSA), who had already been involved in producing five such books. Rosskam, a Jewish émigré from Germany who was sensitive to issues of racial oppression, had read both *Uncle Tom's Children* and *Native Son*. He proposed to his boss, Roy Stryker, that the agency work with Wright on a photo-text collaboration. Stryker knew it would be controversial, but he recognized an opportunity to get FSA photographs of black life before the public. Rosskam approached Viking Press, which offered a substantial advance, and Wright signed on to the project that would lead to publication of his third book, *12*

Million Black Voices. In January 1941, he traveled to Washington, D.C., where he and Rosskam examined thousands of photographs in the agency's files.[71]

In April Wright was back in Chicago again, this time with his new bride, Ellen Poplar, who enjoyed the warm hospitality of Horace and Irma Cayton. Rosskam and FSA photographer Russell Lee were on hand to capture images of the South Side. The remarkable photographs of storefront churches and kitchenette families that appear in *12 Million Black Voices* owe much to Cayton's contacts at every level in the community. Opening his voluminous research files to Wright, Cayton provided a refresher course in sociology. "I've come to write a picture book," he recalled Wright saying. "I want to get into your files. I want your sociological concepts." Cayton explained "the idea . . . of culture versus civilization, of a sacred versus a secular society. . . . the differences between societies in which folkways determine the way of life and those which are governed by contracts rather than promises."[72] Once again, Wright read extensively in sociology. He listed six major sources in the book's preface, five of them published since his reading under Wirth's tutelage, and three by sociologists of the Chicago School: *Black Workers and the New Unions* (1939) by Cayton and Mitchell, *The Negro Family in the United States* (1939) by Frazier, and Wirth's seminal essay "Urbanism as a Way of Life" (1938).

As if in symbolic blessing of the project, Cayton arranged a meeting with Robert Park, who was visiting from Fisk. Park was sitting "in a very large and very comfortable easy chair," Cayton recalled. "When Wright walked into the room Park began a painful struggle to get out of his chair. Wright impulsively asked him not to rise." The old man, insistent on standing, extended his hand to Wright and said, "I want to shake hands with a great writer."[73] Nine months later, Cayton wrote to Wright, "I have never met anyone with whom I could talk as freely. . . . I feel even more at home with you intellectually than I do with all the sociologists with the exception of say, old Dr. Park."[74]

In April 1943, Cayton and Wright boarded a sleeping car on the Zephyr line from Chicago to Nashville. Charles Johnson had invited them to lecture at Fisk. Wright was anxious about speaking before a racially mixed audience in the South and decided, after much thought, to discuss his experiences growing up in the Delta. It was "a clumsy, conversational kind of speech," he recalled. "The audience was terribly still," except for occasional "hysterical, half-repressed . . . laughter." Wright suddenly realized that he "was saying things that Negroes were not supposed to say publicly."[75] Reactions from the faculty were mixed, but students were fascinated and hurled question after question. Two weeks later, Wright received a letter from his host: "Your visit was about as stimulating and delightful as any event in my academic memory here," Johnson wrote. "You won the blasé students and their slightly bored dons completely, needling them to an amazing animation."[76]

Within four years of that trip to Nashville, the three principal figures had scaled new heights. The reactions to Wright's speech convinced him that his next book should be about his own life, and in 1945, he published his brilliant, best-selling memoir *Black Boy*. In the same year, Cayton and Drake published *Black Metropolis*. In 1947 Johnson became the first African American president of Fisk. What had once been a strategic Chicago/ Tuskegee axis had become, by the early 1940s, a Chicago/Nashville/Washington axis, linking—among other institutions—Fisk, the Rosenwald Fund, the Farm Security Admin-istration, Parkway House, the Associated Negro Press, the Illinois Writers' Project, and Chicago's Department of Sociology, and involving such personages as Charles Johnson, Edwin Embree, Will Alexander, Horace Cayton, Claude Barnett, Arna Bontemps, Louis Wirth, and Richard Wright.

The friendship and collaboration of Cayton and Wright affected not only their careers but also the cultural life of Bronzeville. Multifaceted programming at Parkway included classes in writing, music, and dramatics. For a time, one of its meeting rooms housed the Chicago Poets' Class, a writers' workshop where Gwendolyn Brooks and others struggled to master the craft. Visiting luminaries such as Wright, Langston Hughes, Marian Ander-son, and Paul Robeson presented lectures and performances at Parkway, and Hughes founded an important community theater group, the Skyloft Players.[77] Part of Cayton's salary supported South Side visual artists in the most concrete way; he built a personal col-lection of their paintings and sculptures.[78]

Although Wright had moved to New York in 1937, he remained closely connected with Black Chicago's cultural scene. He wrote an essay intended for Cayton's use as a fund-raising vehicle, and he helped arrange a benefit performance of the stage version of Native Son. He also served as patron of an art exhibition to help Bronzeville artists secure representation by New York galleries, assisted the editors of Negro Story to launch their journal, and helped Gwendolyn Brooks secure her first contract.[79] Cayton recalled that, until Wright moved to Paris in 1947, they "were in constant contact, either by letter or his visiting me in Chicago or my going to New York."[80]

The Documentary Spirit

On January 10, 1939, Good Shepherd Church hosted "the first public exhibit" of the Cayton/Warner research. No fewer than five hundred people turned out to view a display of "charts, maps, graphs, photographs, and over 5,000 pages of completed manuscripts" as well as "samples of interview material and statistical processes used for analysis of data."[81] The success of this event, with South Side residents flocking to view exhibits more typi-cal of an academic or government conference, suggests a community curious to learn the precise facts of its physical and social topography. Such curiosity extended to the social processes behind transformation of Chicago's Black Belt—a racially quarantined mass of southern migrants—into Bronzeville—a Black Metropolis with its own institutions, leader-ship class, and emerging cultural and artistic elite. This moment of community self-discovery was also related to a documentary movement that some scholars describe as the dominant form of cultural work in the United States in the 1930s and early 1940s.[82]

The "documents" most commonly associated with this movement belonged to the same photographic files that Rosskam and Wright explored—images of migrant farm workers captured by Dorothea Lange, Walker Evans, Arthur Rothstein, Ben Shahn, and other employees of the FSA's photographic section. Its director, Roy Stryker, a former Columbia University economics instructor, joined the agency when it was established in

1935 as the Resettlement Administration and stayed when it was reorganized two years later as the Farm Security Administration under the leadership of Will Alexander. While the FSA provided assistance to hundreds of thousands of displaced farmers, Stryker's unit was charged with documenting the agency's programs and the devastating agricultural crisis that they addressed. He gathered a team of talented, socially conscious photographers, who followed the trails of migrants, both white and black, out of the southwestern Dust Bowl and the boll weevil-blighted Delta. By 1940 Stryker's unit was distributing about 1,400 images a month to periodicals as diverse as *Life*, *Fortune*, and *Junior Scholastic* and for use in books and public exhibitions.[83]

Reviewing their accomplishments in 1938, Edward Steichen, the most famous photographer of the day, observed that in the process of creating "a picture record of rural America," Stryker's team "also found time to produce a series of the most remarkable human documents that were ever rendered in pictures." These photographs "told stories . . . with such simple and blunt directness that they made many a citizen wince" and left "a feeling of a living experience you won't forget."[84] Steichen's comments focus attention on what William Stott identifies as the two sides of "documentary": a combination of factuality—real people driven from their homes, gaunt with hunger, anxiety etched in their faces—and strategic selection and presentation of facts for maximum audience impact. FSA photographers were recording an unfolding human catastrophe, image by image, to galvanize public support for government intervention to ameliorate such conditions.

"The age of documentation," Paula Rabinowitz writes, "corresponds to the age of mechanical reproduction."[85] The achievements of FSA photographers depended in part on improvements in the means of mechanical reproduction. Smaller, lighter cameras and new types of film allowed faster capture of images, less reliance on controlled lighting, and consequently more spontaneous composition. These advances were equally important in establishment of the mass-circulation magazines that defined the genre of photojournalism. *Life*'s first issue appeared in November 1936, and *Look* premiered three months later. Photographic work for the new magazines and for New Deal agencies often overlapped and provided images of that "one-third of a nation, ill-housed, ill-clad, ill-nourished" described by Franklin Roosevelt in his second inaugural address.

Roosevelt's commitment "to make every American citizen the subject of his country's interest and concern" also helped create a wide audience for a series of photo-documentary books that combined text by some of the nation's best writers with pictures by some of its best photographers: Erskine Caldwell and Margaret Bourke-White, *You Have Seen Their Faces* (1937); Archibald MacLeish, *Land of the Free* (1938); Paul Taylor and Dorothea Lange, *An American Exodus* (1939); and James Agee and Walker Evans, *Let Us Now Praise Famous Men* (1941). These collaborations provided a model for Wright's *12 Million Black Voices*.

The documentary movement, although most closely associated with photography, was certainly not confined to that genre. A broadly similar spirit could be discerned in FSA photographs, *Life* and *Look* photo-essays, social novels, "on-the-road" memoirs, Federal Art Project murals, state guides produced by the Federal Writers' Project, the "living newspapers" of the Federal Theater Project, sociologists' community studies, journalistic exposés, oral histories, government-sponsored documentary films, movie-theater news-reels, live radio news reports, and other diverse cultural forms. The documentary spirit encompassed genres high and low and the work of individual artists as well as creative activities within government agencies, the academy, and popular media. The common denominator was a desire to communicate the reality of America, to record and make comprehensible the lives of all its citizens, to portray the specific tone and texture of places, people, and events. What these diverse enterprises shared, according to proletarian novelist Jack Conroy, was a Whitmanesque commitment to "vivifying the contemporary fact" and serving as "witness to the times."[86]

The empirical methods of the Chicago School helped shape the documentary spirit in a manner suggested by Lloyd Warner's "Methodological Note" to *Black Metropolis*. Praising the work for combining "the research approaches of sociology and social anthropology," he observed that studying a community "as a set of interconnected human beings living in a vast web of vital relations . . . necessitates living with the people being studied, interviewing them, and observing what they do."[87] Following Park's injunction to study "only what you can see, hear, and know" directly, Chicago social scientists favored participant-observation, life-history interviews, case study, and collection of what William Thomas called "personal life-records."[88] The net effect of these qualitative methods was to yield studies intended, in the words of Ernest Burgess, "to admit the reader into the inner experience of other men."[89] Sociological case studies of Chicago's diverse ethnic communities and social subgroups began appearing even before the Depression created a more deeply felt need to understand how and why that "one-third of a nation" lived. These studies established a paradigm of detailed social investigation that influenced documentary work in other fields and genres.[90]

In *Black Metropolis*, for example, statistical and survey generalizations are consistently elaborated and supported by vivid observational descriptions and quotations from hundreds of interviews that serve to "admit the reader into the inner experience" of Bronzeville residents. At times, the writing perches on a thin line where social scientist, journalist, and novelist meet. In one footnote, Cayton and Drake explain: "This account of a doctor's Christmas experience is based on an actual incident witnessed by one of the authors, when he was a participant-observer in a group of lower-class households for six months, and on interviews with the physician involved and his wife. The principal characters' inner thoughts are obviously fictionalized. But the other quoted material . . . has been selected from interview-documents gathered by trained interviewers and has not been subjected to imaginative recasting."[91] Thus did "sincere art and honest science" meet in *Black Metropolis* and more generally in documentary work.

12 Million Black Voices

12 Million Black Voices is a central text of the Black Chicago Renaissance, central in respect to the documentary spirit of the times, to the integration of Chicago sociology and Marxism, and to Wright's grand theme of the migration. The book's subtitle, *A Folk His-*

tory of the Negro, underscores its emphasis on "that which is abiding . . . in Negro experience" and on the lives of "the broad masses."[92] So too does the language. Wright spoke his first draft into a dictaphone in three days, and, despite "months of rewriting," the text retained a quality described by John Reilly as "simulated oral utterance," based on "the spontaneous arts that shape the orations of the preacher."[93]

The book's four sections represent slavery times, the post-Reconstruction rural South, the urban transplantation, and hopeful portents of a future society cleansed of racism. The unavoidable absence of contemporary photographs in Parts One and Four (a pre-camera past and an imagined future) deprive them of the visceral power of the two central sections, which render, in stunning photographs and poetically compressed prose, the contrast between an agrarian/traditional and an industrial/modernizing phase of social development.

Part Two, "Inheritors of Slavery," portrays the plantation system that survived the Civil War and persisted, with declining vigor, into the 1930s. Its salient feature was "a new kind of bondage," whereby the black sharecropper borrowed plow and mule, seed, fertilizer, and food rations from a white landlord and at harvest time found himself, despite his best efforts, deeper in debt than the year before. Widespread illiteracy, disfranchisement, and frequently overt terror perpetuated the system.

12. Cotton buyer and Negro farmer discussing price, Mississippi.
Photo: Marion Post. Library of Congress, Prints & Photographs Division,
FSA-OWI Collection. LC-DIG-fsa-8c10867.

13. Thirteen-year-old sharecropper, Georgia.
Photo: Dorothea Lange. Library of Congress, Prints & Photographs Division,
FSA-OWI Collection. LC-DIG-fsa-8b32269.

But white oppression also fostered black community, built around "a secret life and language." Strong ties of kinship developed. "A child is a glad thing in the bleak stretches of the cotton country, and our gold is in the hearts of the people we love," Wright's narrator intones in the first-person plural used throughout.[94] The church emerged as the central community institution, a mighty fortress in times of trouble, and the book's exact middle contains seven images of worship and a reconstructed passage from a sermon. The following pages portray the Saturday-night dancehall and the sustaining joys of song and laughter. Wright was no romantic partisan of village life, and his autobiographical writing generally presents a bleak picture of rural black experience. Here, however, he paused to celebrate the strength of the folk community and the verdant beauty of southern soil.

Part Three, "Death on the City Pavements," focuses on the encounter of rural southerners with an urban, industrial milieu and their traumatic sensation of suddenly feeling trapped "inside of a machine."[95] Fifteen short, strongly cadenced paragraphs, in effect a prose poem, detail the horrors of cramped, vermin-ridden kitchenette flats. Factories initially confine migrants to "nigger work" or employ them as strike-breakers during labor conflicts. The Promised Land turns out to be a place of violence: the violence of criminals, brutal police, white gangs, and full-scale riots. As in Part Two, this scathing indictment of the social

14. Negro dwelling, Chicago.
Photo: Russell Lee. Library of Congress, Prints & Photographs Division,
FSA-OWI Collection. LC-USF34–038871-D.

system is followed by Wright's tribute to sources of black survival, especially the churches and "blues, jazz, swing, and boogie-woogie . . . our 'spirituals' of the city pavements."[96]

The preacherly oratory of *12 Million Black Voices* is leavened with passages of sociological observation. While Cayton highlighted the salient difference in societies "governed by contracts rather than promises," Wright's narrator says: "For three hundred years we have been forced to accept the word of men instead of written contracts."[97] Wirth identified "the growth of cities and the urbanization of the world [as] one of the most impressive facts of modern times."[98] Wright's narrator comments: "We have heard tell that all over the world men are leaving the land for the streets of the city, so we are leaving too."[99] Wirth described the city as a place where "the bonds of kinship, of neighborliness, and the sentiments arising out of living together for generations under a common folk tradition are likely to be absent or, at best, relatively weak."[100] Wright's narrator declares: "Coming north for a Negro sharecropper involves . . . living on a new and terrifying plane of consciousness. . . . strangers whose lives and thoughts are unknown to us, pressing always close about us."[101] Park maintained: "No other people, in the United States at least, have compressed into a career so brief so many transfigurations of their racial life."[102] Wright's narrator observes: "Three hundred years in the history of our lives are equivalent to two thousand years in the history of the lives of whites! The many historical phases which whites have traversed voluntarily and gradually during the course of Western civilization we black folk have traversed through swift compulsion."[103]

Wright absorbed Chicago sociology the way he absorbed other schools of thought and bodies of literature—passionately and eclectically. His first exposure to sociology through Louis Wirth closely followed his exposure to Marxism through the John Reed Club and the Washington Park Forum. Of the Marxist literature he read, most influential was Joseph Stalin's pamphlet "Marxism and the National Question," which defined a nation as "a historically evolved, stable community of language, territory, economic life, and psychological make-up manifested in a community of culture."[104] At the time Wright joined the Communist Party, it defined blacks as "an oppressed national minority" and advocated that "in the so-called Black Belt of the South, where the Negroes are in the majority, they will have the fullest right to govern themselves."[105] Although Party policy on black self-determination had changed by 1941, Wright continued to describe "a separate nation, stunted, stripped, and held captive within this nation."[106] In *12 Million Black Voices*, he carefully delineated the national characteristics of the southern "Black Belt" and described its historical evolution, distinctive language and psychology, territorial borders, separate economic system, and common folk culture.

Wright understood both Marxism and sociology as looking toward a cosmopolitan future marked by racial equality, a vision embodied in the book's final section, "Men in the Making." Three images encapsulate its spirit: a young black worker in close-up, looking with pride and confidence into the camera, a line of black women picketing the White House to demand an end to lynching, and a black man standing on the back steps of his modest house, looking up as sunlight bathes his face. References to struggles to build integrated industrial unions and free the Scottsboro defendants precede the concluding exhortation:

15. Negro family living in crowded quarters, Chicago.
Photo: Russell Lee. Library of Congress, Prints & Photographs Division,
FSA-OWI Collection. LC-USF34–038621-D.

16. Steelworker, Pittsburgh.
Photo: Arthur Rothstein. Library
of Congress, Prints & Photographs
Division, FSA-OWI Collection.
LC-USF34–026502.

"The ties that bind [blacks and whites] are deeper than those that separate us. . . . Look at us and know us and you will know yourselves, for *we* are *you*, looking back at you from the dark mirror of our lives" (italics original).[107]

The "honest science" of the Chicago School helped Wright "know what [his] story was." He found his plot outlined by thousands of other southern blacks escaping the plantation for the possibilities of the northern city. Just months before his death in 1960, he recalled his move to Chicago as the most traumatic period of his life.[108] In the books he wrote between 1935 and 1945, he created the fullest and deepest rendering of the migration experience of any writer of his generation. Arna Bontemps's contention that the Mississippian was "the most typical as well as the most famous example of the depression-bred WPA writer" rests on Wright's dramatic life experience as a migrant, his embrace of the concepts of Marxism and Chicago sociology to comprehend that experience, his work with the Federal Writers' Project, and his pioneering achievements as a literary artist.

CHAPTER 7

The Documentary Eye

In 1896, English journalist George Steevens memorably captured Chicago's paradoxes: "Queen and guttersnipe of cities. . . . The most beautiful and the most squalid, girdled with a twofold zone of parks and slums; where the keen air from the lake and prairie is ever in the nostrils, and the stench of foul smoke is never out of the throat; . . . widely and generously planned with streets of twenty miles, where it is not safe to walk at night; . . . the most American of American cities, and yet the most mongrel . . . the first and only veritable Babel of the age."[1] Traditionally the city's artists came from the zone of wide streets, verdant parks, and fresh lake air, and they gave back to the privileged classes elegantly wrought images of refinement, grace, and symmetry. Yet Chicago was ever an unruly city, throwing up a countertradition for every tradition. If an itinerant laborer from downstate Illinois could become a great American bard, singing of "the City of the Big Shoulders," could not children of the slums, foul smoke, unsafe streets, and languages of Babel become great artists? Could not the city itself, in all its brutality and teeming human diversity, yield subjects to inspire their creative imaginations?

A foreshadowing of such a cultural shift occurred in 1908, when the Art Institute, generally known for aesthetic conservatism, hosted a touring exhibition of "The Eight," which "excited much attention" with its vigorous portrayals of city streets and rooftops and such plebian entertainments as the barroom, pool hall, vaudeville theater, skating rink, boxing arena, and dance hall.[2] Prominent art teacher Robert Henri led the group, which included John Sloan, George Luks, Everett Shinn, and William Glackens. These artists embraced the city, its surging crowds and soaring skyscrapers, its speed, noise, and constant change, for these were signposts of the Modern. Along with some of Henri's students, such as George Bellows and Edward Hopper, the Eight devolved into a loosely affiliated and stylistically diverse group, which became known, rather derisively, as the "Ashcan School."[3] Their rebellious spirit and urban vision held great appeal for Chicago's young artists, and Bellows became especially influential at the School of the Art Institute (SAIC). His lectures encouraged young African American painter Archibald Motley to turn to the everyday scenes and people of the South Side for his primary subject matter.[4]

New Perspectives for the Black Artist

In the summer of 1930, Archibald Motley returned to Chicago after spending a year in France. Supported by a Guggenheim fellowship, he had rented a studio in Montmartre, studied works of the Old Masters at the Louvre, and produced a dozen or so splendid oils.

The artist found his homeland plunging into depression, and Chicago was especially hard hit. Fewer than a quarter of the unemployed received relief, homeless women slept in Grant and Lincoln Parks, men fought over barrels of garbage behind restaurants, and teachers fed malnourished students, even while the city withheld their paychecks.[5] The market for fine art was decimated, and Motley turned to manual labor to survive.

The presidential election of 1932 changed the political climate dramatically. In the spring of 1933, the administration of Franklin Roosevelt launched the Public Works of Art Project, the first of several programs to benefit desperate artists. Motley was hired and, for about nine years, supported himself largely through wages or commissions from government agencies. He was one of the first African American artists hired by the Illinois unit of the Federal Art Project, organized late in 1935 to provide economic relief for artists and maintain their highly specialized skills. Amy Mooney estimates that he executed "some twenty easel paintings and four murals" for various New Deal projects. The Treasury Department's Section of Painting and Sculpture, overseeing mural projects around the country, tended to be quite prescriptive in its guidelines, whereas the Art Project allowed its employees significant freedom within the framework of a general preference for representations of "the American Scene." These differences likely account for the contrast between the wooden didacticism of Motley's historical murals such as *Progressive America* (1935) and the vibrancy of his South Side scenes.[6]

People-in-crowds became the artist's trademark.[7] A composite of his street scenes might look like this: the crowds are dense, yet somewhat individuated, presenting a cross-section of familiar Bronzeville types. Jitneys, streetcars, automobiles, and traffic lights establish the bustling urban environment in which southern blacks now find themselves. At street level are the business enterprises: drugstore, beauty parlor, chicken shack, barbershop, restaurant, and hotel. Upstairs are lonely, doubly ostracized women of the demimonde, who await their evening customers. Colors are heightened, and the lighting has the artificial quality of a stage set. Broadly considered, such scenes of urban life suggest the workings of a documentary impulse, but filtered through an aesthetic informed by movies, comic strips, and popular music.[8]

The South Side cabarets, as Motley portrays them, are no less crowded than the busy streets. Consider *Nightlife* (1943, color plate 3). Its dynamic composition, strong colors, and echoed shapes create a sense of movement, from the twisting male figure on the bottom left upward diagonally past the dancing couple, the rising plumes of smoke and lurching waiter to the frenetic dancers at top right. Precariously balanced trays, raised hands, and an upturned glass give new meaning to the word "Tipsy." Figures appear to float against a theatrical pale-rose backdrop, punctuated by light bulbs above and beside the bar. Alluding to Edward Hopper's *Nighthawks*, which entered the Art Institute collection in 1942, *Nightlife* shows Motley's ongoing fascination with artificial light. Like his other genre paintings, it stresses mood and scene rather than individual figures, and features are suggested rather than defined. The lively rhythm and upward motion are periodically interrupted. The bald, heavy-set bartender (a figure reappearing in many of Motley's scenes) slouches into his task of skimming foam from a beer mug. Further along, a man slumps onto the bar. Another sits alone at a table, his head resting heavily on his palm. Besides capturing the down cycle of a night on the town, such figures effectively create visual syncopation that evokes the rhythms of jazz. In his nightclub and street scenes, Motley focused on black subjects within an urban milieu; in the process he overturned Victorian taboos and opened fresh perspectives for African American art.

Indicative of the artist's reputation was his participation in the selection juries for the 1940 *Exhibition of the Art of the American Negro*, whose three hundred works represented, according to Alain Locke, "the most comprehensive and representative collection of the Negro's art . . . ever . . . presented to public view."[9] The exhibition was part of the American Negro Exposition, held in Chicago to mark the seventy-fifth anniversary of the abolition of slavery. Other jurors included Art Institute director Daniel Catton Rich, Federal Art Project head Holger Cahill, and noted black sculptor Richmond Barthé. Although Motley had to travel to New York to advance his own career in 1928, twelve years later he served as one of the judges evaluating the work of 115 black artists from around the country, and Bronzeville had established sufficient claim as center of African American political, economic, and cultural life that it was the site for what was, in effect, the first black World's Fair.[10]

"Making Bricks Without Straw"

Describing the early years of Tuskegee Institute and construction of the school's buildings by the students themselves, Booker T. Washington wrote, "I had always sympathized with the 'Children of Israel,' in their task of 'making bricks without straw,' but ours was the task of making bricks with no money and no experience."[11] Washington's epic account of survival through mother wit and gritty determination might well serve as a paradigm to frame a narrative of Bronzeville artists working in the 1930s and 1940s. These children of the Great Migration too often found their dreams circumscribed by poverty and the walls of American apartheid. They seized such opportunities as existing institutions provided and improvised to bridge the gaps, creating new institutions as they went along.

The struggle for survival in this desperate period was compounded for artists, who needed not only food, rent money, and heat but also materials, tuition, and venues to display their work. Sometimes more experienced artists provided guidance and training. One important mentor was George Neal, a Memphis native born in 1906, who worked as a sign painter and illustrator. He taught classes at the South Side Settlement House and in 1932 gathered his most promising young students into a group called the Art Crafts Guild. Neal himself studied evenings at the SAIC and, every Sunday, passed along skills that he had just acquired. His students, according to a contemporary, "followed him from one improvised studio to another as irate landlords threw him out for non-payment of rent."[12] After Neal's death from pleurisy in 1938, he was hailed by the *Defender* as "the foremost Race art instructor in the city."[13]

The Art Crafts Guild sponsored fund-raising parties and exhibitions in parks, churches, and community centers. These proved important to artists whose best hope of survival was being hired by the Federal Art Project, which required catalogs of group shows, individual reviews, dealers' recommendations, or other evidence of talent and experience.[14] Balancing its mission of providing economic relief with hiring artists of demonstrated professional capacity proved difficult for the new organization. During her tenure as first director of the Illinois Art Project, Increase Robinson was repeatedly challenged over this issue by the Chicago Artists Union.[15]

One might suppose that, under ordinary circumstances, organizing artists into a trade union is akin to training cats in close-order drill, yet the Federal Art Project created a truly extraordinary situation: thousands of artists across the country—from mere apprentices to highly accomplished painters, sculptors, illustrators, designers, and crafts workers—were employed full-time by the government to make art. The Artists Union grew alongside the Art Project with the goals of serving as bargaining agent for its employees, increasing hiring quotas, ensuring the participation of artists in all major decisions, and making the project permanent.[16]

The Union's Chicago affiliate grew to 250 members by 1940 and was one of sixteen locals in major cities from Baltimore to Los Angeles. Formed against a backdrop of massive labor unrest and a drive to "organize the unorganized," the Union forged a bond between ideologically committed artists and those primarily concerned with uninterrupted flow of government paychecks to subsidize their creative work. In Chicago both groups shared the goals of expanding federal support and removing the sometimes autocratic Robinson. In November 1937, the Union secured its own exhibition and meeting space on the Near North Side, which quickly became a center for contentious disputes over politics, aesthetics, and Union policies.[17]

Supporters of the Communist Party were often the most vocal and organizationally adept participants in Union meetings. Fed by desperation and rage, the Party's ranks had grown rapidly in the early 1930s, drawing from among the unemployed, blacks, industrial workers, artists, and intellectuals. In 1932 the communists selected an African American, James Ford, as their vice presidential candidate. By the end of that year, the Party had more than four hundred black members in Chicago, by far the largest concentration of any city in the country.[18]

Before his death, George Neal had begun forging an alliance with radical white artists who were active in the Artists Union. Many of them came from the West Side Jewish ghetto, and some were in the orbit of the Communist Party. The Union took up the goal of creating jobs for African Americans on the project, a process that accelerated when George Thorp replaced Increase Robinson as state director in March 1938. During its eight-year existence, the Illinois unit hired at least twenty-six black artists, more than any other state affiliate of the Federal Art Project. The project and the Union provided rich opportunities for collaboration across racial lines and helped create a key Bronzeville institution: the South Side Community Art Center.[19]

An Art Project initiative to establish neighborhood art centers with free classes, lectures, and exhibition space provided an opportunity to realize Neal's dream. Following the national model of project/community collaboration, Thorp offered to staff an art center with project artists and provide funds to renovate a space if South Side leaders raised money to purchase a building and pay for utilities and art materials. He hired Peter Pollack, a former gallery owner, to coordinate the effort. Pollack had contacts among black artists because his Michigan Avenue gallery had been among the first to give them exposure to white collectors. He contacted local movers and shakers, and in the fall of 1938, a sponsors committee was formed, consisting of two rather distinct constituencies. An elite of black business, professional, and society people contributed personal funds, connections, and the necessary air of respectability, while a scruffier group of artists contributed talent, contagious enthusiasm, and much hard work.[20]

The creation of the Art Center broadly resembled the process by which the Wabash Avenue YMCA and other key institutions had been established. Blacks identified a need and approached a white-dominated institution, traditionally the Rosenwald Fund, for financial support. That institution provided seed money while African American leaders raised matching funds, garnered broad-based community support, and assumed responsibility for the ongoing success of the project. Two things had changed: private patronage was replaced by a publicly funded arm of the New Deal and a nascent artistic elite operated in partnership with, but outside the control of, the traditional black business and professional leadership.

The Art Crafts Guild essentially dissolved itself into the campaign and later provided many of the center's teachers and administrators.[21] The sponsoring committee launched a "Mile of Dimes" campaign to raise funds, and young artists stood on Bronzeville street corners, amassing a down payment on a building one coin at a time. Theater performances, card parties, lectures, and art exhibitions also raised funds. The most successful effort began in the fall of 1938 when Frances Taylor Matlock, a socially prominent teacher, chaired the first annual Artists and Models Ball. The gala dinner dance, held at the Savoy Ballroom, quickly became one of the community's premier social events, famous for imaginative themes and contests, beautiful models and extravagant costumes, decorations and artwork.

Finding a site proved daunting, as Pollack complained to Alain Locke: "If someone wants to know just how bad housing is on the south side try searching for an art center. Miserable hell holes have ten or more persons to a flat. We want eight thousand square feet of space; such a property is making somebody rich."[22] In July a contract was signed to purchase a three-story brick building at 3831 South Michigan, once the home of baseball magnate Charles Comisky. Art Project designers and architects drew up plans for renovation, and Bronzeville merchants contributed construction materials. The artists supplied much of the physical labor that turned the dilapidated structure—last used as a kitchenette tenement—into a gallery, classrooms, meeting space, and craft shops.

The center opened to the public in December 1940, and five months later, Eleanor Roosevelt presided over its formal dedication. Police barricaded surrounding streets to traffic, while thousands of spectators jammed into the area, hoping to get a glimpse of the First Lady as she cut the ribbon and toured the building. Following the ceremony, several hundred invited guests adjourned to the Savoy for a nationally broadcast dedication ceremony and banquet. Alain Locke introduced the First Lady and provided his own commentary:

17. Gathering at the South Side Community Art Center, 1948: *standing, left to right*: Marion Perkins, Vernon Jarrett, Robert Lucas; *seated, left to right*: Margaret Brundage, Tom Conroy, Fern Gayden, Gwendolyn Brooks, Margaret Burroughs.
Vivian G. Harsh Research Collection of Afro-American History and Literature, Chicago Public Library. Perkins Family Papers 013.

"For the first time, at least on such a scale with prospects of permanency, a practicing group of Negro artists has acquired a well-equipped working base and a chance to grow roots in its own community soil."[23] A concurrent exhibition brought together sixty-five paintings, drawings, and pieces of sculpture by thirty Bronzeville artists.[24]

For years the Roosevelt administration, Art Project, and Artists Union struggled, each in its own way, to defend expenditures of public money to employ artists and create community art centers. They had to contend with newspaper pundits, conservative congressmen, and others who portrayed the WPA cultural projects as a giant boondoggle or government-funded cover for communist propaganda. "That project . . . was attacked by everybody under the sun," Holger Cahill recalled. "There was a dead cat coming through the window every few minutes."[25]

Seven months after the center's dedication, hundreds of Japanese bombers attacked the U.S. Pacific fleet, an event that dramatically reshaped the futures of millions of Americans. Shortly after the attack on Pearl Harbor, Pollack sat down to write his report on the center's first year of operations. "Considering our recent declaration of war," he began, determined to make the case for continuing an "art program during this emergency." Employees of the Craft, Design, and other divisions of the Illinois Art Project had already been diverted to war-related activities, and Pollack proposed redirecting the center's exhibitions, classes, and meeting spaces to bolster civilian morale and "counteract the grimness of war."[26] To Alain Locke, he described himself "acting instinctively hoping to hold on, fighting damned reactionaries in the district who are trying to wipe out the project. . . . The research and records project . . . , making maps, raided the art project last week and took about 75 of our first rate artists."[27]

Despite the efforts of Pollack and his counterparts around the country, the Federal Art Project was doomed. Its demise was brutally abrupt. Thousands of artists were laid off, and many found reemployment only in military ranks. Records were destroyed, as were many paintings, sculptures, and prints. Other works were randomly distributed to government offices, sold for a pittance, stolen, or simply lost.[28] Art centers in other cities closed their doors after they lost government funding, but Bronzeville rallied to defend its center. The South Side Community Art Center survived not only termination of the Federal Art Project but decades of challenges, large and small, and in the early twenty-first century is the only one of more than one hundred project-supported centers still in existence.[29] A key figure in its creation and survival was Margaret Burroughs.

Margaret Burroughs: Artist and Educator

Margaret Taylor Goss Burroughs was born in 1917 in St. Rose, Louisiana, a few miles upriver from New Orleans. Educational opportunities were scant, as black children missed large parts of each school year to pick cotton or chop cane. In 1922, sometime after a gang of whites kidnapped and murdered a family member, the Taylors moved to Chicago. At first they lived with relatives on Thirty-first Street, but once Alex and Octavia Taylor found employment—in the stockyards and as a domestic—the family could afford their own flat.

They moved many times, always searching for better living conditions. Moving up meant moving south as the Black Belt expanded slowly, block by block, into formerly all-white areas. When the family moved into a house on Sixtieth Street, a transitional area, racial taunts were hurled, bricks were thrown through windows, and finally their front porch was firebombed.

Burroughs attended Englewood High School, gravitated toward art courses, and contributed illustrations to school publications. She also became one of the youngest members of the Art Crafts Guild and one of only two females. After graduation she enrolled at Chicago Normal College (today's Chicago State University) for two years and became a substitute teacher.[30]

Burroughs's earliest involvement in political activism began when she and Englewood classmate Gwendolyn Brooks joined the NAACP Youth Council. The group met weekly at the South Parkway YWCA, where teacher Frances Matlock served as their advisor. Other members included Henry Blakely, whom Brooks later married, and John H. Johnson, future head of the Johnson Publications empire.[31] In one small but spirited march, they walked the streets of Bronzeville wearing paper shackles around their necks and carrying handmade signs denouncing the scourge of lynching and the frame-up of the Scottsboro defendants.[32] Political activism and art work remained closely intertwined throughout Burroughs's career.

In 1939 Burroughs married Bernard Goss, a native of Kansas City, Missouri, and graduate of the University of Iowa. In an *Opportunity* article called "Negro Art in Chicago," Willard Motley described their coach-house flat: "a barn of a place, so many rooms that [their] rude, hand-fashioned fireplace with its stove-pipe chimney and a large coal-burning kitchen stove cannot warm them all in winter. The water is fetched in a pail, the dishes are washed in a clothes-tub. But the studio, a large room, blends the artistic, the Bohemian and the economic charmingly. There are canvases on the wall. There are pieces of sculpture standing on tables. And there are cracked plates, mismatched silver, rickety chairs."[33] Dubbed "little Bohemia," their home was a gathering place for a wide circle of friends and colleagues.

Burroughs poured her energies into the campaign for a neighborhood Art Center and became, at twenty-one, the youngest member of its board. The center's dedication, however, brought to a boil simmering tensions between black society patrons and the artists—most of them poor, many of them radical. When informed that they would not be directly represented in the opening ceremony, they threatened to use well-honed protest tactics to create a disruption. Pollack and other organizers decided to allow a brief statement at the banquet. The artists selected David Ross, a painter and center administrator, to deliver the speech and asked Burroughs to write it.

With Ross facing a crowd of invited guests in formal attire, waiting to hear Eleanor Roosevelt, Burroughs's words had bite: "We were not then and are not now complimented by the people who had the romantic idea that we liked to live in garrets, wear odd clothes and go around with emaciated faces painting for fun. . . . We believed that the purpose of art was to record the times. As young black artists, we looked around and recorded in our various media what we saw. It was not from our imagination that we painted slums and ghettos, or sad, hollow-eyed black men, women and children. These were the people around us. We were part of them. They were us."[34]

George Neal had taught his students to paint all manner of people and places in Bronzeville without shame. He had led sketching tours of the neighborhood and invited local residents to observe his studio classes.[35] Charles White recalled that Neal "got us out of the studio and into the street. He made us conscious of the beauty of those beat-up old shacks . . . conscious of the beauty of black people. He got us away from the old-time movie magazines that some of us, wanting to do illustrations, copied and were influenced by."[36] This documentary spirit may be discerned in the titles of many of Burroughs's paintings: *Washington Park, University Towers, Mother & Child, Street Scene, Neighborhood, Park Scene, Grief,* and *White City*.[37]

Much of Burroughs's early work was in watercolor, a medium chosen "because it was the cheapest thing we could get. We could not afford oils, canvas, stretchers and all that

1. Archibald J. Motley Jr., *Portrait of the Artist's Father,*
c. 1921, oil on canvas, 36 × 29 in.
Collection of Valerie Gerrard Browne. Photograph courtesy Chicago History Museum.

2. Archibald J. Motley Jr., *Blues*, 1929, oil on canvas, 36 × 42 in.
Collection of Valerie Gerrard Browne. Photograph courtesy Chicago History Museum.

3. Archibald J. Motley Jr., *Nightlife*, 1943, oil on canvas, 36 × 48 in.
Art Institute of Chicago. Photograph courtesy Chicago History Museum.

4. Margaret Burroughs, *38th & Wabash*, 1943, watercolor, dimensions unknown.
Courtesy of the artist. Photo: Michael Hays.

5. Charles White,
Kitchenette Debutantes, 1939,
watercolor, 27 × 22.5 in.
Private Collection. © 1939
The Charles White Archives.

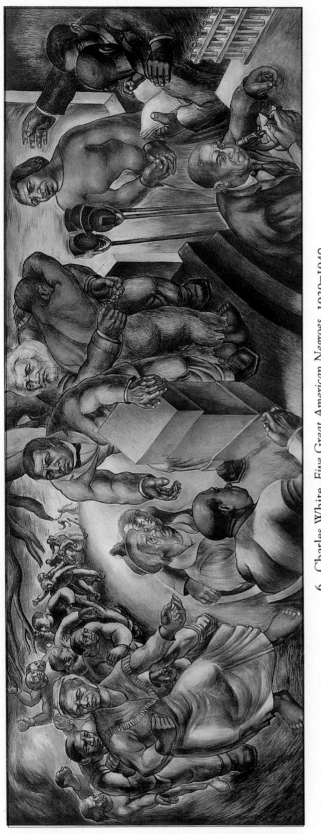

6. Charles White, *Five Great American Negroes*, 1939–1940, oil on canvas mural, 5 ft. × 12 ft. 11 in. Howard University Gallery of Art. © 1940 The Charles White Archives.

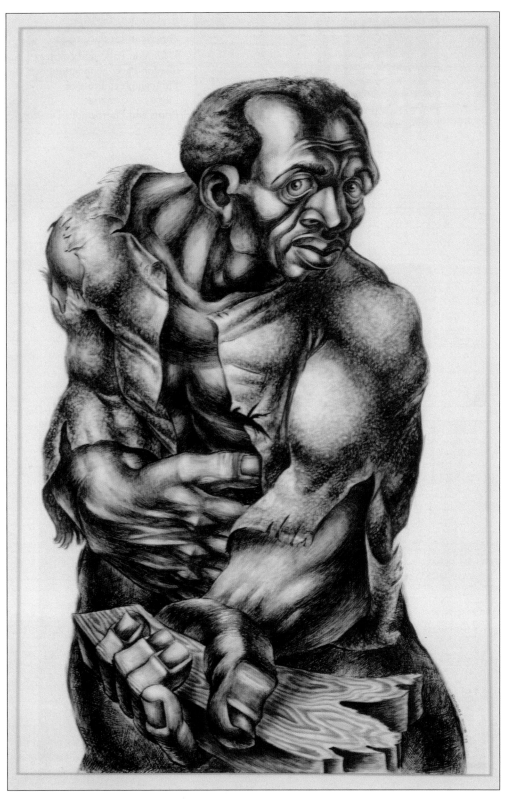

7. Charles White, *Native Son*, 1942, ink on paper, 36 in. × 48 in. Howard University Gallery of Art. © 1942 The Charles White Archives.

8. Gordon Parks,
American Gothic, 1942.
© Gordon Parks and courtesy
Gordon Parks Foundation.
Photograph courtesy of
Library of Congress,
Prints and Photographs Division.

9. Gordon Parks, *Ella Watson and Her Grandchildren*, 1942.
© Gordon Parks and courtesy Gordon Parks Foundation.
Photograph courtesy of Library of Congress, Prints and Photographs Division.

10. Charles Sebree, *Lady MacBeth*, 1942, watercolor, 24 × 20 in.
DuSable Museum of African American History. Photo: Michael Hays.

11. Eldzier Cortor, *Southern Gate*, 1942–1943, oil on canvas, 46.25 × 22 in.
© Eldzier Cortor; courtesy of Michael Rosenfeld Gallery, LLC, New York, NY. Photograph courtesy of Smithsonian American Art Museum, Gift of Mr. and Mrs. David K. Anderson, Martha Jackson Memorial Collection.

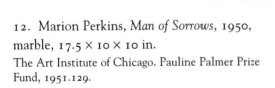

12. Marion Perkins, *Man of Sorrows*, 1950, marble, 17.5 × 10 × 10 in.
The Art Institute of Chicago. Pauline Palmer Prize Fund, 1951.129.

kind of stuff."[38] A 1943 watercolor is representative of her documentary work. *38th &* *Wabash* (color plate 4) portrays a street in the heart of Bronzeville. The scene is dominated by two buildings: an imposing brick church and a three-story wood-frame Victorian. The church's doors open to the street, and a man in hat and suit stands on the landing. A black girl passes by, walking, not running, for this is a sacred precinct. Yet the seeming solidity of this church of spires and stained-glass windows is contrasted with the house to its right, which leans precariously toward it. The eye is drawn to the odd angle of the house's front steps and the jarring red in its curtains and the dress worn by a figure on the second floor. The apparent ordinariness of this scene invites contemplation of the tensions between sacred and secular and perhaps rich and poor.

The church may in fact be St. Thomas Episcopal, described by historian Wallace Best as "the church to attend for [blacks] concerned about social status and style." The congregation had moved to fashionable Wabash Avenue in 1907, vacating an edifice on Dearborn Street "because poor and working-class African Americans had engulfed the area." But as the migrant population continued to swell, "the church found itself again in the middle of the Black Belt."[39] Burroughs used a warm sepia tone to give this painting a nostalgic hue, perhaps hiding contemporary disrepair while evoking the faded glory of Chicago's original Gold Coast, the Near South Side of the churches and mansions of the Armours, Swifts, McCormicks, Ogdens, and other industrial magnates.

Burroughs's "little Bohemia" lost much of its verve after the December 1941 declaration of war began thinning the ranks of Bronzeville's artists. She started a mimeographed letter full of home-front news and mailed it to her many friends who had been drafted. Black soldiers and sailors and a few whites passed copies of *Life with Margaret* from hand to hand. Many wrote back, recounting harrowing tales of racism in the armed forces of American democracy. Incensed by such tales, she began writing impassioned articles for the *Defender* and Associated Negro Press.[40]

Burroughs's writing was also influenced by a course on children's literature taught by librarian Charlemae Rollins. Concerned with the self-image of African American youths, Rollins encouraged them to read exemplary works of biography and literature and authored several herself.[41] In 1947 Viking brought out *Jasper the Drummin' Boy*, the story of a rhythmically hyperkinetic youth, with text and illustrations by Burroughs, who earned both bachelor's and master's degrees at SAIC and in 1946 became a full-time art teacher at DuSable High School.

Margaret and Bernard Goss had lived apart for many years when they divorced in 1947. Two years later, Margaret married Charles Burroughs, whom she met while working as art teacher at Wo–Chi–Ca, an interracial summer camp operated by the Leftist International Workers Order. Charles Burroughs was a handsome black man with a deep baritone voice, who sang soulful Russian folk songs with a perfect Slavic accent. Although he was born in Brooklyn, he grew up in the Soviet Union, the only place that his mother, communist militant Williana Burroughs, believed was free from racial discrimination.[42] Margaret continued teaching at DuSable, where she sought to inspire in her students awareness of their racial heritage. In 1961 she and Charles founded the Ebony Museum of

Negro History, the first such institution in the nation. Today it is the DuSable Museum of African American History and, along with the South Side Community Art Center, marks the legacy of Margaret Burroughs, art educator and institution builder of Bronzeville.[43]

Charles White and Social Realism

Ethelene Gary, daughter of poor Mississippi farmers and granddaughter of slaves, moved to Chicago in 1914 and met Charley White, a construction worker of Creek ancestry, originally from Georgia. Their son Charles Wilbert White was born in 1918.[44] Ethelene worked as a domestic and raised her son in what he described as "a very poor, ramshackle neighborhood." A rather lonely and introspective child, he acquired an early love of reading and drawing, nourishing his imagination and sense of beauty as if to shield himself from poverty and the daily humiliations of race, including the "grotesque stereotypes" of African Americans that he encountered in "books, . . . motion pictures, cartoons, newspapers, 'jokes,' and advertisements."[45] Creating images that capture the beauty and dignity of his people became a lifelong passion.

White attended Englewood High along with Margaret Burroughs, Eldzier Cortor, Charles Sebree, and other aspiring artists, and with them he joined George Neal's Art Crafts Guild. Learning about African American cultural achievements from Locke's *New Negro*, White developed "a kind of secret life, a new world of facts and ideas in diametric opposition to what was being taught in the class rooms and text books." Such private ruminations often incubate revolutionaries or artists. White aspired to be both and challenged teachers who "never mentioned a Negro in history." At odds with most of his teachers and classmates, he grew increasingly rebellious and, instead of attending classes, began to "wander about [the Art Institute's] galleries, looking at paintings, and dreaming of becoming an artist."[46]

Another influence upon White was Morris Topchevsky, a talented painter, communist, and resident art instructor at the Abraham Lincoln Centre.[47] Topchevsky had befriended Richard Wright in the John Reed Club, and his studio at the settlement house became an interracial gathering place.[48] There aspiring creative artists, including Charles White and Margaret Burroughs, discussed modern art trends, current events, African American history, and the writings of Marx, Engels, and Lenin.[49] While still in high school, White began contributing articles to Communist Party publications.[50]

After graduation from Englewood in 1937, White studied on scholarship at SAIC and, a year later, was hired by the Illinois Art Project, where he was initially assigned to the easel division. A representative piece is his 1939 watercolor *Kitchenette Debutantes* (color plate 5). Skillful use of light and shadow, perspective, and color draw the eye to the foregrounded figure at the window and then back into the room to a second female figure. Sinuous lines and swirling background colors define the human element against a rectangular frame. The bitter irony of the title was immediately apparent on the South Side, where tens of thousands of the poorest residents were crowded into dilapidated kitchenette buildings. White's "kitchenette debutantes" may preen in the mirror or await a caller (perhaps a paying customer), but clearly no cotillions or formal gowns lie in their futures, a message underscored by their clothing and the coarse, oversized hand holding a cigarette. Their lives are as tightly bounded as the window that frames their figures and as drearily predictable as the wall of bricks beneath.

White's symbolic use of the kitchenette to evoke the harsh conditions of urban working-class life exemplifies an important element in the iconography of social realism in Bronzeville. If the literary and visual art of the Harlem Renaissance frequently centered on the cabaret or house-rent party, scenes where Langston Hughes's "long-headed jazzers play," the art of Bronzeville often employed imagery of entrapment and deprivation. "The kitchenette is our prison," begins a long passage in Richard Wright's *12 Million Black Voices*. "The kitchenette throws desperate and unhappy people into an unbearable closeness of association. . . . The kitchenette is the funnel through which our pulverized lives flow to ruin and death on the city pavements, at a profit."[51]

The Illinois unit of the Federal Art Project was well known for the work of its muralists, especially Edward Millman and Mitchell Siporin, who gained national attention while painting an epic scene for the St. Louis, Missouri, post office, the largest and most expensive of all twenty-five hundred Art Project murals.[52] They were inspired by the revolutionary Mexican muralists Diego Rivera, David Siquieros, and José Clemente Orozco, whose work represented for them "the idea of a public art, . . . working in close contact with a viewing public and built in a public building."[53] Siporin paid homage to *los tres grandes* for making midwestern artists "aware of the . . . application of modernism toward a socially moving epic art of our time and place . . . the 'big parade' . . . of the past melting into the present, . . . in which each event begs the artistic transformation into a moving sociocultural critique."[54] While hardly a radical, Art Project director Holger Cahill also embraced the principle of "art for the people." He lauded the shift away from "the age-old cleavage between artists and public" and argued that "a naturalization of art in all our communities . . . must be achieved if our art is to be anything more than an effervescence along the Atlantic seaboard." Through its mural, graphics, photography, and poster divisions, the project promoted work in media more available to ordinary citizens than traditional easel painting and sculpture.[55]

Seizing the opportunity to "get a wall," White transferred to the mural division, where he worked with Millman and Siporin before painting his own *Five Great American Negroes* (1939–1940, color plate 6), a five-feet by thirteen-feet, oil-on-canvas work, based on a *Defender* survey identifying the most influential black leaders. Past melts into present as the eye moves left to right, beginning with Sojourner Truth, who leads a "big parade" of freedmen marking the Emancipation. Booker T. Washington leans forcefully across a podium and addresses three well-dressed blacks of the post-Reconstruction era. Beneath the bare branches of a dead tree (conventionally associated with lynching and race terror), Frederick Douglass embraces a fugitive slave, barefoot and shirtless. Tuskegee scientist George Washington Carver peers into a microscope before a bank of test tubes. Famed contralto Marian Anderson sings into broadcast microphones. Only a few months earlier, she had withstood a highly publicized affront when racists blocked her Easter 1939 concert at

18. Charles White at work on mural, c. 1940.
Chicago Public Library, Special Collections and Preservation Division. WPA 132.

Constitution Hall in Washington; Franklin Roosevelt subsequently authorized the event's relocation to the Lincoln Memorial.[56] With its epic sweep through the seventy-five years since the abolition of chattel slavery, White's mural challenged erasure of the African American experience from American history.

Several formal elements invite scrutiny. White's composition creates an illusion of motion through patterns of dark and light, through repetition and echoing of sinuously curving lines, and through the apparent muscular straining of central figures toward the viewer. The sense of movement from the tiny, indistinct figures at the rear of Sojourner Truth's procession to the monumental figures of Carver and Anderson suggests the march of history from the dim past of slavery to brighter present-day racial achievement. Figures are rendered in large blocky masses, creating a sculptural effect reinforced by strategic distortion. Washington's extended arms, for example, are swollen thick as a gnarled tree limb. Similarly stylized rendering of monumental figures and working of epic themes marked the other murals that White completed in these years: *Chaos of the American Negro* (1940), *A History of the Negro Press* (1940), and *The Contribution of the Negro to Democracy in America* (1943).

From July to September 1940, White's work was exhibited at the American Negro Exposition, and he won several awards, including first prize in black-and-white media for the drawing *There Were No Crops This Year*. First prize in sculpture went to Elizabeth Catlett, a faculty member at Dillard University, for her limestone *Negro Mother and Child*.[57] Catlett then spent the summer of 1941 studying lithography at the South Side Community Art Center. She rented a room in Margaret Burroughs's coach-house studio, where artists gathered to argue about politics and art, to eat and drink, and to celebrate each others' successes late into the night. Catlett remembered this artistic circle as much for their politics as for their creative energies: "There was a lot of discussion, they were trying to recruit me into the Communist Party."[58] In December she and White were married at her mother's home in Washington, D.C., and moved to New Orleans, where both taught at Dillard.

In April 1942, White won a Rosenwald fellowship for a project intended to counter the "stereotyped and superficial caricatures of 'uncles,' 'mammies,' and 'pickaninnies.'" His proposal included travel in the South to observe and paint black farmers and laborers and study in Mexico to "take advantage of the best mural techniques available."[59] White's draft board, however, refused him permission to leave the country. Instead he and Catlett moved to New York for the summer, where she studied with abstract sculptor Ossip Zadkine, and he studied with lithographer Harry Sternberg.

The couple lived and traveled in the South for nearly two years, before returning to New York. Their paintings and graphic works of this period bore stylistic similarities, which sometimes led people to mistake Catlett's work for White's. Both were struggling, as were Eldzier Cortor, Jacob Lawrence, Beauford Delaney, and other black artists, to create an aesthetic synthesis—a stylistic vocabulary that would address the African American experience within the representational tradition, while incorporating formal devices such as anatomical distortion, expressive color accents, fractured spatial planes, montage, collage, and surreal juxtapositions of images.[60] Mitchell Siporin had called it "the application of modernism" to "sociocultural critique."

One striking example of this synthesis is White's ink drawing *Native Son* (1942, color plate 7). Bigger Thomas, the "native son" of Richard Wright's 1940 novel, is a murderer, rapist, and fugitive, desperately struggling to avoid capture. In White's rendering, the figure appears to be running. Outsized arm and chest muscles have burst through his shirt, which hangs in tatters. His extended left hand clutches a jagged piece of lumber, the squarish fingernails bearing a marked resemblance to bullets. His haunted eyes seem to transfix and track the viewer. White's Bigger Thomas is a nightmare vision–America's imbruted offspring and the byproduct of its racism. Wright saw his fictional protagonist "as a symbolic figure of American life," one of the casualties of "a dislocated society . . . dispossessed and disinherited."[61] The grotesquely muscled, writhing figure in Charles White's *Native Son* may be said to embody the writhing soul of Richard Wright's Bigger Thomas, who in turn symbolizes a society tortured and distorted by race and class oppression.

In 1944 White and Catlett began teaching at the newly established George Washington Carver School in Harlem, whose curriculum offered a combination of practical skills, high culture, and Marxist politics. White was drafted several months later and contracted tuberculosis when his segregated army unit was put to work controlling floods in the Midwest. He spent two years recovering in a veterans' hospital, while Catlett won her own Rosenwald fellowship to create a series of prints depicting the struggles and achievements of African American women.

After White's release from hospital and renewal of Catlett's fellowship, the couple moved to Mexico City, where they worked at the Taller de Grafica Popular, a graphic arts workshop equally famous for technical excellence and radical politics. Although they shared great talents, Leftist politics, and the heady early days of brilliant careers, their marriage collapsed, and they divorced in 1947. Catlett stayed on, worked in sculpture and graphics, taught at the National University, and became one of Mexico's most accomplished artists, while remaining a leading voice on the social role and responsibilities of African American artists.

White continued working in a figurative mode throughout his career, developing a style more naturalistic in its representation of the black subject, even as the art establishment enshrined abstract expressionism as the quintessence of modern art. He attributed the influence of the Taller artists and of Harry Sternberg to his "stronger leaning for graphics" and "black and white media" as his career progressed.[62] In 1956 he and second wife Frances Barrett moved to Los Angeles to improve his health, and he began teaching at the Otis Art Institute nine years later. Among many honors, he became, in 1975, the second African American elected to the National Academy of Design; the first was Henry O. Tanner.

The Divided Sensibility of Gordon Parks

Gordon Parks lived a long life and reflected and wrote, almost obsessively, about its meaning. His first attempt at autobiography, *A Choice of Weapons* (1965), opens with his mother's burial in a small Kansas town and his own departure for St. Paul, Minnesota. Episodes of violence proliferate, and throughout the book Park interrogates his own survival: "Until the very day that I left Fort Scott . . . , there had been a fair chance of being shot or perhaps beaten to death. I could easily have been the victim of mistaken identity, of a sudden act of terror by hate-filled white men, or, for that matter, I could have been murdered by some violent member of my own race. There had been a lot of killing in the border states of Kansas, Oklahoma and Missouri, more than I cared to remember."[63] The passage goes beyond personal memory to a near-mythic history of violence that began when the first white settlers carried their rifles into the wilderness, and the native inhabitants rose to defend their hunting grounds with bow and arrow. Fort Scott, Park's birthplace, was once part of a network of fortifications that delineated new boundaries and protected ever-expanding white claims on land that was to become the state of Kansas.[64]

"Bleeding Kansas" in the mid-1850s was the site of ruthless guerrilla warfare between pro- and anti-slavery settlers, the latter led by John Brown. When the killing temporarily ceased, on the eve of the Civil War, Kansas entered the Union as a free state.[65] Thenceforth, John Brown's Kansas exerted a strong pull on the imagination of blacks. Following the 1877

Compromise and violent overthrow of Reconstruction, the state drew tens of thousands of former slaves. Like those who poured out of the South two generations later, the Kansas "Exodusters" found far less than their dreams encompassed.[66] Poverty and de facto segregation marked the lives of most black Kansans when Gordon Parks was born in 1912.

At fifteen Parks joined his sister in St. Paul, but a fight with his brother-in-law left him bruised and tossed into the snow during the dead of winter. He slept on a trolley bustling back and forth between the Twin Cities and found whatever work he could, surviving the next few years through luck, grim determination, and an extraordinary gift for music. From an early age, he was encouraged by his mother to practice on an old Kimball upright that graced their farmhouse parlor. After leaving home, he played whenever he found access to a piano, working to improve his technique and composing in the W. C. Handy mode. His song "No Love" caught the ear of white bandleader Larry Funk, who invited him to join the band as vocalist on a national tour.[67] At their final stop in New York, however, Funk abandoned his musicians without paying them. Parks took the A-train to Harlem where he was marooned and jobless again.

Creation of the Civilian Conservation Corps (CCC) in March 1933 took two million young men off streets and breadlines and provided Parks's meal ticket for the next fifteen months. When the corps disbanded, he returned to the Twin Cities and to first wife Sally Arvis. He worked as busboy, waiter, and musician until taking a job on a dining car on the North Coast Limited, running from St. Paul to Chicago and then across the continent to Seattle. On one of those long journeys, Parks found a discarded photo-magazine with images of migrant workers taken by FSA photographers: "Dispossessed, beaten by dust, storms and floods, they roamed the highways in caravans of battered jalopies and wagons between Oklahoma and California scrounging for work." These viscerally powerful images inspired him to buy his first camera.[68]

The Twin Cities had once seemed the Big Time to a Kansas farm boy, but Chicago, a true metropolis, now beckoned. Marva Louis, wife of heavyweight champion Joe Louis, chanced to see some fashion photos by Parks on display in a St. Paul department store and promised to find him work if he moved to Chicago.[69] During a layover in the city, he met David Ross, exhibition manager for the Community Art Center. They discussed his ambitions and soon struck a deal: Parks would serve without pay as official photographer for the center, and in return he would enjoy rent-free workspace. Within weeks, he had relocated his family to Chicago and began work in a fully equipped darkroom and spacious studio. With help from Marva Louis and influential Center board members, his portraits of Bronzeville socialites began appearing in Chicago newspapers.

Parks became friends with Art Center administrators and teachers, and he and the painters influenced one another. The photographer absorbed compositional ideas from the painters while experimenting with unusual shooting angles and lighting techniques in his camera work.[70] Parks grew especially close with Charles White, whose "powerful, black figures" seemed a model for "the kind of photography that I knew I should be doing." They walked the South Side together, photographing and painting the same "ash piles, garbage heaps, tired tenements and littered streets."[71]

19. Painting class at South Side Community Art Center, 1942;
instructor Eldzier Cortor (*standing*), Gordon Parks (*sitting, facing forward*).
Photo: Jack Delano. Library of Congress, Prints & Photographs Division,
FSA-OWI Collection. LC-USW3–000702-D.

White had applied for a Rosenwald fellowship and encouraged Parks to also try his luck. He submitted a photographic portfolio accompanied by support letters from Alain Locke, Horace Cayton, Peter Pollack, and David Ross. To further strengthen Parks's case, Ross arranged an exhibition at the Art Center in November 1941.[72] At the opening reception, Parks recalled, "It seemed that half of Chicago was there," including Rosenwald Fund president Edwin Embree and FSA photographer Jack Delano. "The elite, dressed in their furs and finery, rubbed elbows with some of the people I had photographed in the poor quarter."[73]

Parks's photos included social-documentary work as well as landscapes and portraits. At one point, he observed two figures standing by their respective portraits: a bejeweled white society matron, photographed in a North Side penthouse, and an elderly black woman, wearing a little bonnet, photographed in a storefront church. Reflecting the extremes represented in those images and in the gallery audience itself, Parks's apprentice work established a pattern of social and aesthetic bifurcation that extended throughout his career.

Parks was the first photographer to win a Rosenwald fellowship—testimony to not only individual talent but also the heightened importance of photography in American life. In the 1920s, Edward Steichen's studio portraits of beautiful people in elegant clothes had graced the pages of glossy magazines as if the very definition of the good life. In the 1930s, photographers for New Deal agencies and photo-magazines *Life* and *Look* traveled the country to capture images of the pain wreaked by the Depression.[74]

In Chicago, Parks was mastering both the portraiture epitomized by Steichen's work for *Vanity Fair* and the documentary mode. His memoirs make clear his pragmatic sense that he could always pay the bills with fashion work and portraits, but his strongest drive was to use the camera as Charles White used paint. "I am interested in the social, even the propaganda, angle of painting," White told Willard Motley in 1940. "Paint is the only weapon I have with which to fight what I resent."[75] Parks identified Wright's *12 Million Black Voices* as his "bible" and "inspiration" and the FSA as the best place to continue honing his skills.[76]

A letter from the Rosenwald Fund opened doors at the FSA's photographic unit, and Parks's fellowship allowed him to work there as an unpaid trainee. Director Roy Stryker, a gruff taskmaster and skillful teacher, first sent the young man to discover for himself the hard truth about racial mores in the nation's capital: "Eating houses shooed me to the back door, theaters refused me a seat. . . . Washington . . . was a hate-drenched city." Parks returned to FSA offices seething with humiliation and rage. Stryker calmly urged him to learn to use his camera to "help turn things around."[77]

Later, while exploring photographic files and mulling over Stryker's advice, Parks encountered a thin, gray-haired African American woman named Ella Watson. After an initially awkward meeting, the charwoman poured out her story to the young stranger with a camera: "She had struggled alone after her mother had died and her father had been killed by a lynch mob. She had gone through high school, married and become pregnant." Both her husband and their daughter had died, and Watson was raising her grandchildren "on a salary hardly suitable for one person."[78] She agreed to be photographed, and one of Parks's most famous images resulted.

In *American Gothic* (1942, color plate 8), Ella Watson stares directly into the camera and, through it, at the viewer. Posed like the man in Grant Woods's famous 1930 portrait of a farm couple, Watson's expression is solemn, lucid, stoic. The right side of her face is cast in emblematic darkness. She wears an old smock with buttons missing and holds a broom in one hand, a mop in the other—tools of her actual work but, more broadly, symbols of the status of her people. The American flag, hanging limply in the background, serves as bitterly ironic comment. Its vertical stripes frame Watson's face while its stars echo the polka dots of her dress. A narrow depth of field brings her face and figure into sharp focus. Stryker was unsettled by this deliberately provocative image but encouraged Parks to keep working with Watson. For nearly a month, he recorded the quotidian moments of her life—in worship, work, repose, and kinship.

Ella Watson and Her Grandchildren (1942, color plate 9) is as complex and multi-layered as *American Gothic* is simple and direct in its anger. The scene is neatly bisected by a doorframe, creating two panels, seemingly in dialogue. On the left, Watson tenderly holds her youngest grandchild as the older siblings turn away from a plain meal. Their clothing, chipped plates, and the box lid and barrels serving as dining table and chairs indicate the family's poverty. On the right, Watson's adopted daughter is reflected in the mirror of a carved and lacquered vanity, which displays the portrait of an elegantly dressed couple, presumably the oldest of four generations pictured. Much can be read into this study, especially about familial ties and affections, but the tension between the two panels has unmistakable connotations of straitened circumstances and unfulfilled hopes. Parks's work with the Watson family suggests his particular strengths as a documentary photographer: careful and creative attention to composition, light, texture, and tone; ability to establish trust and gain entry into his subjects' lives; a perspective that was both well-informed and empathic; creation of photographic series with implicit narratives.

When the FSA was disbanded in 1943, Parks followed Stryker into the Office of War Information, and the following year he joined a special photographic unit at Standard Oil of New Jersey. Ongoing work with his mentor and increasing success as a freelancer for *Ebony, Glamour,* and other magazines eventually brought the photographer to the attention of the editors of *Life.* In 1948 they accepted his idea for a photo-essay on a teenage gang leader in Harlem, which Parks later called "the second most important step in my career" (the first was his Rosenwald fellowship).[79]

Typical of the social bifurcation noted earlier, the success of Parks's photo-essay on Harlem gangs led to a staff position at *Life* and a voyage on the *Queen Mary* to France, where he covered the Parisian fashion shows. In the following decades, he photographed whatever caught the attention of his ever-curious eye: American ghettoes and Brazilian favelas; celebrities and fashion models; soldiers in battle; musicians, monks, matadors, and monarchs; cops and criminals; landscapes and cityscapes on four continents; nudes and still lifes; Muhammad Ali, the Black Muslims, and the Black Panthers.[80] He broke new ground for blacks in Hollywood as producer, director, screenwriter, and composer. His work on these and other wide-ranging projects continued to reflect the two sides of a divided sensibility: the personal combativeness and awareness of social conflict that animated his documentary work and the lush romanticism that characterized his fashion and art photography.

Other Visions

The two sides of Gordon Parks's career reveal the conflicting pulls of a purely aesthetic "art for art's sake" approach and a more instrumental "art as weapon" approach (in a less overtly politicized version, the documentary mode). As FSA photographs suggest, however, this is no simple dichotomy. An instrumental approach, in the hands of an artist such as Parks or White (or Honoré Daumier, Francisco Goya, Käthe Kollwitz, or Dorothea Lange) can produce works of great complexity and enduring power. A purely aesthetic or formal approach can allow deeper exploration of a chosen medium and hold great potential satisfaction and achievement for even the most politically committed artist. The choices artists make about subject, medium, technique, and other matters are complexly shaped by many factors. Marxist-inspired social realism was a decisive influence on many

Bronzeville artists, but certainly not the only one. As a group, they constituted less a school of artistic expression or a unified ideology, than a generational milieu, shaped by a particular set of circumstances. A brief look at several other Bronzeville artists illustrates the point.

Charles Sebree was born in Kentucky in 1914 and moved with his mother to Chicago when he was ten.[81] He manifested creative talent at an early age, and a teacher at Burke Elementary brought his work to the Renaissance Society at the University of Chicago, one of the centers of modernist influence in the city. He went to Englewood High School and SAIC, created costumes and stage décors for the Cube theater, danced in several of Katherine Dunham's productions, worked in the easel division of the Illinois Art Project, and studied at the School of Design, founded by Laszlo Moholy-Nagy, an émigré veteran of Berlin's famous Bauhaus.[82]

In 1936, the first year of Inez Cunningham Stark's four-year tenure as Renaissance Society president, Sebree's paintings were exhibited in a two-artist show, and he later participated in several group exhibitions in the Society's gallery.[83] He showed at the annual exhibitions of the Watercolor Society from 1935 to 1942, and his work was hung repeatedly in Katherine Kuh's North Side gallery, including a March 1940 exhibition where it appeared alongside paintings by Léger, Matisse, Modigliani, and Picasso.[84] Willard Motley reported that Sebree "sold more paintings than any other of the [Bronzeville] group. In his teens he was considered a professional artist."[85] Sebree caught the attention of white modernists such as Stark and Kuh, and their support propelled his early successes.

Working in oil, tempera, watercolor, and other media, Sebree achieved a look that was distinctively modern and distinctly his own. The bleeding, layered shadings of browns and grays in his 1942 watercolor *Lady Macbeth* (color plate 10) are indicative of his subtle color sense. The heavily outlined figure is also vintage Sebree, as is the hazy background composed of vaguely suggestive details: a full moon reflected in a near-black sea, a distant villa, a crumpled piece of paper in the middle distance. Everything evokes a theatrical setting, and the black Lady Macbeth may well allude to the 1939 production of *Macbeth* by the Negro division of the Federal Theater Project in New York.

Most important is the enigmatic figure that dominates the scene. Sebree's typical subjects are performers: harlequins, jugglers, acrobats, costumed actors. These nomads and outsiders often seem to look within, as if experiencing and restraining some powerful but ambiguous emotion. One of Sebree's contemporaries, artist and critic James Porter, described Sebree's work as "conceived in a mood of contemplation and recall[ing] . . . Russian icon painting."[86] The artist's representation of Lady Macbeth departs from Renaissance rules of perspective, and the setting is rendered with no attempt to evoke a natural source of light. The androgynous central figure also divides the work into three sections, effectively bridging interior and exterior spaces and imparting a surreal quality to the overall scene. Although Sebree was integrally involved in South Side institutions and social networks, his art showed little affinity for the social-realist or documentary approach; he evidences the range of aesthetic influence and possibility explored by Bronzeville's artists even at the height of cultural radicalism.

Eldzier Cortor also made important contributions to the stylistic diversity and achievements of Bronzeville's visual artists. He was born in Richmond, Virginia, in 1916, but his family moved to Chicago the following year.[87] His father was an electrician and small businessman, who earned a good living until the Depression struck. Cortor was initially interested in becoming a cartoonist but shifted focus to fine arts while studying at Englewood High School.

Cortor's art history teacher at SAIC, Kathleen Blackshear, required students to sketch African sculptures at the Field Museum in order to understand their precise spatial concepts and formal severity. He later cited this experience as a major influence on his "cylindrical and lyrical handling of the human figure."[88] Interested in the relationship between African sculpture and modern art, he began to do abstract work while studying at SAIC, which had a strong Cubist influence in the 1930s. While working at the Illinois Art Project he returned to figurative painting. For several years, he focused on the people and places of Bronzeville, producing memorable genre scenes such as *The Night Letter* (1938), *Coming Home from Work* (c. 1938), *She Didn't Forget* (1939), and *Signs of Times* (1940).

A major exhibition of nineteenth-century French masters impressed Cortor with the "epic style" of Jacques-Louis David and Eugene Delacroix, a quality he perceived as missing from his work for the Project. In the early 1940s, a search for his own epic style and his studies of African sculpture converged in a series of dramatic portrayals of black women, which established his reputation. *Southern Gate* (1942–43, color plate 11) is probably Cortor's most famous oil painting (lithography became his primary medium in his later years). The semi-nude figure of a beautiful young woman is rendered with a rounded sculptural quality and dominates the scene, seemingly detached from the background imagery. Part of the face and body is shaded, reflecting the artist's emphasis on the suggestive quality of that which is only half-seen. The elongated body, impassive expression, and African features are typical of his female figures. Such details as the bird, clustered flowers, and flowing garments on the figure and the iron fence, decayed column, distant church and river in the background further suggest symbolic intent. "The Black woman represents the Black race," Cortor once said. "She . . . conveys a feeling of eternity, and the continuance of life."[89]

Cortor's friend Horace Cayton encouraged him to read recent studies of African cultural survivals among the Gullah people of the Carolina and Georgia Sea Islands. This reading reinforced his interest in the aesthetics of African face and figure, and, with Cayton's support, he secured the first of two consecutive Rosenwald fellowships in 1944. They enabled him to live and work on St. Helena Island, South Carolina, which according to Daniel Schulman, was for Cortor "a South more akin to Gaugin's Tahiti than to Charles White's Alabama." There he "won [the] freedom to completely reimagine and intensify subject matter . . . already examined."[90] This aesthetic freedom was exemplified in Cortor's description of himself as belonging to "the mystic-romantic school of painters."[91] His colleagues, Willard Motley reported, considered him "the most original of the group."

Marion Perkins was born in Arkansas in 1908, but, after his parents died when he was eight, he was sent to live with an aunt in Chicago.[92] He left Wendell Phillips High School in his junior year and began supporting himself as a laborer. His early interest in sculpture competed with an interest in becoming a playwright. He participated with Richard Wright, Margaret Walker, Theodore "Ted" Ward, Arna Bontemps, and others in the South Side Writers' Group and, like Wright and Ward, became a committed communist.

Perkins was initially a self-taught sculptor. While operating a news stand on busy Indiana Avenue, he carved heads and figures from blocks of stone that he "requisitioned" from building demolitions. In 1938 Peter Pollack was driving through the South Side and noticed Perkins working at his curbside pedestal. Impressed by his obvious potential, Pollack brought him to the attention of Art Project sculptor Simon Gordon, who became Perkins's friend and mentor. Developing rapidly, Perkins secured private commissions and exhibited two stone heads at the 1940 American Negro Exposition. When the Community Art Center opened, he began teaching and exhibiting there. In 1942 he was invited to show his powerful limestone *John Henry* at the Art Institute, alongside Edward Hopper's *Nighthawks* and a memorial retrospective of works by Grant Wood. He received a Rosenwald fellowship in 1948, the fund's final year.

Perkins's stylistic range and technical acumen continued to grow and were on full display in his masterwork, the 1950 marble *Man of Sorrows* (color plate 12), which won a purchase award at an Art Institute exhibition the following year. The work also won near-universal acclaim from critics of both the abstraction and anti-abstraction camps. One writer singled out its "simplified forms" and "contrasting textures" for special praise. Perkins himself offered a straightforwardly political interpretation, declaring that his piece "shows the Negro people's conception of Christ as a Negro . . . reflect[ing] the suffering of our people but . . . in a strong and forceful way. The . . . suffering of the Negro people . . . is an acid test of American democracy."[93] *Man of Sorrows* is striking in its manifold interpretive possibilities. Vertical contrasts for example between the finely wrought brow and hairline and the roughly worked mouth and jaw create dynamic tension and allude simultaneously to classical European sculpture and to African sculpture as rendered through the lens of primitivist modernism.

Marion Perkins's comrades, proudly referring to him as a "worker-artist," emphasized both his very real achievements in sculpture and the fact that he supported himself as a laborer for much of his life.[94] His plebian origins, self-education as an artist, and proletarian employment set him apart from some of his peers, but in important ways his career was also representative of the extreme barriers of race and class that his artistic colleagues had to surmount. He had in fact more formal education than Gordon Parks or Richard Wright and shared common formative experiences with other sons and daughters of stockyard workers, domestics, and farmers who created the visual arts of the Black Chicago Renaissance.

Although the art of Bronzeville was stylistically diverse—encompassing social realism, American Scene, and varied modernistic influences—the figurative mode and documentary impulse were dominant. The Art League of William Farrow and Charles Dawson apparently did not survive the onset of the Depression, but all evidence indicates that most artists who emerged from George Neal's Art Crafts Guild would have been profoundly uncomfortable in the older organization. White, Burroughs, Cortor, and the others generally followed

Archibald Motley in finding aesthetic interest in the black subject and the urban milieu, a profound shift in its time, partly reflecting the earlier example of the Ashcan School. The institutions where their sensibilities were shaped—public schools, settlement houses, radical organizations, the Art Project—encouraged them to make art for the people, in their case primarily black people, rather than to impress individual white collectors and patrons. The white colleagues and comrades with whom they interacted also came from plebian backgrounds. The radical Jewish artists—Topchevsky, Gordon, Millman, Siporin—were children of another diaspora, another migration, another ghetto.

Philosophically, Bronzeville artists stood, as modern artists typically do, on the margins of the communities from which they sprang. Their art training and broader education, their lives in a great urban center, their radical political philosophies marked them as cosmopolitans, part of the avant-garde, yet, within their individual or family histories, the static world of the plantation was often living memory. They portrayed contemporary life on the South Side, but many were also drawn to subjects based on African American history and southern folk tradition. In "mongrel" Chicago, "the most American of American cities," black folk culture was transformed through the pressures of and exposure to modern urban life, formal education, and other cultures. Documenting and contributing to this process, the artists of Bronzeville created a representational art of social concern, marked by mastery of technique, intense feeling, and resonant associations of human dignity.

CHAPTER 8

Bronzeville's "Writing Clan"

Bronzeville's writers came of age in hard times and in a hard city, and this was reflected in their literary work—its themes, forms, tropes, and goals. If writers of the Harlem Renaissance tended to turn inward, toward heightened ethnic consciousness and a romantic identification with a southern-rooted folk culture, writers of the Black Chicago Renaissance tended to turn outward, toward social transformation achieved through the cold-eyed documentation of oppressive social realities. Portents of this aesthetic and generational shift could be found as early as 1932 in such works as Langston Hughes's *Scottsboro Limited* and Sterling Brown's *Southern Road* and may also be seen in a series of Marxist-inspired short stories that Hughes began writing in 1934 and in Arna Bontemps's novel of slave revolt, *Black Thunder* (1936).[1]

Bontemps and Hughes, in particular, forged close ties with Bronzeville's young writers and must be regarded as transitional figures whose writings resonate with both the Harlem Renaissance and the Chicago-centered movement that supplanted it. On moving to the South Side in 1935, Bontemps was pleased to discover "a writing clan" with which he quickly affiliated. Richard Wright and Frank Marshall Davis were important members of that clan, and the poems they published in mid-decade signaled Bronzeville's emergence as the hot center of African American literary work.

The Gathering of "A Writing Clan"

Richard Wright arrived in Chicago by train in December 1927. To a youth of nineteen, born on a Mississippi plantation and bred with the austerities of the Seventh-Day Adventist faith, Robert Abbott's "Promised Land" initially seemed more like Babylon than Zion. "My first glimpse of the flat black stretches of Chicago depressed and dismayed me, mocked all my fantasies," he recalled. "Chicago seemed an unreal city whose mythical houses were built of slabs of black coal wreathed in palls of gray smoke, houses whose foundations were sinking slowly into the dank prairie. . . . The din of the city entered my consciousness, entered to remain for years to come."[2] Anxiety was the young migrant's strongest emotion, and he found his initial fears fully justified as he desperately lurched from job to job, attempting to feed and shelter his family. His involvement with the John Reed Club led to publication of such revolutionary poems as "I Have Seen Black Hands," carried in the June 1934 *New Masses*. These publications in turn brought national attention and helped him qualify for a supervisory position in the Chicago office of the Federal Writers' Project.

Frank Marshall Davis arrived by train the same year as Wright. "Santa Fe from the West crawls noisily into Chicago guided by two shining ribbons of steel," he wrote a few months later. "Southside factories look disinterestedly down on moving cars from dirty windows. . . . Moving yellow and red surface cars against the drabness of brown and gray State Street stores—filthy snow piled high on paved Chicago streets—Twenty-eighth Street and one block eastward five stories of red brick house—The Wabash Y."[3] At six-foot-one and well over two hundred pounds, the twenty-one-year-old Kansan was frequently described as "the poet who looks like a prizefighter."[4] He earned his living as a journalist, starting out in Chicago, then moving to Gary, Indiana, and in 1931 becoming managing editor of the *Atlanta World*.[5] On the side, he published verse and pulp fiction in black periodicals.

In 1935, about a year after returning to the South Side, Davis published his first book, *Black Man's Verse*. A lively mix of polemic, satire, jazz improvisation, and lyric, these poems announced the arrival of a new generation of black writers and prompted Alain Locke to declare: "For the new notes and the strong virile accents in our poetry today, we must shift from Harlem to Chicago."[6] Although well-received by critics, *Black Man's Verse* generated little income, and Davis supported himself as an editor at the Associated Negro Press, a service founded in Chicago in 1919 by Tuskegee alumnus/trustee Claude Barnett to provide news and opinion pieces to a national network of African American newspapers.[7]

Wright met another native Mississippian on the Writers' Project.[8] William Attaway, born in 1911 in Greenville, was brought to Chicago at age six.[9] His parents were professionals, a physician and a school teacher, and the arrival of their second child, Ruth, some eighteen months after William's birth, forced a major decision. "My father . . . had a notion," Attaway recalled, "that Negro kids brought up in the South unconsciously accept the whites' estimates of them, and they never get to know what it is to be a human among humans."[10] The Attaways joined other African American professionals and business people who followed their clients and customers north. While the children attended South Side schools, their parents sought to retain kinship ties and assist newly arrived migrants, and Dr. William Attaway became a leading figure in the Mississippi Club, founded in 1923.[11]

Young William was intent on becoming an auto mechanic until he encountered the poetry of Langston Hughes in a high school English class. Inspired, he immersed himself more seriously in academic work and also tried his hand at script-writing for his sister's amateur dramatic groups. He studied English at the University of Illinois and wrote one-act plays and short stories for literary magazines. "I had all the advantages that a self-made man imagines are good for an only son," Attaway said of his adolescence. During his second year at the University life changed abruptly when his father died, an event roughly coinciding with the onset of the worst years of the Depression. "I rebelled and spent my time hoboeing," he recalled.[12] Traveling the country for two years, he worked variously as seaman, salesman, and migrant laborer. After returning home in 1933, he resumed his studies, saw his play *Carnival* produced on campus, and in 1935 joined the Writers' Project.

Wright was introduced to Margaret Walker by Langston Hughes, who had first met her in February 1932 during his tour of southern black colleges. Born in Birmingham in

1915, Walker was raised in New Orleans on the saintly side of the street.[13] Her father, Sigismund, was a Methodist Episcopal minister, who had emigrated from Jamaica to attend college. Her mother, Marion, was southern-born and a music teacher. Both parents taught at New Orleans University (now Dillard). The precocious Walker wrote her first poems at ten and began undergraduate study at fifteen. As Hughes packed his books away after a poetry reading in New Orleans, a diminutive sophomore approached the podium and thrust a sheaf of poems into his hands. Years later, Walker remembered that "he stopped what he was doing, put my poems up on the piano where my sister had sung during his program, and proceeded to go through them one by one for about an hour, talking about them, how they might be improved. He said I had talent. . . . He even urged my parents to send me to school in the North, where I would have more freedom to grow."[14]

Within months the teenager transferred to her father's alma mater, Northwestern University, where she majored in literature. While still an undergraduate, she published a poem in *Crisis* and wrote three hundred pages of fiction based on her maternal grand-mother's tales of slavery. This college creative-writing exercise represented the earliest rough draft of her novel *Jubilee* (1966). Despite Walker's outstanding academic record, graduation into a devastated economy brought only months of frustrating job-hunting until she too found work with the Illinois Writers' Project.

Like Walker, Arna Bontemps moved to Chicago to pursue further education, hoping that a graduate degree from the University of Chicago would help secure a faculty position at a southern black college. Born in Louisiana in 1902, he was raised and educated through the baccalaureate level in California. He participated in the Harlem literary scene from 1924 to 1931, winning awards for his poetry and publishing his first novel. The scattering of Harlem's literati under the blows of the Depression led him to Oakwood Junior College in Alabama. Three years later, he fled the shadow of the Scottsboro trials and found tenuous refuge at his father's home in Los Angeles. Paul Bontemps, a bricklayer and Seventh-Day Adventist minister, was as disapproving of literary aspirations as Richard Wright's family. An advance on a second novel facilitated Arna's relocation from his father's home to Chicago, where he found employment as principal of Shiloh Academy, an Adventist institution.

Bontemps was at first shocked by the crime and appalling poverty that he encountered on the Depression-wracked South Side but soon found "a writing clan that adopted [him] and bolstered [his] courage."[15] When Langston Hughes paid his first visit, the two friends sought out Richard Wright, whose poems in *New Masses* had caught their attention.[16] In April 1936, the writing clan gathered, under the aegis of the Chicago Council of the National Negro Congress, to honor Bontemps's literary achievements with a reception and symposium at the Abraham Lincoln Centre. The focus of the symposium was his recently released second novel, *Black Thunder*. The prestigious speakers' list included Frank Marshall Davis, *Defender* editor Metz Lochard, and Harold Kingsley of Good Shepherd Congregational Church.[17]

Another member of the clan, Willard Motley, joined by a somewhat circuitous route. He was born in 1909 in predominantly white Englewood and raised in the devoutly

Catholic, middle-class home of maternal grandparents Mary and Archibald Motley Sr., a teacher and Pullman porter respectively.[18] Although the family was touched by the terror of the 1919 riots, Willard learned the harsh realities of class and race less from his early years than from a deliberate immersion in poor communities, later serving as the basis for several naturalistic novels.[19]

Willard followed his artist uncle at Englewood High School. Gregarious, athletic, and aching to succeed as a writer, he shared his generation's belief that the open road was the best school for aspiring authors. Shortly after graduation, he set off on a thousand-mile bicycle trip to the East Coast, eager "to have adventures, to feel life beat and caress, to live!"[20] This was the first of several cross-country trips, which Motley meticulously recorded in his diaries. He wrote feverishly throughout the 1930s and collected an impressive pile of rejection letters from newspapers and magazines. In 1938 he began publishing in travel magazines and the Catholic journal *Commonweal*.

Motley moved out of Englewood and into a filthy basement apartment near Hull House, epicenter of the teeming, polyglot West Side slums. He became friends with several white Hull House residents, among them Peter Schenck, a friend and admirer of Carl Sandburg, and Alexander Saxton, an aspiring novelist and student at the University of Chicago. The three founded *Hull-House Magazine*, a mimeographed monthly, in the fall of 1939, and Motley contributed a series of plotless literary sketches of the neighborhood and its down-at-the-heels inhabitants.[21] With a modest publication record and certifiable pauper status, he qualified for the Writers' Project in 1940.

One younger member of the group, Gwendolyn Brooks, was born in her maternal grandparents' home in Topeka, Kansas, in 1917, but her parents were Chicago residents. Her father, David Brooks, spent a year at Fisk in hopes of becoming a doctor but instead worked thirty years as a porter. Keziah Wims Brooks taught fifth grade until her marriage. Raised in a little house with front porch and neat lawn, Gwendolyn was a somewhat lonely child. "I liked to read," she recalled, "and everyone else considered reading a chore. And I like to draw. . . . These things combined to make me seem a rather strange individual." By age eleven, she was writing a new poem each day, prompting her strong-willed mother to declare that she would become "the second Paul Laurence Dunbar."[22]

Shortly after graduating from Englewood High School, Brooks published a poem in the *Chicago Defender*, and some seventy-five more pieces followed during the next four years. While writing for the *Defender*, Brooks studied at Wilson Junior College and became involved in the NAACP Youth Council, the Community Art Center organizing committee, and a group called the Cre-Lit Club. Overlapping membership in these groups included Margaret Burroughs and Brooks's future husband, Henry Blakely. While Brooks's fellow Englewood alumni Burroughs and Charles White remained torn between conflicting demands of political activism and creative expression, Brooks's organizational involvements of the late 1930s added new elements to her imaginative purview without distracting her from focused dedication to her art. She marched with the militant NAACP youth and also joined other Cre-Lit members in articulating her personal poetic credo: "Think how many fascinating human documents there would be now, if all the great poets had written of what happened to them personally—and of the thoughts that occurred to them, no matter how ugly, . . . fantastic, . . . seemingly ridiculous!"[23] The road from the Cre-Lit Club to her first collection, A Street in Bronzeville (1945), led through the Community Art Center's poetry workshop led by Inez Cunningham Stark, who in addition to serving as president of the Renaissance Society was a reader for Poetry. In the early 1940s, Brooks's finely wrought poems about the people and places of Bronzeville began gaining much attention.

Wright, Davis, Attaway, Walker, Bontemps, Motley, and Brooks met and collaborated in such settings as the Abraham Lincoln Centre, the George Cleveland Hall Library, the National Negro Congress, the South Side Writers' Group, the Community Art Center, Parkway Community House, and the Illinois Writers' Project. Besides publishing in black newspapers and Abbott's Monthly, they helped create and published in little magazines such as Challenge, New Challenge, and Negro Story. They sought to ground their work in the realities of African American life, above all in the transformations wrought by the great movement from South to North, field to factory. As literary artists, they laid claim to a broad and multifaceted cultural heritage: black folk traditions and vernacular forms of expression, the free verse of Sandburg and Hughes, the naturalistic novels of Dreiser and Farrell, and the formal innovations of transatlantic modernism. Through their work, Bronzeville entered African American letters as the most representative destination of the Great Migration and as metaphor for cultural flux and confrontation, racial aspiration and disillusion.

The South Side Writers' Group

Wright's poem "I Have Seen Black Hands" is built from densely clustered images of suffering and unrest, which limn the stages of black plebian life from infancy through adolescent recklessness to the thwarted maturity of unemployed laborers whose desperate outbursts are suppressed by prisons or lynch mobs. A brief peroration invokes a vision of militant unity between black and white workers. In the city where the July 1919 bloodbath was living memory, such a vision might have seemed sheer Marxist fantasy were it not coincident with the formation of interracial unions and the massive organizing drives of the CIO.

As the idea of working-class unity across racial and ethnic lines rumbled through midwestern packing houses, steel mills, and automobile plants, Bronzeville hosted a conference described by one participant as "an Olympian protest against racial injustice." Representing trade unions, civil rights organizations, fraternal orders, religious bodies, and civic associations, nearly a thousand delegates met for three days in February 1936 to forge a boldly inclusive alliance of African American groups. Red-lettered banners hung from the walls of the Eighth Regiment Armory: "Defend the Sharecroppers from Landlord Terror"; "Defend Ethiopia from Fascist Invasion and Imperialism"; "Black America Demands an End to Lynching, Mob Violence and Racial Persecution." Speakers included Langston Hughes, Socialist Party leader Norman Thomas, NAACP executive Roy Wilkins, and

Angelo Herndon, a black communist indicted in Georgia for "incitement to insurrection." A. Philip Randolph, preeminent black trade union leader of the era, was elected president in absentia. His statement to the Congress linked racial and class oppression: "Because Negroes are black, they are hated, maligned and spat upon. Because Negroes are workers, they are brow-beaten, bullied, intimidated, robbed, exploited, jailed and shot down."[24]

At this gathering, Richard Wright chaired a panel on "Negro Artists and Writers in the Changing Social Order," sharing the podium with Langston Hughes and Arna Bontemps. The latter outlined the formidable challenges faced by African American writers and urged his audience to support them by reading their books.[25] Afterward Wright circulated among the South Side intellectuals, testing their readiness to form a writers' club. Margaret Walker had come to see Hughes again, four years after they first met in New Orleans. Introducing her to Wright, Hughes added: "If you people really get a group together, don't forget to include this girl."[26] Wright found a receptive audience for his initiative, and the South Side Writers' Group held its first meeting in May.

With Wright as guiding spirit, some twenty black writers, most in the apprentice stage of their careers, met on alternate Sundays to read and criticize each other's work.[27] Participants included writers Wright, Davis, Bontemps, and Walker, playwright/sculptor Marion Perkins, aspiring literary critic Edward Bland, social worker and native Kansan Fern Gayden, playwright Ted Ward (originally from Louisiana), communist youth leader Claude Lightfoot (born in Arkansas), poet Robert Davis (originally from Mobile, Alabama), and anthropology student Marian Minus. They were joined on occasion by the older poet Fenton Johnson.

Walker vividly recalled the first meeting. She arrived late and flustered, just in time to hear Wright "expounding on the sad state of Negro writing . . . and punctuating his remarks with pungent epithets." She "drew back in Sunday school horror, totally shocked by his strong speech."[28] Over the next three years, the sharecropper's son from Mississippi repeatedly shocked the minister's daughter from New Orleans by pretending to drink excessive amounts of beer one day and offering to teach her how to shoplift on another. Her innocence brought out his mischievous side; his worldly confidence stimulated increasingly amorous feelings on her part.[29]

Wright also challenged a state of intellectual innocence that persisted beyond Walker's undergraduate years: "The whole thing sank in gradually that he was a Communist," she recalled. "I honestly didn't know what communism or Marxism meant. I had had no courses in sociology, economics, nor political science." When Wright discovered her ignorance of not only Marxism but also much of literary modernism, he prepared a series of reading lists that she pursued for several years. Wright suggested many works: in the realm of radical politics, John Reed's *Ten Days That Shook the World* and Marx's *Capital*; in modernist fiction, novels by Joyce, Proust, Faulkner, and Stein; among the naturalists, Crane, Dreiser, and Farrell. In poetry, Wright favored Whitman, Yeats, Eliot, Masters, and Sandburg.[30] Walker's literary and political horizons broadened through this course of reading, meetings of the South Side Writers' Group, and informal discussions at Writers' Project offices and studio parties. In the fall of 1937, she joined the Communist Party.[31]

Wright's strenuous autodidacticism, intellectual boldness, and Marxist politics opened a broad realm of new ideas to Walker and other members of the Writers' Group. Even as he sought the guidance of prominent academics such as Louis Wirth, he aroused curiosity, and perhaps ire, among his college-educated colleagues about all that was missing from their conventional academic training.

Meeting in a classroom at Abraham Lincoln Centre where Ted Ward taught speech and drama, the group proved a rich environment for young writers.[32] Ward was working on his first major play, *Big White Fog*, produced by the Chicago unit of the Federal Theater Project in 1938.[33] Wright brought drafts of essays and such stories as "Long Black Song" and "Down by the Riverside," which appeared in his first book, *Uncle Tom's Children*.[34] Davis recalled that after Wright read "Big Boy Leaves Home," "nobody spoke for several minutes. We were too much moved by his power." Davis himself read "I Am the American Negro," the long title poem of his second collection, published in 1937.[35] Walker shared drafts of poems in which she turned attention toward the black masses and her southern roots and began to shape her distinctive approach to free verse. Many of these pieces later appeared in her first collection, *For My People* (1942).[36] Davis also remembered her reading "a chapter from a historical novel she had begun."[37]

Although the South Side Writers' Group met for less than two years, dissolving sometime after Wright's departure for New York, its importance for African American letters far surpasses its brief life span.[38] Like George Neal's Art Crafts Guild, it proved to be a seedbed for the flowering of creative expression in Bronzeville and beyond. Many participants in the Writers' Group, like Guild members, found employment on the WPA cultural projects, won fellowships to further their careers, and played important roles in advancing African American culture. By the time Wright left Chicago in May 1937, he had completed two novels (neither published in his lifetime) and the stories that comprised *Uncle Tom's Children*.[39] His writing and organizational initiatives were influencing Chicago writers, black and white, and, through his achievements and those of his colleagues, Bronzeville's influence soon extended across the nation.

Bronzeville's "Blueprint"

The Writers' Group served as not only workshop for novice writers honing their craft but also testing ground for ideas. Eighteen months after Walker first heard Wright "expounding on the sad state of Negro writing," theories that had been vetted in the group were broadcast in a declaration of generational independence. In H. L. Mencken, Wright first encountered a writer "using words as a weapon, using them as one would use a club."[40] This early lesson informed the opening lines of "Blueprint for Negro Writing": "Generally speaking, Negro writing in the past has been confined to humble novels, poems, and plays, prim and decorous ambassadors who went a-begging to white America . . . dressed in the knee-pants of servility, curtsying to show that the Negro was not inferior, that he was human, and that he had a life comparable to that of other people. For the most part these artistic ambassadors were received as though they were French poodles who do clever tricks."[41] "Blueprint" was meant to drive the last nail into the coffin of the Harlem Renaissance and to rally younger writers around a new aesthetic that joined realistic writing with literary experimentation, radical politics, and organic connection to the lives and language of the black masses.

Wright's essay appeared in *New Challenge*, a journal published in New York in 1937 but unmistakably bearing Bronzeville's imprint. Dorothy West, a Boston-based writer of the Harlem Renaissance generation, had launched its predecessor, *Challenge*, in March 1934, hoping to spark "a rebirth" among New Negro writers as well as to encourage "newer voices."[42] Its six issues had done a bit of both but failed to develop a consistent editorial policy. By 1937 West was looking leftward toward Wright's circle in Chicago. Her March editorial noted the group's "considerable dispraise" of *Challenge* and proposed "a special section in a forthcoming issue that they may show us what we have not done by showing us what they can do." West's offer to Wright was brokered by their mutual friend Marian Minus, a former member of the South Side Writers' Group.[43]

Wright eagerly accepted the opportunity to recreate *Challenge* as an African American literary journal with a Marxist orientation, supported by the Popular Front apparatus of bookstores, organizations, and publications but beyond the Communist Party's direct control. He heralded the journal's transformation in an article for the *Daily Worker*, which had hired him as Harlem correspondent shortly after his move to New York. His piece described a "new audience" for African American writing: "Negro workers, students and intellectuals . . . touched by recent social and economic changes." Wright identified his Chicago colleagues as "the first group whose aims were to render the life of their race in social and realistic terms" and recounted efforts to create a national network "similar . . . to . . . the old John Reed Clubs" and to establish *New Challenge* "as its organ of expression."[44]

When the journal appeared in October, West and Minus were listed as editors; Wright was merely associate editor, a designation that prompted a "surprised" Margaret Walker to offer her sympathy at such an obvious slighting of her friend's central role.[45] Six members of the South Side Writers' Group appeared as *New Challenge* contributors and/or editors, joined by a carefully culled roster of Left-leaning writers, including poet Robert Hayden and poet/dramatist Owen Dodson. Langston Hughes contributed a translation of a Spanish poem. Alain Locke reviewed Claude McKay's latest work, castigating him for "spiritual truancy and social irresponsibility." Sterling Brown contributed "Old Lem," a poem in which a sharecropper speaks of his hardscrabble life. Brown's 1932 collection, *Southern Road*, had pointed a way toward crafting poetry from folk materials and vernacular expression while challenging the demeaning association of dialect poetry with minstrelsy.[46] *New Challenge* included a book review by Ralph Ellison, his first published piece. The former Tuskegee music student moved to New York in 1936, studied sculpture with Richmond Barthé, deepened his musical skills, and entered the orbit of the Communist Party. He met Wright almost immediately upon the latter's arrival in the city and acquired a close friend and mentor, who convinced him that he could write.[47]

Ellison also produced a short story about a black hobo, a piece intended for the journal's second issue, but *New Challenge* 2 never appeared. Evidently piqued at Wright's aggressive approach and disdain for the Harlem generation with which she identified, West withdrew her financial support. Wright was unable to find sufficient support in Party circles or elsewhere to keep the journal afloat.[48] He had succeeded, however, in bringing together elders Locke, Brown, and Hughes, the Chicago group, and other rising writers around his political and aesthetic vision: nominally proletarian but more deeply rooted in the fist-in-the-face nationalism of Bronzeville's migrant masses, descended from literary naturalism but deeply influenced by transatlantic modernism.

Questions of audience, subject matter, and "perspective" lay at the heart of "Blueprint for Negro Writing." The literary manifesto faulted earlier African American writers for addressing "a small white audience" rather than "the Negro masses." Wright's experiences on the South Side in the tumultuous 1930s underpinned his faith in the "consciousness and mobility" of "Negro workers." He argued that black writers must acknowledge "the nationalist character of the Negro people" and "the emotional expression of group-feeling" built upon a separate "Negro way of life in America." If the apogee of consciousness was reached among recently proletarianized blacks in northern cities, then their cultural roots lay in the rural South, especially in the black church and folklore. Wright urged young writers to draw inspiration from "the fluid lore of a great people," to "accept" nationalism and folk culture "in order to change and transcend them."[49] He intended the poems and stories in New Challenge as well as his own fiction to illustrate these views.

"Blueprint" contains a passage that illuminates Wright's personal struggle to be both a loyal Communist Party member and a professional writer: "Negro writers should seek through the medium of their craft to play as meaningful a role in the affairs of men as do other professionals [italics added]. But if their writing is demanded to perform the social office of other professions, then the autonomy of craft is lost. . . . If the sensory vehicle of imaginative writing is required to carry too great a load of didactic material, the artistic sense is submerged."[50] Eventually Wright reached a modus vivendi with the leadership. He retained nominal membership and contributed to Party-affiliated publications and initiatives such as the League of American Writers, but he was free of day-to-day organizational duties while he pursued his writing and ventures such as the Writers' Group and New Challenge.

Wright's attempts to join aesthetic theory and literary practice were reflected in the four novellas that comprise the first edition of Uncle Tom's Children, published in March 1938.[51] These stories spotlight conditions driving African Americans from the South. The characters endure floods, malnutrition, and physical and spiritual violation. They are beaten, raped, shot down, tarred and feathered, whipped, and burned alive. A "long river of blood" haunts Sarah, female protagonist of "Long Black Song": "White men killed the black men because they could, and the black men killed the white men to keep from being killed."[52] All four pieces explore "the nationalist character of the Negro people," which emerged in response to such conditions, and three protagonists kill white men in attempts to defend their lives and dignity.

In several stories, church members, assisting beleaguered brothers and sisters, provide physical relief, moral support, or a veil of secrecy. Wright's treatment of the church as central to "the emotional expression of group-feeling" entails literary attention to the sacred side of the vernacular tradition: sermons and prayers, some in call-and-response mode. Two story titles, "Fire and Cloud" and "Down by the Riverside," derive from spirituals, and singing of the sorrow songs at gatherings evokes the long line of descent that links these characters to unknown forebears. The secular side is evidenced in the ritualized insults of "the dozens" in "Big Boy Leaves Home," in the lullaby Sarah sings to her baby daughter, the tales of trailing blood hounds and other terrors, and the received wisdom that counsels subterfuge rather than direct confrontation with overwhelming white power.

Uncle Tom's Children is not without the flaws of apprentice work and sometimes bears "too great a load of didactic material." The sudden appearance of poor whites joining an interracial protest march near the end of "Fire and Cloud" seems little more than a *Marxus ex machina*. Certain turns of plot in "Down by the Riverside" likewise strain credulity. At times folk materials appear grafted onto rather than organically emerging from plot and characterization. But overall, in its compelling dialogue, crackling narrative tension, rendering of characters' inner states, and use of realistic details to create symbolic resonance, the collection signaled the greatness to come. Its publication, taken in conjunction with the appearance of *New Challenge* and "Blueprint for Negro Writing," represented a turning point. The writers of Bronzeville had seized the initiative and were manifestly in the ascendancy.

Creating the "New Audience"

"Blueprint for Negro Writers" focuses on two central issues: truthful rendering of African American experience by those most familiar with its varied manifestations and creation of a broad audience of black readers for black writers. Contributors to *New Challenge* were committed to representing African American life with greater realism than their predecessors, and some of their attempts are examined in the following chapters. The first issue for consideration, however, is Wright's question: "Shall Negro writing be for the Negro masses?"[53] What sorts of cultural changes and institutions might have quickened his hope that a "new audience" could develop among a predominantly migrant population only a few years removed from rural backwaters and ramshackle schoolhouses?

The Bronzeville reading public supported five weekly newspapers, and Chicago writers as different as Gwendolyn Brooks and Willard Motley received their first exposure through the black press. Reading a newspaper and reading a book, however, especially a work of imaginative literature, are two very different experiences. Charles Johnson reported that only "twenty-five per cent of the homes [in one area of rural Alabama] had some reading matter," mostly "popular magazines and rural life journals." "There are, of course, no libraries," he added, quoting one black youth who borrowed books from the county agent: "If I didn't have these . . . to read, I don't know what I'd do. Things are so dry around here, but with these books to read it seems as if I go into another world entirely. . . . Some day I am going to get away from this place and go where they have some real libraries."[54] While living in Memphis, Wright invented a ploy to borrow books from a segregated library. Not only did he have to pretend to fetch books for a white man, but, to allay the librarian's suspicion that he might read them, the youth had to feign illiteracy as well. He significantly, linked his "hunger . . . for books" with a desire to move north.[55] In Chicago the libraries were open to all, but, when Wright arrived, the South Side did not have a local branch.

That changed in January 1932 when George Cleveland Hall Branch Library opened its doors. With a limestone exterior following Italian Renaissance design, Hall Branch was "said to be the most beautiful in the city."[56] A stone-arched entranceway opened into an octagonal rotunda from which radiated four well-appointed reading rooms. This minor miracle of the Depression was named for the African American surgeon who had served as chief of staff at Provident Hospital until his death in 1930. In the 1920s, Hall was appointed to the Board of the Chicago Public Library and began pressing for a branch library to serve South Side blacks. After protracted negotiations, the board agreed to construct the facility on a plot at Forty-eighth and South Michigan that had been donated by Julius Rosenwald.

Vivian G. Harsh was appointed head librarian, a post she held for twenty-six years. The daughter of two Fisk University graduates, she was born in Chicago in 1890 and initially served as a junior library clerk. She completed a degree in library science in 1921

20. Vivian G. Harsh, c. 1933.
Vivian G. Harsh Research Collection of Afro-American History and Literature,
Chicago Public Library. Hall Branch Archives 019.

and, three years later, became the first African American appointed branch librarian in Chicago. In preparation for her duties as director of the new library, she traveled to several cities in 1931, visiting libraries that served black communities, among them Harlem's 135th Street branch. Active in the Association for the Study of Negro Life and History, she had for some years collected rare books, pamphlets, periodicals, and manuscripts that document African American history. When Hall Branch opened, these became the basis for a Special Negro Collection that Harsh and children's librarian Charlemae Rollins worked tirelessly to expand.[57]

In a speech about Hall Branch, Harsh emphasized efforts to "arouse parents' interests in their children's reading." As "the chief adult activity," she highlighted the Book Review and Lecture Forum, begun in October 1933 "to enrich the leisure time of those who desire to be informed in a cultural and literary way, . . . to draw attention to books and authors and to discover and develop local talent."[58] A committee, including South Side Writers' Group members Margaret Walker and Russell Marshall, planned and advertised its biweekly programs, and attendance climbed steadily, averaging fifty people per meeting in 1937.[59] Guest speakers in the 1930s and 1940s included William Attaway, Arna Bontemps, Gwendolyn Brooks, Horace Cayton, St. Clair Drake, Langston Hughes, Zora Neale Hurston, Alain Locke, Margaret Walker, and Richard Wright. Under Harsh's direction, Hall Branch became an active research and cultural center serving both neighborhood residents and black intellectuals from around the country.

Another important institution was Parkway Community House, directed by Horace Cayton. Besides essential social services, the center provided adult literacy classes, story hours for children, a lending library, cultural outings, and topical reading packets complementing the Parkway Forum lecture series—initiatives intended to make Bronzeville a community of readers. One of the center's meeting rooms hosted the Chicago Poets' Class, which had begun at the Art Center under direction of Inez Cunningham Stark but moved to Parkway sometime after she left Chicago.[60] Prominent intellectuals and artists such as Langston Hughes, Marian Anderson, and Paul Robeson presented well-attended lectures, readings, and performances.[61]

Hughes made a notable contribution by helping found the Skyloft Players as an inhouse theatrical company. He began an extended stay at Parkway in November 1941 after one of the darkest periods of his life. Despite undeniable fame and twenty years in the writers' trade, Hughes had suffered major career setbacks and lost the lease on his Harlem apartment. With a bank balance of $1.20, he was rescued from penury by award of a Rosenwald fellowship. A bed at Parkway, an office at Rosenwald Fund headquarters, and the ample, tasty meals prepared by Alberta Bontemps helped keep Hughes's weary blues at bay while he worked on *The Sun Do Move*, a stirring musical drama about a black soldier in the Union army.[62] The play opened in April 1942 to a packed house. Under their first director, Helen Spaulding, the Skyloft Players produced many more plays at Parkway and at churches, schools, and other community institutions. They sponsored playwriting, essay, and speech contests, performed on the radio, recommended books and authors, and taught classes in acting and stagecraft.[63]

21. Two actors with Langston Hughes discussing script
of new play for Skyloft Players, 1942.
Photo: Jack Delano. Library of Congress, Prints & Photographs Division,
FSA-OWI Collection. LC-USW3–000677-D.

Another Bronzeville-based institution that helped create a new audience for black writing was *Negro Story* magazine, launched in 1944 by Alice Browning and Fern Gayden. Browning was a Chicago native, prominent in African American social circles, a public school teacher, and fiction writer. Stung by a rejection slip from *Esquire*, she conceived the idea of an African American periodical modeled on Whit Burnett's popular *Story* magazine. Browning and Gayden enlisted prominent community members as financial sponsors, members of the Chicago Poets' Class agreed to contribute, and Langston Hughes accepted an invitation to serve as advisor. In March Richard Wright was a guest at Parkway, and Cayton told him about the young women's plans. Over dinner, they asked Wright's help in launching the journal, and he offered reprint rights to "Almos' a Man," which had appeared in *Harper's* in 1940. He also promised to solicit support among friends in New York and to introduce them to Jack Conroy, a white Chicago writer known as editor of Leftist literary journals and as author of the proletarian novels *The Disinherited* (1933) and *A World to Win* (1935).[64]

Browning and Gayden bought some scarce paper stock from the *Defender* and launched *Negro Story* in May. Their first editorial encouraged "stories about Negroes who are real people rather than the types usually seen in print" and expressed optimism "that Negroes have a great opportunity to achieve integration with the best elements of our society."[65] The July editorial cautioned against propagandistic tendencies inherent in "protest" writing but did not eschew socially committed literature, offering as models the novels of Richard Wright and William Attaway, whose "characters . . . help to eradicate the stereotypes in American thinking."[66] In a letter published in the second number, English professor S. I. Hayakawa wrote: "Obviously the time is ripe for such a magazine. The Negro reading public is expanding as more and more people become aware that ideas are weapons in the long, hard struggle for equality."[67]

Many of *Negro Story*'s readers wielded more lethal weapons. The editors identified "our men overseas and in camps" as part of the growing market for black writing and urged readers to send them subscriptions.[68] Contributing authors were often identified by military rank or service branch. Every issue contained at least one story in which the war provided an essential plot element, and more typically three or four used a military setting. These stories ranged widely across genres. Tales of wartime romance and infidelity showed the strong generic influence of popular love-story magazines. Other pieces were realistic, sometimes resembling the plotless sketches found in Leftist journals of the 1930s and often focusing on racist treatment of black soldiers.

Chester Himes, however, translated his indignation into comic plots dependent on role reversals and mutual incomprehension and narrated in the argot of 1940s hipsters. An editorial described his stories as "our most popular," leaving "everyone in the camps in 'stitches.'"[69] Alongside work by aspiring writers whose futures lay elsewhere, Himes's pieces mark the unfolding of a significant talent. His earliest stories had appeared in another Chicago periodical, *Abbott's Monthly*, in 1932 and 1933, and a Rosenwald fellowship in 1944 helped him complete his first novel, *If He Hollers Let Him Go*, published the following year.

Ralph Ellison also contributed several pieces to *Negro Story*, eventually joining Himes and Langston Hughes on the advisory board. An editorial lauded Ellison as "one of the coming writers, [who] will undoubtedly be one of our important young American authors."[70] Other "coming writers" published in the journal included Frank Marshall Davis, Margaret Walker, and Gwendolyn Brooks.

Browning entered the second year of publication without Gayden as coeditor, but with impressively ambitious plans: addition of drama and music sections, a magazine for children, *Negro Story* Clubs in Chicago and New York, and generous literary prizes. The six bimonthly issues of the first year gave way, however, to an erratic publication schedule, as it became clear that Browning had outstripped her financial and human resources. The ninth and final issue appeared in April 1946. For two years, *Negro Story*—published from Browning's South Side home—was a focal point of black writing in America, providing an opportunity for apprentice writers to hone their craft, gain national exposure, and join other young writers in creating a new audience for black literature as the nation and race faced the postwar era.

Later in the 1940s, many Bronzeville residents had their first exposure to Richard Wright, Gwendolyn Brooks, and other black authors not through print media or readings at Parkway or Hall Branch but through the era's most popular medium, radio. Local stations with limited transmission range had offered black-appeal entertainment throughout the 1930s, but, as booming wartime industries sparked a second migratory wave and higher incomes among black Chicagoans, national networks began to take notice.[71] Radio programming for black audiences reached an important milestone with the June 27, 1948, premier of *Destination Freedom* on NBC's Chicago affiliate, WMAQ. The brainchild of Mississippi-born Richard Durham, this weekly series dramatized the struggles and achievements of black creative artists, rebels, political and religious leaders, scholars and educators, entertainers, explorers, scientists, and athletes.[72]

Durham undertook to not only entertain but also educate his audience by presenting historically accurate portrayals that challenged demeaning stereotypes. This necessitated a fight for creative control, which began with the first broadcast, a dramatization of Crispus Attucks's fatal confrontation with British soldiers in Boston. In a letter to the program's white producer/director, Durham criticized his encouragement of the lead actor to display "a certain humbleness." "Your Attucks," the writer complained, "had somewhat the approach of an intelligent pullman porter. Not the biting, fighting hero which would have carried the audience with him. . . . This 'get sympathy' approach is rarely a fact in a dramatic hero who is initiating his own moves and conscious of his direction."[73]

For two years, Durham spent long hours at Hall Branch researching his scripts, pouring over books and documents suggested by Vivian Harsh. *Destination Freedom* emphasized the liberating potential of education, which led one contemporary to note: "Mr. Durham constantly attacks the attitude that 'books and schools are for white folks.'"[74] In a 1949 interview, the writer observed that "somewhere in this ocean of Negro life, with its cross-currents and under-currents, lies the very soul of America." He emphasized a need to "shatter the conventions and traditions which have prevented us from dramatizing the infinite store of material from the history and current struggles for freedom."[75] Durham's commitment to documenting the centrality of African American experience within American history can be traced, at least in part, to one of the institutions where he honed his skills, for, like most of Bronzeville's finest authors, he was a veteran of the Illinois Writers' Project.

The Illinois Writers' Project and the Documentary Spirit

Henry Alsberg became first director of the Federal Writers' Project in July 1935 and was beset by controversy throughout four years in that position. In a few months, Project ranks swelled to exceed 6,500 employees scattered across the nation: impoverished novelists and poets, jobless academics from various disciplines, radical pamphleteers, unemployed journalists, researchers, technical writers, lawyers, and librarians—united only by economic need and their experience, however minimal, in preparing some sort of written material for an audience.[76] Although total expenditures for the Writers' Project between 1935 and 1943 amounted to less than $26 million, a tiny fraction of the $3 billion spent by the WPA as a whole, the agency drew disproportionate public attention.[77] As Alsberg and his staff undertook their massive task, conservative politicians and newspaper editors, violently hostile to the entire New Deal, accused agency employees of inefficiency, incompetence, and/or disseminating communist propaganda. The campaign gained intensity with formation of Martin Dies's House Committee on Un-American Activities in 1938, and Alsberg was forced to resign the following year.[78]

A shambling bear of a man in his mid-fifties, Alsberg brought to this challenging position an eclectic background in law, journalism, and theater, as well as a genial philosophical anarchism. He had once found a natural habitat in pre–World War I Greenwich Village, where his friends Van Wyck Brooks, Waldo Frank, and Alfred Kreymborg trumpeted the need for spiritual rebirth of the nation through its arts. The pointless slaughter in Europe and postwar pressures for conformity only deepened the alienation of younger intellectuals. While some fled to the cosmopolitan centers of the Continent, the Americanist avant-garde turned attention toward the multiple cultural streams that flowed into a common American identity. Alsberg's own commitment to cultural pluralism was evident in his work in the little theater movement. As producer and director, he helped bring to the off-Broadway stage both his own adaptation of the famous Yiddish play *The Dybbuk* and Paul Green's antiracist drama *In Abraham's Bosom*. In rough outline, cultural nationalism and pluralism shaped the intellectual perspective that Alsberg and his top administrators brought to the Federal Writers' Project.[79]

Much had changed in the cultural scene during the years immediately preceding Alsberg's appointment. Granville Hicks, a prominent Marxist critic in the period, recalled that in the 1920s few "literary and artistic people" were "directly interested in politics," but during the Depression, "This business civilization that we had been belaboring on cultural and moral grounds had collapsed." Realizing that "something fundamental" had to be done, many creative artists and intellectuals looked to some form of socialism for a solution.[80] Although nothing could have dislodged Gertrude Stein from France or T. S. Eliot from England, many other expatriates began returning home, retrospectively questioning what critic Malcolm Cowley labeled "the religion of art."[81]

Such changes were echoed among African American intellectuals, as evidenced by a 1935 letter from Charles Johnson to his friend Claude Barnett, director of the Associated Negro Press: "Locke has misread or unread my Shadow of the Plantation to the point of finding it an apology for the system!" complained the famously reserved sociologist. "Negro reviewers who wish to have themselves regarded as economic radicals see some dire implication in the fact that the study was made possible by [the Rosenwald] Fund, . . . suggesting that our research . . . therefore is warped." Johnson reiterated his "utter conviction of the . . . inherently exploitative character of the plantation tenancy system, and the necessity if not inevitability of its destruction." He added, "The thing that riles me is that a conviction arrived at after six years of deliberate investigation in the cotton country can be distorted . . . by pink tea radicals who have never even been South . . . or contributed one mite more to change than a grotesque parroting of an economic philosophy heard third or fourth hand."[82] Some seven years after Johnson and Locke collaborated to organize and publicize the Harlem Renaissance, Locke was publicly sniping at what he called Johnson's "evasive and wheedling gradualism," and Johnson was privately seething at the affront.[83] Locke had moved significantly left while Johnson, in alliance with Edwin Embree and Will Alexander, still pursued a southern-centered strategy of interracial diplomacy and gradual social change.[84]

Prominent black radical Richard Wright played a key role at the second American Writers Congress, held in New York in June 1937. Chairing a panel on contemporary fiction, he warmly introduced panelist Henry Alsberg as "a man who has been associated with one of the most interesting experiments in the history of America."[85] This experiment involved the creation of literary work for unemployed writers at government expense and the equally challenging task of minimizing political opposition from the Right. Alsberg was largely responsible for the American Guide Series, born of the pragmatic need for an undertaking safe enough to deflect further controversy and simple enough that "writers" with minimal or narrow training could fulfill the task. Ostensibly a set of tourist guidebooks, the forty-eight state volumes were intended to gather the raw materials of American history and culture and record the ebb and flow of the nation's life with Whitmanesque inclusiveness. Each state guide followed a standard format, and draft materials, reviewed at state level, were forwarded to the national office for further scrutiny. The production process was sometimes contentious, and published guides ruffled more than a few feathers among local boosters or perennial New Deal opponents. Yet they were remarkable achievements in their comprehensive detail and excellent prose.[86]

In its attempts to document American life, however, the Writers' Project confronted forces, both inside and outside the agency, that would obscure or distort aspects of that reality, especially the real experiences of African Americans. Committed to cultural inclusiveness, Alsberg appointed Howard University professor Sterling Brown as national editor of Negro affairs. For four years, the poet and critic devoted himself to ensuring adequate and accurate coverage of black history and culture and to increasing black employment on the Project. Keenly aware that "The Negro has too seldom been revealed as an integral part of American life," Brown struggled against the tendency to either render blacks invisible or represent them stereotypically. Under his leadership, the Project launched ambitious book-length studies intended to create "a portrait of the American Negro, from earliest days to the present; . . . socially interpretive . . . and accurate; not stodgy but graphic and popular in the best sense."[87] Although he did not win all his battles, Brown won enough to make the publications and research files of the Writers' Project invaluable sources of information about black life on this side of the Middle Passage.[88]

The Illinois unit, directed by John T. Frederick, undertook one such study.[89] An Iowa farmer's son with a passion for regional literature, Frederick taught English at Northwestern, wrote novels, and had promoted midwestern authors since founding an influential journal, *The Midland*, in 1915. Sixteen years later, Frederick moved his journal from Iowa City to Chicago. An editorial citing the city's rich literary tradition asserted that "Chicago seems among American cities most likely to make a challenge to New York's domination immediately effective."[90] Elsewhere he linked the rich diversity of regional literatures with "the work of writers of various large ethnic groups not characteristically expressed in previous decades" and assigned special importance to African American writers.[91] In March 1936, the Illinois Writers' Project employed some two hundred writers, nine of them black, a small percentage but higher than any other state. Eventually at least twenty-three blacks served in the state unit, primarily in Chicago.[92]

Richard Wright was a supervisor in the Chicago office. Shortly before moving to New York, he wrote to Sterling Brown proposing a study of the Negro in Illinois, but he left it to others to carry the work forward.[93] Chief among them was his friend Arna Bontemps. As principal of a Seventh-Day Adventist school, Bontemps was chafing at the same narrow-mindedness he had encountered at similar institutions in New York and Alabama. Forced to choose between losing his job and abandoning "the Devil's work" of imaginative literature, he sought a position on the Writers' Project. Impressed by Bontemps's novel *Black Thunder*, Frederick leaped at the opportunity, bringing him in as one of the approximately 10 percent of experienced writers exempted from the stringent means test (or "pauper's oath") normally required of project employees.[94] Bontemps joined several acquaintances from the South Side Writers' Group as well as such talented white writers as Jack Conroy, Nelson Algren, Sam Ross, Studs Terkel, and Saul Bellow.[95]

Conroy and Bontemps became good friends. "Our desks were about twenty feet apart," Bontemps recalled. "We were both employed as editorial supervisors. . . . Katherine Dunham, Richard Wright, Frank Yerby . . . had worked at these same desks just weeks or months earlier, and some of them returned occasionally to see how things were going."[96] Conroy wrote: "I found myself ensconced with Arna in the former Rosenwald mansion on the South Side as his co-supervisor on a project slated to produce a volume to be called *The Negro in Illinois*. . . . The Rosenwald Foundation was [co-]sponsoring [the] venture." Their offices were separated by a hallway, "down which our field-workers came to report and to deposit the fruits of their labors." Digging through musty files of long-defunct publications, researchers gradually "aggregated a rather comprehensive social history of the colored citizen and his conditions and also yielded significant evidence of prevailing white attitudes toward him." They also conducted interviews and first-hand observations. Conroy described, for example, how "one of our alert Negro field-workers managed not only to obtain the [Moorish-American Science Temple]'s secret rituals but also to be accepted as a member and to take part in some of the meetings."[97]

In this heady atmosphere, diverse academic backgrounds, work histories, aesthetic currents, and political ideologies fruitfully contributed to what is described herein as the documentary mode. In terms of research methods, for example, Dunham's training in anthropological fieldwork complemented the more archival orientation of English major (and future librarian) Bontemps. Conroy, a coal miner's son and self-described "pick and shovel stiff," was largely self-educated and had worked whatever jobs he could while learning the writer's craft. His impeccable working-class credentials and gift for storytelling served him well when Frederick assigned him to collect "industrial folklore"—the tall tales, jokes, and dramatic personal stories that laborers share either in barroom camaraderie or during the workday's tedium. Wright helped lay the basis for the *Negro in Illinois* study with an amateur sociological essay, "Ethnographical Aspects of Chicago's Black Belt." The documentary mission and perceived social utility of the project's work engaged the energies of anthropologist Dunham, cautious race man Bontemps, avowedly proletarian writers Algren, Conroy, and Wright, and literary regionalist Frederick in productive joint enterprise.

While Wright considered government employment of artists a radical social experiment, Algren observed that the Project "gave new life to people who had thought their lives were over . . . [and] lost their self-respect by being out of work. . . . The WPA provided a place where they began to communicate with people again."[98] Bontemps observed that the agency sparked a "revitalization of old timers like the poet Fenton Johnson," who was about fifty when he was hired.[99] Johnson's voice had been silent for nearly two decades when he joined the Writers' Project and began visiting the South Side Writers' Group. His contributions to the *Negro in Illinois* files indicate that he played an important role in researching and writing essays on African American history in Chicago. One day, in the course of delivering field notes to Conroy, Johnson surprised his supervisor "with a sheaf of poems—enough to make a small volume." Bontemps and Conroy excitedly began discussing the possibility of helping their colleague find a publisher, "but Johnson never came back, and inquiry at his rooming house revealed that he had departed without leaving a forwarding address."[100] In 1967 Bontemps responded to a query about Johnson: "He died in an institution a decade or two ago and his manuscript poems were given to me. . . . He left no heirs. . . . His last job, I believe, was under my supervision in the Illinois Writers' Project." Johnson's last collection was never published.[101]

With strong administrative leadership and a significant number of published authors, including editorial supervisors Algren, Bontemps, Conroy, Dunham, and Wright, the agency's Chicago office proved a rich training ground for aspiring writers. On their project hours, they collected and edited information about Illinois, its various municipalities, and its people. On their own time, they reworked these materials into other forms: novels, short stories, poems, popular histories, juveniles, folklore collections, and newspaper and magazine articles. Benjamin Botkin, the Project's national folklore director, observed that work on the guides "trained writers to record what they heard as well as what they saw with an ear for the characteristic phrase and rhythm of the vernacular."[102] Working in a milieu where social history was quickened by the literary imagination and where the literary imagination was nourished by close, careful observation, Wright and his colleagues learned to move fluidly between imaginative literature and the literature of fact. A tall tale might appear in the folklore section of *Illinois: A Descriptive and Historical Guide* and later be transmuted into fictional form for young readers, as in Conroy's and Bontemps's collaborations *The Fast Sooner Hound* (1942) and *Slappy Hooper, The Wonderful Sign Painter* (1946). Wright published his first piece of journalism, "Joe Louis Uncovers Dynamite," while he was working on the project. His story "Big Boy Leaves Home" was included in the prestigious 1936 anthology *New Caravan*, edited by Alfred Kreymborg, Lewis Mumford, and Paul Rosenfeld. It was the first time his work appeared in a book, and Margaret Walker recalled how "his eyes shone with pride" as he unwrapped the book at his office "with an audience to appreciate his first major success as a prose writer."[103]

As a supervisor, Wright had to be in the office each day, but Walker enjoyed greater latitude: "I went downtown twice weekly with my assignments on the *Illinois Guide Book*. . . . I worked at home and went looking for news stories or covered art exhibits and made reports." She was eventually given a highly coveted creative writing assignment, allowing her to work fulltime on a novel and submit draft chapters as project assignments.[104] The manuscript was titled *Goose Island* after the poor Italian and African American neighborhood on the North Side where Walker had lived during her senior year at Northwestern. The seedy neighborhood with its petty criminals, tenements, and giant rats became the setting for a novel patterned on Emile Zola's *L'Assommoir*, the urtext of literary naturalism.[105] While volunteering for a WPA recreation program, Walker had befriended "a group of so-called delinquent girls . . . , primarily . . . shoplifters and prostitutes. Division Street was the street for prostitutes, and I saw them there at night, jangling their keys as they walked."[106] Walker was appalled and fascinated by these "painted" women, as she called them in her poem "Whores." She later described the protagonist of her unpublished novel as "a very talented girl, a musician who became a prostitute." Walker added, "That's what the environment did to her."[107]

While writing *Goose Island*, Walker also drafted many of the poems that comprised her first collection, *For My People*. Wright helped her rework several pieces and read early drafts of her historical novel *Jubilee*. She gave him feedback on revisions of his story "Almos' a Man" and the developing manuscript of a novel called *Lawd Today!*, published posthumously in 1963. "We discussed the difficulties of Negro dialect," Walker recalled, "our interest in Negro spirituals and the work songs and what Wright called the dozens."[108]

Walker and Wright corresponded and remained close friends for two years after he left Chicago. Following the success of *Uncle Tom's Children*, Wright worked on a novel whose protagonist was an impoverished South Side teenager with a "wild and intense hatred of white people," who inadvertently kills the daughter of his white employer.[109] One day he sent a special delivery letter to Walker: "I have just learned of a case in Chicago that has broken there and is exactly like the story I am starting to write. See if you can get the newspaper clippings."[110] Walker sent *Chicago Tribune* articles that covered the case of Robert Nixon with lurid sensationalism and undisguised racism; these became the basis for "many of the newspaper items and some of the incidents in *Native Son*."[111] Walker left Chicago for the Iowa Writers Workshop in 1939. She and Wright served literary apprenticeships in the South Side Writers' Group and the Illinois Writers' Project, and both were on the cusp of national recognition when they left the city.

Although the Federal Writers' Project launched or sustained many important writing careers, it suffered the same ragged, demoralizing termination as the Federal Art Project: the FWP fell victim to ideological enemies, political shifts within the Roosevelt administration, and mobilization of resources for the war.[112] As the Chicago office began shutting down in 1943, Bontemps and the Rosenwald Fund managed to salvage the *Negro in Illinois* files; they gave them to Vivian Harsh for the Special Negro Collection, where much of the research had been conducted.[113] Today they are preserved in the archival collection that bears her name. Thousands of pages of notes contain the work of about one hundred researchers. Topics cover almost two centuries—from the founding of Chicago by a fur trader of African descent named Jean Baptiste Point DuSable to the vibrant contemporary music, art, and literature of Bronzeville. Although the planned volume was never published, some of the research appeared in a ninety-five-page booklet, *Cavalcade of the American Negro*, prepared for the 1940 American Negro Exposition. Five years later, some material was incorporated by Drake and Cayton into *Black Metropolis*, and Bontemps and Conroy used substantially more in their history of black migration, *They Seek a City*. These works of sociology and history stand alongside the fiction and poetry discussed in the following chapters as testament to the upsurge of creative talent and achievement that marked Bronzeville's literary awakening against a backdrop of mass migration, economic crisis, and world war.

CHAPTER 9

Bronzeville and the Novel

Chapter 8 described a Bronzeville of brick and stone—tenements, schools, churches, settlement houses, libraries, and offices—actual places where writers lived and worked and interacted, creating a generational milieu. This chapter explores a Bronzeville of the mind—figurative reconstructions of time and place in works of the literary imagination—Chicago as one of the "invisible cities in the Afro-American novel" that Charles Scruggs discusses.[1] Chapter 9 focuses on five writers associated with Black Chicago—Arna Bontemps, Richard Wright, William Attaway, Alden Bland, and Willard Motley—and considers their novels written during the focal time frame of this study. Each writer lived in other places, but life in Chicago between 1932 and 1950 played a decisive role in shaping the development of his imagination and career. Some worked in more than one genre, but this focus on their novels allows critical and comparative analysis of individual works of fiction and attention to the development of literary form.

Arna Bontemps stands in relation to Bronzeville's "writing clan" much as Archibald Motley stands to the visual artists, a transitional figure whose works span two generations and suggest much about their contrasts and continuities. Richard Wright's first two novels demonstrate not only how the journey from Mississippi plantation to South Side streets stands at the imaginative center of his finest writing but also how this self-taught artist struggled to break new ground at the intersection of conflicting literary genealogies and philosophical traditions. The novels of William Attaway—marked by acute awareness of mobility, change, and loss—represent fictional reworkings of his generational experience of dislocation. *Blood on the Forge* (1941) in particular aspires to render the epic experience of migration in a manner at once realistic and poetic. In *Behold a Cry* by Alden Bland and *Knock on Any Door* by Willard Motley, both published in 1947, the naturalistic form is found on the verge of exhaustion; its very success and longevity planted the seeds for an aesthetic reaction against sociologically influenced fiction.

Arna Bontemps: Spanning the Generations

Arna Bontemps had careers and accomplishments enough for several people. He served as teacher, administrator, and librarian in private schools, a government agency, and universities, and he published some three dozen anthologies and works of poetry, fiction, and nonfiction for both adult and juvenile readers. Three novels appeared in the 1930s. The years between publication of the first, *God Sends Sunday* (1931), and the second, *Black Thunder* (1936), were marked by deep economic misery and sharp social convulsions, by

22. Arna Bontemps at Hall Branch Summer Reading Program, 1941.
Vivian G. Harsh Research Collection of Afro-American History and Literature, Chicago Public
Library. Hall Branch Archives 053.

continued migration and urbanization of blacks, and by emergence of the Scottsboro case
as the decade's most noted manifestation of both racial oppression and antiracist resistance. The works themselves stand on either side of a divide in African American cultural
history, and Bontemps was uniquely positioned to chronicle the generational shift.

In a memoir, Bontemps identified the genesis of *God Sends Sunday* in the spirit,
achievements, and limitations of "renaissance Harlem." Exuberant portrayals of lower-
class black life by Claude McKay, Langston Hughes, Rudolph Fisher, Zora Neale Hurston,
and others had won unprecedented attention, and publishing house doors were beginning
to open. Commercial success largely depended, however, on an exotic vogue among the
jazz-mad and Charleston-loving white cognoscenti who made Carl Van Vechten's *Nigger
Heaven* a best-seller.[2] Just as the owner of the New Gallery had pressed Archibald Motley
in 1928 to produce paintings representing "negro life in its more dramatic aspects," specifically cabarets and voodoo, Bontemps discovered in the following year that white publishers also had strong preferences about types of black subject matter. Fiction that
suggested the sensational and primitive was more likely to find an outlet than "a first novel

with autobiographical overtones about a sensitive black boy in a nostalgic setting." While rejecting his tale of rural childhood, "three of the editors who turned it down . . . went out of their way to praise one of the minor characters," a sharp-dressing little man with a taste for women and whiskey. Seeing the possibility of his first book contract, Bontemps "responded with *God Sends Sunday*."[3]

The more marketably exotic character in Bontemps's unpublished novel was loosely based on Buddy Joe Ward, his great-uncle. In *God Sends Sunday*, Buddy is transformed into Little Augie, a boy "too frail for hard labor" and born, like Ward and the author himself, upriver from New Orleans. Needing a high perch to see the world, the ragged, diminutive orphan moves from the "top-piece" of "the big barn gate" to "a stack of boxes" on the boat landing to "the back of the old lead mare" on Red River Plantation. Atop a good horse, the boy feels big and powerful. He stows away on a side-wheel riverboat and finds a home among a clan of racetrack workers, with whom he learns "to amuse himself like the other Negro hands, drinking whiskey, gambling with dice, and clog-dancing."[4] Augie rises from stable-boy to jockey and races from track to track, win to win, gaining fame and money and an ever-deepening appetite for the pleasures of red-light districts.

The novel derives its overall form from the conventions of the picaresque: a loosely structured, chronologically sequenced plot and a protagonist who escapes a closed society to pursue freedom and experience on the open road.[5] Augie's adventures take him from the plantation to New Orleans and eventually St. Louis, hub of "the Negro sporting wheel."[6] En route, he acquires gold teeth and a flashy wardrobe, witnesses shootings and "catfights," begins to drink heavily, and kills another rounder in a gunfight.

At the end of Part One, Augie loses—all on one ill-fated day—a premier race, his money, his wardrobe, and his "yella gal." He is left "a tiny disconsolate man," walking down the railroad tracks with no particular place to go. In Part Two, he reappears many years later in Mudtown, a black enclave outside Los Angeles, searching for his elder sister Leah, the only family he has ever known. The old woman lives alone except for her fifteen-year-old grandson, Terry, described as "timid" but "smart as a whup," a character recalling the sensitive youth of Bontemps's original manuscript.[7]

To Terry, Augie is at first glance only a "withered man in a frayed and ancient Prince Albert [coat] and a badly battered silk hat, carrying in one hand a dilapidated wicker traveling-bag and in the other the familiar accordion."[8] Yet something about this pathetic figure—perhaps the faded glory of his clothing, his much-traveled bag, or the blues he plays on the accordion—hints at vague mystery, even magic. One evening, in the transforming light of "a big round moon," Terry sees with new eyes: "Augie took on a singular glamour. For the first time [Terry] felt his kinship with his great-uncle."[9] The boy's feelings are complex and mercurial, for Augie represents an aspect of the racial self he has been carefully taught to deny. His stance can only be one of pained ambivalence, of drawing close and pulling away, of laughing to keep from crying.

If Terry's blues come from a divided self, Augie's come from narrowed horizons and shattered dreams—from sometimes *feeling* big but never *being* big, from being "nigger-rich" but never really rich, from pining for the near-white beauty who discards him as she serves a white man's pleasure. These tunes are the singing of a caged bird, and the cage is both Augie's tiny body and the racial caste system.

Terry's blues reflect Bontemps's own youth when he felt torn between two role models: his father, Paul, a brick-mason and Seventh-day Adventist minister, and great-uncle Buddy, an alcoholic, wanderer, and storyteller deeply attached to the rural South. His uncle "loved dialect stories, preacher stories, ghost stories, slave and master stories. He half-believed in signs and charms and mumbo jumbo, and he believed wholeheartedly in ghosts." Paul Bontemps considered Ward and his friends "don't care folk" and "ignorant people." He sent Arna to a white boarding school and, with Buddy's influence in mind, sternly warned the boy, "Now don't go up there acting colored."[10]

Paul Bontemps's anxiety may be seen as a facet of the Great Migration, of transplanted rural southerners admonished by urban relatives, urban newspapers, and the Urban League to "act right"—to lower the voice, improve the language, avoid saloons and poolrooms, attend proper established churches, never wear head rags or overalls in public. "In their opposing attitudes towards roots," Bontemps recalled, "my father and my great-uncle made me aware of a conflict in which every educated American Negro . . . must somehow take sides. . . . One group advocates embracing the riches of the folk heritage; their opposites demand a clean break with the past and all it represents."[11] Bontemps, Hughes, Fisher, and other younger writers of the Harlem Renaissance chose to embrace the folk heritage but were often caught between the Victorian sensibilities of their elders and the sensationalist tastes of white readers.

In deference to the latter, such plot subtleties as the inner conflict of a sensitive black adolescent are relegated to the wings in *God Sends Sunday*. Center stage is held instead by a gaudy procession of bad-mouthing, big-talking characters, whom literary historian Bernard Bell describes as "more caricatures, than realistic portrayals of street people."[12] A contemporary *New York Times* reviewer praised the book for its "gay pageant of pagan color," its representation of "the common speech of a most spontaneous race," its "vivid picturesqueness" and "natural freshness of childish naiveté."[13] In *Opportunity*, Alain Locke cautiously praised the work for its "folk flavor" and suggested that it was "probably the last, and one of the best of the low-life novels . . . for the swing has definitely gone to the problem novel."[14]

The seed idea for Bontemps's second novel was planted during the years he lived in Huntsville, Alabama, not far from Scottsboro. "An opportunity . . . to visit Fisk University" offered "a brief release from tension." In this "oasis," he found "three old friends from the untroubled years of the Harlem Renaissance: James Weldon Johnson, Charles S. Johnson, and Arthur Schomburg." In the Fisk library, Bontemps discovered a substantial trove of slave narratives and "began to read almost frantically" and "ponder the stricken slave's will to freedom."[15] Thus arose his own impulse to strike a blow for freedom through the novelistic medium. "The Scottsboro case was a prologue to what happened to my thinking," he recalled, "and it encouraged me to go ahead with some such statement as *Black Thunder*."[16] The slave narratives contained accounts of resistance on many levels, from malingering, sabotage, and individual flight to open rebellion. Bontemps found the basis for his plot in the documentary record of a revolt led by Gabriel Prosser near Richmond, Virginia, in 1800.

Bontemps's shift to the historical novel was careful and deliberate. He of course hoped to create a salable work, and, as Sterling Brown noted at the time, "The present vogue of historical fiction has given new impetus to the long-standing interest in the Old South and the Negro."[17] Many of those novels, however, were written by whites who continued the plantation tradition in literature by portraying loyal, happy slaves ruined by Reconstruction. "I am interested in themes from Negro history," Bontemps told Harold Jackman. "*Our writers* have neglected them thus far" (italics added).[18] With the new genre came a shift in the manner in which Bontemps employed forms of vernacular expression as well as motifs and character types drawn from the folk tradition. In *God Sends Sunday*, such materials frequently appear in a form suggesting the primitive and exotic. In *Black Thunder*, Bontemps shaped folk sources to echo the tocsin of revolt.

In Bontemps's fictionalized account, Gabriel Prosser's uprising is triggered by the death of Bundy, an aged bondsman, who is savagely beaten for pilfering his master's rum. Winning widespread support among slaves on nearby plantations and free blacks in the town, as well as the passive sympathy of a circle of white radicals, the rebellion gathers strength, and Gabriel plans to take Richmond with an army exceeding a thousand men. His strategy is thwarted, however, by a torrential rainstorm and eleventh-hour betrayal. By the novel's midpoint, the insurrection has aborted, and plot focus shifts to the pursuit and capture of its leaders, the retribution exacted on them, and the stoicism of the defeated hero.

The plot develops in fragments, through dozens of short chapters, each of which abruptly shifts the scene and momentarily focuses on a different character. Major and minor figures alike step briefly into the spotlight and reveal themselves through action, dialogue, and interior monologue. From this constantly shifting point of view, the reader must piece together the entire panorama. Bontemps skillfully uses this approach, reminiscent of the novels of Dos Passos, well-suited to present complex historical events and to deftly give voice to minor characters who represent the otherwise anonymous masses.

Bontemps also makes economical use of realistic details and events to create symbolic resonance. Bundy, for example, is literally trampled into the ground by a master on horseback who berates him as a "lickspittle scavenger." This single horrific scene encapsulates all cruelty of master to slave. The novel also begins and ends with Old Ben serving his master, portraying through the figure of the "contented" house slave a placid surface of normalized oppression that is momentarily shattered by Gabriel's attempted revolution.[19] This framing of events underscores the novel's casting of Gabriel as tragic hero. Further symbolic dimension is contributed by Juba, whose flashing naked thighs astride a black colt signal the start of the rebellion. A slave insurrection, among other things, asserts suppressed manhood, and Bontemps dramatizes this through Juba's challenge: "Always big-talking about what booming bed-men you is. . . . Well, let's see what you is good for sure 'nough. Let's see if you knows how to go free; let's see if you knows how to die."[20]

Gabriel's mind is set on freedom from his first appearance in the novel to his last. Overhearing white Jacobin sympathizers talk of "the equality of man" raises "gooseflesh on

Gabriel's arms and shoulders." He gathers his closest comrades to hear a smuggled call to arms from Toussaint L'Ouverture, leader of Haiti's slave insurrection, and vows "to write up something like that . . . soon's we get our power." When his followers start to fall away during the storm, Juba suggests that the two of them flee. Gabriel replies, "Running away won't do me no good long's the others stays." Akin to "a birthmark" or "a conjure," he perceives his fate is to lead the way to freedom or die trying. He faces interrogation, torture, and execution with stoic dignity, explaining to the exasperated prosecutor, "Something keep telling me that anything what's equal to a gray squirrel wants to be free. That's how it all come about."[21] Gabriel's simple eloquence is echoed by other characters and establishes Bontemps's protagonist as a representative figure and folk hero, described in Richard Wright's review as "endow[ed] with a myth-like and deathless quality."[22]

This masterfully crafted work joined the materials of recorded history, the vernacular folk tradition, and the cathartic power of tragedy. It was, according to Arnold Rampersad, "almost certainly the most advanced novel, in terms of narrative technique, published to that point by an African-American."[23] Black Thunder won praise from literary critics and young radicals alike and was instrumental in Bontemps's winning a Rosenwald fellowship for research in the Caribbean to gather material for his third novel.[24]

Drums at Dusk (1939) is set in the early days of the long struggle that overthrew slavery in the French colony of Saint Domingue, brought Toussaint to power, and eventually won independence for the black republic of Haiti. Just as news of that brutal, bloody conflict filling southern newspapers between 1789 and 1804, gave material shape to the spectral fears of slave-holding whites, the success of the insurrection inspired many blacks in the antebellum period.[25]

From 1915 to 1934, however, the African American press carried accounts of a nation recolonized at gunpoint by U.S. Marines, and some historians and creative artists responded sharply. Langston Hughes visited in the spring of 1931 and was deeply shaken by what he saw; he described Haiti as "a fruit tree for Wall Street, a mango for the occupation, coffee for foreign cups, and poverty for its own black workers and peasants."[26] Such indignation did not find its way into Popo and Fifina (1932), the book about Haitian children Hughes wrote with Bontemps, but it did provoke him into writing his first historical drama, Troubled Island, produced in November 1936 at Cleveland's Karamu House.[27] Three other plays set in Haiti were produced by the Federal Theater Project between 1936 and 1938.[28] Jacob Lawrence painted his acclaimed forty-one-panel series Toussaint L'Ouverture in 1937–1938.[29] C.L.R. James's Marxist historical study Black Jacobins appeared in 1938, just as Bontemps was putting the finishing touches on Drums at Dusk. The novelist visited Haiti in September and October 1938, mailed the finished manuscript to his publisher, Macmillan, on January 16, 1939, and sent his report to the Rosenwald Fund the following day.[30]

Drums at Dusk is at once a tale of revolutionary upheaval and an historical romance. Early scenes establish twin poles of the historical narrative: the brutal treatment of half a million slaves and the elemental rage unleashed in their rebellion. But the novel was hastily carved from material for a larger project, which resulted in significant artistic flaws.[31] Bontemps's efforts to communicate even a minimal sense of the complex events and their international contexts sometimes bloat the exposition or render dialogue ponderously didactic. Evidence of commercial pressures is found in heavy reliance on graphic violence and bodice-ripping sensationalism. The characterization of one protagonist, white abolitionist Diron Desautels, draws on the stock figure of the daring, darkly handsome romantic hero torn between two loves. With the mysterious and dangerous Paulette Viard, Diron dances a heated tango of attraction and repulsion, an even-deeper-South version of Rhett Butler and Scarlett O'Hara.

The second protagonist is Toussaint himself. "The pleasant old coachman" of the early chapters appears "to catch fire" at the outbreak of rebellion "as if he had suddenly laid claim to vast, half-forgotten resources of physical and mental strength. . . . He was riding through groves, crossing fields and leaping fences like the very god of insurrection." Matching intelligence to passion, Toussaint is the cool head in the heat of battle. He recognizes the desperate odds the rebels face and intends "to see discretion and sober wisdom play a part in this thrust for liberty." Through Toussaint's eyes, the reader sees "the wild element in control" during the revolution's first days, "the hungry jackals" who pillage plantations to repay their masters' cruelty. Their fury is personified in "the gigantic, barrel-bellied Boukman," a voodoo priest originally from Jamaica and one of the insurrection's leaders. "You're soft, *vieux* Toussaint," the former field slave tells the former house servant. "Your back is smooth. Look at these scars [of the lash]. I say spare none [of the whites]."[32] Through careful manipulation of point of view, Bontemps distances the reader from Boukman, the incarnation of black rage, thereby creating sympathy for Toussaint.

Toussaint's characterization perhaps drew on elements of self-projection by the author, a cautious man of scholarly disposition. In the radical tumult of 1930s Bronzeville, Bontemps worked amicably with people holding a wide spectrum of views while remaining skeptical of the claims and pressures of all true believers. After the death of Paul Bontemps, Arna received a letter from a church elder, reminding him of his father's desire that "the unique and timeless Truth of the Seventh-day Adventist Message be forever espoused by you."[33] The writer responded coolly: "I'm sure I am my father's son in many ways, including my hardheadedness. But in at least one thing I think I inherit more from my mother. My father never separated the 'spiritual' from the 'sectarian' in his thinking, but my mind has never worked this way."[34] Despite an enduring friendship with Richard Wright, Bontemps was wary of the younger man's zeal. When Wright broke with the Communist Party in 1944, Bontemps commented to mutual friend Jack Conroy: "Perhaps if Dick had worn communism as a loose garment, this sad story would have been less sad. But he gave his heart without reserve, and I doubt that a creative spirit can ever do that— to any organizational group—no matter how deep his sympathy. The creative mind *is* different; it doesn't ever exactly fit" (original italics).[35]

In his two historical novels, Bontemps reinvented his creative project in relation to the aesthetic and political currents swirling through Bronzeville. He engaged the radical spirit of the younger generation while resisting any "sectarian" prescription for African American writing, an intention signaled by his article for the *Chicago Bee*, "Negro Writers of Chicago," describing "three courses . . . open to the writers": "First, they may choose to make a frontal attack on the forces of poverty and want and discrimination. Richard Wright's *Native Son* represents a powerful thrust in this direction. Or, they may take 'the road to Xanadu,' as it has been called, and follow the imagination, forgetting the more immediate world. They may seek escape in laughter and dreams and romance and adventure. Finally, it may be possible for some to find a combination of the two in the manner of the historical novelists who seek to illuminate the present by presenting analogous scenes from the past."[36] Bontemps clearly staked his own claim in the third camp.

In crafting characters through whom to refract great events from the racial past, Bontemps was most successful in rendering the tragic nobility of Gabriel and the cool restraint of Toussaint. It remained to Wright to demonstrate that an African American writer could succeed both critically and commercially, to create fiction from the harsh contemporary reality of kitchenettes and pool rooms, and to realize the inner life of a figure like Boukman, reimagined as a modern antihero named Bigger Thomas.

Richard Wright and the Urban Nightmare

Wright's own accounts of his early years center on themes of deprivation, threat, and fear. Fear of physical annihilation is joined with fear of a life without meaning. After escaping the South, he struggled to acquire the tools to write his way into a world that offered meaning and freedom from physical threat and need. He read voraciously and eclectically, studying novelists as different from one another as Dreiser, Farrell, Dos Passos, Joyce, Dostoevsky, and Proust. In "Blueprint for Negro Writing," he claimed the full range of modern literature as "the heritage of the Negro writer." His early works show the strong influence of naturalistic writers, especially Dreiser, but also create a place for human subjectivity and agency. "The transition from realism/naturalism to modernism," Richard Lehan observes, "effected a radical change in the novel . . . [from a] narrative point of view . . . in which characters are seen from the outside to one in which consciousness and memory dominate the telling."[37] Wright's attempts to synthesize conflicting literary genealogies reveal the African American novel on the cusp of this transition.

Posthumously published in 1963, nearly three decades after it was completed, *Lawd Today!* is more important in documenting the evolution of Wright's career than for its literary achievement. The novel is a palimpsest of diverse influences, initially signaled by epigraphs paying homage to Van Wyck Brooks, Waldo Frank, and T. S. Eliot. The structural model is Joyce's *Ulysses*, portraying a single day in the life of a frustrated, self-deluded protagonist who roams a great city. Dreiser's influence is evident in descriptions of the social setting and emphasis on socially determined behavior, but the interior landscape is explored through dreams and stream of consciousness.

Chicago serves as setting, represented as an industrial wasteland, the midwestern, proletarian counterpart of Eliot's "unreal city" of London. But use of real place names and descriptively accurate details in the perambulations of antihero Jake Jackson creates a virtual Baedeker of Bronzeville, from the policy station where he plays the numbers, to the movie theater, barbershop, Hall Branch Library, and Walgreen's lunch counter. The influence of both literary naturalism and the documentary mode is also reflected in exhaustive depictions of social processes such as placing bets on the policy wheel, playing bridge, or sorting mail.

The first epigraph announces a theme of psychological stagnation, of swirling motion without progress: "a vast Sargasso Sea—a prodigious welter of unconscious life, swept by groundswells of halfconscious emotion." In the opening scene, Jake dreams of endlessly running up stairs without getting anywhere. His marriage to Lil is a study in claustrophobia and emotional ugliness. The plot unfolds on February 12, Abraham Lincoln's birthday, and an ongoing radio tribute to the "Great Emancipator" serves as ironic commentary, for Jackson feels "just like a slave," despite relative material comfort.[38] He has worked in the post office for nine years, owns ten suits, spats and a cane, and lives in an apartment with carpets, "voile curtains," and its own tiled bathroom. Such details exemplify a coworker's observation that "when a black man gets a job in the Post Office he's done reached the top."[39] But Jake is tormented by how low that top actually is, especially when measured by the dreams of prosperity and pleasure offered by the policy wheel, Hollywood movies, and department store windows. He is trapped in a place of inertia, thwarted desire, and venality.

Wright's bleak treatment of the urban scene is relieved by satiric jabs at Jake's ostentatious materialism and by brief glimpses of larger possibilities, such as organized protest movements or the creative realm, represented by Hall Branch and the Art Institute. Ultimately, however, rituals of male camaraderie enable Jake and three coworkers to survive the relentless pace and tedium of their work. "When they grew tired like this," begins the fourth chapter of a section titled "Squirrel Cage," "when most of their workaday preoccupations had been drowned in exhaustion, their basic moods would blend and fuse. . . . And when they talked it was more like thinking aloud than speaking for purposes of communication."[40] For thirty pages, four individual streams of consciousness merge into a torrent of talk: boisterously competitive, leaping erratically from topic to topic, full of banality, scatological humor, and casual misogyny, punctuated by a hellfire religious tract juxtaposed with the profane humor of the dozens. Well-worn stories of ghosts, dreams, sexual conquests, and the strange and ugly ways of white folks exemplify folk values and commonplaces and flow together with ill-digested bits of reading and broadcast news—a mélange deriving from the confrontation of rural southern traditions with urban life.[41]

Despite his best efforts, Wright could not find a publisher. Arnold Rampersad suggests that "quite possibly . . . editors were repulsed by the extreme realism in the novel," especially its frank sexual references.[42] Surely the work's manifest literary flaws must also be considered; one publisher rejected it as "artificially blown up and drawn out."[43] The economics of publishing in the Depression were grim. Arna Bontemps, a prize-winning poet and established novelist, counted himself lucky to have had *Black Thunder* accepted. The path was even steeper for a black apprentice novelist, known only for his revolutionary poems and offering a work that did not fit established literary niches.

A scene in the third chapter of "Squirrel Cage" alludes to a different sort of dilemma facing a Leftist black writer determined to address "the Negro masses." While Jake and his coworkers swap stories during their mail sorting, Al offers a sordid tale about a woman who gave him "the kind of love that would make a wildcat squall." Whenever she criticized or complained, he responded by "beat[ing her] black and blue till she forgot . . . and could cuddleup in my arms for a little love." Jake and the others howl appreciatively at Al's account of sado-sexual domination but then notice a white postal clerk joining in their laughter. "Gee, that was some hot story," he says. "Let's hear another one." This unexpected intrusion leaves the blacks "silent, resentful, hurt."[44]

Wright believed that black writers should offer values to serve black readers as "a guide in their daily living."[45] *Lawd Today!* was intended to provoke and challenge those who might recognize something of themselves in Jake, who internalizes and acts out the worst elements of a dehumanizing environment through consumerist display, racial self-hate, misogyny, and self-defeating violence. Despite Wright's success in creating such a new audience, he had to assume that the majority of his readers would be white, standing in the position of the fictitious postal clerk. Portraying unsavory facets of life among his own people could invite further scorn and ridicule. To write honestly about the South Side as he saw it would require defeating what Wright called his "mental censor—product of the fears which a Negro feels from living in America—standing over me, draped in white, warning me not to write." He would also have to ignore those voices of black propriety that asked: "Why don't you portray in your fiction the *best* traits of our race, something that will show the white people what we have done in *spite* of oppression" (italics original).[46]

The author described his struggles with inner and outer censors in a lecture at the 135th Street library in New York. He had turned down several more prestigious, more lucrative speaking engagements but accepted an invitation from head librarian Ernestine Rose and Schomburg Collection curator L. D. Reddick, an acquaintance from Chicago days.[47] If *Lawd Today!* had found a publisher in 1937, it might well have provoked consternation among race leaders. But Jake Jackson is at bottom a frustrated striver, affronted by restrictive covenants, the job ceiling, and the indignities of second-class citizenship. His simmering rage is constrained by fear of losing his relatively privileged job, and his anger is channeled into forms that are mainly destructive to him and those closest to him. The protagonist of *Native Son*, however, comes from the very bottom layer of black society and has nothing to lose. Wright knew that his portrayal of Bigger Thomas as white America's worst nightmare would jolt white and black readers alike, and his lecture at the Schomburg was an effort to assure that his novel was positively received by Harlem's intelligentsia.

Wright traced Bigger's imaginative genesis to blacks he had encountered in both Mississippi and Chicago: one a "swaggering" bully, another a rebellious "bad nigger," another a lunatic, and so on. Collectively, they represented variations on a social "pattern" or "type" as understood by sociologists.[48] The author insisted on the necessity of focusing on "the environmental factors which made for [their] extreme conduct." With the mobilization of the German and Italian lumpenproletariat by Hitler and Mussolini in mind, Wright described his murderous protagonist as "a symbolic figure of American life," a casualty of "a dislocated society" with counterparts among the "dispossessed and disinherited" of all races and nations. He portrayed his process of composition in classically naturalistic terms: "Why should I not, like a scientist in a laboratory, use my imagination and invent test-tube situations, place Bigger in them, and . . . work out in fictional form an emotional statement and resolution of this problem?"[49] This "laboratory" was an imaginative recreation of the community where he had lived for ten years, served his literary apprenticeship, and first conceived the idea of writing about someone like Bigger Thomas while watching local youths in pool halls and settlement houses. The Bronzeville portrayed in *Native Son* is nightmarish, notably stripped of the few rays of hope that glimmer in the background of *Lawd Today!*

The opening scene of Book I, in which Thomas corners and kills a huge black rat, exemplifies what Michel Fabre describes as "one of the most striking if not original devices of Wright's narrative: the use of a symbolic detail or episode to announce a crisis or future event."[50] As his name suggests, Bigger aspires to something larger than the cramped, vermin-infested confines of a kitchenette and the shared misery of a tightly bounded ghetto. His background is sketched through brief glimpses of his relationships with his family, girl-friend, and gang. When the young men are not shooting pool or planning robberies, they like to "play 'white,'" pretending to be pilots, generals, financial magnates, and government officials. Bigger joins in but pointedly reminds them of their actual situation: "We live here and they live there. We black and they white. They got things and we ain't. They do things and we can't. It's just like living in jail. Half the time I feel like I'm on the out-side of the world peeping in through a knot-hole in the fence."[51]

Bigger's efforts to break through the fences and barriers of his life—geographical, racial, economic, political, and psychological—lead him into violence and criminality.[52] Each of the novel's three books focuses on a key moment related to his criminality: Book I, "Fear," centers on his murder of heiress Mary Dalton; Book II, "Flight," revolves around his mur-der of his girlfriend, Bessie Mears; and Book III, "Fate," portrays his attorney's attempt to present evidence to mitigate the punishment for his crimes.

The first murder occurs inside the "high, black, iron picket fence" surrounding the Dalton mansion in Kenwood/Hyde Park, where Thomas has been dispatched by the relief office to work as a chauffeur. "Fear and hate" are his dominant reactions to the "cold and distant world" of wealthy whites. Mr. Dalton supports the NAACP, and his wife "has a very deep interest in colored people"; yet the young man instinctively feels that he dare not raise his eyes in their presence.[53] Assigned to drive their daughter Mary to the Uni-versity, he learns that instead she is planning to meet her communist lover, Jan, and that she expects the chauffeur's complicity in keeping the tryst secret. After Mary and Jan humiliate Bigger with ostensible gestures of comradeship, he finds himself carrying the drunken white woman to her bedroom. He becomes aroused, and his hands are on her breasts when her blind mother suddenly appears in the doorway. Seized with "hysterical terror" rooted in visceral fear of the lynch mob, he smothers Mary with a pillow to pre-vent her outcry and his discovery. To hide his crime, he dismembers and burns her body.

At first Mary's murder appears the inexorable culmination of a rigidly linked chain of events in which Bigger exercises little agency while his deepest instincts as a Delta-bred black man are triggered. Book II, "Flight," takes a different direction by portraying changes in his consciousness. His friends now seem "far away . . . in another life." He gazes at the single room he shares with his mother, brother, and sister, "seeing it for the first time." He considers whether Mary's death was really an accident or a manifestation of "his will to kill." Transformed in the crucible of crime, Thomas experiences feelings of elation, a newfound sense of purpose and freedom of action. He has "murdered and created a new life for himself . . . something . . . all his own, . . . that others could not take from him."[54] But Bigger's freedom is purchased at the cost of total isolation, epitomized by the coldly deliberate murder of Bessie, who has become a potential hindrance to escape. Bigger rapes her, smashes her head with a brick, and throws her body down an air-shaft. He is now profoundly alone.

With the second murder, Bigger's violence assumes epic dimensions. He is briefly refigured as outlaw folk-hero, a Badman picaro fleeing from street to street, building to building, rooftop to rooftop, vowing to "die shooting every slug he had." Some South Side residents blame him for the repression provoked by the killing of Mary Dalton, but others, unaware of Bessie's murder, cheer his defiance of white authority: "We's all black 'n' we jus' as waal *ack* black, don' yuh see?. . . . Ah'd die 'fo' Ah'd let 'em scare me inter tellin' on tha' man" (italics original).[55]

But Bigger's willful reinvention and his murderous creativity place him outside the normal order, values, and perceptions of both white and black society. With Bessie's blood still drying on his hands, he begins to see hidden meanings in familiar things. Their relationship has been based on little more than an exchange of commodities: she provided sex; he provided money for whiskey. Now "Bessie's whiskey" seems much like "his mother's religion"—two different means to forget their misery. Bigger scorns both women as weak and self-deluded.[56] In philosophical terms, he enters a realm of metaphysical rebellion where lucidity is achieved but hope lost. All his life he has been treated like a cipher, made to feel his nothingness. Now he has killed to assert his being and make the world acknowledge his existence.

Several literary and philosophical traditions converge uneasily at this point in the novel. The naturalist/realist tradition tends toward an exterior, objective portrayal of characters and emphasizes the determining or at least constraining role of social and economic forces. As a Communist and amateur social scientist, Wright gave this intellectual lineage his primary allegiance. Other traditions, associated with such proto-existentialists as Dostoyevsky and Nietzsche and with modernist fiction writers such as Joyce, Proust, and Faulkner, explore the inner life, alienation, memory, and the consequences of human volition in a world bereft of traditional sources of meaning and value. Such ideas, also major elements of Wright's self-education, suggested the future trajectory of his intellectual development, presaged as early as his masterful 1942 short story, "The Man Who Lived Underground," which rests, as Patricia Watkins demonstrates, on a "synergistic relationship" between naturalism and existentialism.[57] In Book II, when Bigger defiantly chooses to embrace an identity as moral outsider, his character seems firmly molded in the existentialist/modernist manner rather than the naturalist/realist, but the novel's core philosophical problem is only held in abeyance by the powerful narrative drive, pushed into the background by the pell-mell rush of a fugitive's flight and eventual capture.

With his arrest, the existential outlaw is momentarily "swallowed in darkness," as inert and helpless as the rat smashed by a skillet in the first scene. Bigger's fate, like the rat's, is death, but not instantaneous and not without conscious mediation, for, in attempting to shape *Native Son* as a novel of ideas, Wright strained at the formal boundaries of naturalism and social realism, just as he strained at the intellectual limits of Parkian social science and Marxist theory. Overwhelming social forces may have brutalized Bigger, causing him to behave brutally, and may have reimprisoned his body, but the author's insistent focus on the interior landscape and the struggle for human agency leaves his protagonist a further road to travel. The picaresque journey is internalized. As Book III opens, Bigger lies in a police-station cell, sunk in despair: "He had reached out and killed and had not solved anything, so why not reach inward and kill that which had duped him?"[58] In the following scenes, Bigger desperately searches for something to grasp, to give meaning to his life and, thereby, to his death. His testing of alternative loyalties, however, is rendered in a manner that sacrifices literary artistry to tendentious argument.

Plot dissolves into improbability and characterization into caricature as Wright reassembles his cast all together in one absurdly overcrowded jail cell. Like characters in a medieval morality play, they enter, singly or in clusters, personifying philosophies or ways of life that contend for Bigger's allegiance: his mother and a preacher urging meekness and faith in a better afterlife, two communists pressing the vision of a new world built by a racially united working class, the paternalistic white-liberal Daltons demanding contrition, and an aggressive district attorney forcing submission to overwhelming power. Thomas is tested and momentarily wavers in his stance of nihilistic defiance. In crafting this scene, Wright was conscious of the artistic risks and defended his approach in his speech at the 135th Street library: "What I wanted that scene to say to the reader was *more important than its surface reality or plausibility*" (italics original).[59]

Bigger's communist lawyer, Boris Max, soon takes center stage with his courtroom plea for the young man's life. Max urges the judge to show mercy in consideration of Bigger's hard circumstances and, more broadly, of the experience of "a separate [Negro] nation, stunted, stripped, and held captive within this nation."[60] The speech is rhetorically powerful and sometimes prescient, yet its great length (some twenty-five pages) and overt didacticism extend a series of literary disasters in Book III. Wright was warned of this problem by his agent, publisher, and friends who read the developing manuscript. He largely ignored their criticisms because he was determined to explicitly present his ideas about race in American society, and he needed the ideologically committed, eloquent lawyer, not the lost, inarticulate black killer, to serve as his spokesman. According to one friend, Wright "anticipated a storm of protest against his Bigger which might silence him for all time. This was, he said, his chance to say what he felt."[61]

In the novel's closing scene, Max continues what amounts to a struggle to save Bigger's soul by offering an optimistic view of humanity's future as secular counterpart to his mother's religion. But the youth ultimately resists all forms of hope and transcendent belief. He finds the strength to die in renewed defiance, in acceptance of the self he has chosen: "I reckon I believe in myself. . . . What I killed for, I *am*!"(italics original). This triumph of existential authenticity is offset by the defeat of human solidarity, and Max reacts in horror at Bigger's willingness to die in total isolation. The youth is left alone in his cell, listening to "the ring of steel against steel as a far door clanged shut."[62]

Native Son did indeed shock readers, as Wright intended. He had written a novel that not only depicted the harsh living conditions of urban blacks but also, through skillful use of limited omniscient point of view, thrust the reader into the blazing furnace of fear and hate inside Bigger Thomas. Instead of being silenced, however, the author found himself lionized, and his novel achieved a degree of commercial and critical success far beyond that accorded any previous literary work by an African American. Within three weeks, Harper & Brothers had sold 215,000 copies, and thereafter 2,000 copies were being sold each day. Major critics hailed it as "strong meat" and "the finest novel as yet written by an American Negro," comparing it with Steinbeck's *Grapes of Wrath*, Dreiser's *American Tragedy*, and Dostoyevsky's *Crime and Punishment*. Some African Americans objected to the book's grim portrayal of life in black communities, but overwhelmingly they applauded Wright's bold indictment of white racism. The NAACP capped his success with award of the prestigious Spingarn Medal for 1940.[63]

Wright remained committed to addressing "the Negro masses," the people from whom he had sprung. He allowed serialization of *Native Son* in the *Chicago Bee* and the Harlem-based *People's Voice*. His friend Ulysses Keys, a prominent South Side attorney, wrote of its local reception: "Your book is raising a 'fog' as to its sociological contribution. Many favor; many do not. But all read it. (That's important.)"[64] Wright found another vehicle for bringing Bigger to a broad audience through collaboration with Orson Welles, John Houseman, and Paul Green to adapt the novel to the stage.[65]

Native Son opened in New York in March 1941. The downtown theater was packed as Harlem artists and intellectuals sat alongside Park Avenue matrons and communist leaders. The play then had a short run uptown at the Apollo Theatre, went on tour, and had its Chicago premier at Horace Cayton's community center. Arna Bontemps described the scene in a letter to Harold Jackman: "*Native Son* opened here last night to a kind of audience it could never have in N.Y. Negroes had taken over the entire house as a benefit for the Good Shepherd Community Church. Only a sprinkling of whites got in, the result being that they giggled all through the early scenes, particularly during Mary Dalton's advances, and went wild during the final speech of Max, the lawyer. Some of them even shouted from the balcony, 'Tell 'em 'bout it!' Altogether it was a lovely night."[66] Boris Max was both Bigger's "mouthpiece" and Wright's, and his monitory vehemence spoke to both the anger and the hopes of Bronzeville on the cusp of World War II.

William Attaway, Elegiac Poet of the Great Migration

The southern exodus provided an impetus for African American writers to turn to themes broadly similar to those found in novels by Frank Norris, Theodore Dreiser, Sinclair Lewis, and other naturalistic writers: the revolt from village life and the movement to a brightly glittering but often brutal reality in the modern city.[67] This turn was a long time coming,

23. William Attaway, c. 1940.
Vivian G. Harsh Research Collection
of Afro-American History and
Literature, Chicago Public Library.
Hall Branch Archives 235.

however. "Despite the imprint of migration . . . on the community of Harlem and the lives of the many writers of its literary culture," observes Lawrence Rogers, "the fiction of the 1920s contains surprisingly little emphasis on . . . the Great Migration. . . . The movement of the southern black masses into Harlem went largely unexplored."[68] Only in the 1930s and 1940s did the transplantation emerge as a central focus of African American novelists, and it was most important to the writers of Bronzeville, foremost among them Mississippi migrants William Attaway and Richard Wright.

Attaway's first significant published fiction, a short story in Dorothy West's *Challenge*, appeared in 1936 while he was working for the Illinois Writers' Project. In "Tale of the Blackamoor," a black servant-boy of another era dances a minuet in fantasy with his mistress's Dresden china doll. This parable is told in treacly prose: "The little blackamoor glanced down at his ridiculous red pantaloons, and the pearls of anguish rolled down his satin-black cheeks."[69] Attaway's own experience of migration and his two years among hoboes and itinerant workers show no trace. The piece seems jarringly discordant with works by such project colleagues as Wright, Bontemps, Motley, Algren, and Conroy, but his two novels provide evidence that Attaway's time on the project planted seeds that later bore fruit.

Let Me Breathe Thunder (1939) reveals an author who, if nothing else, has taken a deep breath of the stormy literary and political atmosphere.[70] He was on the road again, this time as an actor touring with Moss Hart and George Kaufman's *You Can't Take It with You*, when he learned that his manuscript would be published.[71] Influenced by *Of Mice and*

Men, Steinbeck's tale of migrant farmhands, Attaway's first novel tells the story of wanderers Ed and Step, who are "looking for a job of work" and briefly find both work and a dangerous love interest on a ranch in Washington.[72]

The protagonists are white, but the plot involves a variety of interracial situations, allowing the author to highlight a commonality of experience among the dispossessed. In one scene, the shabby pair and a young Mexican companion wait to be served in a railway dining car, uneasily aware that the neatly dressed passengers are staring. Ed, the first-person narrator, thinks: "Everything was so white. The people looked whiter than any I had ever seen before. Once I was in a restaurant in Detroit and a very black boy come in walking hard on his heels. Everybody had looked at him. Now I glanced down at my hands to see if they hadn't turned dark. The waiter hadn't served the black boy."[73] *Let Me Breathe Thunder* is apprentice work; the flowering of Attaway's talents is seen in his powerful novel of migration, *Blood on the Forge.*

Attaway wrote his second novel with financial support from the Rosenwald Fund and dedicated it to his sister, Ruth, a successful actress in New York. He told a Harlem audience, shortly after the work's publication late in 1941, that his first inclination had been "just to do a study" of the migration experience but then he had decided that the theme called for literary, rather than sociological, treatment.[74] Such were the close connections between Chicago social science and naturalist/realist fiction in the intellectual milieu in which Attaway came of age.

At the novel's center are the three Moss brothers. Sharecroppers on a Kentucky hill farm, they are bound, serflike, to the soil, as each crop leaves them deeper in debt than the last. Each has his own way of coping with forces that would strip him of his humanity. Melody, sensitive, thoughtful, and musical, "never had a craving in him that he couldn't slick away on his guitar." Chinatown is irresponsible and playful as a child with "a gold tooth, 'shinin' an' makin' everybody look when Chinatown smile.'"[75] Sober, industrious Big Mat has always wanted to preach, but is stifled by agony over his wife's failure to bear children, which he interprets as God's curse. He is a Joblike figure with a smoldering bitterness and potential for violence and destruction.

The brothers' seemingly endless cycle of toil on the land is disrupted by a series of events beginning with their mother's sudden death behind a plow and ending when Mat is provoked into beating their white "riding boss" to the ground. His panic at the thought of a gathering lynch mob coincides with the appearance of a labor agent in search of recruits for the steel mills of the Monongahela River valley in Pennsylvania. Mat orders his brothers to prepare to board the freight train that will carry them north that very night. As he looks around at the familiar fields for the last time, deep feelings well up, finding voice in words that dramatize his sense of loss and exemplify Attaway's balancing of starkly realist detail with lyrical interludes woven from the folk imagination and vernacular: "Ain't nothing make me leave the land if it good land. . . . Take more 'n jest trouble to run me off the hills. . . . Shareworked these hills from the bad land clean to the mines at Madison. The old folks make crop here afore we was born. Now the land done got tired. . . . The land has jest give up. . . . Now us got to give up too."[76]

Forced to leave his wife Hattie behind, Mat and his brothers, along with dozens of other sharecroppers, board a sealed boxcar at midnight. Such secrecy is intended to prevent interference by local landowners worried about the loss of their workforce, and the train ride briefly seems a flight to freedom. This symbolic framing of the journey is shattered, however, in the novel's second section, wherein graphic details evoke the Middle Passage more than the Underground Railroad. Men squat in total darkness "bunched up like hogs headed for market" as straw soaks up their urine and the boxcar becomes "fetid with man smell and nervous sweat." When the door finally slides open, they are "blinded by the light of a cloudy day," and their ears still ring with "the scream of steel on the curves."[77] The account of this hellish journey, shortest of the novel's five parts, conveys the impression that the brothers and their anonymous companions have crossed a boundary irreversibly separating them from all that they have known.

Part III contrasts the new way of life with the old. Italicized passages render a polyphonic folk voice that registers the migrant's initial shock: *This Allegheny County is an ugly, smoking hell out of a backwoods preacher's sermon. . . . We can't see where nothin' grows around here but rusty iron towers and brick stacks*" (italics original).[78] These "green men" have entered a world that turns all things and people "gray," whose dreary sameness is interrupted only by shooting red flames from the mills. They listen to bunkhouse tales of death from hot steel, and their apprehension grows. Attaway describes the massive steelworks in taut, vivid prose evoking struggle and pain. The migrants discover that the human environment is nearly as hostile as the physical. Their "hunky" neighbors stare with contempt, viewing "new niggers" from the South as strikebreakers. The immigrants' children throw stones.

In this alien and disorienting environment, face-to-face racial subordination gives way to a situation in which blacks stand in rough parity and can compete with white steelworkers. Great machines now loom threateningly above them all: "*Like spiral worms, all their egos had curled under pressure from the giants around them. Sooner or later it came to all the green men: What do we count for against machines that lift tons easy as a guy takes a spoonful of gravy to his mouth?*" (italics original). Twelve-hour shifts leave them jumpy and volatile, prone to sudden outbursts of violence. Defenses that had once sustained the Moss brothers prove useless. "The mills couldn't look at China's gold tooth and smile."[79] Melody experiments with new rhythms but eventually lays aside his guitar. Mat abandons his Bible, then squanders his money, and such loss defeats all hope of sending for Hattie. Under the relentless pounding of the steel, the brothers' personalities, rooted in the soil of southern folkways, begin to disintegrate.

Melody and Mat try to regain their sense of worth through the young "Mex town" prostitute Anna. Melody falls in love with this child-woman with "legs beautiful as fresh-split cedar," but, gripped by a strange mood and too much whiskey, he hesitates to make love to her.[80] Shortly afterward, Mat rescues her from a wild brawl at a dogfight and takes her to his shack. Supplanting Hattie and causing tension between the brothers, Anna symbolizes Mat's rootlessness and the deterioration of family bonds.

Impending disaster dominates Part IV, foreshadowed as Melody transfers to the blast furnaces to replace a man killed in an explosion. The foreman pronounces the area "jinxed," but the company continues rebuilding the blown-out furnace. When Melody injures his hand, his brother Chinatown takes his place. A disabled black steelworker named Smothers assumes a prominent role at this point. He has a gift for discerning the meaning "when cold steel whisper . . . and hot roll steel scream like hell." What Smothers hears is ominous, and, like an Old Testament prophet, he warns his people: *"It's a sin to melt up the ground, is what steel say. It's a sin.* Steel bound to git ever'-body 'cause o' that sin. They say I crazy, but mills gone crazy 'cause men bringin' trainloads of ground in here and meltin' it up" (italics original).[81] Smothers's prophecy comes to pass when the furnace erupts again, taking fourteen lives including his own and leaving Chinatown blinded.

Melody tries to buoy his stricken brother's spirits by conjuring down-home memories of "chitterlin's and cabbage greens" and his proud acquisition of the gold tooth.[82] Anna comforts Chinatown like a child at her breast. His wound and emotional regression are incorporated into an extended metaphor dramatizing the brothers' physical and psychological disintegration. Chinatown loses his sexual confidence with his sight and can no longer enjoy the pleasures of "Mex town." Melody too suffers symbolic castration when he accidentally smashes his "picking hand" at work. Mat is reduced to an "empty paper sack" when Anna stops sleeping with him, and his efforts to regain his lost manhood become the central focus of the novel's closing pages.

The horrific explosion has "helped the cause of the union," with Slavs and Italians joining in large numbers as Steeltown divides into warring camps.[83] Mat views the labor conflict in strictly racial terms, however. The beating by whites of a black foreman named Bo triggers a deep fear with "roots in mob-fearing generations of forebears in the South."[84] Later the brothers discover, somewhat incredulously, that Bo is a company spy responsible for the firings of union activists. While the foreman reports to the mill office, Mat broods outside: "He would not join the union. For a man who had so lately worked from dawn to dark in the fields twelve hours and the long shift were not killing. For a man who had ended each year in debt any wage at all was a wonderful thing. For a man who had known no personal liberties even the iron hand of the mills was an advancement. In his own way he thought these things. As yet he could not see beyond them."[85]

Careful control of tone and aesthetic distance in such passages suggests the author's perspective. Mat's outlook is plausible, given his background and personality, yet it proves self-destructive, a distinction Attaway was eager to communicate to his audience, most especially to black readers hovering between race and class allegiances. Significantly, while Melody expresses much confusion, he shows potential understanding of the union's role in fighting for all workers.

Mat perceives the deepening strife as a chance to "heal his ruptured ego with . . . a sense of brutal power."[86] Hastily "deputized," he joins a group of professional strike-breakers, distinguishing himself by his fearlessness and taste for violent confrontation. Learning that Anna has returned to her former profession, he goes berserk and beats her mercilessly. Minutes later, he leads a raid on union headquarters. Tasting "bitterness towards all things white," Mat batters his way through the crowded office and strangles "a little gray Slav."[87] He is battered in turn and killed by a union man wielding a pickax handle.

Mat's dying moments release him from his blood frenzy. Looking into the "good face" of the union man, he has an epiphany: "It seemed to him that he had been through all of this once before. . . . Yes, once he had beaten down a riding boss. Had that riding boss been as he was now? Big Mat . . . could no longer distinguish himself from these other figures. They were all one and all the same. In that confusion he sensed something true. Maybe somewhere in these mills a new [owner] was creating riding bosses, making a difference where none existed."[88] This abrupt realization strikes a false note that weakens the novel's denouement and contrasts with otherwise sure control of plot and characterization. Alan Wald suggests that such artistic lapses by Leftist black writers are "partly explained by the relationship of art to experience. The experience of . . . racial oppression was vivid, real, and overwhelming . . . [whereas] full-blown interracial class solidarity was by comparison almost a leap forward to a quixotic chimera."[89]

While rooted in the aesthetics of social realism and the documentary impulse, Attaway's narrative of race and class conflict, of dislocation and loss, is graced by a persistent lyrical chord.

A poetic realism dramatizes the confrontation of rural folk imagination with the conditions of modern industrial life, as the author weaves the sounds of southern black speech throughout the novel and at certain moments amplifies their melopoeic rendering.[90] The earliest voicings occur in Part I in the "Hungry Blues" that Melody sings, the "wishing game" he plays with Chinatown, and the "solemn feeling" that spurs laconic Mat to prayerful eloquence while bidding farewell to the red-clay hills. These sounds echo in the polyphonic voice of the "green men" recoiling from a gray world and further resonate in Smothers's prophetic alarums at the violation of nature. Finally, the lyrical strain swells as Melody and Chinatown board another train, this one headed for Pittsburgh.

The tone of the conclusion is unmistakably elegiac. The strike has been defeated. Indian summer is gone, and winter is settling in. The train is taking Melody "away from the mills . . . Anna . . . Chinatown's eyes . . . Big Mat's grave" (ellipses original). He is "beginning to feel the truth: they would never go home." This train ride mirrors the earlier departure from Kentucky, a flight from an unbearably painful situation that brings only new pain. The slender thread of hope is even further attenuated. Melody's family is reduced to the sightless brother at his side. All that marks what he has left behind are "a homemade watch fob and an old backless Bible."[91] Such small details illustrate Sterling Brown's observation that the novel's "mature" style rests on a "veering from naturalistic to symbolic."[92] The Bible was abandoned by Mat in his dark agony. The watch fob was created in a solemn ritual in the black men's bunkhouse, marking Smothers's destruction by the steel monster. Melody wears it for good luck, and Attaway hints that there may yet be some small luck in the future of an adaptable black man gifted with imagination and mother wit and clutching the remnants of family and folk tradition as he makes his way in the city.

Blood on the Forge was published the year after the towering success of *Native Son* and just weeks before the attack on Pearl Harbor. Taken together, these two events likely explain the disappointing sales of this fine novel. "The Negro masses" were not, any more

than the white masses, reading the best works of the literary imagination, and the educated, middle-class, predominantly white audience who read *Native Son* did not rush to
embrace a second major African American author. The outbreak of war impacted the production and sale of books, as it affected every aspect of life on what suddenly became
known as "the home front." Attaway, like other members of his generation, saw his early
years blighted by the Depression, and, just as he was launching a career, a second catastrophe overshadowed his dreams. The July 1944 issue of *Negro Story* notes that the writer
"is in New York City in the United States Army" and adds, "We hope he will write more
novels while there." But Alice Browning and other readers who recognized Attaway's
achievement and potential would be disappointed. Although both his novels were reissued in pocketbook format in the early 1950s, he never published another full-length
work of fiction. Instead, he joined other talented graduates of the Writers' Project working in popular cultural forms. He wrote more than five hundred songs and became a pioneering black scriptwriter for radio, film, and television.

Naturalism in Extremis: Alden Bland and Willard Motley

If Wright and Attaway struggled to bend and shape the naturalistic novel to the expanding reaches of their literary projects, Bronzeville writers Alden Bland and Willard Motley
worked more conventionally within the inherited form. Alden, like his brother Edward,
had participated in the Chicago Poets' Class at the South Side Community Art Center.
He began publishing fiction in *Negro Story* while serving in the navy. His novel *Behold a
Cry* (1947) is, like *Blood on the Forge*, set in the year of Chicago's bloody race riots, but he
takes considerable liberties with the actual chronology.[93]

Centered on the deteriorating familial relations of Ed and Phom Tyler and their two
sons, Bland's plot is strung from three structural poles outlining the historical context.
Chapter one evokes the "millions of restless feet" of the wartime migration.[94] Toward the
middle of the novel, four chapters (out of thirty-seven) portray the 1919 riots, during
which Ed and a coworker are severely beaten. Near the end, four more chapters are
devoted to a stockyard strike, prompting further interracial violence as large numbers of
blacks are employed as strikebreakers. Extended passages of exposition periodically remind
the reader of the shaping force of such epic events.

Characterization depends heavily on a series of polarities that reflect sociological
premises: rural versus urban, naïveté versus sophistication, sacred versus secular, neighborliness versus anonymity, children of the alley versus those of the frontyard. Bland
embodies such polarities in different characters and employs omniscient narration to
reveal how external actions and dialogue reverberate subjectively. At its worst, this technique produces scenes in which ideas are debated with greater tendentiousness than the
most flawed passages in *Native Son* or characters who seem like startled Pinocchios looking up and discovering their strings.

Several characters, however, are developed with sufficient psychological subtlety to
make their conflicts and choices plausible and even moving. Bland generally accomplishes

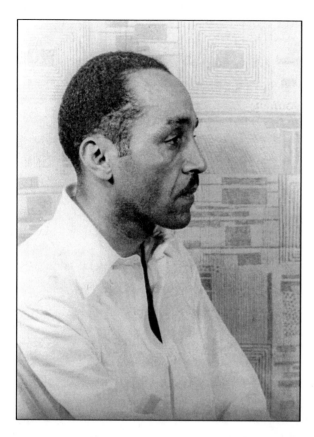

24. Willard Motley, 1947.
Photo: Carl Van Vechten. Library of Congress, Prints & Photographs Division, Carl Van Vechten Collection. LC-USZ62–114424.

this by shifting attention between male and female characters in different circumstances. Ed, for example, migrates to Chicago nearly a year before Phom and their sons, and this span of time creates a barrier between them. On his family's arrival, Ed takes in every detail. His wife "sensed the incongruity of their appearance. While Phom looked about at the well-dressed people, Ed walked slightly ahead feeling conspicuous and on edge."[95] Their neighbors Sam and Clara Brown are involved, respectively, in a stockyard workers' union and a black church. While Sam attempts to win Ed to a prolabor stance, Clara offers Phom the solace of female companionship and the familiar sounds of Baptist worship: "The choir rose to sing. . . . Clara thought of home, of her mother who was dead. Great swells of feeling rose upward to her throat."[96] Despite the occasional strength in characterization, the narrative suffers a persistent slackness that comes from leaving such conflicting pulls and various subplots dramatically unresolved.

Of all Black Chicago's writers, Willard Motley most thoroughly embraced the naturalistic prototype. He began work on his most important novel, *Knock on Any Door*, around 1939 while participating in a writers' group with several white friends. They read extensively in modern literature, including the poetry of Sandburg and Masters and novels by Dos Passos, Hemingway, Joyce, and Anderson. "Dreiser was a big influence," one participant recalled.[97] While working for the Writers' Project, Motley was assigned to do research in "Little Sicily" on young housing-project residents, many of them petty criminals. From this informal sociological study, his sketches of life on the West Side for *Hull-House Magazine*, and his extensive travel diaries, he began to draft a massive novel of the Chicago slums, eventually published in 1947.

Knock on Any Door is the story of Nick Romano, the son of Italian immigrants whose blighted environment pushes him inexorably down the path to delinquency and crime. He is a pious altar boy at the novel's beginning, but when his father's grocery store is lost to the Depression, the family slips into desperate poverty, and the youth begins to break the law. His criminal career progresses from shoplifting to "jackrolling" (mugging) drunks, armed robbery, and eventually the murder of a police officer. Nick moves from the grim confines of a reform school to a county jail, his criminality deepens, and he dies in the electric chair at the age of twenty-one. For nearly a hundred chapters, Motley piles episode upon episode, overwhelming the reader with evidence—detailed, authentic, redundant—of society's responsibility for producing youths like Nick.

Characterization relies primarily on appearance, action, and dialogue. What passes for psychological insight combines Catholic sensibility with Hollywood stereotype. Characters are either sinners or saints, and few saints are found in jail or Skid Row. But Motley insists on the essential goodness of all; sinners must be seen as fallen saints. The chronological detailing of Nick's fall is punctuated by periodic reminders of his violated innocence, typically represented by guilt feelings or paroxysms of tears. Motley renders guilt the way he renders everything, in a clipped, pseudo-Hemingway monotone: "Things tore at him. He couldn't understand them. He felt hurt and alone. For a minute a picture of Father O'Neil stood up in front of him." Romano often forgets "to be hardboiled." Moments before the police apprehend him: "He put his folded thumb between his teeth and pressed hard. Little Nicky Romano the wise guy! Always one ahead of the game! Nick's eyes swam with tears of fear and impotence."[98] Romano is the tough guy with a soft heart, weeping over such other victims as a mouse tormented by a cat or a puppy run down by an automobile. This stereotype has a literary lineage, examined by Leonard Cassuto, in "Dreiser's portraits of emotionally conflicted criminals" swerving between "the sentimental and the hard-boiled."[99]

A well-publicized police dragnet culminating in a murderer's dramatic rooftop capture is but one of several key plot elements for which Motley owes a debt to Wright. Like Bigger Thomas, Nick commits a murder that ironically gives meaning to his own life. "This is what I was born to do," he thinks just before emptying his pistol into the policeman's head.[100] The ensuing chase, trial, and defense strategy of laying blame on society are essentially *Native Son* stripped of racial implications, for Motley's terrain is the multiethnic West Side.

But the differences are as striking as the similarities. Where Wright's treatment is condensed and tersely symbolic, reflecting modernist influences, Motley's is detailed and exhaustive in the older naturalistic style. The ponderous 250,000-word novel had in fact been carved, at the publisher's insistence, from a manuscript of a million words. Romano must be as bad as Motley can make him, on the theory that the deeper his pathology, the deeper society's guilt. But his portrayal is constrained by a need to arouse the reader's pity, hence Romano's guilt and tears. Repeated references to the protagonist saving a tiny mouse portray Nick himself as a cat's paw of society. Bigger, in contrast, is portrayed as the biggest, fiercest rat in the ghetto, for pity is the last thing on Wright's mind.

Knock on Any Door was greeted with extravagant critical acclaim and compared to the work of Dreiser, Farrell, and Wright. Many reviewers explicitly acknowledged its generic lineage. A *New York Times* critic wrote: "No abler recruit has joined the extreme natural-ist school of fiction in a long time than Mr. Motley. The grim effectiveness of his socio-logical reporting is beyond question." The *Harper's* reviewer noted that "the pathos, the shocking inevitability in Nicky's downfall are what make this a novel of power and stature."[101] The public shared the critics' enthusiasm, and sales approached 350,000 within two years. Soaring up the best-seller lists and with few subtleties to complicate smooth translation from page to screen, the novel's commercial success was capped by a 1949 Hollywood film treatment.

The novel's predominantly white cast of characters appears to place it within a post-war trend among black writers toward works avoiding or minimizing explicitly racial sub-ject matter and black characters. Ten of twenty-nine novels by African Americans published between 1946 and 1950 have exclusively or predominantly white characters, a phenomenon that critics have variously correlated with a movement away from literary naturalism or with rising hopes for racial equality spurred by recent legal breakthroughs.[102] Motley's decisions about characters had different roots, however. "Nick's Italian-American ethnicity and the anonymous poverty of the Great Depression serve as metaphors and par-tial cover-ups for being black," recalls Motley's friend and fellow novelist Alexander Sax-ton, who read drafts of the work in progress. "We pushed him to bring his own experience directly into his writing but he would not go in that direction."[103]

Personally, Motley did not "feel at home" with other African Americans. In his 1933 diary, he wrote: "I don't feel that the colored people are a part of me. I've lived in this neighborhood [Englewood] all my life. My friends, my everything have been white people. I don't look down on Negroes but I'm not one of them any more than the Prince of Wales is."[104] Politically, he was an unaffiliated radical and admired the Socialist Party of Eugene Debs, which had been notably oblivious to unique forms of racial oppression.[105]

Aesthetically, Motley was most indebted to Dreiser, but the naturalistic tradition was by 1947 a well-mined literary vein, with a five-decade history centered largely in Chicago. The panoramic novel of rich sociological detail, chronologically organized, populated by characters representing social types, and animated by philosophical determinism was on the verge of displacement by newer forms.

Naturalists of the Second Generation

In *Native Son* and *Blood on the Forge*, Wright and Attaway pushed the boundaries of the naturalistic novel through more extensive formal experimentation, greater symbolic depth, more open-ended philosophical premises, and closer attention to language and characterization than typically found among Dreiser and his contemporaries.[106] Wright was especially conscious of standing at an aesthetic turning point. During a radio interview in late 1941, he discussed the challenges faced by "the Negro writer who treats of new subject matter." While doubting "that realism will be abandoned," he observed that "simple, naïve realism is on the way out" and predicted that novels of the 1940s would exhibit "greater complexity and imaginative depth" and "a new surge of interest in character development." He implied that such new possibilities would build on the prior achievements of the documentary movement: "The '30s were a period of digestion. . . . We know something about our country now, that is, how it actually works and the influence of that working upon personality."[107]

Wright and such contemporaries as Attaway, Bland, Motley, Chester Himes, Carl Offord, Ann Petry, and William Gardner Smith were shaping what Bernard Bell describes as "a disquieting new naturalistic vision in the Afro-American novel between 1937 and 1952."[108] This Afro-naturalist vision embraced words as weapons and books as vehicles for advancing social justice, racial equality, and more broadly modernity among the migrant black masses; a project explicitly announced in "Blueprint for Negro Writing" and, four years later, in the peroration of *12 Million Black Voices*: "Hundreds of thousands of us are moving into the sphere of conscious history. . . . Print compels us. Voices are speaking. Men are moving! And we shall be with them."[109] Afro-naturalism focused on black individuals and families as representative types and set their stories against the backdrop of migration, urbanization, depression, war, and other great events of their time.

Unfortunately, Bell is intent on drumming Wright out of the mainstream of an ostensibly unitary African American literary tradition and reduces his work to nothing more than naturalism and an exclusively pathological view of black life. Rather than acknowledge the existentialist strain in *Native Son* with its attendant claims on human freedom, Bell characterizes the novel's philosophical underpinnings as simply an "interplay between Freudian psychology and Marxist social analysis . . . informed by the belief that the character and history of man can be *completely explained* by biological and socioeconomic facts" (italics added). Bell also ignores the formal experimentation in Wright's early fiction, the satiric elements in *Lawd Today!*, and the many positive estimations of folk culture in "Blueprint for Negro Writing," *Uncle Tom's Children*, and *12 Million Black Voices*.[110]

Nelson Algren's comments to Wright, written just days after publication of *Native Son*, suggest the problems with reductive views like Bell's. The white novelist told Wright that he had previously "assumed [the novel] would deal almost wholly with external situations [and] would prove, competently, the need of change." Instead Algren found that he had "never read anything more psychologically convincing," that *Native Son* could "be read five ways or so, like The Vicar of Wakefield or like Crime and Punishment. It's the best detective story I ever read . . . could be read for its sociology . . . as a political novel . . . as a horror story . . . above all, . . . as an humanitarian work."[111] Two years later, in his introduction to Algren's novel *Never Come Morning*, Wright praised that work not for "prescribing 'pink pills for social ills,' pil[ing] up a mountain of naturalistic detail, [or] draw[ing] blueprints . . . in a call for direct action," but rather for "depict[ing] the intensity of feeling, the tawdry but potent dreams, the crude but forceful poetry, and the frustrated longing for human dignity residing in the lives of the Poles of Chicago's North West Side."

Wright and Algren belonged to a second generation of naturalistic writers redefining and extending the form in relation to their respective ethnic experiences, the felt exigencies of the times, and recent aesthetic and intellectual influences. They attempted to work out, on the literary plane, a series of artistic problems similar to those engaged by practitioners of social realism in the plastic arts such as Chicagoans Charles White, Marion Perkins, and Mitchell Siporin. Andrew Hemingway's comments about Leftist visual artists generally apply to these writers: "Social art was a hybrid and unstable mode. It had to carry the imperative to be an art equal in formal achievement to both the great art of the past and the modern tradition. At the same time it had to suggest a political orientation without becoming overt revolutionary propaganda."[112] Other felt imperatives were to portray the lives of ordinary people and to address mass audiences. As Carla Cappetti notes of Algren's work, such intentions required a precarious balancing of "reportage and nightmare, journalism and surrealism, sociology and poetry."[113]

The best of the second-generation naturalists, black and white, were engaged in such precarious balancing and in the process exploded the form from within. Comparing the evolution of Wright's novels from *Native Son* to *The Outsider* (1953), Richard Lehan observes: "Like [Paul] Bowles and [Norman] Mailer, if Wright had not had the benefit of naturalism, he could not have written his version of the existential novel. . . . By voiding the novel of its moral center and creating the antihero, naturalism allowed protoexistentialists to fill their fiction with Nietzschean overmen."[114]

While Wright's permanent relocation to France in 1947 brought him to the epicenter of existentialist philosophy and enabled his definitive break with literary naturalism, it also removed him from that soil, at once stony and fertile, on which he had shaped his finest works of fiction. In a 1953 letter to Albert Murray, Ralph Ellison characterized Wright's expatriation as an example "of what happens when you go elsewhere looking for what you already had at home. Wright goes to France for existentialism when . . . any blues could tell him things that would make . . . Sartre's head swim."[115] The next stage in the evolution of the African American novel would not be centered in Chicago and would be realized most successfully by such writers as Ellison and Murray, who hewed closely to their cultural roots even as they mastered the technical resources of literary modernism, who defended the art of fiction as embodying a valid epistemology independent of the premises of social science, and who gave evidence of a debt to Wright even as they anxiously repudiated his influence.

CHAPTER 10

Bronzeville and the Poets

Frank Marshall Davis, Margaret Walker, and Gwendolyn Brooks each published books of poetry that proved to be milestones for African American letters. These breakthroughs culminated when Brooks received the 1950 Pulitzer Prize for poetry, the first time a black writer had been so honored and an event that helps establish the final boundary year of this study. As poets and people, the three were quite different, yet Bronzeville—as place and metaphor—was indelibly woven into their experiences, values, allusions, imagery, symbols, tropes, and themes—the very warp and woof of their writing. Twelve years separate the birth dates of Davis and Brooks, and fourteen separate the publication of Davis's *Black Man's Verse* (1935) and Brooks's *Annie Allen* (1949). Such a span affords time enough to gauge both the development of individual careers and the trajectory of broader cultural trends.

In an essay called "New Poets," published in 1950, Walker attempted to delineate the generational experiences of African American writers who first published in the 1930s and early 1940s. Their affinities included a shared rejection of "the status of the exotic, the accidentally unusual." In language that echoed "Blueprint for Negro Writing," Walker criticized poets of the Harlem Renaissance who "lacked social perspective" and "seemed constantly to beg the question of the Negro's humanity." Her generation, she observed, formed "a new school of writers who were no longer isolated because of color, who were integrated around the beliefs that created the New Deal."[1]

Walker referred to herself, Davis, Sterling Brown, Robert Hayden, Melvin Tolson, and others as "poets of social protest" and linked their militant spirit with the CIO's interracial labor organizing and the WPA's cultural projects. She noted that the New Deal agencies supplanted individual patrons while broadening the audience for creative expression. "As a result of free art for all the people," she asserted, "a cultural renaissance in all the arts swept the United States. . . . Consequently, . . . the Negro people themselves grew in intellectual awareness."

Brooks was among the youngest of the poets discussed in the essay, which appeared shortly after she was awarded the Pulitzer. As Walker described her friend's achievements, she set Brooks somewhat apart, in but not entirely of the generation under consideration. She discerned a socially conscious, documentary core in Brooks's 1945 collection, *A Street in Bronzeville*, especially in its "concern with the problems of war," but Walker noted that, four years later, *Annie Allen* was "a marked departure from the note of social protest." Brooks was, by Walker's reckoning, one of the "new poets of the late forties," focusing "attention on craftsmanship with an emphasis on form." Significantly, Walker did not regard this shift in emphasis as an act of political apostasy or aesthetic misdirection; rather, she perceived Brooks's embrace of the increasingly dominant high-modernist aesthetic as laying the basis for her "personal triumph" *and* for "a racial vindication," insofar as "the Negro has finally achieved full status in the literary world as an American poet."

"New Poets" suggests the value of a dual perspective on Brooks's early works, treating them both as exemplars of generational achievement and as harbingers of a new period in African American letters. Walker's essay also underscores the need for closer examination of aesthetic differences among the specific sites where Bronzeville writers served their literary apprenticeships, especially the South Side Writers' Group and the Chicago Poets' Class.

Frank Marshall Davis, Fighting Poet

Frank Marshall Davis's first long poem, "Chicago's Congo," was published in *Abbott's Monthly* in 1931, while he was working as a journalist for the *Atlanta World*.[2] Its title signified on both Carl Sandburg's "Chicago" and Vachel Lindsay's "The Congo." From Lindsay, whose most famous line was "Boomlay, boomlay, boomlay, BOOM!" Davis learned to value dramatic sound effects and to think of poetry as public performance. Thus, he often included orchestral directions in the margins of his poems. Even more influenced by fellow journalist and poet Sandburg, Davis wrote free verse marked by panoramic views of the urban scene, colloquial language, and concrete details from the lives of ordinary people.

"Chicago's Congo" caught the attention of a white socialite, who became Davis's lover and his intermediary with a small North Side publisher.[3] The poem reappeared as the lead piece in *Black Man's Verse*, a collection published in October 1935, about a year after his return to Bronzeville. It gave voice to the bluster and bravado of a rising generation and an expanding Black Metropolis:

> I'm a grown up man today Chicago
> My bones are thick and stout
> (when I moved to new districts bombings couldn't break them). . . .
> I've got a lion's heart and a six-shooter
> I've got a fighter's fist and five newspapers
> I've got an eye for beauty and another for cash
> Nothing you've got I can't have.[4]

Defender editor Lucius Harper hailed Davis as "the acknowledged interpreter in verse of Chicago's South Side."[5] George Schuyler lauded his collection for "depth, thought, sweep and a technique not yet attained by any of our other Aframerican poets."[6] Alain Locke saw it as evidence of an emerging new center of African American writing. He criticized "veteran poets" of 1920s Harlem, who "expect in this day of changing styles and viewpoints to live successfully in the past," and hailed Chicagoans Davis and Wright for following "the Langston Hughes inspiration, . . . go[ing] deeper into the substance of the folk life" and bringing "fresh talent and creative imagination to this waning field."[7]

Black Man's Verse was also well-received by white critics. In the *Saturday Review of Literature*, William Rose Benet highlighted the lyrical notes that punctuate Davis's tendency toward polemic and satire: "His love songs are those of a black Solomon." Kansas editor William Allen White aligned the poet's work with the Whitmanesque celebration of the national life associated with the documentary spirit: "He is singing the songs which some day will rise in the land and become a great American epic."[8]

Poetry editor Harriet Monroe, finding "a good deal of swinging strength" in the volume and identifying "Cabaret" as "the best built and most successful of the longer pieces," noted especially its playful personification of the instruments of a jazz band. She quoted the final stanza approvingly:[9]

> Weave for me a strange garment, O Maker of All!
> Make me a jacket of silver stolen from the cornet's high C,
> Take the violin's tremolo and make me a shimmering golden waistcoat
> Of black, O Maker Of All, the piano has plenty to spare
> Just a little of its bass would make a long thick cloak
> I'll die some day I hope
> Death must be a winsome hermaphrodite
> or men and women would leave those arms
> I'd like, O Maker of All, to wear those garments when I take my last dance
> with Death.

While the Earl Hines NBC Orchestra held the airwaves nightly and Archibald Motley painted energetic portraits of Bronzeville nightclubs, Davis created syncopated verse performances with a mix of free verse and rhyme, arresting imagery, and jaggedly varied line lengths and rhythms.

Four months after publication of his first collection, Davis participated in the founding conference of the National Negro Congress, and Wright subsequently invited him to join the South Side Writers' Group. The group provided a forum in which to try out new poems while grappling with Wright's Marxist aesthetics. In his memoirs, Davis recalled their relationship: "Curious and fascinated, I asked many questions. . . . Quite often I needled him [Wright] about Communism, but he took it all good-naturedly."[10] Davis's earlier journalism reveals him as racially militant yet deeply suspicious of "the sweet bunk of oily tongued Reds," but he grudgingly commended "the International Labor Defense . . . for its conduct of the [Scottsboro] trial." "The very fact that the Communists have taken up the sword in behalf of the Negro," he observed, "and that there exist cases so rank and putrid as the Scottsboro mess could wean this race to the Red banner."[11]

Davis brought a draft of "I Am the American Negro," title poem of his second collection, to the South Side Writers' Group for feedback. In its published version, the piece develops through a sequence of dramatic vignettes centered on "a giant of indeterminate brown, his arms and legs shackled" inside "the temple of America's Social System." Early in the poem, the giant announces:

I, the American Negro, am a rainbow race, a kaleidoscope breed found
only in this land.
In my veins runs the blood of Caucasian Europe and of the Indians of
America. . . .
In me is a monstrous union of many African tribes. . . .
My dream is to be physically white . . . so I straighten my kinks, bleach
my skin and look down on those darker than I. . . . whatever white folks do
I imitate.

At the poem's conclusion, the giant achieves a sudden growth in consciousness through confrontation with the personified "experience" of the "Black man" in America. The awakening comes too late, however, as "the temple falls in a crash . . . and the voice of the giant is stilled" (ellipses original).

"Wright's main criticism" of the poem, Davis recalled, "was what he called its 'hopeless bitterness' and 'lack of a positive resolution for the plight of black people.' He said he would have had his giant crush all opposition."[12] This trope of the shackled and/or avenging giant situates Davis's poem and Wright's criticism of it within an early 1930s iconographic tradition in "*New Masses* and other CPUSA publications where the working class is almost always figured as a large muscular man." James Smethurst further describes this figure as influenced by the "masculinist discourses of modernism [and] African American nationalism" in the 1920s.[13]

I Am the American Negro was published in 1937, the same year that Davis received a Rosenwald fellowship. His grant of $1,500 for "creative writing, especially poetry," was secured with the assistance of his employer, Claude Barnett, who was well connected with Charles Johnson and other principals of the fund.[14] Eleven years passed before Davis published his third collection, *47th Street*. Clearly the demands of his day job as executive editor of the Associated Negro Press partly explain the delay, but his increasing political activism is also pertinent. From 1935 to 1948, Davis wrote much of the ANP's copy and "personally edited or rewrote every item released." He covered sports and politics and reviewed books, plays, and records, through which he developed a special interest in jazz that spilled over into the improvisational style of his poetry.[15]

Activism and creative expression were deeply entwined for Davis, as for many artists of the period. Under Wright's influence, he became active in the League of American Writers and by 1938 was serving as treasurer of the Chicago branch.[16] He became an associate editor of the Leftist literary journal *New Anvil* the following year.[17] His memoirs and scrapbooks document ever-expanding commitments in the 1940s to organizations within the Communist Party orbit, including American Youth for Democracy and the Civil Rights Congress.[18] Whatever may have been the societal value of his activities in the Popular Front milieu of the 1940s, they did little to advance his artistic productivity or craftsmanship.

Opening with a long poem of the same name, *47th Street* offers a panoptic view of Bronzeville's "Broadway": its street cars and sound trucks, its gamblers, preachers, "pigfaced pimps and hogpursed physicians," "garrulous gin gobblers," political protestors, pawnbrokers, numbers bankers, anxious widows, and young men on corners. Leaning heavily on Davis's favorite devices—enumeration, juxtaposition, paradox, and irony—the poem rambles through the sights and sounds of the street, concluding with a satirical flourish:

> Maybe this is the promised land
> Elsewhere they say Opportunity knocks but once. In Chicago Opportunity
> bangs loud enough to rouse the family in the flat below, leaves a calling
> card, then telephones next day to learn whether you got it.
> There is that one who could not vote in Alabama. From his law office
> on 47th Street he went to Washington as a congressman from Illinois
> Or consider this one from Iowa who served 60 days in the county jail for
> stealing a ten cent loaf of bread. He is now in Joliet for 20 years after a
> thousand dollar robbery of a 47th Street currency exchange.
> This is a street of bigger and better things

As both poet and journalist, Davis was above all a chronicler and documentary observer of his time and place.

The collection also contains love poems built of lush, sensuous imagery ("For you I have built a shrine of scented memories—/ Turquoise, ruby and moon yellow.") and delicate lyrics, suggesting another dimension behind the polemic, satire, and documentary:

> Night's brittle song, sliver-thin
> Shatters into a billion fragments
> Of quiet shadows
> At the blaring jazz
> Of a morning sun.

The surprise of such synesthetic imagery underscores Langston Hughes's observation that "when [Davis's] poems are poetry, they are powerful."[19]

47th Street appeared just months before Davis permanently relocated to Hawaii in December 1948. While the energy and intended effect of his poems frequently outpace a disciplined control of language, his work remains an important part of the textual record of Bronzeville's literary awakening. In common with many another Chicago writer, Davis's poetry combines a note of political protest with defiant pride in the *genius loci* of the sprawling industrial giant of the American heartland, in the clash and bang of its relentless materialism and its endless pursuit of the new and the big. This rugged muse inspired a fighting poet.

Margaret Walker: Singing the Martial Songs

Margaret Walker was seventeen when she transferred from New Orleans to Northwestern University. She lived in the Chicago area for seven years, coming of age in the shadow of the Great Migration and Depression and playing an active role in Bronzeville's artistic and intellectual circles. Her father was a Jamaican immigrant, but her mother's family had

25. Margaret Walker, c. 1941.
Vivian G. Harsh Research Collection of
Afro-American History and Literature,
Chicago Public Library. Hall Branch
Archvies 050.

deep roots in southern soil. Walker's emotional attachment to the South and the pain of
dispossession animate her finest writing, and her early poems filter this tension through a
politically radical sensibility shaped in Chicago.

Walker identified her first influences as her mother's music, her father's teaching and
preaching, and "the southern landscape of my childhood and adolescence."[20] Her home
was filled with classical music, church hymns and anthems, spirituals, ragtime, popular
ballads, and even work songs, blues, and jazz. Her father, a religious scholar and Methodist
minister, taught her to read the Bible and wisdom literature of the East and moved her
with his sermons.

At Northwestern, Walker studied Renaissance literature, the English poets, and the
mechanics of prosody, but in the years that followed her friendship with Richard Wright
opened new aesthetic and political vistas. She recalled their collaboration on the Illinois
Writers' Project, South Side Writers' Group, and *New Challenge*: "During those three years
[1936 to 1939] we were struggling to publish for the first time in national magazines and
books. . . . [We] went to some of the same studio parties, read the same books, spent long
evenings talking together, and often walked from the North Side, where the Project was
located, on Erie Street, downtown to the public library, or rode the El to the South Side,
where we lived."[21] Walker brought draft poems to be critiqued at meetings of the Writers'
Group and revised them individually with Wright: "We sat together and worked on the

forms of my poetry, the free verse things, and came up with my long line or strophic form, punctuated by a short line."[22]

In October 1937, Wright published four of Walker's poems in *New Challenge*, and a few weeks later, the piece that was to make her reputation appeared in the pages of *Poetry*.[23] "Shortly after my twenty-second birthday [in July 1937]," she recalled, "I sat down at my typewriter and in fifteen minutes wrote all but the last stanza of the poem 'For My People.'" Wright had just moved to New York so Walker turned to another Writing Project colleague, Nelson Algren, for advice. Wright's former John Reed Club comrade read the first nine stanzas and suggested "how to write the resolution and conclusion."[24]

The "strophic form" that lends shape to the free verse of "For My People" is musical in origin, a method of structuring a piece by creating sections, corresponding to poetic stanzas, and developing them through thematic repetition and variation. Each of the first nine stanzas begins with a long line stating a theme to be developed and commented upon in the following shorter lines. Each begins with the words "For My People" or some variant and consists of a single phrase built by additive detail, extending over four to seven enjambed lines. These devices unify the first nine stanzas, create a sense of anticipation, and prepare for a dramatic break that is both syntactic and semantic.

The first stanza introduces key thematic elements of music and religion and establishes the syntactic pattern of a single long, breathy phrase:

> For my people everywhere singing their slave songs
> repeatedly: their dirges and their ditties and their blues
> and jubilees, praying their prayers nightly to an
> unknown god, bending their knees humbly to an
> unseen power;[25]

Musical references continue in stanza three, where children play "concert" among other games, and in stanza five, where grown men and women "laugh and dance and sing." Religious references reoccur in stanza three, where children are "playing baptizing and preaching," in stanza five, where "religion" is set beside adult pleasures of "play and . . . wine and . . . success," and in stanzas seven and eight, where black people are "shouting when burdened" and "floundering in the dark of churches."

The tenth and final stanza disrupts the established pattern. In place of a single long phrase is a series of short, imperative sentences, beginning: "Let a new earth rise. / Let another world be born. Let a / bloody peace be written in the sky." The thematic element of music continues, but it is transformed along with the syntax: "Let the martial songs be / written, let the dirges disappear." The key word "dirges" (lugubriously elongated in Walker's recorded reading of the poem) suggests both spirituals and blues—harmonic vehicles for surviving and wresting beauty from a world of pain. Implicit in the poem is a coming transfiguration, marked metaphorically by music appropriate to "a second / generation full of courage." Such "martial songs" have the power, so apparent in the anthemlike poem itself, to stir "the pulsing / in [the] spirits and [the] blood" of "a people / loving freedom."

The religious theme continues into the tenth stanza echoing the preacher's invocation of God's wrath on a fallen, sinful world. The voice is prophetic and visionary. For nine stanzas, the speaker has lamented the tribulations of her people—their lives of endless toil and "bitter hours," their blindness and bewilderment, their deaths from "consumption and anemia and lynching." The ninth stanza concludes with "all the adams and eves and their countless generations." From these progenitors of the future will be born the "new earth" of the final stanza. Walker's phrase alludes to the "new earth" and the twelve-gated "new Jerusalem" promised in the biblical Book of Revelation once "the abominable, and murderers, and whoremongers, and sorcerers, and idolaters, and all liars" have been cast "in the lake which burneth with fire and brimstone."[26]

"For My People" merges Christian eschatology with its secular Marxist counterpart, expressed most notably in "The Internationale," the revolutionary anthem that promises "The earth shall rise on new foundations."[27] Walker's hybrid millennialism was of a piece with the struggle of other members of the South Side Writers' Group to forge literary forms that would embody all they had mastered of their craft while speaking for and to "the Negro masses." Her use of carefully modulated rhythms, rise and fall of the voice, striking juxtapositions, syntactic parallelism and repetition, concrete imagery and diction, alliteration and assonance underscores the poem's debt to the oratorical rhetoric of both the down-home preacher and the black communist soap-boxer.

In June 1939, Walker went to New York to attend the third American Writers' Congress and to see Richard Wright again. The trip ended in personal disaster, however, as an apparent misunderstanding on her part provoked Wright into abruptly and brutally severing their relationship.[28] Shortly thereafter she left Chicago for graduate study in creative writing at the University of Iowa. There she worked in the now-famous writers' workshop while submitting fiction to New Anvil, the Leftist literary journal edited by her Chicago friends Jack Conroy, Nelson Algren, and Frank Marshall Davis.[29] In January 1940, she reported to Arna Bontemps, who had recommended her for a Rosenwald fellowship, that her thesis, a collection of poetry, had been approved and she was looking for a publisher.[30] Her bid for a year at Iowa free of economic pressures was unsuccessful, however, and in August, she returned to her parents' home in New Orleans "in a state of collapse" from overwork and malnutrition.[31]

While the poet recovered, her collection found a publisher. Yale University Press issued For My People as the 1942 volume in its prestigious Yale Series of Younger Poets. No African American had ever before received this honor. Consisting of twenty-six poems, many of them written in Chicago, the book is divided into three sections, each exploring a different form: free verse, the folk ballad, and the sonnet.

The first section, which begins with the title poem, holds by far the greatest interest. "I want my body bathed again by southern suns, my soul / reclaimed again from southern land," yearns the speaker in the opening lines of "Southern Song," a poem that had been critiqued in the Writers' Group and previously published in New Challenge. Walker's "song" begins as a pastoral reverie of "grass and hay and clover / bloom," of "rain-soaked earth" and "the smell of soil." Another piece, "Sorrow Home," begins "My roots are deep in southern life" and evokes "a tropic world," embracing "the cotton fields, tobacco and the cane" of the American South, "the palm tree and banana leaf" of her father's Jamaica, and the "rubber trees" of Africa. Walker's tropic images of warmth, moisture, fecundity, color, and light clash with the cold, sterile, smoke-darkened world of migrants in northern tenements, echoing the contrasts in Langston Hughes's early poem "Our Land." In "Sorrow Home," she writes: "I am no hot-house bulb to be reared in steam-heated flats / with the music of El and subway in my ears, walled in / by steel and wood and brick far from the sky." Against these discordant urban strains, the sweet music of homeland and heartland beckons, but the pastoral refrain is no sooner voiced than stifled by nightmare recollection of race terror. "Southern Song" ends: "I want my careless song to strike no minor key; no fiend to / stand between my body's southern song—the fusion of / the South, my body's song and me." The last sentence of "Sorrow Home" similarly recalls "the Klan of hate, the hounds / and the chain gangs."

"I am a child of the valley," the speaker announces in "Delta," the collection's longest piece, described by Eugenia Collier as "the poem that most completely exploits the motif of the South."[32] Ripped from the "mud and muck and misery of lowlands," she mourns the loss of that which her people earned with blood and toil, but "dare not claim"—"these mountains we dare not claim, / . . . this earth we dare not claim, / . . . the river we dare not claim." The wound of dispossession is raw and bleeding and will not be healed by "the honky-tonks . . . and the blues." Each of the poem's three sections ends with an image of regeneration, of a new day and "a new earth." The close of section one recalls the martial songs of "For My People": "If only from this valley we might rise with song! / With singing that is ours." Section two ends "Out of a deep slumber truth rides upon us / . . . and full of a hundred unfulfilled dreams of today / . . . we wish no longer to rest." The poem's final lines include: "Neither earth nor star nor water's host / can sever us from our life to be. . . ."

The yearning, anger, and prophetic oratory of the poems in the collection's first section give way to a series of ballads, drawn from folk sources, including tales of such archetypal figures as Stagolee and John Henry. Neither these pieces nor the sonnets that follow ever approach the power of the first section, for the collection's strength rests squarely, as R. Baxter Miller observes, on the success of the visionary poems.[33] Walker's irregularly rhymed sonnets trace her early life from Birmingham, near the "old Ishkooda mines," and New Orleans "in low cotton country," to Chicago and Iowa. They are imbued with the documentary spirit of the age. "Whores," for example, recalls the time Walker spent on the Illinois Writers' Project writing about Goose Island and Division Street: "When I grew up I went away to work / where painted whores were fascinating sights."

Richard Wright, Walker's one-time friend, mentor, and project colleague, fled the Delta permanently as if pursued, like bluesman Robert Johnson, by "a hellhound on [his] trail." But Walker's life journey brought her back to the beginning, to her roots and her "Sorrow Home." From Iowa she returned South, married, raised four children, and pursued an academic career. Her teaching posts took her from North Carolina to West Virginia and in 1949 to Jackson, Mississippi, where Wright had spent five desperate years and where Walker lived for nearly half a century. After For My People, she did not publish another book for twenty-four years, but Jubilee, her novel of slavery times, appeared at the height of the civil rights movement and helped retrieve her lost audience. Four other books of poems, a biography of Wright, and two collections of essays followed.

In her 1950 essay, "New Poets," Walker discusses, among others, Frank Marshall Davis and Sterling Brown, who published first collections in the 1930s, and Robert Hayden and Melvin Tolson, whose first books appeared in the early 1940s. She observes that, despite the relative prosperity ushered in by wartime industrial production, "The poetry of American Negroes continued to reflect the mood of the thirties" well into the following decade. Although Hayden, a veteran of the John Reed Clubs and Detroit Writers' Project, later became known for a complex, lapidary style, his first collection, *Heart-Shape in the Dust* (1940), fit Walker's generational paradigm through poems on the Scottsboro case and Gabriel Prosser's revolt and use of the hortatory "mass chant" popularized by other radical poets and playwrights.[34] Walker juxtaposes the peroration of "For My People," an excerpt from Hayden's poem "Speech," and the final "movement" of Melvin Tolson's "Dark Symphony" to demonstrate how each poet plays a stylistic variation on a common "note of social protest." Here are the lines from Tolson:

> Out of abysses of Illiteracy,
> Through labyrinths of Lies,
> Across the waste lands of Disease . . .
> We advance!
>
> Out of dead-ends of Poverty,
> Through wildernesses of Superstition,
> Across barricades of Jim Crowism . . .
> We advance!
>
> With the Peoples of the World . . .
> We advance! (ellipses original)[35]

This section of the poem bears the subtitle "Tempo di Marcia," or "in march time," for it too is a martial song, sung by another poet of a militant generation.

Gwendolyn Brooks and the Chicago Poets' Class

With a determined mother behind her, Gwendolyn Brooks set out to become a famous poet, writing at least one new piece a day after she turned eleven. Extensive reading of nineteenth-century English poets strongly influenced her adolescent poems of romantic passion, unrequited love, natural beauty, friendship, and world-weariness. She encountered the poets of the Harlem Renaissance in Countee Cullen's anthology *Caroling Dusk* and in the persons of James Weldon Johnson and Langston Hughes. A letter from Johnson urged her to "study carefully the work of the best modern poets . . . to help cultivate the highest possible standards of self-criticism."[36] She and her mother met Hughes at a poetry reading at Metropolitan Community Church. He read several of her poems and told her: "Keep writing. Some day you'll have a book published."[37]

Brooks contributed dozens of poems to the *Defender*. The very first, "To the Hinderer," appeared in August 1934 and, according to her biographer, George Kent, was a coded response to racial slights by white students at Hyde Park High School.[38] Its mannered style, plodding iambicism, and abstract diction suggest the teenage apprentice attempting to imitate the poetry of an earlier age. She later described her adolescent self as "swimming in Swinburne."[39] Four years later, she published a free-verse poem, "An Old Apartment Building," whose concrete diction, pose of wry puzzlement, and cataloguing of events from the building's past anticipate stylistic and thematic aspects of her impressive first collection, *A Street in Bronzeville*.[40] In the years between these poems, she followed Johnson's injunction and read Sandburg, Eliot, Pound, John Crowe Ransom, and other contemporary poets.

Brooks deepened her engagement with the moderns in a Wednesday evening poetry workshop at the Community Art Center. Its founder, Inez Cunningham Stark, was a white socialite who wrote about art for Chicago newspapers, served as a reader for *Poetry*, and—as president of the Renaissance Society—helped advance the city's cultural avant-garde. With a list provided by the local NAACP, she gathered a group of South Side residents interested in writing. "We have a poetry class here at the Center," Robert Davis wrote to Langston Hughes in October 1941. "There are some 25 persons registered for the class and about 15 attend each session."[41] Besides Davis, a veteran of the South Side Writers' Project, the class included Brooks, her husband, Henry Blakely, Margaret Burroughs, John Carlis, Edward Bland, William Couch, and Margaret Cunningham Danner.[42] It continued into the next decade and was known variously as the Chicago Poets' Class, the Visionaries, and the Creative Writing Forum.[43]

Brooks vividly recalled Stark "tripping in [to meetings], slender, erect, and frosted with a fabulous John Fredericks hat. . . . her arms . . . loaded with books." Typically, Stark announced the evening's topic and read a group of poems to illustrate. "When she had finished, . . . a burst of excitement met her full blast. The 'students' evaluated, criticized, praised, tore. They treated similarly their own precious creations, laboriously evolved during the seven days since the last meeting. Sometimes what we said to each other hurt or stung. We were all . . . desperately earnest."[44]

Stark prodded these young writers to find language that would startle the reader, to explore the elasticity of poetic form, to find subjects in the things and people they knew. She used a poetic handbook that cautioned: "From the technical standpoint no poem is stronger than its weakest word."[45] Brooks described Stark offering advice: "All you need in this poem are the last four lines"; "You must be careful not to list the obvious things. . . . Use them only to illustrate boredom and inanity." Of her own subjects, Brooks wrote, "You had only to look out of a window. There was material always, walking or running, fighting or screaming or singing."[46]

The recollections of other participants provide further glimpses of the group. Painter John Carlis told an interviewer that Stark often played records of poets such as Yeats, Hughes, and Lindsay reading their work. These particular choices suggest that, in common with other members of Chicago's artistic community, she took a broad view of modern art, embracing both transatlantic modernism and the Americanist avant-garde. Carlis also recalled that

26. Poetry class at the South Side Community Art Center, 1942.
Photo: Jack Delano. Library of Congress, Prints & Photographs Division,
FSA-OWI Collection. LC-USW3–000701-D.

participants became good friends and that, when Stark was traveling, the class was sometimes led by her friend, Peter De Vries, an editor at *Poetry* and later a prolific novelist.[47]

"We read our works and there was a critique," Margaret Burroughs remembered. "Some of the class criticized my work as being too political, propaganda, etc. . . . I wrote about . . . Scottsboro and other social themes. . . . I decided to leave the poetry to Gwen and started writing for children."[48] The "marked departure from the note of social protest" that Walker perceived in Brooks's second collection, *Annie Allen*, can be traced in part to the aesthetics of the Poets' Class, where that note might be sounded in many registers, or not at all.

This "departure" could be found as early as 1942 in Brooks's personal statement quoted by Burroughs, who served as poetry editor of a short-lived magazine called *Negro Youth Photo Script*: "I prefer Emily Dickinson, for her consistency in striking at the heart of life. . . . I have no message for poets of this querulous time except—Scrape the stuff of your everyday living into the poetry you write. Don't compel the war theme to serve you. If the war has hit you, it will find its way easily into your work. If not, not. Don't write about bombings you can't imagine, or mass deaths that, in your less giddily patriotic moods, you will admit mean nothing to you personally. Be sincere, even if being that means dealing only with sunsets, your latest love affair, and the smell of limburger cheese."[49] That same year, Brooks wrote to Hughes asking his "opinion regarding the personalized trends that most of the members of the poetry class are taking."[50] The documentary record lends support to George Kent's characterization of Brooks in this period as "attached to the certainties of her upbringing, Christianity, and middle-class democracy," rather than the closet radical some scholars portray.[51]

Another participant in the Poets' Class, Edward Bland, had great influence on Brooks, and his 1944 essay "Racial Bias and Negro Poetry" suggests the sorts of conversations that occurred in and around the group's meetings.[52] Bland's essay characterizes "almost all poetry by Negroes" as distorted by "a provincial view of life and an intensely slanted approach." He attributes these limitations to both "external" and "internal" sources. The external stem from "the defensive maneuvering of a minority" against the "bigoted white world," the internal from "the pre-individualistic thinking of the Negro," which Bland defined as "self-conscious 'race' values which impair and delimit the vision of the artist."[53] The piece reveals a striking evolution of Bland's thinking since his earlier participation in the South Side Writers' Group. In "A Note on Negro Nationalism," published in *New Challenge* in 1937, he had argued that Negro writers allied with "the revolutionary movement" must understand "the true difference between nationalism as a limiting concept and nationalism as a phase which is difficult but rich in the materials for progress into wider channels." That essay makes clear Bland's earlier hope that Leftist black writers might help guide "the Negro masses" from a separatist racial identity to an interracial class identity through a Left-influenced nationalism.[54] By 1944 he was instead emphasizing the necessity of individual artistic vision over group identity of any sort and linking this value to his hope "that the present war will create an environment more favorable to humanistic goals."

Stark encouraged the group's participants to enter their work in poetry contests. Brooks was awarded first prize at the Midwestern Writers' Conference in 1943 and again in each of the following two years. She vividly recalled attending an awards ceremony at Northwestern University and waiting to hear the results announced. When Paul Engle, Margaret Walker's one-time teacher at Iowa, announced that Brooks had won, she sat in stunned amazement: "No one expected a little Negro girl to win. . . . So I just sat there, finding it hard to believe that he was really calling my name, wanting me to come up to the stage to get the first prize. . . . Finally, I walked up there. I'll never forget the gasps that went through the audience. . . . Negroes just didn't win prizes of that sort."[55] Such growing recognition eased the way to the poet's first book contract. By guiding and promoting the apprentice work of aspiring creative artists and by broadening Bronzeville's cultural horizons, the Chicago Poets' Class achieved a place of historical importance alongside Richard Wright's South Side Writers' Group and George Neal's Art Crafts Guild.

A Street in Bronzeville to *Annie Allen*

The letter from Harper Brothers accepting Brooks's first collection was accompanied by Richard Wright's enthusiastic evaluation. Brooks's poems "are hard and real," he wrote. "She easily catches the pathos of petty destinies, the whimper of the wounded, the tiny accidents that plague the lives of the desperately poor, and the problem of color prejudice among Negroes." Wright was especially struck by the way "kitchenette building" portrayed that grim existence he had known and described so powerfully in his prose works. His major reservation was absence of "one really long fine poem around which shorter ones are added or grouped." Brooks wrote to thank Wright for his support and to assure him that she was working on such a piece, which became "The Sundays of Satin-Legs Smith."[56]

A *Street in Bronzeville* appeared on August 15, the same day that Japan's surrender formally ended World War II. If outbreak of war had proved disastrous for such works as Wright's *12 Million Black Voices* and William Attaway's *Blood on the Forge*, its end was auspicious for Brooks's first collection. The book was well received by critics and had good sales for a work of poetry. White reviewers praised it; poet Rolfe Humphries for example highlighted Brooks's "command over both the colloquial and the more austere rhythms."[57] Black writer/critic J. Saunders Redding commended Brooks for "giving the undertone of Negro life without the obvious device of ringing the brazen bell of dialect."[58] Margaret Walker hailed her sophisticated technique and noted "new directions" marked by "internationalism rather than . . . nationalism and racism."[59] A prim review in *The Journal of Negro Education*, however, complained of a focus on "the seamy or pathological side of Negro life" and absence of "Negro homes with lovely lawns and . . . Brown Americans whose conduct is normal."[60]

The collection contains forty-one poems in three groups. It opens with a sequence of twenty lyric poems, deriving from Brooks's initial intention "to take some personality or event, or idea from each (or many of) the approximately thirty houses on a street in this vicinity."[61] This of course is the documentary spirit at work. The pieces that compose the second section are essentially character portraits: four longer poems and a subgroup of five brief "Hattie Scott" pieces. The book ends with twelve poems based on letters that Brooks received from friends in the military. Clustered under the title "Gay Chaps at the Bar," the poems were conceived as "a sonnet series in off-rhyme, because . . . it was an off-rhyme situation."[62]

The book's second poem, "kitchenette building," opens memorably: "We are things of dry hours and the involuntary plan, / Grayed in and gray."[63] The first line alludes to the "noons of dryness" and "involuntary powers" of W. H. Auden's "Lullaby" and less directly to Eliot's "The Hollow Men." The long, Latinate "involuntary" also echoes down centuries of African American experience, from the first slave ship to the invisible barbed-wire fences enclosing Bronzeville. "Grayed-in and gray" suggests the grimy urban environment as well as the indefinite mood. The phrase also sets up a contrastive color scheme with "white and violet," which are associated with "Dream," the poem's key word. Langston Hughes's question, "What happens to a dream deferred?" is revoiced. "Dream" resonates with "a giddy sound," bright colors, a "flutter," an "aria," invocations of yearning for some undefined excitement and creative outlet. The speaker (first-person, plural, female) strains to keep the dream alive amidst the smells and noise and cold and dirt of a squalid kitchenette building but succumbs, at last, to the mundane allure of a bathtub, which serves five flats, suddenly becoming unoccupied. Marked by unobtrusive craftsmanship, "kitchenette building" portrays the defeat of aspiration by circumstance and sounds a note of protest, but in the distinctly minor keys of satire and irony.

Anchoring the collection is "The Sundays of Satin-Legs Smith," a portrait of a ladies' man and dandy—a long, complex work, marked by mercurial shifts in tone and nuance. The opening lines establish a pattern of playing one convention or expectation against another: "Inamoratas, with an approbation, / Bestowed his title. Blessed his inclination." The diction is elegant and Latinate; but, for an extra syllable, this would be iambic pentameter and the perfect heroic couplet. The fustian high style plays against the poem's "low" content: Smith's many lovers enjoy the feel of his smooth skin and applaud his sexual prowess. He wakens of a Sunday, like "a cat / Tawny, reluctant, royal," plans his next "performance," and enters "his bath." The tone is detached, the speaker slightly amused.

After the first four stanzas, the speaker shifts from third- to first-person, and stanza length increases dramatically, two of many shape-shiftings that occur throughout the poem. In a play on Eliot's Prufrock ("Let us go then, you and I. . . ."), the reader is invited to accompany the speaker through the scenes of Satin-Legs' typical Sunday. His "bath" fumes with overpowering scent of "lavender" and "pine," first of many déclassé elements that the speaker notes, to the implied discomfit of the white, middle-class reader. The tour continues into "the innards of [Smith's] closet," contemplates his "drapes"—fabulously colored 1940s zoot suits, topped by "hats / Like bright umbrellas; and hysterical ties." Along with changes in linguistic register, the speaker's perspective seems to shuttle between blushing propriety and warming admiration for the elaborate preening of this ghetto dandy. Her uneasy, shifting mood recalls the speaker of "a song in the front yard"— well-bred, sexually innocent, but longing "to be a bad woman, too / And wear the brave stockings of night-black lace / And strut down the streets with paint on my face."

Amidst the aesthetic contemplation of Smith's "variegated grace" come catalogues of ghetto sounds that "He hears and does not hear" and ghetto sights that "He sees and does not see." Satin-Legs, it appears, survives by self-delusion and isolation, a condition (vide Prufrock) that, while not peculiar to Bronzeville, takes on exaggerated sharpness when physical want joins spiritual want: "Promise piled over and betrayed."

As Sunday comes to an end, the dark knight-errant "Squires his lady to dinner at Joe's Eats." Every Sunday he has a different lady, but the courtly ritual remains the same. The poem ends with the surprise of a lyrical sestet, its altered tone highlighted by italics. The speaker sets all censoriousness aside, closes ironic distance, and acknowledges Smith's frame of reference. His lady becomes his succulent, sensuous meal and their lovemaking his art. Three of six lines begin with "*Her body*"—compared with "*new brown bread*" and "*a honey bowl*" and, in the final lines, with "*summer earth, / Receptive, soft and absolute . . .*" (italics and ellipses original). Sex is the only absolute that Satin-Legs can conceive, and in achieving an acclaimed performance he achieves a small triumph in his small world.

"Gay Chaps at the Bar" serves as title poem of the book's third section, composed of twelve sonnets, based on the experiences of African American soldiers who were Brooks's friends and correspondents. Some pieces address segregation and discrimination in the military; others consider the horror of the war itself. The lead poem opens with a quote from William Couch, formerly of the Poets' Class, now a lieutenant in the South Pacific:

" . . . and guys I knew in the States, young officers, return from the front crying and trembling. Gay chaps at the bar in Los Angeles, Chicago, New York. . . ."

The poet assumes the collective voice of these confident, educated black men, who "knew beautifully how to give to women / . . . the tropics of our love." In an adaptation of the Petrarchan sonnet, the poem "turns" after the first eight lines. The "tropics" of young love in the opening octet link, ironically, with the "islands" of the closing six lines. The poem pivots on the word "but":

> But nothing ever taught us to be islands.
> And smart athletic language for this hour
> Was not in the curriculum. No stout
> Lesson showed how to chat with death. We brought
> No brass fortissimo, among our talents,
> To holler down the lions in this air.

The suave self-assurance of the opening lines fades and fails before "islands" of fear and human isolation in the charnel houses of the Pacific war. What knowledge could possibly prepare these gay chaps "for this hour" and "this air"? Brooks's use of the sonnet to explore this dark night of soul and body shows the same complex subtleties of language, crafty reworkings of form, and deeply humane vision that characterize the entire collection.

In the following years, Brooks received back-to-back Guggenheim Fellowships and worked on two literary projects: a group of poems called "American Family Brown" and another poem cycle focused on someone much like herself. Harper rejected the former in October 1947, and she set the project aside, later recasting it in prose as the basis for her sole novel, *Maud Martha* (1953). She submitted her other collection five months later and received a lukewarm acceptance, accompanied by a detailed, sharply critical evaluation by poet Genevieve Taggard. Her editor's letter observed, "This present collection shows you in transition"; the missive contrasted her first book's "emphasis on content rather than form" with its opposite in the new work. Brooks responded, "I'm surprised that this reaching toward a more careful language should strike anyone as 'a trick and shock device.'"[64]

When Brooks delivered the revised collection early the next year, she highlighted the greater "cohesion" in its treatment of the focal character. According to the poet, *Annie Allen* (1949) "trac[es] the life of a young woman" through three stages of life.[65] The collection contains thirty poems in three sections and is prefaced with a memorial for Edward Bland. The young corporal had died in Germany in 1945 after volunteering in response to "the Army's invitation accepting Negroes into integrated units."[66]

The poet's new direction is apparent from the opening piece, "the birth in a narrow room," which begins: "Weeps out of western country something new. / Blurred and stupendous. Wanted and unplanned." The inverted syntax and extreme truncation of the opening lines puzzle until the title brings them into focus, suggesting a newborn ("something new") crying. The oxymoronic pairings of the second line are equally startling.

The second stanza slides down the rabbit-hole of time: "Now, weeks and years will go before she thinks / 'How pinchy is my room! how can I breathe!'" The perfect child's neologism, "pinchy," is alliteratively echoed two lines later: "But prances nevertheless with gods and fairies." The perceived smallness of this world does not so much evoke societal confinement and deprivation, in the manner of "kitchenette building," as suggest the experience of any child growing in size and imagination. Differences of this sort mark *Annie Allen* as new in both thematic and stylistic emphasis.

"The Anniad," by far the longest poem, comprises the middle section of the book. It consists of forty-three seven-line stanzas, nearly every line composed of seven syllables. The mode is mock heroic, or as Brooks put it, "The girl's name was Annie, and it was my little pompous pleasure to raise her to a height that she probably did not have. I thought of the *Iliad*."[67] To the extent that this poem is related to Homeric epic, the focal character is a Penelope- or Andromache-figure, the wife who remains behind while her husband goes to war. The narrative encompasses adolescent dreams of romance, courtship, marriage, separation through war, reunion, a husband's infidelity, reconciliation, and a final parting through death.

But use of the term "narrative" threatens to mislead the reader. "The Anniad" may be reduced, for ease of discussion, to some such outline of paraphrasable content, especially with the helpful glossing that Brooks provided on various occasions, but the poem is not so much driven by "plot" as by an ambitious young poet's intention to push her technique to its furthest limits. A sampling of the work suggests Brooks's bravura performance. Here is the first stanza:

> Think of sweet and chocolate,
> Left to folly or to fate,
> Whom the higher gods forgot,
> Whom the lower gods berate;
> Physical and underfed
> Fancying on the featherbed
> What was never said and is not.

As these lines suggest, the conventions of the epic are continually evoked and continually undercut. "The Anniad" begins "in medias res," as do the *Iliad* and other epics. The imperative "Think" announces a theme, but "sweet and chocolate" are hardly the conventional stuff of heroic deeds. The gods are invoked, after a fashion, but only to find the subject merely dreaming on her featherbed.

Rhyme is used throughout the poem and, along with stanzaic regularity, suggests a certain traditional symmetry, but as in the slant rhyme of "chocolate" and "fate," symmetry is no sooner suggested than undermined. The metrical pattern likewise varies. Each line begins and ends with a stressed syllable, setting up a brisk trotting rhythm that runs through the poem but is frequently disrupted (for example, by the extra syllable in line six). The dactylic "Fancying" lazily draws out the meter to capture the dreamy mood of the romantic adolescent. Alliteration of "fancying" and "featherbed" deepen the image.

"The Anniad" moves forward episodically as the girl approaches womanhood and first passionate romance. For five stanzas, her dreams are personified by an imaginary lover—called, again in heroic language, a "paladin"—and further described in Homeric epithet as "ocean-eyed." When a real lover arrives in stanza six, he is "a man of tan," linking to a theme of color consciousness that runs through many of Brooks's poems. His "tan" is contrasted with her "chocolate" and, in stanza five, with her "unembroidered brown." In stanza seven, he is associated with "the godhead" and evokes a "hot theopathy," which exactly reverses the courtly tradition insofar as the lady here worships her suitor. Stanzas nine through eleven suggest her sexual initiation. The woman has "thaumaturgic" powers, summoned repeatedly to overcome and transform quotidian experiences that do not match romantic dreams. She is a hero on the plane on which she battles, that of the imagination.

The language becomes even more complex as the poem proceeds. After her sexual "metamorphosis,"

> Doomer, though, crescendo-comes
> Prophesying hecatombs.
> Surrealist and cynical.
> Garrulous and guttural.

Every word is pregnant with multiple connotative, allusive, and figurative possibilities; each is a tiny book. "Doomer" personifies war, names it like some shrieking slayer from an Old English or Norse epic. "Crescendo-comes" functions as verb, epithet, and truncated sentence, and in conjunction with "Doomer," has overtones of Wagnerian climax. Such linguistic compression and complex diction, hallmarks of poetic virtuosity in high-modernist aesthetics, place enormous demands on the reader and run the risk of obscurity. Speaking of "The Anniad," Brooks recalled, "What a pleasure it was to write that poem! . . . I was just very conscious of every word; I wanted every phrase to be beautiful, and yet to contribute sanely . . . to the whole effect. . . . Every stanza . . . was worked on and revised, tenderly cared for."[68]

The years between A Street in Bronzeville and Annie Allen were marked by momentous social and cultural changes. Differences between the two collections reflected those changes, as well as Brooks's evolution as a poet. A Street in Bronzeville has a documentary, realist core. Although the craft is superb, nearly every poem draws attention more to what it is "about" than to how it is made. Brooks described it in a 1977 interview as "a folksy book . . . full of people and story," adding "most people like those qualities in a book of poetry." She described Annie Allen as "a book of extensive experiment" in which she "enjoyed being technically passionate."[69] Brooks named the essential differences, even though the first volume is not without virtuoso displays of technique and the second not without poems reflective of poverty or racial oppression.

Brooks's timing was as eminently successful as her technique. In March Poetry published a selection of poems from the forthcoming work, and in November the editors awarded Brooks the prestigious Eunice Tietjens Memorial Prize. In April 1950, the journal published a long, strongly positive review by Stanley Kunitz, and on May 1 the poet learned that she had been awarded the Pulitzer Prize. The shy singer of Bronzeville had seemingly scaled the pinnacles of the American literary establishment. The broader implications for African American letters are part of the burden of chapter 11.

CHAPTER 11

The Wheel Turns

The scholarly delineation of historically distinct periods is always somewhat arbitrary. A case could be made for closing this narrative a year or two earlier or later, but 1950 stands out as not only the midcentury mark but also the year of Gwendolyn Brooks's symbolically resonant Pulitzer Prize. That award was a highpoint of generational achievement by Black Chicago's writers, but the prize-winning collection, *Annie Allen* (1949), also signaled a shift toward modernist poetics that valued well-honed craft and formal innovation over commitment to portray social realities and address mass audiences. This was one in a series of changes—cultural, political, and institutional—that marked the waning of Bronzeville's dominant role in African American letters, changes that roughly cluster around the year 1950.

Of Poets and Poetics

That year Alain Locke praised Brooks's second collection for "striving . . . to discover the universal in the particulars of a modern woman's experiences of love, motherhood, struggle, frustration." He cited "the birth in a narrow room" as an exemplary piece in which "the racial overtones are all the more poignant and meaningful through being left implicit." The clarion call of the 1920s for distinctively racial expression was notably muted: "The Negro poet is . . . basically a modern poet and an American poet."[1] Equally muted was the tocsin of revolt, as Locke, in a special issue of *Phylon* dedicated to "The Current [Literary] Scene," solidarized with younger black critics who "rightly claim" that "objective universality . . . is the ultimate desideratum for a literature that seeks universal appeal and acceptance."[2] Buoyed by the commercial and critical successes of recent novels, memoirs, and poetry collections by black writers, as well as by a series of significant postwar civil rights victories, critics such as J. Saunders Redding, Blyden Jackson, Hugh Gloster, and Nick Aaron Ford believed they could discern the shape of a future nonracial society, even as they taught at segregated institutions in the South. They shared a cautiously optimistic sense that American society would tear down the walls of apartheid without revolutionary upheaval. They saw broader opportunities in the literary marketplace and expanding aesthetic possibilities beyond black writers' felt need to defend their own humanity. They agreed "that no single period had been as fruitful as that of the thirties and forties."[3]

One essay in *Phylon* cited Gwendolyn Brooks and Frank Yerby "as the literary symbols of these triumphs."[4] If Brooks and Yerby were indeed "symbols," they symbolized very different sorts of "triumphs": in the first case, a black poet's critical recognition by a white literary establishment that valued linguistic play, technical acumen, and erudition; in the second, a black novelist's commercial success in a fictional genre previously the near-exclusive domain of white authors. Both triumphs could be traced to the cultural institutions and energies of Bronzeville, yet paradoxically, each suggested ways in which the next period of African American literary production would be fundamentally different.

Brooks's own brief essay in *Phylon*, "Poets Who Are Negroes," highlighted the exigencies of craft: "The Negro poet['s]. . . . most urgent duty, at present, is to polish his technique, his way of presenting his truths and his beauties."[5] Her statement was emblematic of a shift from emphasis on content to emphasis on form—from a "perspective" (to use a key term in "Blueprint for Negro Writing") in which words are meant to be deployed as weapons to move the Negro masses in struggle against injustice to a perspective in which words are meant to be enjoyed as gemlike artifacts by knowledgeable players in a game of language. Such shifting emphasis was apparent between *A Street in Bronzeville* and *Annie Allen*, and a broadly similar evolution could be found in the work of other black poets, notably Robert Hayden and Melvin Tolson.

Robert Chrisman has examined Hayden's "transition years," which fall precisely between Brooks's first two collections. "What is most striking," Chrisman writes, "is his reformulation of his aesthetic from Left populism to modernism." In 1947, the year Charles Johnson became Fisk's first black president, Hayden was an assistant professor and guiding spirit in "an editing, publishing and ideological group" called Counterpoise. Other key members included fellow poet Myron O'Higgins, then a research consultant at Fisk, and fiction writer William Demby, then an undergraduate studying on the GI Bill. That year both Hayden and O'Higgins held Rosenwald fellowships, which presumably supported the first Counterpoise publication, their slim co-authored collection *The Lion and the Archer* (1948). Hayden's poems, Chrisman observes, "marked a new direction, with rich imagery, complex rhythms, and a highly connotative symbolism, all of which combined to celebrate the play of imagination rather than explicit social statement."[6]

Hayden penned a brief manifesto for Counterpoise: "We are unalterably opposed," it began, "to the chauvinistic, the cultish, to special pleading, to all that seeks to limit and restrict creative expression. . . . We support and encourage the experimental and the unconventional in writing, music and the graphic arts. . . . As writers who belong to a so-called minority we are violently opposed to having our work viewed, as the custom is, entirely in the light of sociology and politics."[7] The Counterpoise writers resisted any pressures or restraints on the autonomy of black artists and any racially condescending or reductively nonliterary practices in publishing or interpreting their work. Hayden was thoroughly familiar with Bronzeville's radical cultural currents, friendly with such figures as Bernard and Margaret Goss (Burroughs), and had appeared "in recital" at the Community Art Center shortly after it opened.[8] As challenges to the aesthetics of Wright's "Blueprint" began to emerge in the 1940s, they often came from artists like Hayden who had previously espoused them.

Melvin Tolson's work underwent similar transition between *Rendezvous with America* (1944) and *Libretto for the Republic of Liberia* (1953). The long and densely allusive ode commemorating Liberia's founding prompted Allen Tate, a preeminent white poet and critic, to write: "For the first time, it seems to me, a Negro poet has assimilated completely the full poetic language of his time and, by implication, the language of the Anglo-American poetic tradition." Tolson commented in a letter to Horace Bond, president of Lincoln University: "[Tate] is the toughest of the New School of Criticism. . . . At long last, it seems, a black man has broken into the ranks of T. S. Eliot and Tate! We have been completely ignored heretofore."[9] J. Saunders Redding, however, greeted *Libretto* with "fundamental objections to poetry which the author must himself interpret for his readers in an addendum of notes" and suggested that the poet might be "deliberately uncommunicative and obscure." Tolson responded sharply in the Baltimore *Afro-American*: "Every art and every science have reached an amazing state of complexity today. . . . If one wants to be a modern poet, one must study modern poets. . . . I have done this for twenty years. . . . Mr. Redding has a fetishism for 'simple lines.' . . . Away with the simple Negro! This is a book to be chewed and digested."[10]

In the 1950s, Brooks's emphasis on polished technique, Hayden's objections to reading the work of black writers through sociological and political lenses, and Tolson's defense of complexity and insistence on a place in the mainstream of American letters would be reflected in not only black poetry but also novels by Ralph Ellison, James Baldwin, William Demby, and Brooks herself, all of which signaled new directions in African American literature as a whole. Other expanding possibilities for black writers could be found in the commercial "triumph" of Frank Yerby.

"The Road to Xanadu"

Yerby's first major success as a fiction writer, a story called "Health Card," appeared in *Harper's* in 1944 and won the O. Henry Award the following year. The piece portrays the racist treatment of a black army private and his girlfriend in a southern town. This and other stories that Yerby published between 1939 and 1946 exhibit the same taut fury and realistic detail as Richard Wright's short fiction, but social realism did not make him perhaps the most commercially successful African American writer of all time.[11]

Born in Augusta, Georgia, in 1915, Yerby spent summers in Chicago and then enrolled at the University in 1938 for doctoral study in English. He met Frank Marshall Davis, who admired his "grim and realistic short stories about discrimination" and arranged for one to appear in *New Anvil* in1939.[12] He also secured a position with the Illinois Writers' Project, working on Katherine Dunham's study of black religious cults.[13] Discussing the writer's trade with Project colleagues one day, Yerby announced: "You intellectuals can go ahead and write your highbrow stuff. I'm going to make a million."[14] His time on the project and his academic training helped develop the writing and research skills and disciplined work habits that would enable him to meet his goal. Failing to find a publisher for a novel focused on the struggles of a well-educated black protagonist, Yerby decided that the road to "a million" was not paved with protest, and he leapt unhesitatingly into the world of pulp fiction, specifically historical romance.

The Foxes of Harrow (1946), Yerby's first published novel, served up a sensational plot set on an antebellum Louisiana plantation with a red-haired, blue-eyed adventurer as protagonist. Few readers were initially aware of the author's racial identity. *Defender* book reviewer Gertrude Martin described the ingredients in Yerby's formula for commercial success: "an irresistible dashing Southerner loved madly by two or more beautiful women. . . . a maximum of bloodshed. . . . sex and history . . . mixed . . . in the proper proportions— much sex and history enough to hang a plot on."[15] The historical settings for the thirty-two novels that followed ranged widely, from the antebellum South to the French and American revolutions, the Middle Ages, the time of Christ, and ancient Greece. Most titles were book-club selections, twelve became bestsellers, and three were adapted to film. Following what Arna Bontemps called "the road to Xanadu," Yerby's books attained worldwide sales of nearly sixty million copies.

Reviewers in the African American press made much of Yerby's race and noted, accurately, that the black characters hovering in the background of his southern tales are portrayed with somewhat more humanity than the amiable buffoons in Margaret Mitchell's *Gone with the Wind*. But Yerby's ultimate importance does not lie in any aesthetic qualities found in his novels.[16] More to the point than his fictional characters were his real millions in royalties, his villa in Madrid, and photospreads in *Ebony* showing his sumptuous home redecoration and adventurous leisure pursuits. As Adam Green observes, Yerby's career and lifestyle stood as convenient case in point for Chicago publisher John Johnson's promotion of a "concept of black celebrity, . . . evocative of deep shifts in racial notions of selfhood since the 1940s." Such celebrity was associated with a moneyed "leisure ethic," displacing traditional points of reference: "activism, . . . uplift. . . . achievement, productivity, and reputation."[17]

Yerby also demonstrated that a black writer who began by working the terrain mapped out in "Blueprint" could pursue a lucrative career writing genre novels, a path later followed by Chester Himes with a successful series centered on black detectives Coffin Ed Johnson and Gravedigger Jones.[18] Both Yerby and Himes felt the sting of American apartheid deeply but refused to be confined to the niche of protest writing. In 1951 Yerby told an interviewer: "If [a novelist] wants to preach he should go on the pulpit."[19] Two years later, Himes was living in Paris and struggling to escape the long shadow of Wright's *Native Son* and *Black Boy*. He told one publisher: "I don't want to get caught within the limited evaluation of racial protest writing and have my work used exclusively as ammunition in a propaganda campaign."[20] In the trajectory of Yerby's and Himes's commercial ascent as genre writers (and expatriates) could be limned one source of Bronzeville's declining role as focal point of African American letters. The cultural climate of the Cold War was another.

Big Chill

If Richard Wright's generation of artists was forged amidst the social unrest and politically charged cultural movements of the depression, it was tempered in the late 1940s when the

Cold War displaced the wartime Soviet-American alliance and its domestic repercussions fractured the labor-liberal-Left coalition of the New Deal years. Winston Churchill had joined Franklin Roosevelt and Joseph Stalin at Tehran and Yalta to forge the terms of their alliance. On March 5, 1946, eleven months after Roosevelt's death, Churchill announced in Fulton, Missouri, that "an iron curtain has fallen across the continent" of Europe. Henceforth, American- and Soviet-dominated spheres of influence would be locked in a struggle for hearts and minds and, more strategically, for military superiority and territorial control. Churchill warned of "Communist fifth columns . . . [that] work in complete unity and absolute obedience to the directions they receive from the Communist center. . . . [and] constitute a growing challenge and peril to Christian civilization." This established the rationale for domestic persecution of organizations and individuals often charged with little more than sympathy for Soviet-style communism or opposition to racial injustice.[21]

Alan Wald, who studies the literary Left, highlights the following events in an unfolding chronology of political and cultural repression: "1947: House Committee on Un-American Activities (HUAC) investigates Hollywood, resulting in conviction of the 'Hollywood Ten' for 'contempt of Congress.' . . . 1948: Communist Party leaders arrested under the Smith Act. 1949: CIO expels all known Communists and Communist-led unions. . . . 1950: Alger Hiss convicted of perjury. . . . 1951: HUAC investigation in Hollywood creates blacklist of hundreds of screenwriters, actors, etc. . . . 1953: . . . Julius and Ethel Rosenberg executed for alleged espionage."[22] These high-profile events were but the tip of an iceberg of surveillance, subpoenas, interrogations, slanders, blacklists, firings, and trials that ruined careers and lives across the country. A spectrum of organizations and individuals from the far Left to the liberal mainstream came under attack, chilling the exercise of basic civil liberties and artistic freedom. As a major center of radical influence, Black Chicago was deeply affected.

Early in 1948, Bronzeville sculptor Marion Perkins wrote to his friend and comrade Theodore Ward: "I have been permanently divorced from my post office job under Mr. Truman's fascist so-called disloyalty act. This was not entirely unexpected on my part."[23] In December Frank Marshall Davis left Chicago and, seeking safe haven, permanently relocated to Hawaii. As a prominent voice of interracial collaboration and Henry Wallace's Progressive Party, he was under investigation by the FBI, and some libraries even removed his books from their shelves.[24]

In November 1949, radio dramatist Richard Durham told Langston Hughes that, despite censorship pressures, he was "refusing to blue-pencil anything that . . . inspir[ed] Negroes to a more militant struggle." The station managers suggested, in response, that he "'must be Red.'" "Can you imagine that?" Durham asked. "White folks will call you 'Red' in a minute."[25] As a serial target of anticommunist persecution, Hughes would have had no trouble imagining such a thing. Nine months later, after 102 weekly broadcasts and multiple awards, Durham's series, *Destination Freedom*, was abruptly cancelled.

The Chicago Board of Education enacted a loyalty oath and withheld paychecks from teachers who refused to sign. In 1952 Margaret Burroughs was summoned to an interview at board headquarters and questioned about her political associations. Under pressure to identify other teachers of Left-wing sympathies and fearing possible dismissal, she took a one-year sabbatical in Mexico.[26] Around the same time, the executive board of the Community Art Center decided "in a move to curtail rumors of 'un-American' activities . . . to banish artists and their associates from the Center." In response Burroughs and other artists who had founded the center protested on its steps before establishing a new workshop of their own across the street.[27]

To date, the most detailed account of this aspect of Black Chicago's history appears in an energetic study by Bill Mullen that usefully draws attention, in this conservative era, to the power Marxist ideas held for many black intellectuals and artists of the 1930s and 1940s. Mullen tends, however, to draw a seamless web between politics and creative expression and to oversimplify a complex history in order to attribute Bronzeville's cultural flowering to the effects and "echoes" of the Communist Party's Popular Front strategy. He generally ignores creative artists who don't fit the contours of his narrative—for example, Katherine Dunham, Charles Sebree, and Eldzier Cortor—and he misreads the careers and biographies of central figures, such as Horace Cayton and Gwendolyn Brooks.

Signs of a modernist turn in black aesthetics were locally evident at least as early as the formation of the Chicago Poets' Class in 1941. While Cold War witch hunts unquestionably stifled much radically inspired creative expression and destroyed the careers of Leftist artists such as Paul Robeson, it does not follow that modernist ideas and techniques were somehow imposed on black artists at the metaphorical tip of fascist bayonets, as Mullen seems sometimes to imply. Bronzeville's avant-garde had, as rising artists always do, their own individual passions and motives for discarding established forms and exploring what they perceived as the most innovative, productive, and challenging possibilities in their artistic genres.[28]

Social and Institutional Changes

Much had changed in Black Chicago by 1950, and many forces driving the changes had their roots in the war. As Adam Green puts it: "Formal mobilization of black men, and to a lesser extent, black women during World War II coincided with the renewal of racial migration driven by war production to effect the greatest dislocation of African Americans since the antebellum domestic slave market."[29] Many of the South Side's male artists were drafted. The war cut short the promising career of Edward Bland and destroyed Charles White's health.

The Federal Art Project and Federal Writers' Project were also casualties of the mobilization of resources for the war effort. For a time, the projects—despite their many limitations—had provided economic sustenance, colleagues and mentors, and creative outlets for the work of their employees thus leveling the cultural playing field and reducing the gravitational pull of New York's publishing, art, and theater industries as well as Hollywood's film industry. But the projects were long gone by 1950, and only about half of the eighteen artists and intellectuals who are the focus of this study still resided in Chicago.

The war also spurred a second massive influx of southern migrants. Between 1940 and

1950, Chicago's black population grew from 277,731 to 492,265 and would continue growing rapidly. In 1940 blacks constituted 8.2 percent of Chicago's total population. The figure rose to 13.6 percent in 1950 and 22.9 percent in 1960.[30] At first the swelling black
population was largely contained within existing racial boundaries and crowded into
already overcrowded, deteriorating housing, which produced in some areas population
densities and living conditions that sometimes seemed to rival the misery of Calcutta.

Black Chicago continued, however, to be characterized by extreme contrasts. Labor
shortages, union organization, and government pressures to end discrimination brought
substantial employment gains and higher wages in the industrial sector. New opportunities were also opening for black entrepreneurs and professionals. "As the housing short-
age became more critical," writes Arvarh Strickland, "and after [restrictive] covenants
were declared unenforceable by the U.S. Supreme Court, Negroes began to break out of
the ghetto in large numbers. Neighborhoods adjacent to the 'Black Belt' remained in a
state of siege." The specter of 1919 hovered as "hysteria seemed to pervade white communities." Individual attacks, bombings, and mob violence by whites kept the city in
turmoil for years. But change proved inevitable. Black Chicago spread south, west, and
east, with rising prosperity generally associated with home ownership in newer areas of
residence.[31]

The implications of such changes for the core institutions of what is today known as
"historic Bronzeville" were dramatic. People can move; buildings cannot. Vivian Harsh's
annual reports on Hall Branch Library document a changing neighborhood. In 1945 she
noted "a decrease in the use of books by adults as compared with 1940" and added that
"many of our former adult readers now live in the vicinity of the Sub. Br[anch]." In 1947
Harsh reported that the Book Review and Lecture Forum, once a center of Bronzeville's
creative energies, "still has a following, small compared to former years." But 1948 was
marked by "a general loss in adult, juvenile and foreign circulation." In 1951 Harsh wrote,
"Many former patrons have moved either east of Cottage Grove or south of Sixty-third
Street." Her 1955 report was marked by palpable demoralization: "The community served
by Hall Branch is residential and transient. There are many kitchenettes and small apartments, most of which have been converted from larger housing units. . . . The community
is not now essentially a reading community. Some few years ago it was but our steady
patrons have moved away." In 1956 the Book Review and Lecture Forum ended after
twenty-three years.[32]

This is not to suggest that black Chicago was simply turning into one giant slum. On
the contrary, both class stratification and geographical dispersion were rapidly accelerat-
ing. "Everybody has a new car," Langston Hughes observed of "moneyed Southsiders" in
1949.[33] But institutions that had been central to the Bronzeville Renaissance remained
where they were built in earlier years as their immediately surrounding neighborhoods
grew increasingly poor and overcrowded and existing housing was razed to "make way for
expressway routes, low-rent public housing, and private redevelopment projects."[34]

The Rosenwald Fund, while not a black-controlled organization, was nevertheless an
essential element, through its fellowship program and institutional partnerships, in

Bronzeville's creative flowering. In 1948 it reached the preordained end of its twenty-year tenure. The fund's strategic importance was illustrated by Marion Perkins's predicament that year. Writing to Theodore Ward, the sculptor noted: "I received my dismissal [from the Post Office] a month before my Rosenwald fellowship began, so I am not worrying about it as I have a year before me in which I can halfway enjoy some freedom."[35] Edwin Embree and Charles Johnson, hardly radicals, were nevertheless willing to ignore Perkins's political difficulties in recognition of his evident artistic promise, realized two years later when he completed his masterwork, *Man of Sorrows*. The Rosenwald Fund provided financial support to many of black Chicago's leading intellectuals and artists, but Perkins belonged to the very last cohort of fellows.[36] Edwin Embree, the fund's president for twenty years, died in 1950.

Seeds and Legacies

If the earlier discussion of "conservation of [cultural] energy" with regard to the so-called Tuskegee machine has any validity, a broadly similar transformation, rather than disappearance, of Bronzeville's creative energies of the 1930s and 1940s should be expected. Indeed numerous instances might be cited. To some extent, black Chicago's radical cultural ferment persisted into the next decade with the emergence of such new artists as Frank London Brown and Lorraine Hansbury. In 1959 Brown's powerful novel *Trumbull Park* was published, and Hansbury's play *A Raisin in the Son* debuted on Broadway to stunning success. Both works found their subject matter in the violent white resistance to desegregation of Chicago's housing; both were rooted in the political militancy and naturalist/realist aesthetics of the earlier period. But taking the long view, the modernist aesthetics of Gwendolyn Brooks and younger black Chicago fiction writers Clarence Major and Leon Forrest seem more strongly indicative of the direction of African American letters.[37]

Some seeds were planted that blossomed in less predictable form. By 1967 Gwendolyn Brooks had published six books with Harper: four poetry collections for adults, a collection for children, and a novel. But change was once again in the air, and it would touch her deeply. The heroic sacrifices of the southern-based civil rights movement had achieved significant legal victories and token institutional changes but left larger issues of racial oppression and poverty untouched. New voices—among them Stokely Carmichael, Malcolm X, and Amiri Baraka—were each in their own ways turning attention to the hopes, frustrations, and anger of millions of ordinary blacks, North and South. The call for Black Power spurred a "Black Arts Movement," which, according to Larry Neal, was "radically opposed to any concept of the artist that alienates him from his community."[38] Richard Wright's question "Shall Negro writing be for the Negro masses?" resounded, amplified tenfold, through black intellectual and artistic circles.

Brooks had been teaching young black writers for some time, but "until 1967," she wrote, "I had sturdy ideas about writing. . . . My own blackness did not confront me with a shrill spelling of itself." That year she attended the Fisk University Black Writers' Conference and encountered "a new black . . . different from any the world has known . . . a tall-walker . . . understood by no white." Discovering for herself "a surprised queenhood in the new black sun," Brooks became the friend, mentor, and champion of Chicago's "new black" writers such as Haki Madhubuti, Carolyn Rodgers, and Johari Amini.[39] She never abandoned her dedication to craft, to word magic, never forgot that "Man visits art, but squirms. / Art hurts." But she reenvisioned her poetry as a "call" to "all black people" and, leaving Harper, made her work widely available in inexpensive editions from black-owned, community-oriented publishers—Broadside Press in Detroit and Third World Press in Chicago.[40]

Some seeds blossomed far afield. Charles Sebree, for example, settled in Washington, D.C., in the mid-1950s. The first of Bronzeville's younger painters to achieve critical attention and significant sales, he was, like many of his peers, creative in several realms. In the postwar years, theatrical work increasingly absorbed him, and his play Mrs. Patterson had a successful run on Broadway from 1954 to 1955. Several years later, Sebree was participating in a writers' group with Howard University faculty, including his friend from 1940s Chicago, poet/dramatist Owen Dodson. A very young English instructor hesitantly offered a piece for critique, a story about a black girl who prays that God will turn her eyes blue. The group commented positively, but Sebree in particular "hounded" her to keep polishing it. "He saw some special ability that needed to be nurtured and coaxed," Toni Morrison recalled decades later, long after those few draft pages had metamorphosed into her first novel The Bluest Eye (1970). Sebree, said the Nobel laureate, "was the first person that made me think that I could be a writer. And I paid attention."[41]

In the early 1970s, an adolescent boy was living in Hawaii with his maternal grandparents. His father, Barack Obama Sr., lived in his native Kenya; his Euro-American mother, Ann Dunham, was in Indonesia completing fieldwork for a doctorate in anthropology. One of only three African Americans at elite Punahou Academy, young Obama was probing his racial identity with few black role models immediately available. His white grandfather sometimes took the youth along to poker games with several black friends, among them Frank Marshall Davis. By then "pushing eighty, with . . . an ill-kempt gray Afro that made him look like an old, shaggy-maned lion," Davis shared his poetry and stories of life on the South Side with Obama. After an upsetting, racially tinged incident involving his grandmother, the youth sought Davis out. The dashiki-clad old man offered his hard-won racial wisdom, including the counsel to constantly "be vigilant for . . . survival." Later, as Obama prepared to leave for college in Los Angeles, Davis cautioned against "leaving [his] race at the door" and "leaving [his] people behind."[42]

In 1985 Obama was driving the streets of the South Side, where he had just begun working as a community organizer: "I remembered the whistle of the Illinois Central, bearing the weight of the thousands who had come up from the South so many years before. . . . I imagined Frank in a baggy suit and wide lapels, standing in front of the old Regal Theater. . . . The mailman I saw was Richard Wright, delivering mail before his first book sold. . . . I made a chain between my life and the faces I saw, borrowing other people's memories. In this way I tried to take possession of the city, make it my own."[43]

Embarking on a journey that would take him from black Chicago to the White House, Obama would negotiate his own route, drawn to neither Davis's Marxist certainties of the 1940s nor his Black Power militancy of the 1960s. Nevertheless, the memories "borrowed" by a biracial young man learning what it meant to be African American drew ineluctably on the legacies of the great black Metropolis and the hot center of black creative expression that was Bronzeville.

Artists of Bronzeville

Henry Avery*
Margaret Burroughs
John Carlis
William Carter*
Edward T. Collier
Eldzier Cortor*
Charles Davis*
Charles Dawson*
Katherine Dorsey
Walter Ellison*
Ramon Gabriel*
Rex Gorleigh
Bernard Goss*
Charles Haig*
Fred Hollingsworth*
Frederick D. Jones
Joseph Kersey*
Clarence Lawson*

Lonnie Moore*
Archibald Motley*
Frank Neal*
George Neal*
Gordon Parks
Marion Perkins*
Kenneth Prince
David Ross*
William Edouard Scott*
Charles Sebree*
William Stewart*
Jennelsie Walden
Earl Walker*
Charles White*
Oscaretta Winn*
Vernon Winslow*
Leon Wright*

*Employed by the Illinois Unit of the Federal Art Project

This list was compiled from exhibition catalogues in the William McBride Papers and in consultation with Charles A. Davis and Clarice Davis Durham.

African Americans Employed by Illinois Writers' Project

William Attaway
Arna Bontemps
Alvin Cannon
Kitty Chappell (aka Katherine de la Chappelle)
Robert Davis
Katherine Dunham
Richard Durham
Barefield Gordon
Fenton Johnson
Harry Jones
Robert Lucas
Willard Motley
Andrew Paschal
Laurence Dunbar Reddick
Chauncey Spencer
Onah Spencer
Bertha Swindall
Luther Townsley
Margaret Walker
Robert Walker
Richard Wright
O.C. Wynn
Frank Yerby

This list was compiled from various primary sources and in consultation with Charles A. Davis and Clarice Davis Durham.

NOTES (( ))

Abbreviations

AAA	Archives of American Art, Smithsonian Institution, Washington, D.C.
AANB	*African American National Biography.* Edited by Henry Louis Gates Jr. and Evelyn Brooks Higginbotham. New York: Oxford University Press, 2008.
Bontemps Papers	Arna Bontemps Papers, Special Collections Research Center, Syracuse University Library.
BWA	*Black Women in America: An Historical Encyclopedia.* 2d ed. Edited by Darlene Clark Hine. New York: Oxford University Press, 2005.
Cayton Papers	Horace Cayton Papers, Vivian G. Harsh Research Collection of Afro-American History and Literature, Chicago Public Library.
CD	*Chicago Defender.*
DANB	*Dictionary of American Negro Biography.* Edited by Rayford W. Logan and Michael R. Winston. New York: Norton, 1982.
EAACH	*Encyclopedia of African-American Culture and History.* Edited by Jack Salzman, David Lionel Smith, and Cornel West. New York: Simon and Schuster, 1996.
Hall Branch Archives	George Cleveland Hall Branch Library Archives, Vivian G. Harsh Research Collection of Afro-American History and Literature, Chicago Public Library.
Harsh Collection	Vivian G. Harsh Research Collection of Afro-American History and Literature, Chicago Public Library.
Hughes Papers	Langston Hughes Papers, Yale Collection of American Literature, Beinecke Rare Book and Manuscript Library, Yale University.
Johnson Papers	Charles S. Johnson Papers, Special Collections, Fisk University Library.
Locke Papers	Alain Locke Papers, Manuscript Division, Moorland-Spingarn Research Center, Howard University.
McBride Papers	William McBride Papers, Vivian G. Harsh Research Collection of Afro-American History and Literature, Chicago Public Library.
NAAAL	*The Norton Anthology of African American Literature.* 2d ed. Edited by Henry Louis Gates Jr. and Nellie Y. McKay. New York: Norton, 2004.
Rosenwald Papers	Julius Rosenwald Papers, Special Collections Research Center, University of Chicago Library.
SCRBC	Schomburg Center for Research in Black Culture, New York Public Library.
Taylor Papers	Graham Taylor Papers, Midwest Manuscript Collection, Newberry Library, Chicago.
Wirth Papers	Louis Wirth Papers, Special Collections Research Center, University of Chicago Library.
Wright Papers	Richard Wright Papers, Yale Collection of American Literature, Beinecke Rare Book and Manuscript Library, Yale University.

Preface

1. Robert Bone, "Richard Wright and the Chicago Renaissance," *Callaloo* 9 (Summer 1986): 446–468.
2. Robert Bone, *Down Home: Origins of the Afro-American Short Story* (1975; New York: Columbia University Press, 1988), 284–287. Bone cites Arna Bontemps, "Famous WPA Writers," *Negro Digest* (June 1950): 43–47.
3. For example, David Levering Lewis, *When Harlem Was in Vogue* (1981; New York: Penguin, 1997); Amritjit Singh, *The Novels of the Harlem Renaissance: Twelve Black Writers, 1923–33* (University Park: Pennsylvania State University Press, 1976); Nathan Huggins, *Harlem Renaissance* (New York: Oxford University Press, 1971).
4. Carla Cappetti, *Writing Chicago: Modernism, Ethnography, and the Novel* (New York: Columbia University Press, 1993); Bill V. Mullen, *Popular Fronts: Chicago and African-American Cultural Politics, 1935–46* (Urbana: University of Illinois Press, 1999); Maren Stange, *Bronzeville: Black Chicago in Pictures, 1941–1943* (New York: New Press, 2003); Anne Meis Knupfer, *The Chicago Black Renaissance and Women's Activism* (Urbana: University of Illinois Press, 2006); Adam Green, *Selling the Race: Culture, Community, and Black Chicago, 1940–1955* (Chicago: University of Chicago Press, 2007); Davarian Baldwin, *Chicago's New Negroes: Modernity, the Great Migration, and Black Urban Life* (Chapel Hill: University of North Carolina Press, 2007).
5. Randi Storch, *Red Chicago: American Communism at Its Grassroots, 1928–35* (Urbana: University of Illinois Press, 2007); Mullen, *Popular Fronts*, 23.
6. Cappetti, *Writing Chicago*, 2.

Introduction

1. St. Clair Drake and Horace R. Cayton, *Black Metropolis: A Study of Negro Life in a Northern City* (1945; Chicago: University of Chicago Press, 1993), 382.
2. Besides *Black Metropolis*, this portrait of the South Side draws on Drake and Cayton, "Bronzeville," *Holiday* (May 1947): 34–38, 130–133.
3. Peter M. Rutkoff and William B. Scott, "Pinkster in Chicago: Bud Billiken and the Mayor of Bronzeville, 1930–1945," *Journal of African American History* 89, no. 4 (Fall 2004): 316–330.
4. A debt is owed to Michael Flug, senior archivist of the Vivian G. Harsh Collection, for the phrase "precocious discipline."
5. Table 1 in Drake and Cayton, *Black Metropolis*, 8.
6. Drake and Cayton, "Bronzeville," 36.
7. Charles Johnson, "Countee Cullen Was My Friend," address at dedication ceremonies of the Countee Cullen Regional Library, New York City, 12 September 1951, Johnson Papers.
8. Langston Hughes's connections with black Chicago began as early as 1918 and lasted until his death in 1967. The South Side appears frequently in both his prose and poetry, and he befriended and mentored many Bronzeville artists. His visits were frequent and often extended, yet, strictly speaking, he never resided in Chicago so he cannot fairly be included in a roster of Bronzeville luminaries. The historical record indicates, however, that his visits, his weekly column for the *Chicago Defender*, and his many friendships and professional collaborations on the South Side were clearly both a result of and a contribution to Bronzeville's creative flowering.
9. On backgrounds of the Harlem writers, see George E. Kent, "Patterns of the Harlem Renaissance," in *The Harlem Renaissance Remembered*, ed. Arna Bontemps (New York: Dodd, Mead, 1972), 27–50.
10. Richard A. Courage, essay and artist biographies in *Convergence: Jewish and African American Artists in Depression-era Chicago* (Des Plaines, Ill.: Koehnline Museum of Art, 2008).
11. Bone, "Richard Wright and the Chicago Renaissance," 448.
12. This statement appears in *NAAAL*, 962, and was presumably written by Arnold Rampersad, the editor of the Harlem Renaissance section.
13. This statement appears in *EAACH*, s.v. "Harlem Renaissance," an article written by David Levering Lewis.
14. Henry Louis Gates Jr., "Harlem on Our Minds," *Critical Inquiry* 24 (Autumn 1997): 2.

1 (The Tuskegee Connection

1. Edward Ayers, *The Promise of the New South: Life after Reconstruction* (1992; New York: Oxford University Press, 2007); Michael Perman, *Struggle for Mastery: Disfranchisement in the South, 1888–1908* (Chapel Hill: University of North Carolina Press, 2001); Keith Ian Polakoff, *The Politics of Inertia: The Election of 1876 and the End of Reconstruction* (Baton Rouge: Louisiana State University Press, 1973).

2. Tillman and Vardaman quoted in Adam Fairclough, *A Class of Their Own: Black Teachers in The Segregated South* (Cambridge, Mass.: Harvard University Press, 2007), 135, 145.

3. Louis Harlan, *Booker T. Washington: The Making of a Black Leader, 1856–1901* (New York: Oxford University Press, 1972), 116–117. Except as noted, the facts of Washington's career are based on Harlan's two-volume biography.

4. Booker T. Washington, *Up from Slavery*, in *Three Negro Classics* (New York: Avon, 1965), 57.

5. Harlan, *Making of a Black Leader*, 58–66.

6. Ibid., 112.

7. Nell Irvin Painter, *Exodusters: Black Migration to Kansas after Reconstruction* (New York: Norton, 1992).

8. Washington incorporated his Atlanta Exposition address into *Up from Slavery*, 146–150.

9. Quoted in Harlan, *Making of a Black Leader*, 222; Washington, *Up From Slavery*, 151.

10. On Washington's largely secret initiatives to resist racial segregation, see Louis Harlan, *Booker T. Washington: The Wizard of Tuskegee, 1901–1915* (New York: Oxford University Press, 1983), 422–436.

11. Ibid., 128–142.

12. W.E.B. Du Bois, *The Souls of Black Folk*, in *W.E.B. Du Bois Writings*, ed. Nathan Huggins (New York: Library of America, 1986), 393, 404.

13. Harlan, *Wizard of Tuskegee*, 107.

14. For an interpretation of Washington as rhetorical trickster, hitting the proverbial "straight lick with a crooked stick," see Houston A. Baker Jr., *Modernism and the Harlem Renaissance* (Chicago: University of Chicago Press, 1987), 25–36. Also see Raymond Smock, ed., *Booker T. Washington in Perspective: Essays of Louis R. Harlan* (Jackson: University Press of Mississippi, 2006); Donald Cunnigen, Rutledge M. Dennis, and Myrtle Gonza Glascoe, eds., *The Racial Politics of Booker T. Washington* (Bingley, UK: Emerald, 2006).

15. Alan Trachtenberg, *The Incorporation of America: Culture and Society in the Gilded Age* (New York: Hill & Wang, 1982).

16. Gilbert Osofsky observed that although "Progressivism as a political movement . . . bypass[ed] the Negro," Progressive-affiliated "social workers and industrial and municipal reformers" demonstrated "serious, positive and hopeful interest . . . in Negro welfare." "Progressivism and the Negro: New York, 1900–1915," *American Quarterly* 16, no. 2, Part 1 (Summer 1964): 153–154 n. 2. On white Progressives' general acceptance of racial segregation, see Michael McGerr, *A Fierce Discontent: The Rise and Fall of the Progressive Movement in America, 1870–1920* (New York: Simon and Schuster, 2003), 182–220.

17. Washington, *Up from Slavery*, 145.

18. This observation refers not only to railroad executives such as William Baldwin and Collis Huntington, president of the Southern Pacific, but less obviously to men like steel magnate Andrew Carnegie, who began as a railroad telegraph operator, and Julius Rosenwald, who understood that railroad transportation was the lifeblood of the mail-order industry.

19. On William Baldwin's life, see John Graham Brooks, *An American Citizen: The Life of William Henry Baldwin Jr.* (Boston: Houghton Mifflin, 1910); George Nutter, "William Henry Baldwin, 1863–1905," in *Sons of the Puritans: A Group of Brief Biographies* (Boston: American Unitarian Association, 1908), 231–244.

20. On Ruth Standish Baldwin's life, see Roger Baldwin, "Reminiscences," typescript, Oral History Project, Rare Book Room, Columbia University Library, Vol. I, 1–12; Nancy Weiss, *The National Urban League, 1910–1940* (New York: Oxford University Press, 1974), 39–40.

21. M. R. Werner, *Julius Rosenwald: The Life of a Practical Humanitarian* (New York: Harper, 1939), 107.

22. Quoted in Nutter, "William Henry Baldwin," 238.

23. Harlan, *Making of a Black Leader*, 215.

24. Brooks, *American Citizen*, 177, 246–247.

25. Harlan, *Making of a Black Leader*, 313.

26. Harlan, *Wizard of Tuskegee*, 135–137.

27. For various estimations of Baldwin, see Eric Anderson and Alfred Moss, *Dangerous Donations: Northern Philanthropy and Southern Black Education, 1902–1930* (Columbia: University of Missouri Press, 1999), 63–87; David Levering Lewis, *W.E.B. Du Bois: Biography of a Race* (New York: Henry Holt, 1993), 240–241, 267–273; Harlan, *Wizard of Tuskegee*, 190–191; Brooks, *American Citizen*, 172–240.

28. On origins of the Urban League, see Weiss, *Urban League*, 15–46; Guichard Parris and Lester Brooks, *Blacks in the City: A History of the National Urban League* (Boston: Little Brown, 1971), 3–40.

29. Ralph Ellison, "William L. Bulkley," unpublished WPA Writers' Project manuscript, SCRBC; Weiss, *Urban League*, 21–24; Osofsky, "Progressivism," 163–167.

30. Also present was W.E.B. Du Bois, then being courted by Washington and the Baldwins for a position at Tuskegee. Lewis, *Biography of a Race*, 273–276.

31. A founding member of both the Niagara Movement and the NAACP, William Bulkley was a strong supporter of Du Bois, yet in matters educational, he was an advocate of industrial training for the black masses.

32. *EAACH*, s.v. "George Edmund Haynes"; Parris and Brooks, *Blacks in the City*, 23–31.

33. Haynes's dissertation was published as *The Negro at Work in New York* (New York: Columbia University Press, 1912).

34. Weiss, *Urban League*, 60–64; Parris and Brooks, *Blacks in the City*, 33, 483 n. 7.

35. "An Autobiographical Note," in *The Collected Papers of Robert Ezra Park*, vol. 1: *Race and Culture*, ed. Everett C. Hughes, Charles S. Johnson, Jitsuichi Masuoka, Robert Redfield, and Louis Wirth (Glencoe, Ill.: Free Press, 1950), vii.

36. On Park's life, see Winifred Raushenbush, *Robert E. Park: Biography of a Sociologist* (Durham, N.C.: Duke University Press, 1979); Fred H. Matthews, *Quest for an American Sociology: Robert E. Park and the Chicago School* (Montreal: McGill-Queen's University Press, 1977).

37. Paul J. Baker, ed., "The Life Histories of W. I. Thomas and Robert E. Park," *American Journal of Sociology* 79, no. 2 (September 1973): 254.

38. Quoted in Matthews, *Quest*, 11.

39. Luigi Tomasi, "The Contribution of Georg Simmel to the Foundation of Theory at the Chicago School of Sociology," in *The Tradition of the Chicago School of Sociology*, ed. Luigi Tomasi (Aldershot, UK: Ashgate Publishing, 1998), 25–35; Gary Jaworski, *Georg Simmel and the American Prospect* (Albany: State University of New York Press, 1997), 30–36.

40. Published in English as *The Crowd and the Public* (Chicago: University of Chicago Press, 1972).

41. An early version of Georg Simmel's famous essay on social conflict, "Der Streit," was translated by Albion Small, founding chairman of the sociology department at the University of Chicago, and published in the *American Journal of Sociology* 9, nos. 4–6 (January, March, and May, 1904).

42. "Autobiographical Note," vi.

43. Raushenbush, *Robert E. Park*, 36–42; Matthews, *Quest*, 57–61; Stanford M. Lyman, "The Gothic Foundation of Robert E. Park's Conception of Race and Culture," in Tomasi, *Tradition*, 13–23.

44. Quoted in Raushenbush, *Robert E. Park*, 39.

45. Harlan, *Wizard of Tuskegee*, 270–271.

46. Raushenbush, *Robert E. Park*, 39–40.

47. Robert E. Park, "Agricultural Extension Among the Negroes," reprinted in Stanford M. Lyman, *Militarism, Imperialism, and Racial Accommodation: An Analysis and Interpretation of the Early Writings of Robert E. Park* (Fayetteville: University of Arkansas Press, 1992), 255.

48. Quoted in Matthews, *Quest*, 60.

49. Rauschenbush, *Robert E. Park*, 70–72.

50. "Autobiographical Note," vii. On Park's views on industrial education, see Matthews, *Quest*, 67–71.

51. Harlan, *Wizard of Tuskegee*, 291–293.

52. Ibid., 304–308

53. Georg Simmel, "Conflict as a Type of Social Interaction," in *Introduction to the Science of Sociology*, ed. Robert Park and Ernest Burgess (Chicago: University of Chicago Press, 1921), 582–586.

54. Baker, "Life Histories," 253–255.

55. Booker T. Washington, with Robert E. Park, *The Man Farthest Down: A Record of Observation and Study in Europe* (Garden City, N.Y.: Doubleday, 1912), 13.

56. Quoted in Raushenbush, *Robert E. Park*, 67. Also see Harlan, *Wizard of Tuskegee*, 275–276.

57. Edward Shils, "Some Academics, Mainly in Chicago," *American Scholar* 50 (Spring 1981): 188.

58. Peter Ascoli, *Julius Rosenwald: The Man Who Built Sears, Roebuck and Advanced the Cause of Black Education in the American South* (Bloomington: Indiana University Press, 2006), 1–22; Werner, *Julius Rosenwald*, 1–30.

59. Ascoli, *Julius Rosenwald*, 27.

60. Ibid., 32–36, 47–48.

61. Ibid., 42–45, 73–75; Werner, *Julius Rosenwald*, 51–53, 58–60.

62. Ascoli, *Julius Rosenwald*, 52; Werner, *Julius Rosenwald*, 86–87.

63. Irving Cutler, *The Jews of Chicago: From Shtetl to Suburb* (Urbana: University of Illinois Press, 1996), 33–34.

64. Ibid., 34, 94–98, quote at 96. Also see Ascoli, *Julius Rosenwald*, 51–54.

65. Quoted in Werner, *Julius Rosenwald*, 88.

66. Jane Addams, introduction to *Religion in Social Action*, by Graham Taylor (New York: Dodd, Mead, 1913), xx.

67. Quoted in Helen Lefkowitz Horowitz, "Hull-House as Women's Space," in *A Wild Kind of Boldness: The Chicago History Reader*, ed. Rosemary Adams (Chicago: Chicago Historical Society, 1998), 203.

68. Jane Addams, *Twenty Years at Hull House* (New York: Macmillan, 1910), 252, 323–324.

69. Anne Meis Knupfer, *Reform and Resistance: Gender, Delinquency, and America's First Juvenile Court* (New York: Routledge, 2001), 79–83.

70. Louise Wade, *Graham Taylor: Pioneer for Social Justice, 1851–1938* (Chicago: University of Chicago Press, 1964), 70–160.

71. Quoted in Allan Spear, *Black Chicago: The Making of a Negro Ghetto, 1890–1920* (Chicago: University of Chicago Press, 1967), 95. Also see Terrell Dale Goddard, "The Black Social Gospel in Chicago, 1896–1906: The Ministries of Reverdy C. Ransom and Richard R. Wright, Jr.," *Journal of Negro History* 84, no. 3 (Summer 1999): 227–246; Dempsey J. Travis, *An Autobiography of Black Chicago* (Chicago: Urban Research Institute, 1981), 2.

72. Anne Meis Knupfer, *Toward a Tenderer Humanity and a Nobler Womanhood: African American Women's Clubs in Turn-of-the-Century Chicago* (New York: New York University Press, 1996), 44, 51, 116–117; Thomas Lee Philpott, *The Slum and the Ghetto: Immigrants, Blacks, and Reformers in Chicago, 1880–1930* (1978; Belmont, Calif.: Wadsworth, 1991), 318–320.

73. A biographical profile of Jenkin Lloyd Jones appears in *Unity* 101, no. 1 (5 March 1928).

74. In 1918 the Chicago School of Civics and Philanthropy encountered financial difficulties and eventually was absorbed by the University of Chicago as its Graduate School of Social Service Administration. Edith Abbott was dean from 1924 to 1942. Ellen Frances Fitzpatrick, *Endless Crusade: Women Social Scientists and Progressive Reform* (New York: Oxford University Press, 1990); Mary Jo Deegan, *Jane Addams and the Men of the Chicago School* (Piscataway, N.J.: Transaction, 1990), 74–75; Wade, *Graham Taylor*, 161–185.

75. Taylor to Jane Addams, 20 August 1912, Taylor Papers, Box 6, Folder 45.

76. Ascoli, *Julius Rosenwald*, 110–115.

77. Werner, *Julius Rosenwald*, 107. Paul Sachs became a founding board member of the National Urban League and subsequently a professor of fine arts at Harvard University and director of its Fogg Museum.

78. Quoted in Ascoli, *Julius Rosenwald*, 79.

79. *DANB*, s.v. "Jesse Edward Moorland."

80. Ascoli, *Julius Rosenwald*, 77–82.

81. "YMCA Makes World Wind Close with $68,841.32," *CD*, 21 January 1911.

82. Ascoli, *Julius Rosenwald*, 161–165.

83. Werner, *Julius Rosenwald*, 121–124.

84. Ascoli, *Julius Rosenwald*, 135–153.

85. Edwin R. Embree and Julia Waxman, *Investment in People: The Story of the Julius Rosenwald Fund* (New York: Harper, 1949), 12.

2   ⟨   Charles S. Johnson and the Parkian Tradition

1. On Dewey's and Mead's influence on Chicago sociology, see Neil Gross, "Pragmatism, Phenomenology, and Twentieth-Century American Sociology," in *Sociology in America: A History*, ed. Craig J. Calhoun (Chicago: University of Chicago Press, 2007), 183–224; Lawrence A. Young and Lynn J. England, "One Hundred Years of Methodological Research: The Example of Chicago," in Tomasi, *Tradition*, 129–146; J. David Lewis and Richard L. Smith, *American Sociology and Pragmatism: Mead, Chicago Sociology, and Symbolic Interaction* (Chicago: University of Chicago Press, 1980); Robert E. L. Faris, *Chicago Sociology, 1920–1931* (San Francisco: Chandler, 1967), 88–99.

2. Baker, "Life Histories," 259–260.

3. Raushenbush, *Robert E. Park*, 77.

4. Herbert Blumer, quoted ibid., 100.

5. Park's studies of race relations form the first of three volumes of essays collected after his death by several former students. See Hughes et al., *Race and Culture*.

6. Park's most sustained discussion of the race relations cycle appeared in *Introduction to the Science of Sociology*, the famous textbook coauthored with his younger colleague Ernest Burgess. See chapters 5, 9, 10, and 11.

7. Ibid., 574–576.

8. For a brief survey of the biological racism that dominated Anglo-American sociological theory before the rise of the Chicago School, see Pierre Saint-Arnaud, *African American Pioneers of Sociology: A Critical History* (Toronto: University of Toronto Press, 2009), 15–44.

9. On Park's race relations cycle, see ibid., 49–84; Richard Rees, *Shades of Difference: A History of Ethnicity in American* (New York: Rowman & Littlefield, 2007), 71–83; Lyman, *Militarism, Imperialism*, 81–125; Stow Persons, *Ethnic Studies at Chicago, 1905–45* (Urbana: University of Illinois Press, 1987), 60–97; W. J. Cahnman, "Robert E. Park at Fisk," *Journal of the History of the Behavioral Sciences* 14 (1978): 328–336; Matthews, *Quest*, 157–174.

10. A second work in immigration studies, *Old World Traits Transplanted* (1921), bears the names of Robert Park and Herbert Miller but was written primarily by W. I. Thomas, Park's friend and mentor. In 1918 Thomas was involved in a sexual scandal, which led to his dismissal by the University of Chicago and removal of his name from the book by the Carnegie Corporation. Raushenbush, *Robert E. Park*, 88–93.

11. Ibid., 91.

12. Robert E. Park, Ernest Burgess, and Roderick McKenzie, eds., *The City* (Chicago: University of Chicago Press, 1925), 2.

13. Robert Park, "The City: Suggestions for the Investigation of Human Behavior in the Urban Environment," *American Journal of Sociology* 20 (March 1915): 577–612. *The City* by Park et al. opens with a revised version of this essay and includes five other pieces by Park, two by Burgess, one by McKenzie, and a bibliography by Louis Wirth.

14. Raushenbush, *Robert E. Park*, 191.

15. On Johnson's life, see Patrick J. Gilpin and Marybeth Gasman, *Charles S. Johnson, Leadership Beyond the Veil in the Age of Jim Crow* (Albany: State University of New York, 2003); Richard Robbins, *Sidelines Activist: Charles S. Johnson and the Struggle for Civil Rights* (Jackson: University

Press of Mississippi, 1996); Edwin Embree, *Thirteen Against the Odds* (New York: Viking, 1944), 47–70; Charles S. Johnson, "A Spiritual Autobiography," typescript, n.d., Charles Spurgeon Johnson Collection, Fisk.

16. Johnson, "Spiritual Autobiography," 1.
17. Embree, *Thirteen Against the Odds*, 50–51.
18. Johnson, "Spiritual Autobiography," 2.
19. Johnson, "Spiritual Autobiography," fragmentary version, 2, Johnson Collection.
20. Gilpin and Gasman, *Charles S. Johnson*, 3–5.
21. Johnson, "Spiritual Autobiography," 7.
22. Quoted in Raushenbush, *Robert E. Park*, 101.
23. Quoted ibid., 97.
24. Quoted ibid., 73.
25. Arvarh Strickland, *History of the Chicago Urban League* (Urbana: University of Illinois Press, 1966), 42–43.
26. Ibid., 43.
27. Johnson, "Spiritual Autobiography," 7.
28. James R. Grossman, *Land of Hope: Chicago, Black Southerners, and the Great Migration* (Chicago: University of Chicago Press, 1989), 15–16.
29. Frank Hobbs and Nicole Stoops, *Demographic Trends in the 20th Century*, U.S. Census Bureau, Census 2000 Special Reports (Washington, D.C.: Government Printing Office, 2000), 82–83.
30. Grossman, *Land of Hope*, 4.
31. Ibid., 66–88.
32. Roi Ottley, *The Lonely Warrior: The Life and Times of Robert S. Abbott* (Chicago: Henry Regnery, 1955), 85–88, 132–139, 159–172.
33. Doug McAdam, *Political Process and the Development of Black Insurgency, 1930–1970* (1982; Chicago: University of Chicago Press, 1999), 77–79.
34. Albert Murray, *Stomping the Blues* (New York: McGraw-Hill, 1976), 118, 124. Also see Samuel A. Floyd Jr., *The Power of Black Music: Interpreting Its History from Africa to the United States* (New York: Oxford University Press, 1995), 221–225.
35. Toni Morrison, *Jazz* (New York: Alfred A. Knopf, 1992), 32.
36. See map of the Illinois Central Railroad in Grossman, *Land of Hope*, 100–101.
37. Ibid., 4.
38. Spear, *Black Chicago*, 12.
39. On founding the Chicago Urban League, see Strickland, *Chicago Urban League*, 25–33; Horace Bridges, "The First Urban League Family," in *Two Decades of Service* (Chicago: Chicago Urban League, 1936), Archives of the Chicago History Museum.
40. AANB, s.vv. "Thomas Arnold Hill," "Eugene Kinckle Jones."
41. Jones was a founding member of the first chapter of Alpha Phi Alpha, established at Cornell University in 1906.
42. On Park's criticisms of "self-righteous meddling," see Knupfer, *Reform and Resistance*, 13–20; Raushenbush, *Robert E. Park*, 22–23, 38, 97; Matthews, *Quest*, 16–17, 114–117, 176–179; Faris, *Chicago Sociology*, 9–13, 26, 40–41, 130–133. Although likely tainted by sexism, Park's views of predominantly female social reformers also appear motivated by his goal of establishing sociology "as a fundamental science and not a mere congeries of social-welfare programs and practices" (Raushenbush *Robert E. Park*, 97). This required establishing clear boundaries between professional work in his discipline and the networks of Social Gospel preachers, social workers, and Progressive reformers who influenced his department in its earliest years.
43. Bridges, "First Urban League Family."
44. Graves was hired in 1912 and oversaw Rosenwald's philanthropic initiatives until 1927, while relying heavily on the advice of George Cleveland Hall. Graves joined the board of the Chicago Urban League in 1917 and served as his employer's direct link to that organization. Ascoli, *Julius Rosenwald*, 122; Strickland, *Chicago Urban League*, 32–33, 36–38, 98.

45. Robert Park, introduction to *First Annual Report of the Chicago League on Urban Conditions among Negroes, For the Fiscal Year Ended October 31, 1917*, 3, Chicago Urban League Records, University of Illinois, Special Collections, Box 1, Folder 1.

46. Grossman, *Land of Hope*, 181–245.

47. Ibid., 186.

48. Strickland, *Chicago Urban League*, 38.

49. On Hall's early life, see William H. Hartshorn, "An Era of Progress and Promise, 1863–1910," Title #120, in *Black Biographical Dictionaries 1790–1950*, ed. Randall Burkett, Nancy Burkett, and Henry Louis Gates Jr. (Alexandria, Va.: Chadwyck-Healey, 1991). For a version of Hall's mature years, see Helen Buckler, *Doctor Dan: Pioneer in American Surgery* (Boston: Little Brown, 1954), 77, 175–177, 236–258.

50. Christopher Robert Reed, *Black Chicago in the Early Twentieth Century, 1900–1919* (DeKalb: Northern Illinois University Press, 2011).

51. Buckler, *Doctor Dan*, 245, 248–249, 267.

52. Ibid., 264–265.

53. Werner, *Julius Rosenwald*, 274.

54. Jacqueline Goggin, *Carter G. Woodson: A Life in Black History* (Baton Rouge: Louisiana State University Press, 1997), 32–65; Patricia Watkins Romero, "Carter G. Woodson: A Biography" (Ph.D. diss., Ohio State University, 1971), 92–103.

55. Romero, *Carter G. Woodson*, 102–103.

56. Bridges, "First Urban League Family," 3.

57. Strickland states flatly, "It was Rosenwald's financial assistance that enabled the Chicago Urban League to meet its obligations during the first year." He contributed one third of the annual budget in 1917 and remained a major patron for a dozen years. *Chicago Urban League*, 32, 97.

58. One recent study emphasizes the central role of Park and the Chicago School in providing the philosophical underpinnings for the Urban League but minimizes the link with Tuskegee. Touré F. Reed, *Not Alms But Opportunity: The Urban League and the Politics of Racial Uplift, 1910–1950* (Chapel Hill: University of North Carolina Press, 2008), 11–26, 199 n. 1.

59. Matthews, *Quest*, 176–177.

60. On Johnson's journey, see Embree, *Thirteen Against the Odds*, 55.

61. This refers to Béla Kun's short-lived Soviet Republic of Hungary, overthrown by Admiral Horthy; the Spartacist uprising in Berlin, crushed by the Social Democrats; and the seizure of factories in Turin and Milan, followed by the rise of Mussolini's Black Shirts. See Ivo Banac, ed., *The Effects of World War I: The Class War after the Great War* (New York: Columbia University Press, 1983); F. L. Carsten, *Revolution in Central Europe, 1918–1919* (Berkeley: University of California Press, 1972).

62. William Tuttle, *Race Riot: Chicago in the Red Summer of 1919* (Urbana: University of Illinois Press, 1970), 14–20.

63. Diaries, Taylor Papers, Box 4.

64. Tuttle, *Race Riot*, 3–10.

65. Quoted ibid., 40.

66. Chicago Commission on Race Relations, *The Negro in Chicago: A Study of Race Relations and a Race Riot* (Chicago: University of Chicago, 1922), 1–52; Tuttle, *Race Riot*, 32–66. For personal recollections of the violence, see Travis, *Autobiography of Black Chicago*, 25–26.

67. A copy of the letter sent to the mayor and chief of police by "a joint committee of the Union League Club and the Chicago Urban League" on July 28, 1919, may be found in the Rosenwald Papers, Box 6, Folder 4.

68. Christopher Robert Reed, *The Chicago NAACP and the Rise of Black Professional Leadership, 1910–1966* (Bloomington: Indiana University Press, 1997), 46–48; Arthur Waskow, *From Race Riot to Sit-in: 1919 and the 1960s* (New York: Doubleday, 1966), 42–48.

69. The broader Tuskegee Machine became involved when Johnson was formally suggested as a candidate for executive secretary of the commission in a letter to Rosenwald from Robert Moton, Booker T. Washington's successor at Tuskegee. Minutes of the Chicago Commission on Race Relations, 9 October 1919, Rosenwald Papers, Box 6, Folder 4; hereinafter Minutes.

70. Embree, *Thirteen Against the Odds*, 56.

71. Strickland, *Chicago Urban League*, 61; Waskow, *Race Riot*, 60–62. For Taylor's membership in the Urban League, see Philpott, *Slum and the Ghetto*, 395.

72. Ascoli, *Julius Rosenwald*, 245–246. Also see Waskow, *Race Riot*, 60–70.

73. Wade, *Graham Taylor*, 151–152; Graham Romeyn Taylor to Graham Taylor, 20 September 1919, Taylor Papers, Box 27, Folder 1427.

74. Taylor was appointed at an annual salary of $5,000, while Johnson as associate executive secretary received $3,500. Minutes, 28 November 1919.

75. Minutes, 23 January 1920.

76. Minutes, 12 March 1920.

77. Johnson never completed a doctorate, but that did not prevent him from authoring sixteen scholarly books.

78. Martin Bulmer, "Charles S. Johnson, Robert E. Park, and the Research Methods of the Chicago Commission on Race Relations, 1919–1922: An Early Experiment in Applied Research," *Ethnic and Racial Studies* 4, no. 3 (July 1981): 289–306; Waskow, *Race Riot*, 80–81; Raushenbush, *Robert E. Park*, 95.

79. Minutes, 8 January 1920.

80. Minutes, 12 March 1920.

81. Robert Park, "A Race Relations Survey: Suggestions for a Study of the Oriental Population of the Pacific Coast," *Journal of Applied Sociology* 8 (1923): 196.

82. Werner, *Julius Rosenwald*, 273–274. Also see Gilpin and Gasman, *Charles S. Johnson*, 34.

83. On philosophical continuities and discontinuities between Park's work and Johnson's work, see Saint-Arnaud, *African American Pioneers*, 157–167; Gilpin and Gasman, *Charles S. Johnson*, 49–59; Robbins, *Sidelines Activist*, 31–32.

84. Quoted in Ralph L. Pearson, "Charles S. Johnson: The Urban League Years. A Study of Race Leadership" (Ph.D. diss., Johns Hopkins University, 1970), 72–76. The other two types Johnson identified, "combative propaganda" and "radical propaganda," would be central to the work of Richard Wright and his circle a generation later.

85. Gilpin and Gasman, *Charles S. Johnson*, 15; Weiss, *National Urban League*, 216–221.

86. Robert Park, "Methods of Teaching," in Lyman, *Militarism, Imperialism*, 317.

87. Arnold Rampersad, "Racial Doubt and Racial Shame in the Harlem Renaissance," in *Temples for Tomorrow: Looking Back at the Harlem Renaissance*, ed. Genevieve Fabre and Michel Feith (Bloomington: Indiana University Press, 2001), 35.

88. On the racial pseudoscience of the American academy, see Nell Irvin Painter, *The History of White People* (New York: Norton, 2010), 191–227, 256–290, 301–326; Stephen Jay Gould, *The Mismeasure of Man* (New York: Norton, 1981); Thomas Gossett, *Race: The History of an Idea in America* (1963; New York: Oxford University Press, 1997), 370–408.

89. Gilpin and Gasman, *Charles S. Johnson*, 15–19; Pearson, *Charles S. Johnson*, 117–126.

90. Gilpin and Gasman, *Charles S. Johnson*, 15–16, 19–20; Abby Johnson and Ronald Johnson, *Propaganda and Aesthetics: The Literary Politics of Afro-American Magazines in the Twentieth Century* (Amherst: University of Massachusetts Press, 1979), 49–50.

91. James Weldon Johnson, *Book of American Negro Poetry* (New York: Harcourt, 1922), vii.

92. "An Opportunity for Negro Writers," *Opportunity* 2, no. 9 (September 1924): 258.

93. Celeste Tibbets, *Ernestine Rose and the Origins of the Schomburg Center* (New York: New York Public Library, 1989); George Sylvan Bobinski, Jesse Hauk Shera, and Bohdan S. Wynar, eds., *Dictionary of American Library Biography* (Littleton, Colo.: Libraries Unlimited, 1978), s.v. "Ernestine Rose."

94. George Hutchinson, *In Search of Nella Larsen: A Biography of the Color Line* (Cambridge, Mass.: Harvard University Press, 2006), 132–159, 170–177; BWA, s.v. "Librarianship."

95. Lewis, *When Harlem Was in Vogue*, 105.

96. *Dictionary of American Library Biography*, 123.

97. Walrond to Arthur Schomburg, 13 November 1924, Schomburg Papers, SCRBC, Box 7, Folder 55.

98. James Tuttleton, "Countee Cullen at 'The Heights,'" in *The Harlem Renaissance: Re-evaluations*, ed. Amritjit Singh, William Shriver, and Stanley Brodwin (New York: Garland, 1989), 101–137.

99. Robert Bone and Louis Parascandola, "An Ellis Island of the Soul: Eric Walrond and the Turbulent Passage from Garveyite to New Negro," *Afro-Americans in New York Life and History* 34 (July 2010): 34–53. Walrond reconnected with Garvey and published in his journal *Black Man* while both were living in London in the late 1930s.

100. For a generous sampling of Walrond's journalism and short fiction, see Louis J. Parascandola, ed., *"Winds Can Wake Up the Dead": An Eric Walrond Reader* (Detroit: Wayne State University Press, 1998).

101. "West Indian Labor," *International Interpreter*, 14 July 1923; "The Negro Comes North," *New Republic*, 18 July 1923; "Negro Migration to the North," *International Interpreter*, 18 August 1923; "Negro Exodus from the South," *Current History*, September 1923; "The Negro in Northern Industry," *International Interpreter*, 21 February 1924.

102. Johnson and Johnson, *Propaganda and Aesthetics*, 53–54; Lewis, *When Harlem Was in Vogue*, 123; Weiss, *National Urban League*, 229.

103. Johnson to Alain Locke, 7 March 1924, Locke Papers, Box 164–40, Folder 25. As literary editor of *The Crisis*, Fauset was allied with Johnson's primary editorial competitor, W.E.B. Du Bois. See Lewis, *When Harlem Was in Vogue*, 121–125; George Hutchinson, *The Harlem Renaissance in Black and White* (Cambridge, Mass.: Harvard University Press, 1995), 167.

104. The following are specifically named as sponsors: Countee Cullen, Eric Walrond, Langston Hughes, Jessie Fauset, Gwendolyn Bennett, Harold Jackman, and Regina Anderson. *Opportunity* 2, no. 5 (May 1924): 143. Despite his association with Harlem's younger writers, however, Hughes was actually in Paris when the Civic Club banquet was held. On the poet's European sojourn, see Arnold Rampersad, *The Life of Langston Hughes*, Volume 1: *1902–1941*, *"I, Too, Sing America"* (New York: Oxford University Press, 1986), 81–96.

105. The origins of Kellogg's *Survey Graphic* can be traced to Chicago and New York of the Progressive Era and more specifically to a 1905 merger between Graham Taylor's newsletter, *The Commons*, and a similar journal, *Charities*, published in New York. See Clarke Chambers, *Paul Kellogg and The Survey: Voices for Social Welfare and Social Justice* (Minneapolis: University of Minnesota Press, 1971), 12–117; Wade, *Graham Taylor*, 152–158.

106. Lewis, *When Harlem Was in Vogue*, 94–95, 115–117.

107. Johnson to Ethel Ray, 24 March 1924, Johnson Papers.

108. Ethel Ray Nance, interviews by Ann Allen Shockley, 18 November and 23 December 1970, Fisk University Library; David Levering Lewis, *W.E.B. Du Bois: The Fight for Equality and the American Century, 1919–1963* (New York: Holt, 2000), 166–167.

109. Lewis, *When Harlem Was in Vogue*, 127.

110. Bontemps, "The Awakening," in Bontemps, *Harlem Renaissance Remembered*, 18–20, quotation at 20.

111. "An Opportunity for Negro Writers," *Opportunity* 2, no. 9 (September 1924): 199.

112. *Opportunity* 3, no. 6 (June 1925): 176.

113. George Hutchinson makes a case that it became easier to find outlets with the emergence of such new publishing houses as Alfred A. Knopf, Boni & Liveright, and Harcourt and Brace, firms attuned to recent cultural pluralist ideas and more inclined to take risks on black authors. *Harlem Renaissance*, 342–386. Also see Cary Wintz, *Black Culture and the Harlem Renaissance* (Houston, Tex.: Rice University Press, 1988), 155–177.

114. Johnson, "Countee Cullen Was My Friend."

115. Details of Locke's life are based on Jeffrey Stewart, "A Biography of Alain Locke: Philosopher of the Harlem Renaissance" (Ph.D. diss., Yale University, 1979).

116. Ibid., 202–206.

117. Locke's 1916 pamphlet is reprinted in Jeffrey Stewart, *The Critical Temper of Alain Locke* (New York: Garland Publishing, 1983), 407–413, Park citation at 410.

118. Alain Locke, ed., *The New Negro: An Interpretation* (1925; New York: Simon and Schuster, 1999), 7.

119. Robert E. Park, "Racial Assimilation in Secondary Groups with Particular Reference to the Negro," *American Journal of Sociology* 19, no. 5 (March 1914): 622, 620.

120. Charles Scruggs notes the Parkian contribution to Locke's thought and suggests that Wallace Thurman named the Locke figure "Dr. Parkes" in *Infants of the Spring* as ironic acknowledgment of the connection. See Scruggs, *Sweet Home: Invisible Cities in the Afro-American Novel* (Baltimore: Johns Hopkins University Press, 1993), 50–53, 245 n. 35.

121. Brent Hayes Edwards explores the significance of Locke's international connections among intellectuals of African descent. "Three Ways to Translate the Harlem Renaissance," in Fabre and Feith, *Temples for Tomorrow*, 288–313.

122. Alain Locke, "The Negro's Contribution to American Art and Literature," *Annals of the American Academy of Political and Social Science* 140 (1928): 234–247; reprinted in Stewart, *Critical Temper*, 439–450.

123. Hutchinson, *Harlem Renaissance*, 84–87.

124. On Locke's aesthetics and cultural pluralism, see Mary Ann Calo, *Distinction and Denial: Race, Nation, and the Critical Construction of the African American Artist, 1920–1940* (Ann Arbor: University of Michigan Press, 2007), 23–66; Hutchinson, *Harlem Renaissance*, 55, 78–124. On the Harlem/Greenwich Village axis of the 1920s, see Lewis, preface to the Penguin Edition, *When Harlem Was in Vogue*, xv–xxv; Ann Douglas, *Terrible Honesty: Mongrel Manhattan in the 1920s* (New York: Farrar, Straus, 1995).

125. Michael North, *The Dialect of Modernism: Race, Language, and Twentieth-Century Literature* (New York: Oxford University Press, 1994), 128. North is in fact sharply critical of the Americanist avant-garde and their treatment of black writers and black vernacular, asserting that the cross-racial relationship was marred by white bohemians engaging in "racial masquerade" and "racial ventriloquism" as a mode of rebellion. For more positive assessments, see Hutchinson, *Harlem Renaissance*; Scruggs, *Sweet Home*, 58–59, 226 n. 9.

126. Huggins, *Harlem Renaissance*, 60–65.

127. Scruggs, *Sweet Home*, 3–4, 55.

128. Bone, *Down Home*, 212–222.

129. All quotes from Locke, "The Negro's Contribution."

3 ⟨ The New Negro in Chicago

1. Quotes from Waskow, *Race Riot*, 39–40.

2. "Reaping the Whirlwind," CD, 2 August 1919.

3. Quoted in Robert T. Kerlin, *The Voice of the Negro: 1919* (New York: Dutton, 1920), 66–67.

4. Ibid., 23.

5. Quoted in Lorenzo Thomas, *Extraordinary Measures: Afrocentric Modernism and Twentieth-Century American Poetry* (Tuscaloosa: University of Alabama Press, 2000), 39.

6. Louis Harlan, "Booker T. Washington and the National Negro Business League," in Smock, *Booker T. Washington*, 101, 103.

7. Henry Louis Gates Jr., "The Trope of the New Negro and the Reconstruction of the Image of the Black," *Representations* 24 (Fall 1988): 147. Also see Henry Louis Gates Jr. and Gene Andrew Jarrett, eds., *The New Negro: Readings on Race, Representation, and African American Culture, 1892–1938* (Princeton, N.J.: Princeton University Press, 2007); Jeffrey C. Stewart, "The New Negro as Citizen," in *The Cambridge Companion to the Harlem Renaissance*, ed. George Hutchinson (Cambridge: Cambridge University Press, 2007), 13–27; Anne Elizabeth Carroll, *Word, Image, and the New Negro: Representation and Identity in the Harlem Renaissance* (Bloomington: Indiana University Press, 2005); Barbara Foley, *Spectres of 1919: Class and Nation in the Making of the New Negro* (Cambridge, Mass.: Harvard University Press, 2004); Martha Jane Nadell, *Enter the New Negroes: Images of Race in American Culture* (Cambridge, Mass.: Harvard University Press, 2004); J. Martin Favor, *Authentic Blackness: The Folk in the New Negro Renaissance* (Durham, N.C.: Duke University Press, 1999); William J. Maxwell, *New Negro, Old Left: African-American Writing and Communism between the Wars* (New York: Columbia University Press, 1999); Wilson Jeremiah Moses, *The Golden Age of Black Nationalism 1850–1925* (New York: Oxford University Press, 1988).

8. Christopher Reed makes a strong argument for political heterogeneity and blurred allegiances as defining features of the South Side's civic leadership. *Chicago NAACP*, 11–16.

9. Grossman, *Land of Hope*, 128–131; Spear, *Black Chicago*, 71–89; Reed, *Chicago NAACP*, 59–65.

10. "Booker T. Washington Takes Chicago By Storm," *CD*, 10 December 1910.

11. Drake and Cayton, *Black Metropolis*, 391.

12. Washington to Abbott, 19 December 1913, in *Booker T. Washington Papers, Volume 12, 1912–1914*, ed. Louis R. Harlan and Raymond W. Smock (Urbana: University of Illinois Press, 1982).

13. Reed, *Chicago NAACP*, 72–73.

14. This phrasing draws on the titles of chapters 11 and 12 of Gilpin and Gasman, *Charles S. Johnson*.

15. Grossman, *Land of Hope*, 130.

16. Ottley, *Lonely Warrior*, 17–99; AANB, s.v. "Robert Abbott"; DANB, s.v. "Robert Abbott."

17. "The Old and the New," *CD*, 3 January 1920.

18. On Abbott and Wright, see Harold Gosnell, *Negro Politicians: The Rise of Negro Politics in Chicago* (1935; Chicago: University of Chicago Press, 1967), 100–103. Quotation from Carl Sandburg, *The Chicago Race Riots* (New York: Harcourt Brace, 1919), 2–3.

19. Gosnell, *Negro Politicians*, 153–195; Reed, *Chicago NAACP*, 62–65; Tuttle, *Race Riot*, 184–207; Drake and Cayton, *Black Metropolis*, 342–351.

20. Blyden Jackson, *The Waiting Years: Essays on American Negro Literature* (Baton Rouge: Louisiana State University Press, 1976), 113.

21. Davarian Baldwin shifts focus from associations of the New Negro with the black elite and argues instead for the centrality of the mass consumer marketplace and black leisure pursuits as keys to understanding the movement. *Chicago's New Negroes: Modernity, the Great Migration, and Black Urban Life* (Chapel Hill: University of North Carolina Press, 2007).

22. Michael W. Homel, *Down from Equality: Black Chicagoans and the Public Schools, 1920–41* (Urbana: University of Illinois Press, 1984), 108–116; Grossman, *Land of Hope*, 246–258; Spear, *Black Chicago*, 44–46, 203–205.

23. Robert E. Fleming, *Willard Motley* (Boston: Twayne, 1978), 17–19.

24. On the opening of the Regal and its significance, see Clovis E. Semmes, *The Regal Theater and Black Culture* (New York: Palgrave, 2006), 15–42.

25. "4000 at Party," *CD*, 24 November 1928.

26. Daniel Mark Epstein, *Nat King Cole* (Boston: Northeastern University Press, 1999), 28–31.

27. Rutkoff and Scott, "Pinkster in Chicago," 316–330.

28. William Howland Kenney, *Chicago Jazz: A Cultural History, 1904–1930* (New York: Oxford University Press, 1992), 5–8, 47; Gosnell, *Negro Politicians*, 127–128.

29. Kenney, *Chicago Jazz*, 3–5, 11–14; Grossman, *Land of Hope*, 95, 146, 150; Ted Vincent, "The Community That Gave Jazz to Chicago," *Black Music Research Journal* 12, no. 1 (Spring 1992): 43–55; Baldwin, *Chicago's New Negroes*, 47–49.

30. Eileen Southern, *The Music of Black Americans: A History*, 3d ed. (New York: Norton, 1997), 342–345, 350–351; Kenney, *Chicago Jazz*, 12–13.

31. Kenney, *Chicago Jazz*, 35–60.

32. Quoted Ibid., 18.

33. Langston Hughes, *The Big Sea: An Autobiography* (1940; New York: Hill and Wang, 1993), 33.

34. DANB, s.v. "Joseph 'King' Oliver"; Frederic Ramsey, "King Oliver and His Creole Jazz Band," in *Jazzmen*, ed. Frederic Ramsey and Charles Edward Smith (1939; New York: Harcourt Brace, 1967), 59–91; Kenney, *Chicago Jazz*, 3–4, 17–21.

35. Armstrong's own recollections of his Chicago years are found in *Louis Armstrong in His Own Words: Selected Writings*, ed. Thomas Brothers (New York: Oxford University Press, 1999), 25–29, 47–67, 72–76, 84–104, 128–136.

36. James Lincoln Collier, *Louis Armstrong: An American Genius* (New York: Oxford University Press, 1985), 124–134; Scott Yanow, *Jazz: A Regional Exploration* (New York: Greenwood, 2005), 34–35.

37. On Erskine Tate and other classically trained orchestra leaders on the South Side, see Thomas Hennessey, "The Black Chicago Establishment 1919–1930," *Journal of Jazz Studies* 2 (December 1974): 15–45; Southern, *Music of Black Americans*, 350–351.

38. Kenney, *Chicago Jazz*, 116–146.

39. Collier, *Louis Armstrong*, 169–198; William Russell, "Louis Armstrong," in Ramsey and Smith, *Jazzmen*, 128–138.

40. Derek Vaillant, *Sounds of Reform: Progressivism and Music in Chicago, 1873–1935* (Chapel Hill: University of North Carolina Press, 2003), 202–213; Kenney, *Chicago Jazz*, 16–19, 21, 23–25, 147–148, 154; Dempsey Travis, *An Autobiography of Black Jazz* (Chicago: Urban Research Institute, 1983), 33, 70–71.

41. Stanley Dance, *The World of Earl Hines* (New York: Scribner, 1977), 7–32.

42. Ibid., 33–56.

43. To honor the 2001 Armstrong Centennial, Columbia Records issued the four-CD set *Louis Armstrong: The Complete Hot Five and Hot Seven Recordings*. Disc 4 contains all nineteen titles that memorialize the Armstrong/Hines collaboration of 1928.

44. Epstein, *Nat King Cole*, 9. Also see Kenney, *Chicago Jazz*, 139–140; Ted Gioia, *The History of Jazz* (New York: Oxford University Press, 1997), 63–66; Floyd, *Power of Black Music*, 123–125.

45. Travis, *Black Jazz*, 76–109; Kenney, *Chicago Jazz*, 162–164; Green, *Selling the Race*, 58–60.

46. Kenney, *Chicago Jazz*, 148–153.

47. Ibid., 164; *Armstrong in His Own Words*, 103–106.

48. Lewis, *When Harlem Was in Vogue*, 173.

49. Charles S. Johnson, "Illinois: Mecca of the Migrant Mob," *The Messenger* 5 (December 1923), 933. Also see Kenney, *Chicago Jazz*, 17.

50. Kenney, *Chicago Jazz*, 26. On Old Settlers and the Great Migration, see Grossman, *Land of Hope*, 123–160. Christopher Reed restricts the term to those who moved to Chicago prior to the 1893 World's Columbian Exposition. See *Black Chicago's First Century*, Volume I, *1833–1900* (Columbia: University of Missouri Press, 2005), 40, 65; and Reed's forthcoming *Black Chicago in the Early Twentieth Century, 1900–1919*.

51. Kenney, *Chicago Jazz*, 15.

52. Vincent, "Community That Gave Jazz to Chicago," 45–48.

53. Floyd, *Power of Black Music*, 119.

54. Peter Marzio, "A Museum and a School: An Uneasy but Creative Union," *Chicago History* 8, no. 1 (Spring 1979): 20–23, 44–52.

55. Daniel Schulman, "'White City' and 'Black Metropolis': African American Painters in Chicago, 1893–1945," in *Chicago Modern, 1893–1945: Pursuit of the New*, ed. Elizabeth Kennedy (Chicago: Terra Museum of American Art, 2004), 38–51; "Colored Artists of Chicago and Vicinity," in *Intercollegian Wonder Book*, Volume 1: *The Negro in Chicago, 1779–1927*, ed. Frederick H. Robb (Chicago: Washington Intercollegiate Club of Chicago, 1927), 83.

56. Charlotte Moser, "'In the Highest Efficiency': Art Training at the School of the Art Institute of Chicago," in *The Old Guard and the Avant-Garde: Modernism in Chicago, 1910–1940*, ed. Sue Ann Prince (Chicago: University of Chicago Press, 1990), 193–208. Also see Helen Lefkowitz Horowitz, *Culture and the City: Cultural Philanthropy in Chicago from the 1880s to 1917* (Lexington: University of Kentucky Press, 1976).

57. Schulman, "'White City,'" 43–44.

58. Daniel Schulman, "African American Art and the Julius Rosenwald Fund," in *A Force for Change: African American Art and the Julius Rosenwald Fund*, ed. Daniel Schulman (Chicago: Spertus Institute of Jewish Studies and Northwestern University Press, 2009), 57–58.

59. Schulman, "'White City,'" 44–45.

60. Charles Dawson, "Celebrated Negro Artists," in *Intercollegian Wonder Book*, Volume 2: *The Negro in Chicago, 1927–1929*, ed. Frederick H. Robb (Chicago: Washington Intercollegiate Club of Chicago, 1929), 27–28; Lisa Meyerowitz, "The Negro in Art Week: Defining the 'New Negro' Through Art Exhibition," *African American Review* 31, no. 1 (Spring 1997): 75–89; Romare Bearden and Harry Henderson, *A History of African-American Artists from 1792 to the Present* (New York: Pantheon, 1993), 116–117.

61. Schulman, "'White City,'" 46; 50 n. 39.

62. Sources on Motley's life are Amy Mooney, *Archibald J. Motley Jr.* (San Francisco: Pomegranate, 2004); Theresa Jontyle Robinson and Wendy Greenhouse, *The Art of Archibald J. Motley Jr.* (Chicago: Chicago Historical Society, 1991); Archibald Motley Jr., interview by Dennis Barrie, 23 January 1978, AAA.

63. *History of Englewood High School: 1874–1935* (Chicago: privately printed, 1935), Englewood High School Records, Box 1, Special Collections, Harold Washington Central Library, Chicago Public Library.

64. Motley, Interview.

65. Ibid.

66. Moser, "'Highest Efficiency,'" 194, 202–204.

67. Mooney, *Archibald J. Motley*, 83, 86.

68. Elaine Woodall, "Looking Backward: Archibald J. Motley and The Art Institute of Chicago, 1914–1930," *Chicago History* 8 (Spring 1979): 55.

69. Margaret Rose Vendryes, *Barthé: A Life in Sculpture* (Jackson: University Press of Mississippi, 2008), 25–26.

70. *New York Times*, 25 February 1928. Twenty years earlier, in fact, Henry O. Tanner had a single-artist exhibition of religious paintings at New York's American Art Gallery.

71. Comparing Motley's work with the Harmon exhibition, critic Worth Tuttle declared: "There was no one to equal Mr. Motley in imagination and in emotion." "Negro Artists Are Developing True Racial Art," *New York Times*, 9 September 1928. On the Harmon Foundation, see Gary Reynolds and Beryl Wright, eds., *Against the Odds: African American Artists and the Harmon Foundation* (Newark, N.J.: Newark Museum of Art, 1987); Bearden and Henderson, *African-American Artists*, 124–125, 250–259.

72. Robinson and Greenhouse, *Art of Archibald Motley*, 11–12.

73. Alain Locke, "The Legacy of the Ancestral Arts," in *New Negro*, 255–256.

74. Edward Alden Jewell, "A Negro Artist Plumbs the Negro Soul," *New York Times*, 25 March 1928.

75. Theresa Leininger-Miller, *New Negro Artists in Paris: African American Painters and Sculptors in the City of Light, 1922–34* (New Brunswick, N.J.: Rutgers University Press, 2001), 147–154.

76. Archibald J. Motley Jr., "Plans for Study," application for Guggenheim Foundation Fellowship, 1928. This material is found in the Archibald J. Motley Jr. Collection, temporarily housed in the Women and Leadership Archives, Loyola University, Chicago, and made available courtesy of Valerie Gerrard Browne, daughter-in-law of the artist.

77. Quoted in Jan Pinkerton and Randolph H. Hudson, eds., *Encyclopedia of the Chicago Literary Renaissance* (New York: Facts on File, 2004), s.v. "H. L. Mencken."

78. Lisa Woolley argues, however, that black and female voices were marginalized or distorted within the multiplicity of dialects heard in the literature of the first Chicago Renaissance. *American Voices of the Chicago Renaissance* (DeKalb: Northern Illinois University Press, 2000).

79. Harriet Monroe and Alice Corbin Henderson, eds., *The New Poetry: An Anthology* (New York: Macmillan, 1917), vi.

80. A useful chronology of the decade's other mileposts appears in Pinkerton and Hudson, *Encyclopedia of the Chicago Literary Renaissance*, 405–407.

81. Quoted in Kenny J. Williams, "An Invisible Partnership and an Unlikely Relationship: William Stanley Braithwaite and Harriet Monroe," *Callaloo* 32 (Summer 1987): 523. Williams explores the parallel contributions of black Bostonian Braithwaite and white Chicagoan Monroe to the development of early twentieth-century American poetry. Also see Thomas, *Extraordinary Measures*, 45–73.

82. Ellen Williams, *Harriet Monroe and the Poetry Renaissance: The First Ten Years of Poetry, 1912–1922* (Urbana: University of Illinois Press, 1977); Robin Schultze, "Harriet Monroe's Pioneering Modernism: Nature, National Identity, and *Poetry: A Magazine of Verse*," *Legacy* 21, no. 1 (2004): 50–67.

83. On Johnson's life, see Thomas, *Extraordinary Measures*, 11–44; DANB, s.v. "Fenton Johnson"; Fenton Johnson, "The Story of Myself," in *Tales of Darkest America* (Chicago: Favorite Magazine, 1920), 5–8.

84. Arna Bontemps, *American Negro Poetry* (New York: Hill and Wang, 1974), 222.
85. On "Mushmouth," Elijah, and Eudora Johnson, see Travis, *Autobiography of Black Jazz*, 25–30; Spear, *Black Chicago*, 74–77; Gosnell, *Negro Politicians*, 125–128, 173.
86. Lorenzo Thomas traces a "theme of glory and race redemption through . . . self-sacrifice" in Johnson's poetry and prose. *Extraordinary Measures*, 19–22.
87. James de Jongh, *Vicious Modernism: Black Harlem and the Literary Imagination* (Cambridge: Cambridge University Press, 1990), 15.
88. Quoted in Johnson and Johnson, *Propaganda and Aesthetics*, 220 n. 35.
89. Quoted in Thomas, *Extraordinary Measures*, 36.
90. Suzanne W. Churchill, *The Little Magazine OTHERS and the Renovation of Modern American Poetry* (Farnham, UK: Ashgate, 2006). Frank Marshall Davis credited *Others* with introducing him to "the new revolutionary style called free verse." John Edgar Tidwell, "An Interview with Frank Marshall Davis," *Black American Literature Forum* 19, no. 3 (Autumn 1985): 105.
91. Jean Wagner, *Black Poets of the United States* (Urbana: University of Illinois Press, 1973), 182. Wagner was likely influenced by Sterling Brown's emphasis on Johnson's "pessimism." See Brown's *Negro Poetry and Drama* (1937: New York: Arno, 1969), 61–62.
92. "Chicago Art: 'Letters,'" in Robb, *Intercollegian Wonder Book*, Volume 1, 83.
93. Frank Marshall Davis, *Livin' the Blues: Memoirs of a Black Journalist and Poet*, ed. John Edgar Tidwell (Madison: University of Wisconsin Press, 1992), 131.
94. Rampersad, *Life of Langston Hughes*, Volume 1, 138. On *Fire!!*, see Eleonore van Notten, *Wallace Thurman's Harlem Renaissance* (Amsterdam: Rodopi, 1994), 131–158.
95. Richard Wright, *Black Boy [American Hunger]* in *Richard Wright: Later Works*, ed. Arnold Rampersad (1945 [1977]; New York: Library of America, 1991), 272.
96. Davis, *Livin' the Blues*, 103.
97. Ibid., 103–131.
98. Bernard Duffey, *The Chicago Renaissance in American Letters: A Critical History* (East Lansing: Michigan State College Press, 1954), 127–142; Susan Noyes Platt, "The Little Review: Early Years and Avant-Garde Ideas," in Prince, *The Old Guard and the Avant-Garde*, 139–154; Steven Watson, *Strange Bedfellows: The First American Avant-Garde* (New York: Abbeville Press, 1991), 24–26.
99. Dunham was one of the editors of *The Philosophy of the Act*, a 1938 collection of Mead's unpublished papers.
100. "Masque," in Robb, *Wonder Book*, Volume 1, 83; "Publicity Director," CD, 14 January 1928; Knupfer, *Chicago Black Renaissance*, 56. On Browne's Little Theater, see Dale Kramer, *Chicago Renaissance: The Literary Life in the Midwest, 1900–1930* (New York: Appleton, 1966), 155–163; Watson, *Strange Bedfellows*, 23, 402.
101. Terry Harnan, *African Rhythm, American Dance: A Biography of Katherine Dunham* (New York: Alfred A. Knopf, 1974), 44.
102. Dave Peyton, "The Musical Bunch," CD, 12 January 1929; "Start 'Little Theater' in Chicago," CD, 1 February 1929.
103. Knupfer, *Chicago Black Renaissance*, 56; Albert Dunham to Alain Locke, 24 February 1928, Locke Papers, Box 164–26, Folder 20. Also see Dunham to Locke, 2 January 1929; Locke to Dunham, 4 February 1929.
104. "The Negro in Illinois," Illinois Writers' Project, Harsh, Box 47, Folder 7.
105. Harnan, *African Rhythm*, 44.
106. Katherine Dunham, excerpt from "Minefields," in *Kaiso!: Writings by and about Katherine Dunham*, eds. VeVe A. Clark and Sara E. Johnson (Madison: University of Wisconsin Press, 2005), 87.
107. Ann Barzel, Mark Turbyfill, and Ruth Page, "The Lost Ten Years: The Untold Story of the Dunham-Turbyfill Alliance," in Clark and Johnson, *Kaiso!*, 177–188. Barthé's first one-artist show was held in Chicago in 1930. Vendryes, *Barthé*, 45–50.
108. Mark Turbyfill, "Shall We Present to the World a New Ballet?" *Abbotts's Monthly* 1, no. 2 (November 1930): 62–64, 93.

109. Maude George, "News of the Music World," CD, 17 December 1932; "Modern Dancers Praised at Stevens," CD, 24 December 1932.
110. A complete list of Rosenwald Fellows appears in Schulman, Force for Change, 157–172.
111. Thomas Elsa Jones, Light on the Horizon: The Quaker Pilgrimage of Tom Jones (Richmond, Ind.: Friends United Press, 1973), 87–94.
112. Walter A. Jackson, Gunnar Myrdal and America's Conscience: Social Engineering and Racial Liberalism, 1938–1987 (Chapel Hill: University of North Carolina Press, 1990), 31–32; Ellen Lagemann, The Politics of Knowledge: The Carnegie Corporation, Philanthropy, and Public Policy (Middletown, Conn.: Wesleyan University Press, 1989), 6–7, 60–63, 69–70.
113. Memorandum, Johnson to Jones, 29 September 1928, Thomas Elsa Jones Papers, Fisk University Library; Reply, Jones to Johnson, 10 October 1928, Jones Papers.
114. Wayne Urban, Black Scholar: Horace Mann Bond 1904–1972 (Athens: University of Georgia Press, 1992), 40–48.
115. DANB, s.v. "E. Franklin Frazier"; G. Franklin Edwards, "E. Franklin Frazier," in Black Sociologists: Historical and Contemporary Perspectives ed. James E. Blackwell and Morris Janowitz (Chicago: University of Chicago Press, 1974), 85–117.
116. Blyden Jackson, "A Postlude to a Renaissance," Southern Review 25, no. 4 (1990): 746–765. Also see Stanley H. Smith, "Sociological Research and Fisk University: A Case Study," in Black Sociologists, ed. Blackwell and Janowitz, 164–190.
117. A list of Rosenwald Fund trustees appears in Edwin R. Embree and Julia Waxman, Investment in People: The Story of the Julius Rosenwald Fund (New York: Harper, 1949), 235–236.
118. On Embree's life, see Alfred Perkins, "Investment in Talent: Edwin Rogers Embree and the Julius Rosenwald Fellowships," in Schulman, Force for Change, 24–35; Charles S. Johnson, "Edwin Rogers Embree," Phylon 7, no. 4 (Fourth Quarter 1946): 317–334. On John Fee, see Edwin Embree, Brown Americans: The Story of a New Race (1931; New York: Viking, 1943), 57–71.
119. Ascoli, Julius Rosenwald, 216–218, 300–302.
120. Edwin Embree, Julius Rosenwald Fund, 1917–1936 (Chicago: Julius Rosenwald Fund, 1937), 3–4.
121. Ibid., 12, 16.
122. Embree and Waxman, Investment in People, 273, 156, 153.
123. Wilma Dykeman and James Stokeley, Seeds of Southern Change: The Life of Will Alexander (Chicago: University of Chicago Press, 1962).
124. Alexander quoted Ibid., 42.
125. Ibid., 182–183. On the Rosenwald Fund's work in the South, see John H. Stanfield, "Dollars for the Silent South: Southern White Liberalism and the Julius Rosenwald Fund, 1928–1948," in Perspectives on the American South, Volume 2, ed. Merle Black and John Shelton Reed (New York: Gordon and Breach, 1984), 117–138.
126. Daniel Schulman, introduction to Force for Change, 13.

4 ⟨ Year of Transition

1. Lewis, When Harlem Was in Vogue, 165–170, 265–266; Hughes, Big Sea, 245–247.
2. Hughes, Big Sea, 247.
3. EAACH, s.v. "A'Lelia Walker"; Lewis, Fight for Equality, 285.
4. Lewis, Fight for Equality, 174–182.
5. Alain Locke, "The Year of Grace: Outstanding Books of the Year in Negro Literature," Opportunity 9, no. 2 (February 1931): 48.
6. Kirkland C. Jones, Renaissance Man from Louisiana: A Biography of Arna Wendell Bontemps (Westport, Conn.: Greenwood, 1992), 72–74.
7. Eventually, the Bontemps family included six children.
8. Arna Bontemps, introduction to Black Thunder (1936; Boston: Beacon, 1992), xxiv.
9. Dan T. Carter, Scottsboro: A Tragedy of the American South (1969; Baton Rouge: Louisiana State University Press, 1979), 11–12.
10. Bontemps, Introduction, xxiv.

11. Quoted in Jones, *Renaissance Man*, 75.
12. Bontemps to Hughes, n.d. [Fall 1931] in *Arna Bontemps—Langston Hughes Letters, 1925–1967*, ed. Charles H. Nichols (New York: Oxford University Press, 1986), 17–18.
13. This brief account is based on Carter, *Scottsboro*; James Goodman, *Stories of Scottsboro* (New York: Pantheon, 1994).
14. William Leuchtenburg, *Franklin D. Roosevelt and the New Deal: 1932–1940* (New York: Harper, 1963), 2.
15. Quoted in Rampersad, *Langston Hughes*, Volume 1, 214.
16. Ibid., 215–220. Hughes's play was included in a slim volume called *Scottsboro Limited: Four Poems and a Play in Verse* (New York: Golden Stair Press, 1932). Also see Alan M. Wald, *Exiles from a Future Time: The Forging of the Mid-Twentieth Century Literary Left* (Chapel Hill: University of North Carolina Press, 2002), 84–95; James Edward Smethurst, *The New Red Negro: The Literary Left and African-American Poetry, 1930–1946* (New York: Oxford University Press, 1999), 93–115.
17. Arna Bontemps, *The Old South: "A Summer Tragedy" and Other Stories of the Thirties* (New York: Dodd, Mead, 1973), 157–169.
18. Arna Bontemps, "Why I Returned," in *The Old South*, 18.
19. Drake and Cayton, *Black Metropolis*, 217–218 n.
20. "3 Chicago Banks Closed," *CD*, 9 August 1930.
21. "We Must Have Faith," *CD*, 24 May 1931; "Hard Times," *CD*, 12 September 1931.
22. Lizabeth Cohen examines the Depression-induced unraveling of traditional "patterns of loyalty" in ethnic, working-class communities across the city. *Making a New Deal: Industrial Workers in Chicago, 1919–1939* (Cambridge: Cambridge University Press, 1990), 213–249.
23. "Democratic Landslide Beats Thompson," *CD*, 11 April 1931.
24. Mitchell was the first black Democratic congressman in American history. Christopher Robert Reed, "A Study of Black Politics and Protest in Depression-decade Chicago, 1930–1939" (PhD diss., Kent State University, 1982), 220–231; Gosnell, *Negro Politicians*, 89–92.
25. Strickland, *Chicago Urban League*, 104–107.
26. Reed, "Black Politics and Protest," 146–161.
27. Drake and Cayton, *Black Metropolis*, 415, 418–422.
28. Gosnell, *Negro Politicians*, 319–356; Storch, *Red Chicago*, 50–54, 76–78, 111–114.
29. Gosnell, *Negro Politicians*, 328.
30. Horace Cayton, "The Black Bugs," *The Nation* (9 September 1931): 255–256.
31. Storch, *Red Chicago*, 99–101.
32. Bontemps, "Famous WPA Authors," 43–47.

5 ⓒ Birthing the Blues and Other Black Musical Forms

1. Nora Douglas Holt, "News of the Music World," *CD*, 24 September 1921.
2. On Bonds's life, see Helen Walker-Hill, *From Spirituals to Symphonies: African-American Women Composers and Their Music* (Urbana: University of Illinois Press, 2007), 141–188.
3. Reed, *Black Chicago's First Century*, Volume 1, 54, 85, 130, 133, 205, 315–325, 403–409; Wallace Best, *Passionately Human, No Less Divine: Religion and Culture in Black Chicago, 1915–1952* (Princeton, N.J.: Princeton University Press, 2005), 100–102; Spear, *Black Chicago*, 91–97.
4. Margaret Bonds, "A Reminiscence," *The Negro in Music and Art*, ed. Lindsay Patterson (New York: Association for the Study of Negro Life and History, 1967), 191–193.
5. On Price's life, see Rae Linda Brown, "Lifting the Veil: The Symphonies of Florence B. Price," in *Florence Price: Symphonies Nos. 1 and 3*, vol. 19, *Music of the United States of America*, ed. Rae Linda Brown and Wayne Shirley (Middleton, Wis.: A-R Editions, 2008), xv–lii.
6. Rae Linda Brown, "Florence B. Price's 'Negro Symphony,'" in *Temples for Tomorrow*, ed. Fabre and Feith, 89–90.
7. Bonds, "Reminiscence," 192.
8. "Modern Dancers Praised at Stevens," *CD*, 24 December 1932.
9. Maude George, "News of the Music World," *CD*, 18 February 1933.

10. "This Week," CD, 24 June 1933.

11. Rae Linda Brown, "William Grant Still, Florence Price, and William Dawson: Echoes of the Harlem Renaissance," in Black Music in the Harlem Renaissance, ed. Samuel A. Floyd Jr. (Knoxville: University of Tennessee Press, 1993), 71. Also see Southern, Music of Black Americans, 425, 427, 431–434; Floyd, Power of Black Music, 109–110, 120–121.

12. AANB, s.v. "William Levi Dawson."

13. Quoted in Brown, "Price's 'Negro Symphony,'" 94.

14. On Broonzy's life, see Roger Randolph House III, "Keys to the Highway: William 'Big Bill' Broonzy and the Chicago Blues in the Era of the Great Migration" (Ph.D. diss., Boston University, 1999); William Broonzy with Yannick Bruynoghe, Big Bill Blues: William Broonzy's Story (1955; New York: Oak, 1964).

15. House, "Keys to the Highway," 20.

16. Ibid., 63.

17. See Broonzy's own account of his wartime experience in Alan Lomax, The Land Where the Blues Began (New York: New Press, 2002), 433–438.

18. Farah Jasmine Griffin, "Who Set You Flowin'?": The African-American Migration Narrative (New York: Oxford University Press, 1995), 52–61; BWA, s.v. "Blues and Women"; House, "Keys to the Highway," 90.

19. Albert Murray created a literary portrait of the rambling bluesman in the figure of Luzana Cholly, hero of Train Whistle Guitar (1974).

20. Southern, Music of Black Americans, 332–338.

21. W. C. Handy, Father of the Blues: An Autobiography (1941; New York: DaCapo, 1969), 74, 76. Arna Bontemps served as ghostwriter on this project.

22. Murray, Stomping the Blues, 70.

23. William Kornblum, "Discovering Ink: A Mentor for an Historical Ethnography," Annals of the American Academy of Political and Social Science 595 (September 2004): 176–189; Green, Selling the Race, 53–55.

24. Griffin, "Who Set You Flowin'?" 48–99.

25. Elijah Wald, Escaping the Delta: Robert Johnson and the Invention of the Blues (New York: Harper, 2004), 14–42; William Barlow, Looking Up at Down: The Emergence of Blues Culture (Philadelphia: Temple University Press, 1990), 292–294.

26. House, "Keys to the Highway," 94.

27. Samuel Charters, The Country Blues (New York: DaCapo, 1975), 135–137.

28. Green, Selling the Race, 70–72.

29. House, "Keys to the Highway," 86.

30. Barlow, Looking Up, 300.

31. Wald, Escaping the Delta, 41.

32. Barlow, Looking Up, 310–314; Griffin, "Who Set You Flowin'?" 52–61.

33. House, "Keys to the Highway," 202–204. Also see John Hammond, On Record: An Autobiography (New York: Ridge, 1977), 199–206.

34. Muddy Waters, as told to Alfred Duckett, "Got a Right to Sing the Blues," CD, 26 March 1955.

35. Green, Selling the Race, 72–79; Barlow, Looking Up, 324, 328–330.

36. On Dorsey's life, see Michael W. Harris, The Rise of Gospel Blues: The Music of Thomas Andrew Dorsey in the Urban Church (New York: Oxford University Press, 1994).

37. Ibid., 117–124; Best, Passionately Human, 94–100.

38. Harris, Gospel Blues, 178.

39. BWA, s.v. "Mahalia Jackson."

40. Jules Schwerin, Got to Tell It: Mahalia Jackson, Queen of Gospel (New York: Oxford University Press, 1992), 28–29, 31.

41. Studs Terkel, Talking to Myself: A Memoir of My Times (New York: New Press, 1995), 261.

42. Quoted in Laurraine Goreau, Just Mahalia Baby: The Mahalia Jackson Story (Waco, Tex.: World Books, 1975), 54–55.

43. Harris, Gospel Blues, 257–261.

44. Terkel, *Talking to Myself*, 259.
45. For a list of Jackson's records on the Apollo label, see Schwerin, *Got to Tell It*, 191–193.
46. Richard Wright, "Amusements in Districts 38 and 40," Box A880, Federal Writers' Project: Negro Studies Project, Manuscript Division, Library of Congress, Washington, D.C.; reprinted in Stange, *Bronzeville*, 193–195.
47. Albert Murray, *South to a Very Old Place* (New York: McGraw-Hill, 1971), 124.
48. Dance, *Earl Hines*, 58.
49. Quoted Ibid., 61.
50. Ibid., 66–67.
51. Travis, *Black Jazz*, 39–45; Epstein, *Nat King Cole*, 10–11.
52. Travis, *Black Jazz*, 45–46; Dance, *Earl Hines*, 95.
53. Dance, *Earl Hines*, 94.
54. Studs Terkel, *Giants of Jazz* (1957; New York: New Press, 1975), 158–162.
55. Quoted in Travis, *Black Jazz*, 338.
56. Quoted in Dance, *Earl Hines*, 89–90.
57. "Modern Dancers Praised at Stevens," CD, 24 December 1932.
58. Katherine Dunham, excerpt from "Minefields," in *Kaiso!*, ed. Clark and Johnson, 87.
59. Katherine Dunham, "The Anthropological Approach to the Dance (1942)," in *Kaiso!*, ed. Clark and Johnson, 508.
60. Joyce Aschenbrenner, *Katherine Dunham: Dancing a Life* (Urbana: University of Illinois Press, 2002), 28–38.
61. Barzel et al., "Lost Ten Years," 187–188.
62. Quoted in Julia L. Foulkes, "'My Feet Are Again on This Earth': Dance and the Julius Rosenwald Fund," in Schulman, *Force for Change*, 143–144.
63. Harnan, *African Rhythm*, 54–56.
64. Aschenbrenner, *Katherine Dunham*, 44–46.
65. Dunham, "Anthropological Approach," 509.
66. St. Clair Drake, "Honoring Katherine Dunham," in *Kaiso!*, ed. Clark and Johnson, 575. On Hurston's tumultuous relationship with the Rosenwald Fund, see Valerie Boyd, *Wrapped in Rainbows: The Life of Zora Neale Hurston* (New York: Simon and Schuster, 2003), 260–276.
67. Quoted in Aschenbrenner, *Katherine Dunham*, 64.
68. The term "Rada-Dahomey," or "old-Dahomey," refers to the ancient kingdom of Dahomey in coastal West Africa. The kingdom, said to be the birthplace of voodoo, occupied territories co-extensive with modern Togo and Benin.
69. Katherine Dunham, *Island Possessed* (Garden City, N.Y.: Doubleday, 1969), 60–61.
70. Ibid., 132.
71. For a contemporary anthropologist's assessment of Dunham's fieldwork, see Aschenbrenner, *Katherine Dunham*, 43–90. For a mentor's view, see Melville J. Herskovits, *The Myth of the Negro Past* (1941; Boston: Beacon Press, 1958), 270.
72. Harnan, *African Rhythm*, 97.
73. Katherine Dunham, *Journey to Accompong* (New York: Holt, 1946).
74. Dunham, "Minefields," 88.
75. Ibid., 89–90.
76. Ibid., 97.
77. Aschenbrenner, *Katherine Dunham*, 124–127; Harnan, *African Rhythm*, 101–106.
78. On the cultural context within which *Stormy Weather* was produced, see Scruggs, *Sweet Home*, 10–12.
79. Harnan, *African Rhythm*, 121–123.
80. Some scholars have likewise examined commonalities in the work of Wright and Hurston—often construed as polar opposites in their treatment of black folk culture—as a consequence of their common intellectual debts to contemporary social scientific theories. See Maxwell, *New Negro, Old Left*, 153–178; Cappetti, *Writing Chicago*, 182–197.
81. Dunham, "Thesis Turned Broadway," in *Kaiso!*, ed. Clark and Johnson, 216.

6 (Bronzeville and the Documentary Spirit

1. Horace Cayton et al., "Reflections on Richard Wright: Symposium on an Exiled Native Son," in *Anger, and Beyond: The Negro Writer in the United States*, ed. Herbert Hill (New York: Harper, 1966), 196–197.

2. Richard S. Hobbs, *The Cayton Legacy: An African American Family* (Pullman: Washington State University Press, 2002), 40, 67; Horace R. Cayton, *Long Old Road* (New York: Simon and Schuster, 1963), 1–3, 7, 172–174.

3. Quoted in Margaret Walker, *Richard Wright, Daemonic Genius: A Portrait of the Man, A Critical Look at His Work* (New York: Amistad, 1988), 13.

4. Hazel Rowley, *Richard Wright: The Life and Times* (New York: Holt, 2001), 1–49; Michel Fabre, *The Unfinished Quest of Richard Wright* (New York: Morrow, 1973), 1–72. Except as noted, all biographical details on Wright come from Rowley and Fabre.

5. Cayton, *Long Old Road*, 175–176.

6. Hobbs, *Cayton Legacy*, 105

7. Richard Wright, *Black Boy [American Hunger]*, in *Richard Wright: Later Works*, ed. Arnold Rampersad (1945 [1977]; New York: Library of America, 1991), 249.

8. Rowley, *Richard Wright*, 50–60; Fabre, *Unfinished Quest*, 73–82.

9. Cayton, *Long Old Road*, 190.

10. Ibid., 189–206.

11. Rowley, *Richard Wright*, 11–13, 35–36.

12. Fabre, *Unfinished Quest*, 82–87.

13. Wright, *Black Boy*, 285.

14. Cayton, "Black Bugs," 255–256.

15. For memoirs of the John Reed Clubs, see Malcolm Cowley, *The Dream of the Golden Mountains: Remembering the 1930s* (New York: Penguin, 1981), 134–148; Wright, *Black Boy*, 300–333. For a provocative analysis, see Michael Denning, *The Cultural Front: The Laboring of American Culture in the Twentieth Century* (London: Verso, 1997), 205–211.

16. Rowley, *Richard Wright*, 74–81; Fabre, *Unfinished Quest*, 88–90, 95–103.

17. Wirth to Howard Odum, 27 April 1948, Wirth Papers.

18. Roger A. Salerno, *Louis Wirth: A Bio-Bibliography* (New York: Greenwood, 1987), 3–49.

19. Cayton, "Reflections," 196–197.

20. Quoted in Malcolm Cowley, "A Natural History of American Naturalism," in *The Portable Malcolm Cowley*, ed. Donald W. Faulkner (New York: Penguin, 1990), 181.

21. Richard Lehan, *Realism and Naturalism: The Novel in an Age of Transition* (Madison: University of Wisconsin Press, 2005), 99–205.

22. Quoted in Cowley, "Natural History," 177.

23. Carl S. Smith, *Chicago and the American Literary Imagination, 1880–1920* (Chicago: University of Chicago Press, 1984), 62.

24. Charles Scruggs, *The Sage in Harlem: H. L. Mencken and the Black Writers of the 1920s* (Baltimore: Johns Hopkins University Press, 1984); Hutchinson, *Harlem Renaissance*, 313–341.

25. Wright, *Black Boy*, 237–239.

26. Lewis Coser, *Masters of Sociological Thought: Ideas in Historical and Social Context*, 2d ed. (New York: Harcourt, 1977), 381, 371.

27. Ronald Gottesman, introduction to Upton Sinclair, *The Jungle* (1906; New York: Penguin, 1985), xiv–xxviii; Smith, *Chicago and the American Literary Imagination*, 164–170.

28. Lehan, *Realism and Naturalism*, 224.

29. Raushenbush, *Robert E. Park*, 178.

30. Cappetti, *Writing Chicago*, 21–23.

31. Raushenbush, *Robert E. Park*, 17.

32. Park and Burgess, *Introduction to the Science of Sociology*, 144.

33. Cappetti, *Writing Chicago*, 26–33.

34. James T. Farrell, *The Young Manhood of Studs Lonigan*, in *Studs Lonigan: A Trilogy* (New York: Modern Library, 1938), 306–315.

35. On Farrell and the Chicago School, see Cappetti, *Writing Chicago*, 108–143.

36. Wright, introduction to *Black Metropolis*, xvii–xviii.

37. Jerre Mangione, *The Dream and the Deal: The Federal Writers' Project, 1935–1945* (Syracuse, N.Y.: Syracuse University Press, 1996), 29–50.

38. Mary Wirth, interview by Horace Cayton, compact disk, Cayton Papers.

39. Richard Wright, "The Chicago Urban League," typescript, 8 January 1936; "A Survey of the Amusement Facilities of District #35," and "Amusements in Districts #38 and #40," typescripts, n.d.; Boxes A875 and A876, Federal Writers' Project: Negro Studies Project, Manuscript Division, Library of Congress.

40. Richard Wright, "Ethnological Aspects of Chicago's Black Belt," 11 December 1935, typescript, Illinois Writers' Project, Negro in Illinois Papers, Box 53, Harsh.

41. Wright, *Black Boy*, 315–323; Rowley, *Richard Wright*, 95–101; Fabre, *Unfinished Quest*, 105–107, 113–114, 121–122, 134–135.

42. Richard Wright, *Native Son*, in *Richard Wright: Early Works*, ed. Arnold Rampersad (1940; New York: Library of America, 1991), 514–515.

43. On Ickes's background, see Reed, *Chicago NAACP*, 52–55.

44. Robert H. Zieger, *The CIO, 1935–1955* (Chapel Hill: University of North Carolina Press, 1995), 6–110; Cohen, *Making a New Deal*, 333–349.

45. Hobbs, *Cayton Legacy*, 105–106; Cayton, *Long Old Road*, 207.

46. Johnson to Cayton, 25 September 1934, Cayton Papers.

47. Cayton to Wirth, 15 October 1935, Wirth Papers, Box 2, Folder 5.

48. Cayton to Wirth, 31 March 1936, Wirth Papers, Box 2, Folder 5.

49. Raushenbush, *Robert E. Park*, 149–57; Gilpin and Gasman, *Charles S. Johnson*, 99–103; Cahnman, "Robert E. Park at Fisk," 328–336.

50. Quoted in Gilpin and Gasman, *Charles S. Johnson*, 40.

51. Cayton's most important research project failed to yield a Ph.D. degree.

52. Wright, Introduction, xviii. Also see Hobbs, *Cayton Legacy*, 109–115.

53. Cayton to Wirth, 31 March 1936, Wirth Papers, Box 2, Folder 5.

54. Drake and Cayton, *Black Metropolis*, 383.

55. Ibid., 394.

56. Horace Cayton, "A Program of Action," CD, 13 May 1939.

57. Langston Hughes, "A Character," *Pittsburgh Courier*, 12 June 1948.

58. Cayton, *Long Old Road*, 249.

59. "The Parkway Community Center," CD, 6 July 1946. Also see Hobbs, *Cayton Legacy*, 116–118; Knupfer, *Chicago Black Renaissance*, 34–38.

60. Rowley, *Richard Wright*, 184–185, 190–191.

61. A cogent analysis of and primary documents pertaining to the Popular Front period may be found in Albert Fried, ed., *Communism in America: A History in Documents* (New York: Columbia University Press, 1997), 227–336.

62. For a participant's account of the Congress, see Cowley, *Dream*, 269–278; on Wright's role, see Fabre, *Unfinished Quest*, 118–121; Rowley, *Richard Wright*, 105–107.

63. Franklin Folsom, *Days of Anger, Days of Hope: A Memoir of the League of American Writers, 1937–1942* (Niwot: University Press of Colorado, 1994), 332–333.

64. Quoted in Rowley, *Richard Wright*, 189.

65. Cayton, *Long Old Road*, 248.

66. Cayton's papers contain carbon copies or other evidence of more than two dozen stories, some in fictional treatments, as well as a draft introduction and table of contents, suggesting that, sometime in the late 1940s, he had hopes of publishing a volume of episodic tales based on his early years.

67. Susie Revels Cayton to Horace Cayton, c. 1932, Susan Cayton Woodson Papers, Harsh.

68. Horace Cayton, "White Man's War," *Pittsburgh Courier*, 30 January 1942; Cayton, "Fighting for White Folks?" *The Nation* 155 (26 September 1942): 267–270; Cayton, "The Negro Challenge," *The Nation* 157 (3 July 1943): 10–11; Cayton et al., "Roundtable: Have Communists Quit Fighting for Negro Rights?" *Negro Digest* 3, no. 2 (December 1944): 57–70; Drake and Cayton, *Black Metropolis*, 734–740. Also see Hobbs, *Cayton Legacy*, 123–124, 157–159; Maurice Isserman, *Which Side Were You On? The American Communist Party during the Second World War* (Middletown, Conn.: Wesleyan University Press, 1982), 117–119, 141–143, 166–169. For primary sources, see Fried, *Communism in America*, 325–336.

69. Cayton to Wright, 22 October 1944 and 5 May 1945, Wright Papers, Box 95, Folder 1254. Also see Fabre, *Unfinished Quest*, 255–261, 266–268.

70. Davis, *Livin' the Blues*, 242–243.

71. William Stott, *Documentary Expression and Thirties America* (1973; Chicago: University of Chicago Press, 1986), 231–235; Rowley, *Richard Wright*, 236–237; Nicholas Natanson, *The Black Image in the New Deal: The Politics of FSA Photography* (Knoxville: University of Tennessee Press, 1992), 142–145.

72. Cayton, "Reflections on Richard Wright," 198.

73. Horace Cayton, "Robert Park," *Pittsburgh Courier*, 26 February 1944.

74. Cayton to Wright, 23 January 1942, Wright Papers, Box 95, Folder 1254.

75. Quoted in Fabre, *Unfinished Quest*, 249.

76. Johnson to Wright, 22 April 1943, Wright Papers, Box 99, Folder 1409.

77. Hobbs, *Cayton Legacy*, 116–118, 127; Knupfer, *Chicago Black Renaissance*, 34–38.

78. Cayton showed part of his collection at the Collector's Exhibit at the South Side Community Art Center in June 1948 and contributed the catalogue essay. McBride Papers, Box 24.

79. The commercial exhibition of black artists was held at New York's Downtown Gallery in December 1941; see Bearden, *History of African-American Artists*, 241. On Wright's role, see Alain Locke to Peter Pollack, 5 September 1941, Locke Papers, Box 164–78, Folder 6.

80. Cayton, *Long Old Road*, 250.

81. "First Public Exhibition of WPA Race Research Project in Chicago," CD, 14 January 1939; "Community in Charts, Maps Seen by 500," CD, 21 January 1939.

82. Stott, *Documentary Expression*; Paula Rabinowitz, *They Must Be Represented: The Politics of Documentary* (London: Verso, 1994), 35–104.

83. Robert Hirsch, *Seizing the Light: A History of Photography* (New York: McGraw-Hill, 2000), 237–251, 283–293, 319; Maren Stange, *Symbols of Ideal Life: Social Documentary Photography in America, 1890–1950* (Cambridge: Cambridge University Press, 1989), 108–111; F. Jack Hurley, *Portrait of a Decade: Roy Stryker and the Development of Documentary Photography in the Thirties* (Baton Rouge: Louisiana State University Press, 1972), 12–14.

84. Quoted in Stott, *Documentary Expression*, 11.

85. Rabinowitz, *They Must Be Represented*, ix.

86. Douglas Wixson, *Worker-Writer in America: Jack Conroy and the Tradition of Midwestern Literary Radicalism, 1898–1990* (Urbana: University of Illinois Press, 1994), 340.

87. Lloyd Warner, methodological note to *Black Metropolis*, 770, 772.

88. Park quoted in Stott, *Documentary Expression*, 164.

89. Quoted Ibid., 199.

90. Ibid., 152–170.

91. Drake and Cayton, *Black Metropolis*, 564.

92. Richard Wright, preface to *12 Million Black Voices: A Folk History of the Negro in the United States* (1941; New York: Thunder's Mouth, 2002), xx.

93. Richard Wright, "Readers and Writers" (1941 interview by Edwin Seaver), in *Conversations with Richard Wright*, ed. Keneth Kinnamon and Michel Fabre (Jackson: University Press of Mississippi, 1993), 47; John M. Reilly, "Richard Wright Preaches the Nation: *12 Million Black Voices*," *Black American Literature Forum* 16, no. 3 (Autumn 1982): 117.

94. Wright, *12 Million*, 59.

95. Ibid., 100.

96. Ibid., 131, 128.
97. Ibid., 48.
98. Louis Wirth, "Urbanism as a Way of Life," *American Journal of Sociology* 44, no. 1 (July 1938): 2.
99. Wright, *12 Million*, 93.
100. Wirth, "Urbanism," 11.
101. Wright, *12 Million*, 99–100.
102. Robert Park, untitled review essay, *American Journal of Sociology* 31, no. 6 (May 1926): 821–824.
103. Wright, *12 Million*, 145.
104. Joseph Stalin, "Marxism and the National Question," in *Marxism and the National and Colonial Question* (1935; Honolulu: University Press of the Pacific, 2003), 8. In preparing *12 Million Black Voices* for publication, Wright eliminated seven of the thirteen sources listed in an earlier draft. These included *Marxism and the National and Colonial Question*. See Patricia Hills, *Painting Harlem Modern: The Art of Jacob Lawrence* (Berkeley: University of California Press, 2009), 302 n. 37.
105. William Z. Foster, *Toward Soviet America* (New York: International, 1932), 303–304.
106. Wright, *Native Son*, 818.
107. Wright, *12 Million*, 143, 146.
108. Rowley, *Richard Wright*, 52.

7   The Documentary Eye

1. Quoted in Cutler, *The Jews of Chicago*, 56–57.
2. Susan Weininger, "Completing the Soul of Chicago: From Urban Realism to Social Concern, 1915–1945," in Kennedy, *Chicago Modern*, 54.
3. Rebecca Zurier, *Picturing the City: Urban Vision and the Ashcan School* (Berkeley: University of California Press, 2006), 23–44.
4. Mooney, *Archibald J. Motley*, 3.
5. David A. Shannon, ed., *The Great Depression* (Englewood Cliffs, N.J.: Prentice-Hall, 1960), 14–15, 40, 52–3, 99–103; T. H. Watkins, *The Hungry Years: A Narrative History of the Great Depression in America* (New York: Holt, 1999), 57.
6. Mooney, *Archibald J. Motley*, 65, 70–72, 76–77, 99, 110–111. Also see George Mavigliano and Richard Lawson, *The Federal Art Project in Illinois, 1935–1943* (Carbondale: Southern Illinois University Press, 1990), 3–26.
7. Among the best of Motley's street scenes are *Black Belt* (1934), *Chicken Shack* (1936), *Carnival* (1937), *The Argument* (1940), *Gettin' Religion* (1948), and *Bronzeville at Night* (1949).
8. Mooney, *Archibald J. Motley*, 96, 98.
9. Alain Locke, introduction to *Exhibition of the Art of the American Negro, 1851–1940*, 4 July–2 September 1940, American Negro Exposition, Claude Barnett Papers, Chicago History Museum.
10. Green, *Selling the Race*, 18–48.
11. Washington, *Up from Slavery*, 109. The allusion is to *Exodus* 5:7.
12. Quote from Norman MacLeish, "Negro Art in Chicago," *Exhibition of Negro Artists of Chicago*, Howard University Gallery of Art, 1–25 February 1941, McBride Papers, Box 24. Also see Andrea D. Barnwell, *Charles White* (San Francisco: Pomegranate, 2002), 17; Margaret Burroughs, interview by Anna M. Tyler, 11 November and 5 December 1988, AAA.
13. "George Neal, Artist, Dies; Rites Held," *CD*, 3 September 1938.
14. Bearden and Henderson, *History of African-American Artists*, 230, 232.
15. Mavigliano and Lawson, *Federal Art Project*, 11.
16. Ibid., 30–45; Francis V. O'Connor, introduction to *Art for the Millions: Essays from the 1930s by Artists and Administrators of the WPA Federal Art Project*, ed. Francis V. O'Connor (Boston: New York Graphic Society, 1975), 26–28; Gerald Monroe, "The '30s: Art, Ideology and the WPA," *Art in America* (November/December 1975): 64–67.
17. Mavigliano and Lawson, *Federal Art Project*, 30–33.
18. The 412 black Party members in Chicago in 1932 compared with 74 in New York. Storch, *Red Chicago*, 39.

19. Courage, *Convergence: Jewish and African American Artists in Depression-era Chicago*; Mullen, *Popular Fronts*, 75–81; Mavigliano and Lawson, *Federal Art Project*, 68–69.

20. Margaret Goss Burroughs, "Chicago's South Side Community Art Center: A Personal Recollection," in *Art in Action: American Art Centers and the New Deal*, ed. John Franklin White (Metuchen, N.J.: Scarecrow Press, 1987), 131–144; Anna M. Tyler, "Planting and Maintaining a 'Perennial Garden': Chicago's South Side Community Art Center," *International Review of African American Art* 11, no. 4 (1994): 31–37; Mullen, *Popular Fronts*, 81–84; Robert Davis, "A Community Adventure," *CD*, 1 March 1941.

21. Margaret Burroughs, interview by Richard Courage, 18 March 2006.

22. Pollack to Locke, 2 May 1940, Locke Papers, Box 164–78, Folder 5.

23. Alain Locke, "Chicago's New Southside Art Center," *Magazine of Art* 34, no. 7 (August-September 1941): 370–374.

24. *We Too Look at America: Exhibition of Paintings, Sculpture, Drawings*, South Side Community Art Center, May 1941, McBride Papers, Box 24.

25. Holger Cahill, interview by John Morse, 12 April 1960, AAA.

26. Peter Pollack, Director's Report for 1941, South Side Community Art Center, 3–4, McBride Papers, Box 24.

27. Pollack to Locke, 10 March 1942, Locke Papers, Box 164–78, Folder 7.

28. Mavigliano and Lawson, *Federal Art Project*, 77–80.

29. Tyler, "Planting and Maintaining," 35–36; Knupfer, *Chicago Black Renaissance*, 69–72.

30. Margaret T. G. Burroughs, *Life with Margaret: The Official Autobiography* (Chicago: In Time Publishing, 2003), 27–42; Carline Evone Williams Strong, "Margaret Taylor Goss Burroughs: Educator, Artist, Author, Founder, and Civic Leader" (Ph.D. diss., Loyola University, 1994), 25–36.

31. George E. Kent, *A Life of Gwendolyn Brooks* (Lexington: University Press of Kentucky, 1990), 42–43.

32. Burroughs, interview by Courage.

33. Willard Motley, "Negro Art in Chicago," *Opportunity* 18, no. 1 (January 1940): 20.

34. Burroughs, "Community Art Center," 137–138.

35. Burroughs, *Life with Margaret*, 161.

36. Quoted in Bearden and Henderson, *History of African-American Artists*, 407.

37. Titles culled from *Exhibition of Negro Artists of Chicago*, Howard University, February 1941; *We Too Look at American*, South Side Community Art Center, May 1941; *Negro Artists of Chicago*, Art Institute of Chicago, June–August 1943; *Collector's Exhibit*, South Side Community Art Center, June 1948; all found in McBride Papers, Box 24. White City was an amusement park built on the former grounds of the 1893 World's Columbian Exposition and had earlier been the informal name of the exposition itself.

38. Burroughs, interview by Courage.

39. Best, *Passionately Human*, 39.

40. Burroughs, *Life with Margaret*, 94.

41. Knupfer, *Chicago Black Renaissance*, 19, 61–62.

42. June Levine and Gene Gordon, *Tales of Wo-Chi-Ca: Blacks, Whites and Reds at Camp* (San Rafael, Calif.: Avon Springs Press, 2002), 17.

43. On the DuSable Museum, see Burroughs, *Life with Margaret*, 95–101, 149–153.

44. On White's life, see Barnwell, *Charles White*; Charles White, interview by Betty Hoag, 9 March 1965, AAA; Charles White, "Path of a Negro Artist," *Masses & Mainstream* 8, no. 4 (April 1955): 33–44.

45. White, "Path," 34.

46. Ibid., 35–36.

47. Larry Forhman, "Portrait of an Artist: Morris Topchevsky (1899–1947)," *New Masses* (22 July 1947): 9–10; Weininger, "Completing the Soul of Chicago," 59–60.

48. Fabre, *Unfinished Quest*, 96–97, 110.

49. Margaret Burroughs, "He Will Always Be a Chicago Artist to Me," *Freedomways* 20, no. 3 (Third Quarter 1980): 152–153.

50. Stacy I. Morgan, *Rethinking Social Realism: African American Art and Literature, 1930–1953* (Athens: University of Georgia Press, 2004), 49.

51. Wright, *12 Million*, 106, 108, 111.

52. Patricia Hills, *Social Concern and Urban Realism: American Painting of the 1930s* (Boston: Boston University Art Gallery, 1983), 11, 71.

53. Mitchell Siporin, interview by Geoffrey Swift, 11 November 1965, AAA.

54. Mitchell Siporin, "Mural Art and the Midwestern Myth," in O'Connor, *Art for the Millions*, 64.

55. Holger Cahill, "The Federal Art Project," in *Theories of Modern Art: A Source Book by Artists and Critics*, ed. Herschel B. Chipp (Berkeley: University of California Press, 1968), 471–473. Also see Victoria Grieve, *The Federal Art Project and the Creation of Middlebrow Culture* (Urbana: University of Illinois, 2009), 83–109.

56. Watkins, *Hungry Years*, 499.

57. *Negro Mother and Child* was Catlett's carving for her master's thesis at the University of Iowa, where she studied with Grant Wood.

58. Quoted in Melanie Anne Herzog, *Elizabeth Catlett: An American Artist in Mexico* (Seattle: University of Washington Press, 2000), 26.

59. Quoted in Barnwell, *Charles White*, 29–30.

60. Herzog, *Elizabeth Catlett*, 40–45.

61. Richard Wright, "How Bigger Was Born," in *Richard Wright: Early Works*, 866–867.

62. White, Interview, 12.

63. Gordon Parks, *A Choice of Weapons* (1965; St. Paul: Minnesota Historical Society Press, 1986), 2–3.

64. Kenneth Davis, *Kansas: A Bicentennial History* (New York: Norton, 1976), 28–34; William Frank Zornow, *Kansas: A History of the Jayhawk State* (Norman: University of Oklahoma Press, 1957), 51–54.

65. David S. Reynolds, *John Brown, Abolitionist* (New York: Random House, 2005), 138–178; Davis, *Kansas*, 37–71.

66. Nell Irvin Painter, *Exodusters: Black Migration to Kansas after Reconstruction* (1976; New York: Norton, 1992).

67. Funk is identified by his real name in *Voices in the Mirror* (1990) but is called Larry Duncan in *A Choice of Weapons* and *A Hungry Heart* (2005), one of numerous puzzling discrepancies in names, dates, and other details among Parks's memoirs.

68. Parks, *Choice*, 170–175, quote at 174.

69. Ibid., 199.

70. Frederick D. Jones, interview by Arlene Williams, 8 and 10 November 1988, AAA.

71. Parks, *Choice*, 208.

72. *An Exhibition of Creative Photography by Gordon Roger Parks*, November 2–15, 1941, South Side Community Art Center, McBride Papers, Box 24.

73. Parks, *Choice*, 215.

74. Hirsch, *Seizing the Light*, 237–251, 283–293, 319.

75. Motley, "Negro Art," 22.

76. Gordon Parks, *Voices in the Mirror* (New York: Doubleday, 1990), 85.

77. Ibid., 81–82.

78. Parks, *Choice*, 230–231.

79. Ibid., 45.

80. See "List of Plates" in Gordon Parks, *Half Past Autumn: A Retrospective* (New York: Bulfinch, 1998), 357–359.

81. On Sebree's life and career, see Melvin Marshall and Blake Kimbrough, "Above and Beyond: The Life and Art of Charles Sebree," *International Review of African American Art* 18, no. 2 (2002): 2–17.

82. Lloyd C. Engelbrecht, "Modernism and Design in Chicago," in *The Old Guard and the Avant-Garde*, ed. Prince, 119–138.

83. Sebree shared the 1936 exhibition with white artist John Pratt, who married Katherine Dunham. Joseph Scanlan, ed., *A History of the Renaissance Society: The First Seventy-five Years* (Chicago: Renaissance Society, 1993), 141–146.

84. Avis Berman, "The Katherine Kuh Gallery: An Informal Portrait," in *The Old Guard and the Avant-Garde*, ed. Prince, 155–169.

85. Motley, *Negro Art*, 29.

86. James A. Porter, *Modern Negro Art* (1943; New York: Arno, 1969), 132.

87. Corinne Jennings, "Eldzier Cortor: The Long Consistent Road," in *Three Masters: Eldzier Cortor, Hughie Lee-Smith, Archibald John Motley, Jr.*, Kenkeleba Gallery, 22 May–17 July 1988, 12–16; Bearden and Henderson, *History of African-American Artists*, 272–279.

88. Quoted in Bearden and Henderson, *History of African-American Artists*, 274.

89. Quoted in Jennings, "Eldzier Cortor," 15.

90. Daniel Schulman, "African American Art and the Julius Rosenwald Fund," in *Force for Change*, 70, 72.

91. Eldzier Cortor, artist's biography, c. 1947, Chicago Artists' Files, Harold Washington Library, Chicago Public Library.

92. Daniel Schulman, "Marion Perkins: Chicago Sculptor Rediscovered," *Selections from the Art Institute of Chicago: African Americans in Art*, AIC Museum Studies 24, no. 2 (1999): 220–243.

93. Quoted ibid., 238–239.

94. Victoria Steele, "Marion Perkins: Worker-Artist," *Masses and Mainstream* 5, no. 8 (August 1952): 17–18.

8 ⟨ Bronzeville's "Writing Clan"

1. For an analysis of Hughes's Marxist stories, see Bone, *Down Home*, 260–265; Denning, *Cultural Front*, 216–219.

2. Wright, *Black Boy*, 249.

3. J. M. Davis, "Entering Chicago," in *Intercollegian Wonder Book*, ed. Robb, Volume 1, 16. Internal and external evidence, vetted by John Edgar Tidwell, indicates that this piece was authored by Frank Marshall Davis.

4. Tidwell, "Interview with Frank Marshall Davis," 105.

5. For an overview of Davis's journalistic career, see John Edgar Tidwell, introduction to *Writings of Frank Marshall Davis: A Voice of the Black Press* (Jackson: University of Mississippi Press, 2007), xiii–xxxii.

6. Alain Locke, "Deep River, Deeper Sea: Retrospective Review of the Literature for 1935," *Opportunity* 14, no. 1 (January 1936): 10.

7. Barnett was Tuskegee's first African American trustee. Adam Green, *Selling the Race*, 92–127; Lawrence D. Hogan, *A Black National News Service: The Associated Negro Press and Claude Barnett, 1919–1945* (Rutherford, N.J.: Fairleigh Dickinson University Press, 1984).

8. Fabre, *Unfinished Quest*, 127.

9. Trudier Harris, ed., *Dictionary of Literary Biography*, Volume 76: *Afro-American Writers, 1940–1955*, s.v. "William Attaway."

10. Quoted in Milton Meltzer, "William Attaway, Negro Novelist," *Daily Worker*, 26 June 1939.

11. "Mississippians Organize to Promote Racial Uplift," *CD*, 1 September 1923.

12. Quoted in James B. Lloyd, ed., *Lives of Mississippi Authors, 1817–1967* (Jackson: University Press of Mississippi, 1981), s.v. "William Alexander Attaway."

13. On Walker's life, see Maryemma Graham, chronology and "'I Want to Write, I Want to Write the Songs of My People': The Emergence of Margaret Walker," in *Fields Watered with Blood: Critical Essays on Margaret Walker*, ed. Maryemma Graham (Athens: University of Georgia Press, 2001), xix–xxvii, 11–27.

14. Quoted in Rampersad, *Langston Hughes*, Volume 1, 232.

15. Bontemps, "Why I Returned," 18. On this period of Bontemps's life, see Jones, *Renaissance Man*, 85–99.

16. Arna Bontemps et al., "Reflections on Richard Wright: Symposium on an Exiled Native Son," in *Anger, and Beyond*, ed. Hill, 199.

17. Jones, *Renaissance Man*, 88, 93. On the Chicago Council of the National Negro Congress, see Reed, "Study of Black Politics and Protest," 285–290.

18. On Motley's life, see John A. Garraty and Mark C. Carnes, eds., *American National Biography* (New York: Oxford University Press, 1999), s.v. "Willard Francis Motley"; Fleming, *Willard Motley.*

19. On the Motley family and the 1919 riots, see Woodall, "Looking Backward," 56.

20. Jerome Klinkowitz, ed., *The Diaries of Willard Motley* (Ames: Iowa State University Press, 1979), 35.

21. On *Hull-House Magazine*, see Fleming, *Willard Motley*, 27–30.

22. Gwendolyn Brooks, interview by Roy Newquist, 1967, in *Conversations with Gwendolyn Brooks*, ed. Gloria Wade Gayles (Jackson: University of Mississippi Press, 2003), 27, 29.

23. Gwendolyn Brooks, "How I Think Poetry Should Be Written with an Original Poem," 11 September 1938, typescript, Gwendolyn Brooks Papers, Carton 3, Bancroft Library, University of California, Berkeley.

24. Louis Emanuel Martin, "The National Negro Congress," *Challenge* 1, no. 5 (June 1936): 30–34.

25. "Ask Leisure Class to Aid Race Culture," *CD*, 22 February 1936.

26. Margaret Walker, "Richard Wright," in Walker, *How I Wrote Jubilee and Other Essays on Life and Literature*, ed. Maryemma Graham (New York: Feminist Press, 1990), 35.

27. Rowley, *Richard Wright*, 115–118; Fabre, *Unfinished Quest*, 128.

28. Walker, "Richard Wright," 35.

29. Rowley, *Richard Wright*, 168.

30. Walker, "Richard Wright," 36–39. Also see Michel Fabre, "Richard Wright's First Hundred Books," *CLA Journal* 16, no. 4 (June 1973): 458–474.

31. Walker to Wright, 29 September and 9 October 1937 and 2 April and 1 June 1938, Wright Papers, Box 107, Folder 1667.

32. *AANB*, s.v. "Theodore (Ted) Ward."

33. On *Big White Fog*, see Rena Fraden, *Blueprints for a Black Federal Theatre, 1935–1939* (Cambridge: Cambridge University Press, 1996), 115–135.

34. Fabre, *Unfinished Quest*, 128.

35. Davis, *Livin' the Blues*, 240.

36. Walker, "Richard Wright," 35–36, 39–40.

37. Davis, *Livin' the Blues*, 240.

38. Walker described the personal conflicts leading to the group's demise in letters to Wright dated 5 June, 1 July, 10 July, 24 August, 29 September, and 24 November 1937; Wright Papers, Box 107, Folder 1667. Also see Davis, *Livin' the Blues*, 241.

39. Rowley, *Richard Wright*, 131–133.

40. Wright, *Black Boy*, 237.

41. Richard Wright, "Blueprint for Negro Writing," *NAAAL*, 1403.

42. Quoted in Johnson and Johnson, *Propaganda and Aesthetics*, 113.

43. Rowley, *Richard Wright*, 134–135.

44. Richard Wright, "Negro Writers Launch Literary Quarterly," *Daily Worker*, 8 June 1937.

45. Walker to Wright, 24 November 1937, Wright Papers, Box 107, Folder 1667.

46. Henry Louis Gates Jr. observes: "Brown's book of poetry, even more profoundly than the market crash of 1929, truly ended the Harlem Renaissance, primarily because it contained a new and distinctly black poetic diction and not merely the vapid and pathetic claim for one." *Figures in Black: Words, Signs, and the 'Racial' Self* (New York: Oxford University Press, 1987), 227.

47. Arnold Rampersad, *Ralph Ellison: A Biography* (New York: Alfred A. Knopf, 2007), 81–100; Lawrence Jackson, *Ralph Ellison: Emergence of Genius* (New York: Wiley, 2002), 161–236.

48. Verna Mitchell and Cynthia Davis, "Introduction: Dorothy West and Her Circle," in *Where the Wild Grape Grows: Selected Writings, 1930–1950, Dorothy West*, ed. Mitchell and Davis (Amherst: University of Massachusetts Press, 2005), 34, 37–41; Rowley, *Richard Wright*, 134–138; Johnson and Johnson, *Propaganda and Aesthetics*, 112–120.

49. Wright, "Blueprint," 1403–1410.

50. Ibid., 1409.

51. A second edition was published in 1940 with addition of a fifth novella, "Bright and Morning Star," and an introductory essay, "The Ethics of Living Jim Crow."

52. Richard Wright, "Long Black Song," in *Wright: Early Works*, 346, 352.

53. Wright, "Blueprint," 1405.
54. Charles S. Johnson, *Growing Up in the Black Belt: Negro Youth in the Rural South* (1941; New York: Schocken, 1967), 180–181.
55. Wright, *Black Boy*, 233–242.
56. "Center of Attraction," photocaption, CD, 23 January 1932.
57. *AANB*, s.v. "Vivian Gordon Harsh"; *BWA*, s.v. "Vivian Gordon Harsh"; Donald Franklin Joyce, "Resources for Scholars: Four Major Collections of Afro-Americana," *Library Quarterly* 58, no. 1 (1988): 67–70.
58. Vivian G. Harsh, "Hall Branch," emended typescript, c. 1939, Hall Branch Archives.
59. Vivian G. Harsh, Annual Report 1937, Hall Branch Archives.
60. S. I. Hayakawa, "Second Thoughts," CD, 9 October 1943; "Chicagoans Included in New Poetry Anthology," CD, 27 December 1952.
61. Hobbs, *Cayton Legacy*, 127.
62. Rampersad, *Langston Hughes*, Volume 2, 3–43.
63. Knupfer, *Chicago Black Renaissance*, 46–47.
64. This account of the founding of *Negro Story* is based on Fern Gayden to Robert Bone, 19 October 1980; Alice Browning to Bone, 21 October 1980. For an analysis of the journal that attempts to demonstrate its "radical roots" and "revolutionary aspirations," see Mullen, *Popular Fronts*, 106–125.
65. *Negro Story* 1, no. 1 (May-June 1944): 1.
66. *Negro Story* 1, no. 2 (July-August 1944): 1.
67. Ibid., 4. Readers familiar with S. I. Hayakawa's history as a conservative Republican senator from California in the late 1970s might be surprised by the reforming zeal of his letters to *Negro Story* and his columns in the *Chicago Defender* in the 1940s.
68. *Negro Story* 1, no. 1 (May-June 1944): 1, 50.
69. *Negro Story* 1, no. 5 (March-April 1945): 57.
70. *Negro Story* 1, no. 3 (October-November 1944): 2.
71. Green, *Selling the Race*, 80–89.
72. Fred MacDonald, ed., *Richard Durham's Destination Freedom: Scripts from Radio's Black Legacy, 1948–1950* (New York: Praeger, 1989); Barbara Dianne Savage, *Broadcasting Freedom: Radio, War, and the Politics of Race, 1938–1948* (Chapel Hill: University of North Carolina Press, 1999), 260–270.
73. Durham to Homer Heck, 27 June 1948, Richard Durham Papers, Harsh, Box 6, Folder 7.
74. Hugh Cordier, "A History and Analysis of Destination Freedom" (Seminar report: Problems in Radio, Northwestern University, 1949), 38, Richard Durham Papers, Box 6, Folder 4.
75. Quoted ibid., 24, 26.
76. Mangione, *Dream and the Deal*, 3–26, 53–59; Monty Noam Penkower, *The Federal Writers' Project: A Study in Government Patronage of the Arts* (Urbana: University of Illinois Press, 1977), 18–20.
77. Mangione, *Dream and the Deal*, 369 n.
78. Ibid., 289–326.
79. Jerrold Hirsch, *Portrait of America: A Cultural History of the Federal Writers' Project* (Chapel Hill: University of North Carolina Press, 2003), 2–40; Mangione, *Dream and the Deal*, 49–50.
80. Granville Hicks, "Writers in the Thirties," in *As We Saw the Thirties: Essays on Social and Political Movements of a Decade*, ed. Rita James Simon (Urbana: University of Illinois Press, 1969), 78–10, quotations at 82–84. On 1930s radicalism and the WPA's cultural agencies, see Mangione, *The Dream and the Deal*, 29–50. For discussions of pre-Depression radicalism and continuities between the 1920s and 1930s, see Maxwell, *New Negro, Old Left*, 1–124; Smethurst, *New Red Negro*, 3–9, 16–21.
81. Malcolm Cowley, "Art Tomorrow," epilogue to the 1934 edition of *Exile's Return*, in Faulkner, *The Portable Malcolm Cowley*, 275.
82. Johnson to Barnett, 9 March 1935, Claude Barnett Papers, Box 233, Folder 4, Chicago History Museum.

83. "Wheedling gradualism" appears in Alain Locke, "God Save Reality! Retrospective Review of the Literature of the Negro: 1936," Part II, *Opportunity* 15, no. 2 (February 1937), reprinted in Stewart, *Critical Temper*, 252. Johnson's 1935 letter to Barnett was prompted by Locke's discussion of *Shadow of the Plantation* in "The Eleventh Hour of Nordicism: Retrospective Review of the Literature of the Negro for 1934," Part I, *Opportunity* 13, no. 1 (January 1935).

84. On Locke's relation to the Left, see Wald, *Exiles from a Future Time*, 276–279. On Johnson's political perspective during the Depression, see Gilpin and Gasman, *Charles S. Johnson*, 61–70; Robbins, *Charles S. Johnson*, 68–80.

85. Quoted in Michael Szalay, *New Deal Modernism: American Literature and the Invention of the Welfare State* (Durham, N.C.: Duke University Press, 2000), 70. Also see Rowley, *Richard Wright*, 125–126.

86. Penkower, *Federal Writers' Project*, 21–29, 75–95; Hirsch, *Portrait of America*, 41–106.

87. Sterling Brown to Richard Wright, 5 March 1937, Wright Papers, Box 95, Folder 1238.

88. Joanne V. Gabbin, *Sterling A. Brown: Building the Black Aesthetic Tradition* (Charlottesville: University Press of Virginia, 1994), 67–85; Lauren Rebecca Sklaroff, *Black Culture and the New Deal: The Quest for Civil Rights in the Roosevelt Era* (Chapel Hill: University of North Carolina Press, 2009), 81–122; Charles H. Rowell, "'Let Me Be with Ole Jazzbo': An Interview with Sterling A. Brown," in *After Winter: The Art and Life of Sterling A. Brown*, ed. John Edgar Tidwell and Steven C. Tracy (New York: Oxford University Press, 2009), 299–302.

89. Frederick directed the Illinois Writers' Project until 1939, when he was succeeded by Curtis MacDougall, a journalism professor at Northwestern. Mangione, *Dream and the Deal*, 128.

90. Ronald Weber, *The Midwestern Ascendancy in American Writing* (Bloomington: Indiana University Press, 1992), 176–182, 190–191, quotation at 190.

91. John T. Frederick, introduction to *Anthology of American Negro Literature*, ed. Sylvestre C. Watkins (New York: Modern Library, 1944), xv.

92. The figure of nine blacks employed by the Illinois Writers' Project is based on a survey conducted by Alsberg. Rowley, *Richard Wright*, 108, 538 n. 15. Of course, individuals joined and left at various times, so the total number was significantly higher. See Appendix B.

93. Rowley, *Richard Wright*, 108–109, 122. Brown responded by noting that Wright's "splendid" idea "crosses a project we have already started" and inviting him to "serve editorially" on the Negro studies. Brown to Wright, 5 March 1937; also 1 June and 15 June 1937, Wright Papers, Box 95, Folder 1238.

94. Bontemps, Introduction, *Black Thunder*, xv.

95. Mangione, *Dream and the Deal*, 84–85, 119–131. Also see David A. Taylor, *Soul of a People: The WPA Writers' Project Uncovers Depression America* (Hoboken, N.J.: Wiley, 2009), 39–67.

96. Arna Bontemps, preface to Arna Bontemps and Jack Conroy, *Anyplace But Here* (Columbia: University of Missouri Press, 1997), v. First published 1945 as *They Seek a City*.

97. Jack Conroy, "Memories of Arna Bontemps: Friend and Collaborator," *Negro American Literature Forum* 10 (Summer 1976): 53–57.

98. Quoted in Bettina Drew, *Nelson Algren: A Life on the Wild Side* (New York: Putnam, 1989), 100.

99. Bontemps, preface to *Anyplace But Here*, vi.

100. Conroy, "Memories of Arna Bontemps," 55–57.

101. Bontemps to Abraham Chapman, 15 July 1967, Bontemps Papers, Box 5. Researchers have since established that Johnson died in 1958. On the fate of Johnson's WPA poems, see Lauri Ramey, *The Heritage Series of Black Poetry, 1962–75: A Research Compendium* (Aldershot, England: Ashgate, 2008), 134–135.

102. Quoted in Drew, *Nelson Algren*, 101.

103. Walker, *Richard Wright*, 81–82.

104. Walker, "Richard Wright," 36, 40.

105. On Walker's debt to Zola, see Walker to Wright, 7 August 1937, Wright Papers, Box 107, Folder 1667. On *L'Assommoir*, see Lehan, *Realism and Naturalism*, 115–116.

106. Walker, *Richard Wright*, 125–126.

107. Margaret Walker, interview by Claudia Tate, in Graham, *Fields Watered with Blood*, 34.

108. Walker, "Richard Wright," 39.

109. Wright, "How Bigger Was Born," 870.

110. Walker, "Richard Wright," 42–43.

111. Wright, "How Bigger Was Born," 875.

112. Mangione, *Dream and the Deal*, 329–348.

113. Arna Bontemps to Jack Conroy, 14 September 1943, Bontemps Papers, Box 5.

9   (Bronzeville and the Novel

1. Scruggs, *Sweet Home*.

2. Emily Bernard, "The Renaissance and the Vogue," in *Cambridge Companion to the Harlem Renaissance*, ed. Hutchinson, 28–40; Amritjit Singh, "Black-White Symbiosis: Another Look at the Literary History of the 1920s," in *The Harlem Renaissance Re-examined*, ed. Victor A. Kramer (New York: AMS, 1987), 31–42; Singh, *Novels of the Harlem Renaissance*, 22–27, 55–57.

3. Bontemps, "The Awakening," 1–26.

4. Arna Bontemps, *God Sends Sunday* (1931; New York: Washington Square Press, 2005), 15.

5. On the crosscurrents of picaresque and pastoral conventions in Harlem Renaissance fiction, see Bone, *Down Home*, 113–137.

6. Bontemps, *God Sends Sunday*, 52.

7. Ibid., 121.

8. Ibid., 122.

9. Ibid., 129.

10. Bontemps, "Why I Returned," 9–10.

11. Ibid., 11. On Bontemps's conflicting role models, also see Jones, *Renaissance Man*, 31–41, 47–48. On admonitions to recent migrants, see Grossman, *Land of Hope*, 144–155.

12. Bernard Bell, *The Afro-American Novel and Its Tradition* (Amherst: University of Massachusetts Press, 1987), 102.

13. "A Negro Jockey," *New York Times Book Review*, 15 March 1931, 7, 18.

14. Alain Locke, "We Turn to Prose: A Retrospective Review of the Literature of the Negro for 1931," *Opportunity* 10, no. 2 (February 1932): 43.

15. Bontemps, Introduction, *Black Thunder*, xxv–xxvi.

16. "Arna Bontemps," in *Interviews with Black Writers*, ed. John O'Brien (New York: Liveright, 1973), 11–12.

17. Sterling Brown, *The Negro in American Fiction* (1937; New York: Arno, 1969), 189.

18. Bontemps to Jackman, 25 January 1935, Bontemps Papers, Box 15.

19. Arnold Rampersad suggests, in his introduction to the 1992 edition of *Black Thunder*, that Bontemps created fearful Ben "as if to challenge himself and . . . his own limitations of radical spirit," xiv.

20. Bontemps, *Black Thunder*, 81.

21. Ibid., 21, 67, 108, 210.

22. Richard Wright, "A Tale of Folk Courage," review of *Black Thunder*, *Partisan Review and Anvil* (April 1936): 31.

23. Rampersad, introduction to the 1992 edition, *Black Thunder*, vii–viii.

24. Jones, *Renaissance Man*, 89.

25. EAACH, s.v. "The Haitian Revolution."

26. Langston Hughes, "People without Shoes," *New Masses* 7 (October 1931): 12. Haiti's revolutionary history was entwined with Hughes's family history. His mother's uncle John Mercer Langston, one of the most prominent blacks of the nineteenth century, had served as American minister to Haiti. Rampersad, *Langston Hughes*, Volume 1, 204–209.

27. Joseph McLaren, *Langston Hughes, Folk Dramatist in the Protest Tradition, 1921–1943* (Westport, Conn.: Greenwood, 1997), 101–106; Rampersad, *Langston Hughes*, Volume 1, 330–331.

28. Fraden, *Black Federal Theater*, 16–17, 98, 152–164, 156, 179–180; Denning, *Cultural Front*, 395–397.

29. Hills, *Painting Harlem Modern*, 57–74.

30. Arna Bontemps, Report to Julius Rosenwald Fund, typescript, 17 January 1939, Bontemps Papers, Box 24.

31. Bontemps described the more ambitious project as "a broad-canvas novel based on Haitian participation in the American Revolution during the Siege of Savannah." Ibid.

32. Arna Bontemps, *Drums at Dusk* (New York: Macmillan, 1939), 160, 149–151.

33. Garland J. Millet to Bontemps, 15 August 1960, Bontemps Papers, Box 21. Millet was president of Oakwood College from 1954 to 1963.

34. Bontemps to Millet, 21 August 1960, Bontemps Papers, Box 21.

35. Bontemps to Conroy, 4 August 1944, Papers of Jack Conroy, Newberry Library, Chicago, Box 3, Folder 151.

36. Arna Bontemps, "Negro Writers in Chicago," *Chicago Sunday Bee*, clipping c. 1940, Bontemps Papers, Box 34.

37. Lehan, *Realism and Naturalism*, 207.

38. Richard Wright, *Lawd Today!* in *Wright: Early Works*, 19.

39. Ibid., 118.

40. Ibid., 158.

41. Michael Denning focuses on this "powerful virtuoso passage" as exemplifying Wright's "promise of community," *Cultural Front*, 253. George Kent describes it as "a poem, a device which breaks the novel's tight realism and gives its rendering power a new dimension," "Blackness and the Adventure of Western Culture," *CLA Journal* 12 (June 1969): 338.

42. Arnold Rampersad, "*Lawd Today!*" in *Richard Wright: A Collection of Critical Essays*, ed. Arnold Rampersad (Englewood Cliffs, N.J.: Prentice-Hall, 1995), 125.

43. Fabre, *Unfinished Quest*, 136.

44. Wright, *Lawd Today!*, 153–157.

45. Wright, "Blueprint," 1403.

46. Wright, "How Bigger Was Born," 867, 869.

47. Wright repeated this lecture at Columbia University on 12 March 1940. Fabre, *Unfinished Quest*, 180.

48. Wright, "How Bigger Was Born," 854–861.

49. Ibid., 866–867.

50. Fabre, *Unfinished Quest*, 182. Such symbolic realism had an important, although peripheral, lineage among Left-wing artists and intellectuals, traceable for example through the ideas of Chicago muralist Edward Millman and critic Kenneth Burke. Millman, "Symbolism in Wall Painting," in *Art for the Millions*, ed. O'Connor, 67; Burke, "Revolutionary Symbolism in America," in *Communism in America*, ed. Fried, 278–281.

51. Richard Wright, *Native Son*, in *Wright: Early Works*, 459–463, quotation at 463.

52. On the different "cognitive maps" that underpin various characters' experiences of Chicago in *Native Son*, see Scruggs, *Invisible Cities*, 75–85.

53. Wright, *Native Son*, 486, 489.

54. Ibid., 541, 542.

55. Ibid., 652, 681.

56. Ibid., 670–671.

57. Patricia D. Watkins, "The Paradoxical Structure of 'The Man Who Lived Underground,'" in *Richard Wright*, ed. Rampersad, 148–161. Also see Robert Bone, *Richard Wright* (1969; Minneapolis: University of Minnesota Press, 2009), 25–31; Charles H. Nichols, "The Slave Narrators and the Picaresque Mode: Archetypes for Modern Black Personae," in *The Slave's Narrative*, ed. Charles T. Davis and Henry Louis Gates Jr. (New York: Oxford University Press, 1985), 283–298.

58. Wright, *Native Son*, 701.

59. Wright, "How Bigger Was Born," 878.

60. Wright, *Native Son*, 818.

61. Jane Newton quoted in Rowley, *Richard Wright*, 156. Also see ibid., 153–56, 163, 165; Fabre, *Unfinished Quest*, 169–178.

62. Wright, *Native Son*, 848–850.

63. Rowley, *Richard Wright*, 191–194.

64. Quoted ibid., 198.

65. On the stormy collaboration of Wright, Welles, Houseman, and Green, see ibid., 213–225, 233–248.

66. Bontemps to Jackman, 11 November 1941, Bontemps Papers, Box 15.

67. For the specific importance of Chicago to these themes, see Timothy B. Spears, *Chicago Dreaming: Midwesterners and the City, 1871–1919* (Chicago: University of Chicago Press, 2005), 111–146, 174–273.

68. Lawrence R. Rodgers, *Canaan Bound: The African American Great Migration Novel* (Urbana: University of Illinois Press, 1997), 77–78.

69. William Attaway, "Tale of the Blackamoor," *Challenge* 1, no. 5 (June 1936): 3–4.

70. Alan Wald describes Attaway as "a committed Communist from the late 1930s well into the Cold War era." *Exiles from a Future Time*, 281.

71. Darryl Pinckney, introduction to William Attaway, *Blood on the Forge* (1941; New York: New York Review of Books, 2005), viii.

72. William Attaway, *Let Me Breathe Thunder* (1939; repr. as *Tough Kid*, New York: Lion Books, 1955), 14.

73. Ibid., 18.

74. "'Blood on Forge' Author Replies to Book's Critics," CD, 13 December 1941.

75. Attaway, *Blood on the Forge*, 1, 41.

76. Ibid., 36–37.

77. Ibid., 38, 41.

78. Ibid., 45.

79. Ibid., 56, 84.

80. Ibid., 73.

81. Ibid., 150.

82. Ibid., 161–162.

83. Ibid., 167.

84. Ibid., 174.

85. Ibid., 176–177.

86. Ibid., 212.

87. Ibid., 230–231.

88. Ibid., 232–233.

89. Wald, *Exiles from a Future Time*, 295.

90. Bernard Bell observes that "like Wright, Attaway has an acute ear for the distinctive phonological and syntactic patterns of black speech." *Afro-American Novel*, 169.

91. Attaway, *Blood on the Forge*, 234–235.

92. Sterling Brown, "The New Negro in Literature (1925–1955)," in *A Son's Return: Selected Essays of Sterling A. Brown*, ed. Mark A. Sanders (Boston: Northeastern University Press, 1996), 196.

93. Lawrence Rogers provides one of the few serious analyses of Bland's novel but places it, inaccurately, among works "that rejected Wright's 1930s brand of naturalism." *Canaan Bound*, 133, 141–142. Wright, rather than Bland, was reworking and ultimately discarding the naturalistic model.

94. Alden Bland, *Behold a Cry* (New York: Scribner's, 1947), 2.

95. Ibid., 13–14.

96. Ibid., 150.

97. Alexander Saxton to Richard Courage, 22 March 2009.

98. Willard Motley, *Knock on Any Door* (1947; DeKalb: Northern Illinois University Press, 1989), 153, 185, 342.

99. Leonard Cassuto, *Hard-Boiled Sentimentality: The Secret History of American Crime Stories* (New York: Columbia University Press, 2009), 26.

100. Motley, *Knock on Any Door*, 326.

101. Quoted in Fleming, *Willard Motley*, 59, 60.
102. The list of novels upon which these numbers are based may be found in Edward Margolies and David Bakish, *Afro-American Fiction, 1853–1976: A Guide to Information Sources* (Detroit: Gale, 1979), 112–113. For analyses, see Bell, *Afro-American Novel*, 187–191; Bone, *Negro Novel*, 166–170.
103. Saxton to Alan Wald, 12 June 1993. Saxton generously shared a copy of this letter and further recollections with Richard Courage in June 2009.
104. Klinkowitz, *Diaries of Willard Motley*, 72.
105. Saxton to Courage, 22 March 2009.
106. Michel Fabre, "Beyond Naturalism," in *The World of Richard Wright*, ed. Fabre, (Jackson: University Press of Mississippi, 1985), 56–76.
107. Richard Wright, interview by Edwin Seaver, "Readers and Writers," 23 December 1941, in *Conversations with Richard Wright*, ed. Keneth Kinnamon and Michel Fabre (Jackson: University of Mississippi Press, 1993), 43–48.
108. Bell, *Afro-American Novel*, 151.
109. Wright, *12 Million*, 147.
110. Bell, *Afro-American Novel*, 150–167, 185–187, quotation at 167. For more nuanced discussions of Wright's work in relation to literary naturalism and so-called "protest literature," see Lehan, *Realism and Naturalism*, 206–234; Jerry W. Ward, "Everybody's Protest Novel: The Era of Richard Wright," in *Cambridge Companion to the African American Novel*, ed. Maryemma Graham (Cambridge: Cambridge University Press, 2004), 173–188; Cappetti, *Writing Chicago*, 2–5, 190–197, 212 n. 7, 213 n. 14; Scruggs, *Sweet Home*, 68–99. For a classic statement on existentialism's conception of freedom, see Jean-Paul Sartre, "Existentialism Is a Humanism," in *Existentialism from Dostoevsky to Sartre*, ed. Walter Kaufmann (New York: New American Library, 1956), 287–311.
111. Algren to Wright, 12 March 1940, Wright Papers, Box 93, Folder 1167. Algren's multiple ways of reading *Native Son* have kept a legion of literary critics busy (and at odds) for seven decades.
112. Andrew Hemingway, *Artists on the Left: American Artists and the Communist Movement, 1926–1956* (New Haven: Yale University Press, 2002), 144.
113. Cappetti, *Writing Chicago*, 156. See her illuminating discussion of Algren's *Never Come Morning*, ibid., 156–181.
114. Lehan, *Realism and Naturalism*, 224.
115. Ellison to Albert Murray, 9 April 1953, in *Trading Twelves: The Selected Letters of Ralph Ellison and Albert Murray*, ed. John F. Callahan (New York: Vintage, 2001), 43.

10   Bronzeville and the Poets

1. Margaret Walker, "New Poets," *Phylon* 11, no. 4 (1950): 345–354. Reprinted under the title "New Poets of the Forties and the Optimism of the Age," in Walker, *How I Wrote Jubilee*, 102–113.
2. "Chicago's Congo" appears in *Abbott's Monthly* 2, no. 3 (March 1931).
3. Davis, *Livin' the Blues*, 215–226.
4. All quotations from Davis's poems taken from Frank Marshall Davis, *Black Moods: Collected Poems*, ed. John Edgar Tidwell (Urbana: University of Illinois Press, 2002). Used with permission of the poet's literary executor and the University of Illinois Press.
5. Lucius Harper, "Young Poet Strikes a New Chord in Verse," *CD*, 10 September 1938.
6. George Schuyler, "Views and Previews," *Pittsburgh Courier*, 19 December 1935.
7. Locke, "Deep River, Deeper Sea," 10.
8. Benet and White are quoted in Harper, "Young Poet."
9. Harriet Monroe, "A New Negro Poet," *Poetry: A Magazine of Verse* 48, no. 5 (August 1936): 293–295.
10. Davis, *Livin' the Blues*, 240.
11. Frank Marshall Davis, "Touring the World," *Atlanta World*, 2 October 1932 and 9 April 1933; Frank Marshall Davis Collection, Archives of the DuSable Museum of African American History.

12. Davis, *Livin' the Blues*, 240.

13. Smethurst, *New Red Negro*, 56, 51.

14. Davis, *Livin' the Blues*, 252–253.

15. Ibid., 226–227.

16. Ibid., 244–249; Nahum Daniel Brascher, "Fan Fare," *CD*, 25 June 1938.

17. Wixson, *Worker-Writer in America*, 441.

18. Davis describes his increasing wartime activism in *Livin' the Blues*, 275–283. Leftist organizations for which he served as guest speaker, sponsor, and/or officer included American Youth for Democracy, the Midwest Negro People's Assembly, the White Collar and Professional Wartime Legislative Conference, Friends of the *New Masses*, the National Committee to Combat Anti-Semitism, the Civil Rights Congress, the Midwest Committee to Re-elect Franklin Roosevelt, and the Abraham Lincoln School. See miscellaneous fliers in the Davis Collection at the DuSable Museum. John Edgar Tidwell reports that he joined the Communist Party sometime in the 1940s. Tidwell, introduction to Davis, *Black Moods*, xxxiv–xxxvii.

19. Quoted in Tidwell, Introduction, xxi.

20. Margaret Walker, preface to *This Is My Century: New and Collected Poems* (Athens: University of Georgia Press, 1989), xii.

21. Walker, "Richard Wright," 33–34.

22. Ibid., 39.

23. Walker's initial publication was partly facilitated by the proximity of the offices of *Poetry* and the Writing Project on Erie Street and the fact that both Walker and *Poetry* editor George Dillon belonged to the Chicago chapter of the League of American Writers. Brascher, "Fan Fare."

24. Walker, Preface, xiv.

25. All quotes from Walker's poems are taken from *This Is My Century: New and Collected Poems*, copyright 1989 by Margaret Walker Alexander, used by permission of the University of Georgia Press.

26. Revelation 21: 1–8 (King James Version).

27. English version from Upton Sinclair, ed., *The Cry for Justice: An Anthology of the Literature of Social Protest* (Philadelphia: Winston, 1915), 800–801.

28. Walker described this event in a lengthy excerpt from her 1939 diary incorporated verbatim into *Richard Wright: Daemonic Genius*, 127–146. More objective accounts are found in Rowley, *Richard Wright*, 168–172; Fabre, *Unfinished Quest*, 195.

29. The first story Walker published in a nationally circulated magazine was "The Satin Dress" in *New Anvil*. Wixson, *Worker-Writer in America*, 441.

30. Walker to Bontemps, 20 January 1940, Bontemps Papers, Box 28. Walker's other two Rosenwald sponsors were Illinois Writing Project director John T. Frederick and Langston Hughes. She eventually won a fellowship in 1944.

31. Walker, interview by Claudia Tate, 28.

32. Eugenia Collier, "Fields Watered with Blood: Myth and Ritual in the Poetry of Margaret Walker," in *Fields Watered with Blood*, ed. Graham, 101.

33. R. Baxter Miller, "The 'Etched Flame' of Margaret Walker: Literary and Biblical Re-Creation in Southern History," in *Fields Watered with Blood*, ed. Graham, 81–97.

34. Smethurst, *New Red Negro*, 188–194; Robert Hayden, "From *The Life*: Some Remembrances," in *Collected Prose: Robert Hayden*, ed. Frederick Glaysher (Ann Arbor: University of Michigan Press, 1984), 25–26.

35. Melvin B. Tolson, "Dark Symphony," *Rendezvous with America* (New York: Dodd Mead, 1944). Originally published in *Atlantic Monthly* (September 1941). Copyright 1941, 1944 by Melvin B. Tolson, renewed © 1969, 1972 by Ruth S. Tolson. Reprinted with the permission of Melvin B. Tolson, Jr. c/o The Permissions Company, www.permissionscompany.com.

36. Quoted in Gary Smith, "Gwendolyn Brooks' A Street in Bronzeville," in *Gwendolyn Brooks*, ed. Harold Bloom (Philadelphia: Chelsea, 2000), 57–58.

37. E. Ethelbert Miller, "Gwendolyn Brooks on Langston Hughes," *The Langston Hughes Review* 15, no. 2 (Winter 1997), 92–109.

38. Kent reports that Brooks attended three high schools. At Hyde Park, she was shocked at the icy aloofness of white students. At overwhelmingly black Wendell Phillips, she was isolated "because of her lack of social and athletic skills and her dark skin." Englewood, with a roughly 70/30 mix of whites and blacks and its more upwardly mobile or creatively inclined black students, proved the most comfortable environment for the young poet. *Life of Gwendolyn Brooks*, 24–25.
39. Miller, "Gwendolyn Brooks," 94.
40. Gwendolyn Brooks, "An Old Apartment House," *CD*, 20 August 1938.
41. Davis to Hughes, 17 October 1941, Hughes Papers, Box 53.
42. Henry Blakely published a collection called *Windy Place* in 1974. John Carlis became a painter and moved to California. Robert Davis had a successful acting career under the screen name Davis Roberts. William Couch went on to a distinguished academic career. Margaret Danner became associate editor of *Poetry* (another first for African American writers), was poet-in-residence at several universities, and published important collections, including *Iron Lace* (1968) and *The Down of a Thistle* (1976).
43. Kent, *Life of Gwendolyn Brooks*, 59–61; Gwendolyn Brooks, *Report From Part One*, 65–68; S. I. Hayakawa, "Second Thoughts," *CD*, 9 October 1943; "Chicagoans Included in New Poetry Anthology," *CD*, 27 December 1952, 8; Rex Goreleigh to Arna Bontemps, 8 September 1945, Bontemps Papers, Box 4; "Our Contributors," *Negro Story* 1, no. 2 (July-August 1944): 2. Freelance writer and editor Marjorie Peters Long became instructor of the class after Stark left Chicago and, in 1947, she moved it from the Art Center to Parkway Community House. Brooks and Burroughs assumed leadership roles in keeping the class intact immediately after Stark's departure. Brooks to Hughes, form letter, 7 September 1943; Brooks to Hughes, 16 September 1943, Hughes Papers, Box 23.
44. Gwendolyn Brooks, *Report From Part One* (Detroit: Broadside Press, 1972), 66.
45. Robert Hillyer, *First Principles of Verse* (Boston: The Writer, Inc., 1938), 3.
46. Brooks, *Report From Part One*, 66, 69.
47. John Carlis, interview by Henri Ghent, September 1968, AAA.
48. Burroughs to Robert Bone, 28 May 1981.
49. Quoted in Margaret Burroughs, "Personals from the Poetry Editor," *NYPS Magazine*, August 1942, Gwendolyn Brooks Vertical Files, Archives of the DuSable Museum of African American History. The monthly *Negro Youth Photo Script*, edited by Ruth Apilado, was launched in March 1942 and appears to have been published in Chicago for about fifteen months. "Youth Magazine Makes Its Debut," *CD*, 11 April 1942.
50. Brooks to Hughes, 11 March 1942, Hughes Papers, Box 23.
51. Kent, *Life of Gwendolyn Brooks*, 54–57. A different view is found in Mullen, *Popular Fronts*, 148–180; Smethurst, *New Red Negro*, 164–179.
52. Kent, *Life of Gwendolyn Brooks*, 48–49.
53. Edward Bland, "Racial Bias and Negro Poetry," *Poetry* 63 (March 1944): 328–333.
54. Allyn Keith (pseudonym of Edward Bland), "A Note on Negro Nationalism," *New Challenge* (Fall 1937): 65–69.
55. Gwendolyn Brooks, interview by Roy Newquist, in Gayles, *Conversations*, 31.
56. Kent, *Life of Gwendolyn Brooks*, 62–63.
57. Rolfe Humphries, "Bronzeville," *New York Times Book Review*, 4 November 1945, 8.
58. Quoted in Marjorie Peters, "Poetess Brooks Calmly Greets Book's Success in Kitchenette," *CD*, 1 September 1945.
59. Quoted in Kent, *Life of Gwendolyn Brooks*, 66.
60. John Parker, "New Singer from the Middle West," *Journal of Negro Education* 15, no. 2 (Spring 1946): 200–201.
61. Quoted in Kent, *Life of Gwendolyn Brooks*, 71.
62. Brooks, *Report From Part One*, 156.
63. All lines from Brooks's poems are reprinted by consent of Brooks Permissions.
64. Kent, *Life of Gwendolyn Brooks*, 76–77.
65. Gwendolyn Brooks, interview by Studs Terkel, in Gayles, *Conversations*, 7.

66. *Poetry* 66 (June 1945): 174.

67. Brooks, *Report From Part One*, 159.

68. Ibid., 159.

69. Gwendolyn Brooks, interview by Gloria T. Hull and Posey Gallagher, in Gayles, *Conversations*, 96.

11 (**The Wheel Turns**

1. Alain Locke, "Wisdom De Profundis: The Literature of the Negro, 1949, Part I," *Phylon* 11, no. 1 (First Quarter 1950): 11–13.

2. Alain Locke, "Self-Criticism: The Third Dimension of Culture," *Phylon* 11, no. 4 (Fourth Quarter 1950): 392.

3. C. Mozell Hill and M. Carl Holman, "Preface," *Phylon* 11, no. 4 (Fourth Quarter 1950): 296.

4. G. Lewis Chandler, "A Major Problem of Negro Authors in their March toward Belles-Lettres," *Phylon* 11, no. 4 (Fourth Quarter 1950): 386.

5. Gwendolyn Brooks, "Poets Who Are Negroes," *Phylon* 11, no. 4 (Fourth Quarter 1950): 312.

6. Robert Chrisman, "Robert Hayden: The Transition Years, 1946–1948," in *Robert Hayden: Essays on the Poetry*, ed. Laurence Goldstein and Robert Chrisman (Ann Arbor: University of Michigan Press, 2004), 129–154.

7. "Counterpoise," in *Collected Prose: Robert Hayden*, ed. Glaysher, 41–42.

8. Hayden to Bernard and Margaret Goss, 22 February 1940, Margaret Burroughs Papers, Archives of the DuSable Museum of African American History; "Youth Group to Present Poet," 2 February 1941, typescript press release, McBride Papers, Box 24.

9. Robert M. Farnsworth, *Melvin B. Tolson, 1898–1866: Plain Talk and Prophetic Prophecy* (Columbia: University of Missouri Press, 1984), 136–151, quotations at 146. Farnsworth notes the "blandly patronizing tone" of Tate's preface to Tolson's *Libretto*.

10. Ibid., 166–167. Also see Gary Lenhart, *The Stamp of Class: Reflections on Poetry and Social Class* (Ann Arbor: University of Michigan Press, 2006), 64–84. Both Farnsworth and Lenhart make clear that Tolson's embrace of modernist aesthetics did not constitute a renunciation of his radical "Christo-Marxist" politics.

11. Gene Andrew Jarrett, *Deans and Truants: Race and Realism in African American Literature* (Philadelphia: University of Pennsylvania Press, 2007), 143–166; *Concise Oxford Companion to African American Literature*, s.v. "Frank Yerby."

12. Davis, *Livin' the Blues*, 249–250.

13. Dunham, "Minefields," 89.

14. Quoted in Mangione, *The Dream and the Deal*, 126.

15. Gertrude Martin, "Bookshelf," *CD*, 3 May 1947.

16. For a spirited case to the contrary, see Jarrett, *Deans and Truants*.

17. Green, *Selling the Race*, 152–154. Also see Maren Stange, "'Photographs Taken in Everyday Life': *Ebony*'s Photojournalistic Discourse," in *The Black Press: New Literary and Historical Essays*, ed. Todd Vogel (New Brunswick, N.J.: Rutgers University Press, 2001), 207–227.

18. Edward Margolies and Michel Fabre, *The Several Lives of Chester Himes* (Jackson: University of Mississippi Press, 1997), 39–111; Cassuto, *Hard-Boiled Sentimentality*, 226–235.

19. Frank Yerby, interview by Harvey Breit, 13 May 1951, reprinted in *Popular Culture*, ed. David Manning White (New York: New York Times, 1975), 61–62.

20. Quoted in Margolies and Fabre, *Several Lives*, 81.

21. Joel Kovel, *Red Hunting in the Promised Land: Anticommunism and the Making of America* (New York: Basic Books, 1994); Walter LaFeber, *America, Russia, and the Cold War, 1945–1992*, 7th ed. (New York: McGraw-Hill, 1993); David Caute, *The Great Fear: Anti-Communist Purges under Truman and Eisenhower* (New York: Simon and Schuster, 1978); Richard J. Walton, *Henry Wallace, Harry Truman, and the Cold War* (New York: Viking, 1973).

22. Wald, *Exiles from a Future Time*, 328–329.

23. Perkins to Ward, undated letter on exhibit in *To See Reality in a New Light: The Art and Activism of Marion Perkins*, 31 January–31 December 2009, Harsh.

24. Davis, *Livin' the Blues*, 304; Tidwell, introduction to Davis, *Black Moods*, xxx.

25. Quoted in Savage, *Broadcasting Freedom*, 269.

26. The FBI surveillance file on Burroughs, opened in 1937, grew to five hundred pages by the 1980s. Burroughs, *Life with Margaret*, 71–75.

27. Tyler, "Planting and Maintaining," 35.

28. Although not specific to Black Chicago, Alan Wald's more nuanced account of the many-sided interactions of Leftist writing and modernist aesthetics offers a useful corrective to Mullen's analysis. *Exiles from a Future Time*, 299–325.

29. Green, *Selling the Race*, 149.

30. Strickland, *Chicago Urban League*, 157.

31. Ibid., 155–163, quotes at 158. Also see Arnold R. Hirsch, *Making the Second Ghetto: Race and Housing in Chicago, 1940–1960* (1983; Chicago: University of Chicago Press, 1998); Janet L. Abu-Lughod, *Race, Space, and Riots in Chicago, New York, and Los Angeles* (New York: Oxford University Press, 2007), 67–72; Reed, *Chicago NAACP*, 147–156.

32. Vivian G. Harsh, Annual Reports, 1945, 1947, 1948, 1951, 1955, 1956; Hall Branch Archives, Box 23.

33. Langston Hughes, "Things I Like about Chicago I Like, and What I Don't, I Don't," CD, 18 June 1949.

34. Strickland, *Chicago Urban League*, 158.

35. See note 23.

36. Twelve of the eighteen artists at the center of this study were Rosenwald Fellows. Two others were winners of Guggenheim grants, three belonged to the habitually self-supporting clan of musicians, and the eighteenth was schoolteacher Margaret Burroughs.

37. Keith Byerman, "Vernacular Modernism in the Novels of John Edgar Wideman and Leon Forrest," in *Cambridge Companion*, ed. Graham, 253–267; Edward Michael Pavlic, *Crossroads Modernism: Descent and Emergence in African-American Literary Culture* (Minneapolis: University of Minnesota Press, 2002), 79–173; Craig Hansen Werner, *Playing the Changes: From Afro-Modernism to the Jazz Impulse* (Urbana: University of Illinois Press, 1994), 241–262.

38. Larry Neal, "The Black Arts Movement," in *NAAAL*, 2039.

39. Brooks, *Report*, 73–86

40. On Brooks and the Black Arts Movement, see Kent, *Gwendolyn Brooks*, 170–258; James Edward Smethurst, *The Black Arts Movement: Literary Nationalism in the 1960s and 1970s* (Chapel Hill: University of North Carolina Press, 2005), 198–200, 209–215, 228–230, 237–238.

41. Quoted in Marshall and Kimbrough, "Above and Beyond," 13. Also see James V. Hatch, *Sorrow Is the Only Faithful One: The Life of Owen Dodson* (Urbana: University of Illinois Press, 1995), 195–197, 324 n. 3.

42. Barack Obama, *Dreams from My Father: A Story of Race and Inheritance* (New York: Three Rivers Press, 1995), 72–98; quotations at 76, 90, 97.

43. Ibid., 145–146.

Aschenbrenner, Joyce. *Katherine Dunham: Dancing a Life*. Urbana: University of Illinois Press, 2002.

Ascoli, Peter. *Julius Rosenwald: The Man Who Built Sears, Roebuck and Advanced the Cause of Black Education in the American South*. Bloomington: Indiana University Press, 2006.

Attaway, William. *Blood on the Forge*. New York: Doubleday, 1941; repr. New York: New York Review of Books, 2005.

———. *Let Me Breathe Thunder*. New York: Doubleday, 1939; repr. as *Tough Kid*, New York: Lion Books, 1955.

Baker, Paul J., ed. "The Life Histories of W. I. Thomas and Robert E. Park." *American Journal of Sociology* 79, no. 2 (September 1973): 243–260.

Baldwin, Davarian. *Chicago's New Negroes: Modernity, the Great Migration, and Black Urban Life*. Chapel Hill: University of North Carolina Press, 2007.

Barlow, William. *Looking Up at Down: The Emergence of Blues Culture*. Philadelphia: Temple University Press, 1990.

Barnwell, Andrea D. *Charles White*. San Francisco: Pomegranate, 2002.

Bearden, Romare, and Harry Henderson. *A History of African-American Artists from 1792 to the Present*. New York: Pantheon, 1993.

Bell, Bernard. *The Afro-American Novel and Its Tradition*. Amherst: University of Massachusetts Press, 1987.

Best, Wallace. *Passionately Human, No Less Divine: Religion and Culture in Black Chicago, 1915–1952*. Princeton, N.J.: Princeton University Press, 2005.

Bland, Alden. *Behold a Cry*. New York: Scribner, 1947.

Bone, Robert. *Down Home: Origins of the Afro-American Short Story*. New York: Putnam, 1975; Morningside ed., New York: Columbia University Press, 1988.

———. *The Negro Novel in America*. New Haven: Yale University Press, 1958; rev. ed., New Haven: Yale University Press, 1966.

———. "Richard Wright and the Chicago Renaissance." *Callaloo* 9 (Summer 1986): 446–468.

Bontemps, Arna. *Black Thunder*. New York: Macmillan, 1936; repr. Boston: Beacon, 1992.

———. *Drums at Dusk*. New York: Macmillan, 1939.

———. "Famous WPA Writers." *Negro Digest*. (June 1950): 43–47.

———. *God Sends Sunday*. New York: Harcourt, 1931; repr. New York: Washington Square Press, 2005.

———. *The Old South: "A Summer Tragedy" and Other Stories of the Thirties*. New York: Dodd, Mead, 1973.

———, ed. *The Harlem Renaissance Remembered*. New York: Dodd, Mead, 1972.

Brooks, Gwendolyn. *Annie Allen*. New York: Harper, 1949.

———. *Report from Part One*. Detroit: Broadside Press, 1972.

———. *A Street in Bronzeville*. New York: Harper, 1945.

Burroughs, Margaret Goss. "Chicago's South Side Community Art Center: A Personal Recollection." In *Art in Action: American Art Centers and the New Deal*. Ed. John Franklin White. Metuchen, N.J.: Scarecrow Press, 1987.

———. *Life with Margaret: The Official Autobiography*. Chicago: In Time Publishing, 2003.

Cahnman, W. J. "Robert E. Park at Fisk." *Journal of the History of the Behavioral Sciences* 14 (1978): 328–336.

Cappetti, Carla. *Writing Chicago: Modernism, Ethnography, and the Novel*. New York: Columbia University Press, 1993.

Carter, Dan T. *Scottsboro: A Tragedy of the American South*. Baton Rouge: Louisiana State University Press, 1969; rev. ed., Baton Rouge: Louisiana State University Press, 1979.

Cayton, Horace R. *Long Old Road*. New York: Simon & Schuster, 1963.

Clark, Veve A., and Sara E. Johnson, eds. *Kaiso!: Writings by and about Katherine Dunham*. Madison: University of Wisconsin Press, 2005.

Cohen, Lizabeth. *Making a New Deal: Industrial Workers in Chicago, 1919–1939*. Cambridge: Cambridge University Press, 1990.

Courage, Richard, and Nathan Harpaz. *Convergence: Jewish and African American Artists in Depression-era Chicago*. Des Plaines, Ill.: Koehnline Museum of Art, 2008.

Cowley, Malcom. *The Dream of the Golden Mountains: Remembering the 1930s*. New York: Penguin, 1981.

———. "A Natural History of American Naturalism." In *The Portable Malcolm Cowley*, ed. Donald W. Faulkner. New York: Penguin, 1990.

Cutler, Irving. *The Jews of Chicago: From Shtetl to Suburb*. Urbana: University of Illinois Press, 1996.

Dance, Stanley. *The World of Earl Hines*. New York: Scribner, 1977.

Davis, Frank Marshall. *Black Moods: Collected Poems*. Ed. John Edgar Tidwell. Urbana: University of Illinois Press, 2002.

———. *Livin' the Blues: Memoirs of a Black Journalist and Poet*. Ed. John Edgar Tidwell. Madison: University of Wisconsin Press, 1992.

Denning, Michael. *The Cultural Front: The Laboring of American Culture in the Twentieth Century*. London: Verso, 1997.

Drake, St. Clair, and Horace R. Cayton. *Black Metropolis: A Study of Negro Life in a Northern City*. New York: Harcourt, 1945; rev. and enlarged ed., Chicago: University of Chicago Press, 1993.

Drew, Bettina. *Nelson Algren: A Life on the Wild Side*. New York: Putnam, 1989.

Dykeman, Wilma, and James Stokeley. *Seeds of Southern Change: The Life of Will Alexander*. Chicago: University of Chicago Press, 1962.

Embree, Edwin. *Thirteen Against the Odds*. New York: Viking, 1944.

Epstein, Daniel Mark. *Nat King Cole*. Boston: Northeastern University Press, 1999.

Fabre, Genevieve, and Michel Feith, eds. *Temples for Tomorrow: Looking Back at the Harlem Renaissance*. Bloomington: Indiana University Press, 2001.

Fabre, Michael. *The Unfinished Quest of Richard Wright*. New York: Morrow, 1973.

Faris, Robert E. L. *Chicago Sociology, 1920–1931*. San Francisco: Chandler, 1967.

Fleming, Robert E. *Willard Motley*. Boston: Twayne, 1978.

Floyd, Samuel A. Jr. *The Power of Black Music: Interpreting Its History from Africa to the United States*. New York: Oxford University Press, 1995.

Folsom, Franklin. *Days of Anger, Days of Hope: A Memoir of the League of American Writers, 1937–1942*. Niwot: University Press of Colorado, 1994.

Fraden, Rena. *Blueprints for a Black Federal Theatre, 1935–1939*. Cambridge: Cambridge University Press, 1996.

Fried, Albert, ed. *Communism in America: A History in Documents*. New York: Columbia University Press, 1997.

Gayles, Gloria Wade, ed. *Conversations with Gwendolyn Brooks*. Jackson: University of Mississippi Press, 2003.

Gilpin, Patrick J., and Marybeth Gasman. *Charles S. Johnson: Leadership Beyond the Veil in the Age of Jim Crow*. Albany: State University of New York Press, 2003.

Glaysher, Frederick, ed. *Collected Prose: Robert Hayden*. Ann Arbor: University of Michigan Press, 1984.

Gosnell, Harold. *Negro Politicians: The Rise of Negro Politics in Chicago*. Chicago: University of Chicago Press, 1935; repr. Chicago: University of Chicago Press, 1967.

Graham, Maryemma, ed. *Cambridge Companion to the African American Novel*. Cambridge: Cambridge University Press, 2004.

———, ed. *Fields Watered with Blood: Critical Essays on Margaret Walker*. Athens: University of Georgia Press, 2001.

Green, Adam. *Selling the Race: Culture, Community, and Black Chicago, 1940–1955*. Chicago: University of Chicago Press, 2007.

Griffin, Farah Jasmine. *"Who Set You Flowin'?": The African-American Migration Narrative*. New York: Oxford University Press, 1995.

Grossman, James R. *Land of Hope: Chicago, Black Southerners, and the Great Migration.* Chicago: University of Chicago Press, 1989.

Harlan, Louis. *Booker T. Washington: The Making of a Black Leader, 1856–1901.* New York: Oxford University Press, 1972.

———. *Booker T. Washington: The Wizard of Tuskegee, 1901–1915.* New York: Oxford University Press, 1983.

Harnan, Terry. *African Rhythm, American Dance: A Biography of Katherine Dunham.* New York: Knopf, 1974.

Harris, Michael W. *The Rise of Gospel Blues: The Music of Thomas Andrew Dorsey in the Urban Church.* New York: Oxford University Press, 1994.

Herzog, Melanie. *Elizabeth Catlett: An American Artist in Mexico.* Seattle: University of Washington Press, 2000.

Hill, Herbert, ed. *Anger, and Beyond: The Negro Writer in the United States.* New York: Harper, 1966.

Hills, Patricia. *Painting Harlem Modern: The Art of Jacob Lawrence.* Berkeley: University of California Press, 2009.

Hirsch, Jerrold. *Portrait of America: A Cultural History of the Federal Writers' Project.* Chapel Hill: University of North Carolina Press, 2003.

Hobbs, Richard S. *The Cayton Legacy: An African American Family.* Pullman: Washington State University Press, 2002.

House, Roger Randolph III. "Keys to the Highway: William 'Big Bill' Broonzy and the Chicago Blues in the Era of the Great Migration." Ph.D. diss., Boston University, 1999.

Hughes, Everett C., Charles S. Johnson, Jitsuichi Masuoka, Robert Redfield, and Louis Wirth, eds. *The Collected Papers of Robert Ezra Park,* Vol. 1: *Race and Culture.* Glencoe, Ill.: Free Press, 1950.

Hughes, Langston. *The Big Sea: An Autobiography.* New York: Knopf, 1940; repr. New York: Hill and Wang, 1998.

Hutchinson, George, ed. *The Cambridge Companion to the Harlem Renaissance.* Cambridge: Cambridge University Press, 2007.

———. *The Harlem Renaissance in Black and White.* Cambridge: Harvard University Press, 1995.

Jackson, Blyden. *The Waiting Years: Essays on American Negro Literature.* Baton Rouge: Louisiana State University Press, 1976.

Johnson, Abby, and Ronald Johnson. *Propaganda and Aesthetics: The Literary Politics of Afro-American Magazines in the Twentieth Century.* Amherst: University of Massachusetts Press, 1979.

Jones, Kirkland C. *Renaissance Man from Louisiana: A Biography of Arna Wendell Bontemps.* Westport, Conn.: Greenwood, 1992.

Kennedy, Elizabeth, ed. *Chicago Modern, 1893–1945: Pursuit of the New.* Chicago: Terra Museum of American Art, 2004.

Kenney, William Howland. *Chicago Jazz: A Cultural History, 1904–1930.* New York: Oxford University Press, 1993.

Kent, George E. *A Life of Gwendolyn Brooks.* Lexington: University Press of Kentucky, 1990.

Knupfer, Anne Meis. *The Chicago Black Renaissance and Women's Activism.* Urbana: University of Illinois Press, 2006.

———. *Reform and Resistance: Gender, Delinquency, and America's First Juvenile Court.* New York: Routledge, 2001.

———. *Toward a Tenderer Humanity and a Nobler Womanhood: African American Women's Clubs in Turn-of-the-Century Chicago.* New York: New York University Press, 1996.

Lehan, Richard. *Realism and Naturalism: The Novel in an Age of Transition.* Madison: University of Wisconsin Press, 2005.

Lewis, David Levering. *W.E.B. Du Bois: Biography of a Race, 1868–1919.* New York: Holt, 1993.

———. *W.E.B. Du Bois: The Fight for Equality and the American Century, 1919–1963.* New York: Holt, 2000.

———. *When Harlem Was in Vogue.* New York: Knopf, 1980; repr. New York: Penguin, 1997.

Lyman, Stanford M. *Militarism, Imperialism, and Racial Accommodation: An Analysis and Interpretation of the Early Writings of Robert E. Park.* Fayetteville: University of Arkansas Press, 1992.

Mangione, Jerre. *The Dream and the Deal: The Federal Writers' Project, 1935–1945.* Boston: Little, Brown, 1972; repr. Syracuse: Syracuse University Press, 1996.

Marshall, Melvin, and Blake Kimbrough. "Above and Beyond: The Life and Art of Charles Sebree." *The International Review of African American Art* 18, no. 2 (2002): 2–17.

Matthews, Fred H. *Quest for an American Sociology: Robert E. Park and the Chicago School.* Montreal: McGill-Queen's University Press, 1977.

Mavigliano, George, and Richard Lawson. *The Federal Art Project in Illinois, 1935–1943.* Carbondale: Southern Illinois University Press, 1990.

Maxwell, William J. *New Negro, Old Left: African-American Writing and Communism between the Wars.* New York: Columbia University Press, 1999.

Mooney, Amy. *Archibald J. Motley, Jr.* San Francisco: Pomegranate, 2004.

Motley, Willard. *Knock on Any Door.* New York: Appleton-Century, 1947; repr. DeKalb: Northern Illinois University Press, 1989.

———. "Negro Art in Chicago." *Opportunity* 18, no. 1 (January 1940): 19–22, 28–31.

Mullen, Bill V. *Popular Fronts: Chicago and African-American Cultural Politics, 1935–46.* Urbana: University of Illinois Press, 1999.

Murray, Albert. *Stomping the Blues.* New York: McGraw-Hill, 1976.

Nichols, Charles A., ed. *Arna Bontemps–Langston Hughes Letters, 1925–1967.* New York: Oxford University Press, 1986.

O'Connor, Francis V., ed. *Art for the Millions: Essays from the 1930s by Artists and Administrators of the WPA Federal Art Project.* Boston: New York Graphic Society, 1975.

Ottley, Roi. *The Lonely Warrior: The Life and Times of Robert S. Abbott.* Chicago: Henry Regnery, 1955.

Park, Robert E., and Ernest Burgess. *Introduction to the Science of Sociology.* Chicago: University of Chicago Press, 1921.

Parks, Gordon. *A Choice of Weapons.* New York: Harper, 1965; repr. St. Paul: Minnesota Historical Society Press, 1986.

———. *Voices in the Mirror.* New York: Doubleday, 1990.

Parris, Guichard, and Lester Brooks. *Blacks in the City: A History of the National Urban League.* Boston: Little, Brown, 1971.

Pearson, Ralph L. "Charles S. Johnson: The Urban League Years, A Study of Race Leadership." Ph.D. diss., Johns Hopkins University, 1970.

Penkower, Monty Noam. *The Federal Writers' Project: A Study in Government Patronage of the Arts.* Urbana: University of Illinois Press, 1977.

Philpott, Thomas Lee. *The Slum and the Ghetto: Immigrants, Blacks, and Reformers in Chicago, 1880–1930.* New York: Oxford University Press, 1978; repr. Belmont, Calif.: Wadsworth, 1991.

Prince, Sue Ann, ed. *The Old Guard and the Avant-Garde: Modernism in Chicago, 1910–1940.* Chicago: University of Chicago Press, 1990.

Rampersad, Arnold. *The Life of Langston Hughes,* Vol. 1: 1902–1941, "I, Too, Sing America." New York: Oxford University Press, 1986.

———. *Langston Hughes,* Vol. 2: 1941–1967, "I Dream a World." New York: Oxford University Press, 1988.

———, ed. *Richard Wright: A Collection of Critical Essays.* Englewood Cliffs, N.J.: Prentice Hall, 1995.

Raushenbush, Winifred. *Robert E. Park: Biography of a Sociologist.* Durham, N.C.: Duke University Press, 1979.

Reed, Christopher Robert. *Black Chicago's First Century,* Vol. 1, 1833–1900. Columbia: University of Missouri Press, 2005.

———. *The Chicago NAACP and the Rise of Black Professional Leadership, 1910–1966.* Bloomington: Indiana University Press, 1997.

———. "A Study of Black Politics and Protest in Depression-decade Chicago, 1930–1939." Ph.D. diss., Kent State University, 1982.

Robbins, Richard. *Sidelines Activist: Charles S. Johnson and the Struggle for Civil Rights.* Jackson: University Press of Mississippi, 1996.

Robinson, Theresa Jontyle, and Wendy Greenhouse. *The Art of Archibald J. Motley, Jr.* Chicago: Chicago Historical Society, 1991.

Rodgers, Lawrence R. *Canaan Bound: The African American Great Migration Novel.* Urbana: University of Illinois Press, 1997.

Rowley, Hazel. *Richard Wright: The Life and Times.* New York: Holt, 2001.

Saint-Arnaud, Pierre. *African American Pioneers of Sociology: A Critical History.* Toronto: University of Toronto Press, 2009.

Savage, Barbara Dianne. *Broadcasting Freedom: Radio, War, and the Politics of Race, 1938–1948.* Chapel Hill: University of North Carolina Press, 1999.

Schulman, Daniel, ed. *A Force for Change: African American Art and the Julius Rosenwald Fund.* Chicago: Spertus Institute of Jewish Studies and Northwestern University Press, 2009.

Scruggs, Charles. *Sweet Home: Invisible Cities in the Afro-American Novel.* Baltimore: Johns Hopkins University Press, 1993.

Singh, Amritjit. *The Novels of the Harlem Renaissance: Twelve Black Writers, 1923–33.* University Park: Pennsylvania State University Press, 1976.

Smethurst, James Edward. *The New Red Negro: The Literary Left and African-American Poetry, 1930–1946.* New York: Oxford University Press, 1999.

Smock, Raymond, ed. *Booker T. Washington in Perspective: Essays of Louis R. Harlan.* Jackson: University Press of Mississippi, 2006.

Southern, Eileen. *The Music of Black Americans: A History.* 3rd ed. New York: Norton, 1997.

Spear, Allen. *Black Chicago: The Making of a Negro Ghetto, 1890–1920.* Chicago: University of Chicago Press, 1967.

Stange, Maren. *Bronzeville: Black Chicago in Pictures, 1941–1943.* New York: New Press, 2003.

Stewart, Jeffrey. *The Critical Temper of Alain Locke.* New York: Garland Publishing, 1983.

Storch, Randi. *Red Chicago: American Communism at Its Grassroots, 1928–35.* Urbana: University of Illinois Press, 2007.

Stott, William. *Documentary Expression and Thirties America.* New York: Oxford University Press, 1973; repr. Chicago: University of Chicago Press, 1986.

Strickland, Arvarh. *History of the Chicago Urban League.* Urbana: University of Illinois Press, 1966.

Strong, Carline Evone Williams. "Margaret Taylor Goss Burroughs: Educator, Artist, Author, Founder, and Civic Leader." Ph.D. diss., Loyola University, 1994.

Thomas, Lorenzo. *Extraordinary Measures: Afrocentric Modernism and Twentieth-Century American Poetry.* Tuscaloosa: University of Alabama Press, 2000.

Tomasi, Luigi, ed. *The Tradition of the Chicago School of Sociology.* Aldershot, U.K.: Ashgate Publishing, 1998.

Travis, Dempsey. *An Autobiography of Black Jazz.* Chicago: Urban Research Institute, 1983.

Tuttle, William. *Race Riot: Chicago in the Red Summer of 1919.* New York: Atheneum, 1970; Illini Books ed., Urbana: University of Illinois Press, 1996.

Tyler, Anna M. "Planting and Maintaining a 'Perennial Garden': Chicago's South Side Community Art Center." *International Review of African American Art* 11, no. 4 (1994): 31–37.

Vendryes, Margaret Rose. *Barthé: A Life in Sculpture.* Jackson: University Press of Mississippi, 2008.

Wade, Louise. *Graham Taylor: Pioneer for Social Justice, 1851–1938.* Chicago: University of Chicago Press, 1964.

Wald, Alan M. *Exiles from a Future Time: The Forging of the Mid-Twentieth Century Literary Left.* Chapel Hill: University of North Carolina Press, 2002.

Walker, Margaret. *How I Wrote Jubilee and Other Essays on Life and Literature.* Ed. Maryemma Graham. New York: Feminist Press, 1990.

———. *Richard Wright, Daemonic Genius: A Portrait of the Man, A Critical Look at His Work.* New York: Amistad, 1988.

———. *This Is My Century: New and Collected Poems.* Athens: University of Georgia Press, 1989.

Waskow, Arthur. *From Race Riot to Sit-in: 1919 and the 1960s.* New York: Doubleday, 1966.

Watson, Steven. *Strange Bedfellows: The First American Avant-Garde.* New York: Abbeville Press, 1991.

Weiss, Nancy. *The National Urban League, 1910–1940.* New York: Oxford University Press, 1974.

Werner, M. R. *Julius Rosenwald: The Life of a Practical Humanitarian.* New York: Harper, 1939.

White, Charles. "Path of a Negro Artist." *Masses & Mainstream* 8, no. 4 (April 1955): 33–44.

Wixson, Douglas. *Worker-Writer in America: Jack Conroy and the Tradition of Midwestern Literary Radicalism, 1898–1990.* Urbana: University of Illinois Press, 1994.

Wright, Richard. *12 Million Black Voices: A Folk History of the Negro in the United States.* New York: Viking, 1941; repr. New York: Thunder's Mouth, 2002.

———. *Richard Wright: Early Works.* Ed. Arnold Rampersad. New York: Library of America, 1991.

———. *Richard Wright: Later Works.* Ed. Arnold Rampersad. New York: Library of America, 1991.

INDEX

Note: Boldface italic page numbers indicate illustrations.

Abbott, Edith, 29, 40, 243n74

Abbott, Edna, **63**

Abbott, Lyman, 23

Abbott, Robert Sengstacke: background of, 61; black ballet troupe and, 81; "Bookerism sui generis" view of, 60; Chicago Urban League role of, 40; illustration, **63**; on "The Negro in Music" program, 96; politics of, 62; on race riot commission, 47–49. *See also Abbott's Monthly; Chicago Defender*

Abbott's Monthly, 81, 116, 174, 208

Abraham Lincoln Centre, 29, 115, 148, 163, 165, 167

Abyssinian Baptist Church (New York), 89

Achebe, Chinua, xi

Adams, Charles Francis, 19

Addams, Jane, 28, 29, 40. *See also* Hull House

Adler, Dankmar, 27

African Americans: audience of, 91, 170–176, 191, 200–201, 232; grotesque visual stereotypes of, 148, 151; in Locke's global perspective, 55–56; racial progress strategies of, 59–61; shifting political loyalties of, 92–93; upward mobility among, 185; as veterans, 46, 59, 84, 98, 221–222. *See also* dance; documentary movement; institutions; literature; migrants; music; New Negro movement; theater; visual arts

African Methodist Episcopal Church, 28–29

Agee, James, 131

Alabama. *See* Scottsboro case (1931)

Alexander, Black Bob, 99–100

Alexander, Will, 84, 85, 131

Algren, Nelson: advice for Walker, 213; as editor of *New Anvil* journal, 128, 214; Federal Writers' Project and, 178, 179; on *Native Son*, 205, 271n111; naturalistic vision of, 7, 205–206; WORK: *Never Come Morning*, 205

Allen, Frederick Lewis, 51

Alpha Phi Alpha (black fraternity), 40, 245n41

Alsberg, Henry, 176, 177

Altheimer, Josh, 100

American Conservatory of Music, 95, 97

American Federation of Musicians, Local 208, 4, 66–67, 107, 108

Americanization, 28, 34–35

American Journal of Sociology, 120

American Magazine, 25

American Negro Exposition (Coliseum), 7–8, 141, 151, 159, 181

American Sociological Association (ASA), 35, 36

American Writers' Congress, 127, 177, 214

American Youth for Democracy, 210

Ames, Jessie Daniel, 85

Amini, Johari, 233

Ammons, Albert, 102

Anderson, Margaret, 79

Anderson, Marian: Chicago connections of, 130; community lecture by, 172; White's depiction of, 149–150, *plate 6*

Anderson, Nels, 35

Anderson, Regina, 50, 51, 52, 248n104

Anderson, Sherwood, 57, 75, 79, 115, 202

Angell, James Rowland, 82

ANP (Associated Negro Press), 147, 162, 210

anthropology, 109–113

"anxiety of influence," xiv

Apex Club, 64, 67, 68

Apilado, Ruth, 273n49

Apollo Records, 106

Apollo Theater, 107

Armstrong, Lil Hardin, 66

Armstrong, Louis "Satchmo": achievements of, 2, 94; background of, 65–66; Chicago venues played by, 66–67; mob connections of, 107; WORKS: "Cornet Chop Suey," 66; "Gut Bucket Blues," 66; "Heebie Jeebies," 66; "Potato Head Blues," 66; "Weather Bird," 67; "West End Blues," 67

Armstrong, Samuel Chapman, 14, 60

Armstrong Association, 21

"art as weapon vs. art for art's sake" dichotomy, 156–157

Art Crafts Guild: fund-raising for artists by, 141–142; members of, 145, 148, 159–160; South Side Community Center and, 143

Art Institute of Chicago: access to, 148; Bellows's exhibition and lectures at, 71–72; Chicago-area artists annual exhibition of, 72; collection of, 140; "The Eight" exhibition at, 139; "Negro in Art Week" exhibition of, 70–71; Perkins's work at, 159; referenced, 190; reputation of, 69. *See also* School of the Art Institute of Chicago (SAIC)

Artists and Models Ball (1938), 143

Artists Union, Chicago affiliate, 142, 144

Art of the American Negro (exhibition), 141

Cullen, Countee: background of, 51; circle of, 52; as Civic Club event sponsor, 248n104; literary award for, 54; publications of, 50; WORK: *Caroling Dusk*, 216

dance: choices of form, 108–109; Dunham's role in, 109–113; influences on development, 79–81; overview of, 2. *See also* Dunham, Katherine
Danner, Margaret Cunningham, 217, 273n42
Darwin, Charles, 119
Davis, Frank Marshall: background of, 162; centrality of, 3; circle of, 161, 163, 227, 233; economic struggles of, 79; FBI investigation of, 229; fellowship for, 81, 210; as fighting poet, 208–209; on free verse, 253n90; generation of, 6, 207–208; journal coedited by, 214; as journalist and poet, 210–211; on *Letters* group, 78; *Negro Story* contributions of, 175; photography by, 128; politics and wartime activism of, 209, 210, 272n18; in South Side Writers' Group, 166; Walker on, 216; WORKS: *Black Man's Verse*, 3, 162, 207, 208–209; "Cabaret," 209; "Chicago's Congo," 208; *47th Street*, 210–211; "I Am the American Negro," 167, 209–210
Davis, Robert (aka Davis Roberts), 166, 217, 273n42
Dawson, Charles, 69, **70**, 70–71, 159
Dawson, William Levi, 95, 96–97
Delaney, Hubert T., **53**
Delano, Jack, 154
DeLemarter, Eric, 81
Dell, Floyd, 75, 79
Demby, William, 226, 227
Democratic Party, 92, 255n24
demographics: black migration and South Side growth, 4, 38, 39, 40, 115, 230–231; black population in South, 38; black

unemployment (1931), 92. *See also* generational milieu
Denning, Michael, 269n41
Deppe, Lois, 66
Depression era: artists' survival in, 140, 141–145; crime and poverty of, 163; documentary movement in, 130–132, 155–156; early jazz venues in context of, 67–68; generational milieu of, 6–8; hardest year in (1931), 89–93; response to unemployment in, 121; writers' survival in, 114, 117
DePriest, Oscar, 60, 62, 92
Destination Freedom (radio program), 175–176, 229. *See also* Durham, Richard
De Vries, Peter, 218
Dewey, John, 22, 33, 37
Dickerson, Carroll, 66–67
Dickinson, Emily, 218
Dies, Martin, 176
Diggs, Arthur, 69
Dillard, James H., 44
Dillon, George, 272n23
documentary movement: concept of, 3; focus on African American lives, 128–129, 177–178; historical context of, 7–8; photographers' achievements in, 128, 130–131, 154–156; "scientific reporting" ideal and, 25; social realism linked to, 148–152; visual artists' achievements in, 131–132, 139, 140–141, 146–147; writers' achievements in, 131–132, 146–147, 176–181. *See also* federal agencies; sociology; *12 Million Black Voices* (Wright)
Dodds, Baby (drummer), 66
Dodds, Johnny (clarinetist), 66
Dodson, Owen, 168, 233
"Don't Spend Your Money Where You Can't Work" campaign, 92
Doolittle, Hilda ("H.D."), 75
Dorsey, Thomas Andrew "Georgia Tom": background of, 102–103; centrality of, 2, 8; gospel movement fostered by,

104–106; performances of, 98; sacred/secular blend of, 103–104; WORKS: "It's Tight Like That," 99, 103; "Riverside Blues," 103; "Take My Hand, Precious Lord," 8, 94, 103
Dos Passos, John, 186, 189, 202
Dostoevsky, Fyodor, 189, 193, 195
Douglas, Aaron, 52, 72, 82
Douglas, Memphis Minnie, 99–100
Douglass, Frederick: death of, 15; F. Johnson's tribute to, 76; White's depiction of, 149–150, *plate 6*
Downtown Gallery (New York), 130, 260n79
Doyle, Bertram, 36
Drake, St. Clair: circle of, 80; community lecture by, 172; fellowship for, 81, 110; research materials of, 181; on South Side community, 1, 4; university recruitment of, 36; WORK: *Black Metropolis* (with Cayton), 36, 48, 125, 126, 132, 181
Dreamland Café (club), 64–66
Dreiser, Theodore: as influence, 7, 119, 189, 202, 203, 204; move to Chicago, 75; themes of, 195; WORKS: *An American Tragedy*, 120, 195; *Jennie Gerhardt*, 119, 120; *Sister Carrie*, 119, 120
Du Bois, W.E.B.: on Atlanta race riot, 25; as Civic Club event supporter, 51; as C. Johnson's competition, 248n103; F. Johnson's tribute to, 76; legacy of, 126; Locke compared with, 55; shifting focus of, 89; Washington's differences with, 16–17, 60; WORKS: "A Litany of Atlanta," 25; *The Souls of Black Folk*, 16–17. *See also Crisis, The*
Duffey, Bernard, 79
Dunbar, Paul Lawrence, 76
Dunham, Albert (Katherine's brother), 78, 79, 80, 81
Dunham, Katherine: achievements of, 7–8, 94, 112–113; anthropology studies of, 109–111; background of, 2,

Opportunity: art style advocated by, 71; awards competitions of, 50–52, 54, 89, 95; on Bontemps's *God Sends Sunday*, 185; on Burroughs's home, 146; competition of, 248n103; C. Johnson's editorship of, 33, 40; Locke's work in, 54–55, 56–58; proposal and funding for, 49; racial inequality challenged in, 50
Orozco, José Clemente, 149
Ory, Edward "Kid," 66
Osofsky, Gilbert, 241n16
Others (journal), 57, 76, 77, 253n90
Otis Art Institute (Los Angeles), 153
Overton, Anthony, 60
Owen, Chandler, 60

Pace, Harry, 99
Page, Ruth, 109
Palmer, A. Mitchell, 45, 59
Paramount record label, 99, 103
Park, Robert Ezra: activities of, 5; background of, 22–23, 33–34, 120; Cayton's Tuskegee visit and, 116, 125; Chicago Urban League role of, 40, 41, 42, 44; circle of, 117; Fisk role of, 125; as influence, xvi, 2, 55–56; National Urban League role of, 21; Progressive efforts of, 17–18; race relations (acculturative) cycle of, 34–35, 37, 113, 122, 244n6; on race relations destabilizing, 59; race riot commission and, 46–47, 48; research department under, 37–38; Rosenwald and Hall's collaborations with, 43–45, 48–49; Rosenwald's collaborations with, 26, 30; scientific ethos of, 25, 37, 245n42; on sociological methodology, 132; Tuskegee role of, 21, 22, 24–26, 43; University of Chicago role of, 33, 34, 120; urban sociology research of, 35–36; Washington's

relationship with, 21, 22, 23–26; Wright's meeting with, 129; WORKS: *The City* (with others), 244n13; "Cruelty in the Congo Country" (ghost-written by Park), 24; *The Immigrant Press and Its Control*, 35; *Introduction to the Science of Sociology* (with Burgess), 120, 244n6; *The Isle of Enchantment*, 120; *The Man Farthest Down* (with Washington), 25, 26, 44; *Masse und Publikum* (*The Crowd and the Public*), 23; *Old World Traits Transplanted* (with Miller and Thomas), 244n10
Parker, Charlie, 107–108
Parks, Gordon: achievements of, 3; background of, 152–153; circle of, **154**; fellowship for, 154–155; generation of, 6; subjects of, 155–156; two sides of career of, 154, 155, 156–157; WORKS: *American Gothic*, 155, **plate 8**; *A Choice of Weapons*, 152, 263n67; *Ella Watson and Her Grandchildren*, 155–156, **plate 9**; *A Hungry Heart*, 263n67; "No Love," 153
Parkway Community House: development of, 126–127; facilities and programming of, 130, 172; Skyloft Players of, 130, 172, **173**; Wright's *Native Son* produced at, 195; writers' circle associated with, 165. *See also* Chicago Poets' Class
Patton, Charley, 99
Peabody, George Foster, 44
Pekin Theater, 64, 76
People's Voice, 195
Perkins, Marion: achievements of, 3; background of, 158–159; circle of, **144**; fellowship for, 159, 232; generation of, 6; postal job lost, 229; social realism of, 159, 206; in South Side Writers' Group, 166; WORKS: *John Henry*, 159; *Man of Sorrows*, 159, 232, **plate 12**

Perry, Edward, 89
Peterson, Sadie (Delaney), 50
Petry, Ann, 205
Phelps-Stokes, J. G., 44
Phelps-Stokes Fund, 85
Phillips, Henry, 21
photography: documentary impulse in, 128, 130–131, 154–156. *See also* Farm Security Administration (FSA); Parks, Gordon; *12 Million Black Voices* (Wright)
Phylon (journal), 225–226
Pilgrim Baptist Church, 104
Pins and Needles (musical), 112
Pious, Robert, 69
Pitts, Lucia Mae, 78
Plant, Phil, 103
poetry: achievements touted in 1920s, 50; activism and creativity combined in, 209–211; Braithwaite and Monroe compared in, 252n81; circle of writers in, 161–165; dispossession, southern attachments, and radical politics in, 212–216; generational change in, 207–208; interracial class identity and, 219; modernist shift of, 225–227, 274n10; New Negro movement and, 75–79; overview of, 3; as public performance, 208, 217–218; shift from Harlem to Chicago influence in, 162; unsavory facets depicted in, 220; Walker's reflections on, 207–208, 216; white challenges to traditions of, 74–75. *See also* Chicago Poets' Class; South Side Writers' Group; *and specific poets*
Poetry: avant-garde and modern in, 75; on Davis's *Black Man's Verse*, 209; literary traditions rejected in, 57; CONTRIBUTORS: Brooks, 165, 224; F. Johnson, 76, 77; Walker, 213, 272n23
politics: anticommunist, 176, 228–230, 275n26; approach to radical, xvi; Double-V strategy in, 128; poets' generation and,

ABOUT THE AUTHORS

Robert Bone (1924–2007) was a professor of languages and literature at Columbia University Teachers College and a pioneering scholar of African American literature. He was best known for *The Negro Novel in America* (1958), *Richard Wright* (1969), and *Down Home: Origins of the Afro-American Short Story* (1975). His seminal essay "Richard Wright and the Chicago Renaissance" continues to be cited extensively in studies of early twentieth-century African American writing.

Richard A. Courage is a professor of English at Westchester Community College/SUNY. He has published scholarly articles on African American narrative and visual arts, distance learning, and the teaching of writing and has contributed educational reporting and opinion pieces to the *New York Times* and other newspapers.